Representation and Mind
Hilary Putnam and Ned Block, editors

Furnishing the Mind

Concepts and Their Perceptual Basis

Jesse J. Prinz

A Bradford Book
The MIT Press
Cambridge, Massachusetts
London, England

This book was set in Sabon by SNP Best-Set Typesetter Ltd., Hong Kong, and was printed and bound in the United States of America.

First printing, 2002

Library of Congress Cataloging-in-Publication Data
Prinz, Jesse J.
 Furnishing the mind : concepts and their perceptual basis / Jesse J. Prinz.
      p.   cm.
 "A Bradford book."
 Includes bibliographical references and index.
 ISBN 0-262-16207-5 (hc.)
 1. Philosophy of mind. 2. Concepts. 3. Perception. 4. Empiricism. I. Title

BD418.3 .P77   2002
121′.4—dc21

                                                    2001056245

To the memory of Joachim Prinz

Contents

Acknowledgments

One accumulates debts while writing a book. Many people have assisted me through comments and conversations along the way. This project is an outgrowth of my doctoral dissertation, and I am very grateful to those who counseled me on that project. Josef Stern got me thinking about propositional-attitude ascriptions, which got me thinking about attitudes, which got me thinking about the concepts that comprise them. Murat Aydede was a great ally who always had challenging comments on my work. My discussions of Frege cases in this book owe to our many valuable conversations and to Murat's penetrating research on mental-state individuation. My largest debt is to Larry Barsalou. Larry has been incredibly generous and a constant source of inspiration. His work on conceptual instability and his recent crusade for concept empiricism are the models upon which this project is based. The views defended here are an extension of Larry's research.

I also owe special thanks to University of Maryland at College Park, where I spent a wonderful semester as a postdoctoral fellow. Among my many gracious hosts there, I owe the most to Georges Rey. This book has benefited immeasurably from our many heated conversations.

I am also indebted to the outstanding philosophical community at Washington University. Bill Bechtel has been extremely supportive and has worked tirelessly to cultivate an ideal interdisciplinary working environment. I am equally grateful to Andy Clark for his kind encouragement and infectious philosophical curiosity. Andy offered helpful comments on an earlier draft of this book. Red Watson also deserves my gratitude for steering me away from countless stylistic imperfections. Any remaining flaws in form might have been eliminated had I followed his suggestions more fully. Thanks are also due to my colleague Eric Brown for exposing me to the empiricists of the ancient world and to my former colleague Brian Keeley for sharing his valuable work sense modalities.

Numerous others have offered helpful feedback or support. I thank Marshal Abrams, Guy Dove, James Hampton, Stephen Horst, Dominic Murphy, Philip Robbins, David Rosenthal, Richard Samuels, Whit Schonbein, Brandon Towl, Dan Weiskopf, participants in the research meetings of the Philosophy-Neuroscience-Psychology Program, and students in my concepts seminars. I am especially grateful to Fiona Cowie and Eric Margolis for reading a draft of this book. Their detailed comments and prompted significant improvements. Some of Eric's trenchant objections will have to be addressed in a sequel. I am indebted to the MIT Press, the outstanding anonymous reviewers for the press, Carolyn Anderson, and Tom Stone for welcoming me so graciously. Alan Thwaits deserves special thanks for his intelligent and meticulous copyediting. I also thank Kluwer Academic Publishers for allowing me to reproduce the figures and some content from Prinz 2000b in chapters 9 and 10.

Finally, I want to thank my supportive family. I have been inspired by my mother's keen eye for new trends, my father's deep sense of conviction, and my brother's astonishing creativity. My deepest gratitude is reserved for my wife, Rachel, who has been by my side from the first word to the last. Without her, this book would have been impossible.

1

Desiderata on a Theory of Concepts

How comes [the mind] to be furnished? Whence comes it by that vast store which the busy and boundless fancy of man has painted on it with an almost endless variety? Whence has it all the materials of reason and knowledge? To this I answer, in one word, from EXPERIENCE.
Locke (1690, II.i.2)

1.1 Introduction

Without concepts, there would be no thoughts. Concepts are the basic timber of our mental lives. It is no wonder, then, that they have attracted a great deal of attention. Attention, but not consensus. The nature and origin of concepts remain matters of considerable controversy. One item of agreement, however, is that Locke's theory of concepts is wrong. Locke claims that all concepts (or, in his idiom, "ideas") are the products of experience. They are perceptually based. Reason gets its materials from the senses. Those mental states by which we see, hear, and smell the world are used to furnish the faculties by which we think, plan, and solve problems. This position goes by the name "empiricism."

Empiricism is a phoenix in the history of philosophy. It has been perpetually invented, destroyed, and reinvented. In the eyes of some, philosophers resist empiricism only because they suffer from an occupational distaste for the obvious. In the eyes of others, empiricism is a terrible mistake that philosophers have had to rediscover time and again. In the present climate, the latter perspective prevails. Many philosophers and researchers in other fields assume that empiricism has been decisively refuted.

I defend a dissenting view. While certain traditional forms of empiricism are untenable, a properly modernized empiricist account shows tremendous promise. It turns out that Locke's thesis can be reconciled with, and even supported by, the findings of cognitive science. More to the point, a modernized version of concept empiricism can outperform its rivals. A modernized empiricism can counter objections to older empiricist theories *as well as* objections to nonempiricist theories. Arriving at this heretical conclusion will take some time. It must first be shown that the leading nonempiricist theories are inadequate.

It helps to begin with a neutral characterization of concepts so we can home in on the items of disagreement. One such characterization is found in Locke's apt phrase that concepts are the "materials of reason and knowledge." A similar sentiment is expressed by the assertion that concepts are constituents of thoughts. My thought that aardvarks are nocturnal, for example, contains the concept AARDVARK and the concept NOCTURNAL.[1] This characterization leaves open this possibility that there could be thought constituents that are not concepts, and it leaves open the possibility that concepts can occur outside thoughts. Perhaps one can simply token the concept AARDVARK, as in an episode of free association, without having a full-fledged thought.[2] The characterization also says nothing about what thoughts are and what it is to be a constituent. It is sometimes said that concepts are to thoughts as words are to sentences, but this analogy is misleading if one does not buy into the view that thoughts are sentencelike.

The claim that concepts are thought constituents shows why they are so fundamental to a theory of the mind. Psychological theories seek to explain behavior. In both folk and scientific psychology, this is typically done be ascribing thoughts. We negotiate our environments by thinking about them. Thinking itself subsumes such abilities as planning, reasoning, problem solving, deciding, and recalling. To provide an adequate theory of these abilities, we need a theory of thoughts, and a theory of thoughts requires a theory of what thoughts are made of. If concepts are the constituents of thoughts, then they must play a foundational role in any complete theory of cognition. About this, there is considerable agreement.

There is also considerable agreement about some of the further properties that concepts must have. There are certain phenomena that are widely recognized as explanatory goals for a theory of concepts. These can be used to form a wish list—a list of desiderata that a theory of concepts would ideally explain. These desiderata can serve as a litmus test for a theory of concepts. It will be my contention that none of the leading theories satisfies all of the desiderata. This opens a space for an alternative.

1.2 Desiderata

The desiderata I present are widely accepted among philosophers and psychologists.[3] They include the phenomena that have motivated the postulation of concepts in the first place. They are the stuff of textbooks: explanatory goals so widely embraced that they are tedious to review.

Of course, full consensus is too much to hope for. Some might think that no account of concepts can satisfy each of the desiderata I discuss. To insist that an adequate theory of concepts must explain them all would beg the question against those who have more modest explanatory goals. Instead, I offer a conditional thesis: *if* a theory of concepts can accommodate all of the desiderata, then it has an explanatory advantage over its more modest competitors.

1.2.1 Scope

An adequate theory of concepts must have sufficient expressive power or breadth to accommodate the large variety of concepts that we are capable of possessing. The human conceptual repertoire ranges from the sensory to the abstract. We have concepts of readily observable states within ourselves, like PAIN; theoretically derived concepts, such as ELECTRON; and seemingly formal concepts, such as NUMBER. We have concepts of natural kinds, such as FROG; artifacts, such as BOAT; and social kinds, such as MOTHER or DEMOCRACY. This diversity cannot be neglected. Some theories are particularly adept at handling one kind of concept and embarrassingly poor at dealing with others.

1.2.2 Intentional Content

Concepts represent, stand in for, or refer to things other than themselves. My AARDVARK concept is about aardvarks; it refers to all and only aardvarks. Philosophers call this property "intentionality." To say that concepts have intentionality is to say that they refer, and those things to which they refer, I call their intentional contents. Intentional states can refer to both actual things and merely possible things. I can have a concept that represents unicorns.

An adequate theory should help us understand how concepts attain their intentional contents. Many philosophers are explicit about this desideratum. Psychologists tend to be less explicit, but they almost always assume that concepts have intentionality and identify concepts by their intentional contents. For example, the concept FROG is so called because it is the concept that represents frogs.

The intentionality of concepts plays important explanatory roles. Our ability to represent things contributes to an explanation of our ability to behave in ways that are sensitive to those things. The actions of certain simple organisms might not require the mediation of intentional mental states, because they are fully and directly determined by stimuli present in their environments. But our minds are more powerful. We can act with flexibility and forethought, choosing between different courses of action and anticipating future consequences. These abilities seem to demand representations that stand in for extramental objects. Representations can be manipulated by the mind independently of the things they represent. As a result, we can engage in behavior that is sensitive to extramental objects even when those objects are not present. For example, by manipulating a FROG representation, one can devise, mentally test, and ultimately act on a plan to catch a frog.

Despite the consensus that concepts refer, there is some controversy about what they refer to. These days, most philosophers assume that many of our concepts refer to categories whose boundaries are determined by nature. My FROG concept refers not to the set of things I take to be frogs, but to the set of frogs.[4] The set of frogs, in turn, is determined by nature, not by us. It is a natural kind. Some researchers may be inclined to resist this kind of realism. They think that category boundaries are imposed on the world by our concepts. On this view, so-called natural-kind concepts really pick out categories that depend on human thoughts and practices. For some, being a frog is something like being tasty, being a chair, or being the U.S. president. All these categories are real in some sense, but they depend on human cognitive abilities, goals, or social practices. Placing natural kinds in this group makes them dependent on us. On a more radical version of the view, my concepts refer only to what I categorize under them, regardless of the practices of other individuals. If I fail to identify some odd-looking species as frogs, despite the fact that science does, my FROG concept simply excludes them.

I presuppose a strong form of realism. I assume that my FROG concept really refers to a naturally delineated category, despite the fact that I might misclassify a few instances. If I were to insist that some odd looking species is not a frog and then subsequently discover that it shares the same underlying properties as the things I admit are frogs, I would change my original judgment. I would not say that the species changed its ontological identity as a consequence of my discovery. It was a frog species all along. I had simply been fooled by appearances. If such changes in my categorization decisions implied that the reference of my concept had changed, there would be no way to explain why I took my original view to be erroneous and changed my mind. If reference is determined merely by how I actually categorize, there could be no such thing as error.

Opponents of strong realism can try to handle such cases by appeal to ideal observation conditions or scientific consensus. I do not think this will suffice. I side with those who say that my FROG concept can refer to frogs even if there are certain instances that *no one* reliably identifies as such, even under ideal conditions. Just as I can imagine my own errors in categorization, I can imagine systematic errors throughout my community, even under the best circumstances. This is not to say that such errors would actually occur. The strong realist intuition only requires that they could occur. It is even conceivable that human cognitive limitations prevent us from ever discovering certain of nature's joints. In such cases, I believe, we can still pick out kinds whose borders are defined by such joints. Little will hinge on this strong realist claim, but I state it for the record. The weaker claim, according to which my concepts can have intentional contents that neither I nor any member of my community can articulate *at present* is important. It is a principle underlying many scientific pursuits and is implicit in experimentally demonstrable human categorization tendencies.

1.2.3 Cognitive Content

There are well-known reasons for thinking that concepts cannot be individuated by intentional content alone. Two closely related arguments derive from Frege's (1893) philosophy of language. First, Frege draws our attention to the fact that a true identity statement involving two distinct terms can be informative despite the fact that those terms have a common referent. For example, it can be surprising to discover that Lewis Carroll is Charles Dodgson. If we grasped these names by grasping their referents (i.e., intentional contents), the surprise would be inexplicable because their referents are the same. Second, Frege observes that we cannot freely substitute coreferring terms in some linguistic contexts. "Sally believes that Charles Dodgson is a logician" and "Sally believes that Lewis Carroll is a logician" can differ in truth value, even though "Carroll" and "Dodgson" corefer. If reference exhausted the content of terms, these sentences would have the same truth value.

Frege offers these arguments for the limitations of reference in developing an account of linguistic meaning, but parallel examples can be constructed without mentioning language. As with terms, the identification of two coreferring concepts can be informative, and as with sentences, we can have a belief containing one of a pair of coreferring concepts without having a corresponding belief containing the other. This suggests that conceptual content too cannot be exhausted by reference. Peacocke (1992) uses this Fregean insight in discussing identity conditions on concepts. He stipulates that two concepts count as distinct just in case substituting one for the other can render an uninformative thought informative. This is true, he says, even in cases where concepts corefer. This fact about concepts may offer the best explanation of informative identities and substitution failures in language. The linguistic cases may arise as a result of the fact that some coreferential terms are associated with distinct concepts.

This is essentially Frege's position. He solved his puzzle cases by introducing the notion of sense. "Carroll" and "Dodgson" have different senses, but the same referent. In grasping these terms, we grasp the sense, and thereby fail to discover the identity of their referents. The sense of an expression is a part of its content other than its referent. Beyond that, it is not always clear what Frege meant by "sense." What is the ontological status of a sense? How do senses relate to reference? Frege uses the term "sense" in several ways (see Dummett 1981). On one standard interpretation, which is discussed in the next chapter, senses are definitional abstract objects that determine what our concepts refer to. This view has come under attack. For example, some philosophers of language argue that reference is determined by a term's causal history (e.g., Kripke 1980, Donnellan 1972, Putnam 1975). On this theory, a term refers to what its originators were pointing two at the moment the term was introduced. I call this the etiological theory. Defenders of the etiological theory often claim that the information we associate with a term is not part of its meaning. Meaning is exhausted by reference. Defenders of other recent semantic theories share this opinion.

Even if these reference-based accounts are correct, Frege is surely right to say that reference cannot exhaust our *understanding* of terms. When we consider the *psychology* of language, or when we consider the non-linguistic cases just described, the need for a kind of content that transcends reference is manifest. Even if one insists that such contents should play no part in a theory of linguistic semantics, they are indispensable for understanding the concepts we deploy in thought. I return to this point below.

To say that we need a construct that individuates concepts more finely than referents does not entail that we must adopt Frege's notion of sense. In particular, it does not mean that we must say that all concepts are associated with definitional abstract objects. We do, however, need *some* kind of content other than reference, or intentional content, as it was called in the last section. I call this further requirement, "cognitive content." Cognitive content is what allows two coreferential representations, be they terms or concepts, to seem semantically distinct to a cognitive agent.

This is only a first approximation. In addition to explaining how coreferential terms can seem different, cognitive content is needed to explain how concepts that are not coreferential can seem alike. Putnam (1975) introduced a celebrated counterpart to the cases introduced by Frege. He imagines a world, Twin Earth, which is almost exactly like our own world. Every one here has a doppelgänger on Twin Earth. The only difference is that the stuff that has all the superficial properties of water on Twin Earth is not H_2O but some other compound called XYZ. On Twin Earth, XYZ is the clear, tasteless liquid that fills rivers and streams. The concept that I express by "water" refers to H_2O, even if I am ignorant of chemistry, because I apply it to stuff that happens to be H_2O. The concept that my Twin Earth doppelgänger expresses by his word "water" refers to XYZ because that is the local waterlike stuff in his world. Nevertheless, there is some intuitive sense in which our two extensionally distinct concepts are alike. They have the same cognitive content. An adequate account of concepts should explain how coreferential concepts can differ and how divergently referential concepts can be alike.

1.2.4   Acquisition

A fourth desideratum is that a theory must ultimately support a plausible explanation of how concepts are acquired. This requirement has two facets. On the one hand, we need to accommodate ontogenetic acquisition. How does an individual come to possess a given concept? Concepts that are thought to be learned rather than innate must be learnable. A theory of concepts must allow for this.

In addition, an adequate theory must be commensurable with a phylogenetic story. It must lend itself to an explanation of how innate concepts (if such exist) entered the human genome and how we evolved to be able to acquire those concepts that are not innate. Just as we must be able to explain how the language faculty evolved, we must be able to tell a story about how the conceptual faculty evolved. The difficulty of meeting this requirement is proportionate to the degree to which one's theory links concepts to faculties whose evolution is already well understood.

This is not to say that a theory of concepts must come prepackaged with a theory of concept evolution or even a theory of concept learning. A theory of concepts should merely lend itself to such acquisition theories. If one theory of concepts is compatible with a more plausible, independently motivated theory of acquisition then it should be preferred over an incompatible theory.

1.2.5 Categorization

Reference is a semantic relation, but it also has an epistemic counterpart. In addition to the set of things to which a given concept refers, there is a set of things to which a concept is *taken to* refer. We have mechanisms for forming beliefs about what things fall under our concepts, mechanisms of categorization. Concepts are often identified with such mechanisms.

As I use the term, categorization encompasses two different, but closely connected abilities. "Category identification" is manifested when a person identifies the category under which an object belongs. Various kinds of experimental tasks involve category identification. In some experiments, subjects are asked to verbally identify a verbally described or visually presented object. In other experiments, subjects are asked to confirm a categorization judgment, as in "True or false: canaries are birds."

Second, "category production" is manifested when a person identifies which attributes an object possesses if it is a member of a given category. Experiments often assess this by asking subjects to describe categories or to decide whether members of a given category have some specific attribute. In other experiments, subjects are asked to rate the similarity between two categories or to draw inferences about features possessed by category members.

Recognition (identification) and production can work in concert. For example, when tracking an object, one must recognize it across different transformations, but to do that, one must often anticipate what form those transformations will take. Such strategic tracking depends on category production. Another combination of these abilities is category hypothesis confirmation. Once one has tentatively identified the category of a partially concealed object by using available attributes, one can produce knowledge about concealed attributes, and then confirm the original identification by searching for those concealed attributes.

Psychologists widely believed that a theory of concepts should explain these abilities in a way that is consistent with empirical findings. For example, experiments have shown that not all members of a category are created equal. Instead, one finds many "typicality effects." People readily rate some category members as more typical than others (Rosch 1973, Rosch 1975, Mervis, Catlin, and Rosch 1976). These typical members are categorized faster and produced more readily during category production tasks (Smith, Shoben, and Rips 1974, Rosch 1978). Likewise, some attributes are rated as more typical for a category and are produced more readily (Rosch and Mervis 1975). Category members possessing many typical attributes are rated as highly typical (Hampton 1979).

Furthermore, not all categories are created equal. Any given object can fall under many different categories. For example, a single object can be a rottweiler, a dog, an animal, a living thing, and so on. It turns out that the intermediate level of abstraction is privileged (Brown 1958, Berlin and Kay 1969, Rosch, Mervis, Gray, Johnson, and Boyes-Braem 1976). Rosch and her colleagues call this the "basic level" of categorization. Subjects can usually identify an object as a dog faster than they can identify it as a rottweiler (the subordinate level) or as an animal (the superordinate level). They also seem to acquire the concept DOG earlier in development. An adequate theory of categorization should predict and explain these asymmetries.

It might be objected that the categorization desideratum, and these results in particular, introduces an unfair bias in favor of certain theories of concepts. Philosophers rarely try to accommodate such psychological findings when developing their theories. In fact, some philosophers think that a theory of concepts need not explain categorization at all. The constituents of thoughts, they contend, may have little to do with the mechanisms by which we classify objects under the conditions psychologists explore. It is certainly conceivable that we have one set of representations for forming thoughts about frogs and another for picking them out in a crowd (Armstrong, Gleitman, and Gleitman 1983). If concepts are thought constituents, it might be best to remove the explanation of categorization from the list of desiderata.

I address such dissenting opinions more fully in chapters 2 and 4. As a preliminary response, however, I emphasize two points. First, psychologists have found evidence that the effects found in categorization studies appear in other contexts as well. For example, studies have shown typicality effects in inductive inference (Sloman 1993, see also Smith 1989). We are more likely to draw an inference about a property from one subordinate-level category to another if the former is a typical instance of the basic-level category that subsumes them. Such findings support the contention that categorization representations coincide with representations used in thinking.

Second, eliminating the categorization desideratum would strongly bias the case against psychological theories of concepts. In psychology, an enormous amount of the research on concepts has focused on categorization. Concepts are often stipulated to be the cognitive mechanisms by which we categorize. If a theory of concepts were absolved of its obligation to explain categorization, most psychological accounts would be rendered moot. Categorization certainly stands in need of an explanation. If psychological theories were to satisfy all desiderata including categorization and philosophical theories were to satisfy all but categorization, psychological theories would have an explanatory advantage. This does not mean that we should disqualify theories that cannot explain categorization. Instead, we should say that the ability to explain categorization is an asset and that theories lacking this asset are able to defeat their rivals only if they outperform them on other desiderata.

A further objection against the categorization desideratum is that some concepts refer to classes whose members we cannot directly recognize. For example, most of us who possess the concept ELECTRON cannot recognize electrons. Perhaps, then, it is too stringent to demand that a theory of concepts explain categorization. I think this objection fails. First, to take the present example, an inability to recognize electrons would not rule out our ability to engage in electron-categorization behavior broadly conceived. Categorization includes category production, an ability possessed by many of those who could never recognize electrons. If a theory of concepts explains why someone with an ELECTRON concept is likely to characterize electrons as negatively charged particles, it satisfies the desideratum under discussion. Second, even if some concepts never involve categorization (no examples come to mind), the desideratum would not be threatened. *When categorization does occur*, it involves concepts: categorizing something is placing it under a concept or characterizing it by means of concepts. It is natural to hope for and give preference to a theory of concepts that accounts for these abilities.

1.2.6 Compositionality

In many important respects, our cognitive capacities are unbounded. There appears to be no upper limit on the number of distinct beliefs we can entertain, plans we can devise, and sentences we can comprehend. Every day we entertain a breathtaking number of novel thoughts. These are induced by our experiences, tailored by our goals, or awakened by our casual musings. This hyperfertility is achieved using finite means. As finite beings, we have finite minds. Finite minds can only store a limited stock of concepts. Myriad thoughts must somehow be derivable from that limited stock. There is a highly plausible explanation of this. A finite set of concepts can engender a boundless capacity for unique thoughts if those thoughts are derived by combining concepts compositionally.

Concepts are compositional just in case compound concepts (and thoughts) are formed as a function of their constituent concepts together with rules of combination. For example, a compositional system allows one to form the thought that aardvarks are nocturnal by combining one's AARDVARK concept with one's NOCTURNAL concept using the very same combination rule used for forming other thoughts, such as the thought that cows are herbivorous, or that politicians are egomaniacal. Likewise, the very same concepts, AARDVARK and NOCTURNAL, can be used to form other thoughts in a compositional system, e.g., the thought that aardvarks eat insects and bats are nocturnal. The same rules and the same stock of primitives can be used to form different combinations.

Compositionality explains the extreme fertility, or, as it is often called, productivity, of thought, because in principle a finite set of concepts and a finite set of combination rules can be used to generate an infinite number of distinct compounds. Compositional combination becomes infinitely productive when the rules allow for an endless variety of novel combinations. The simplest examples of such rules are recursive functions in logic and grammar. The word "and," for instance, can be iterated indefinitely; we can say "*A* and *B*," "*A* and *B* and *C*," "*A* and *B* and *C* and *A*," and so on. With a handful of recursive rules and a stock of primitives, the variety of possible thoughts becomes staggering. The ability to form novel thoughts can be explained within a compositional framework. If a person knows the constituent concepts and the combination rules, then she can use them to form thoughts that have never been entertained before. Chomsky (1968) gives a seminal presentation of this kind of argument for compositionality in the context of language. Fodor has argued aggressively for its inclusion among the nonnegotiable conditions on a theory of concepts (e.g., Fodor 1981, 1994, 1998).

Fodor and his colleagues also offer another argument for compositionality. They say that it provides the best explanation for what they call the systematicity of thought (e.g., Fodor 1987, Fodor and Pylyshyn 1988, Fodor and Lepore 1992). Our ability to form certain thoughts, such as the thought that Oscar ate the squid, seems to carry with it the ability to form certain others, such as the thought that the squid ate Oscar. Anyone who can entertain the first thought can entertain the second. This fact can be explained if concepts are compositional. The ability to think that Oscar ate the squid co-occurs with the ability to form the thought that the squid ate Oscar because these two thoughts are comprised of the same concepts and generated using the same combination rules. If we needed to learn separate combination rules for forming each thought, such systematic relations would not arise. A similar insight underlies Evans's (1982) defense of what he calls the Generality Constraint on concept possession. According to Evans, a person possesses the nominal concept *a* and the predicative concept *F* only if she can form the thoughts that *a* is *G* for any possessed predicate concept *G* and that *b* is *F* for any possessed nominal concept *b*. It follows naturally from the Generality Constraint that anyone who can form certain thoughts is able to form other thoughts by use of the same concepts and combination rules.

The compositionally requirement stands in need of one clarification. I said that concepts are compositional if compounds are generated as a function of their constituent concepts. Some standard formulations are stated in terms of contents. It is often said that the *content* of a thought (or compound concept) is compositional just in case it is a function of the *contents* of the concepts constituting that thought together with rules of combination. In other words, the claim that compounds are formed from constituents carries with it the idea that constituents contribute their contents to compounds. But what does "content" mean here? This question is complicated by the fact that I distinguish two distinct kinds of content, intentional and cognitive. What kind of content does compositionality pertain to?

I answer that both intentional and cognitive content must be compositional because both kinds of content are implicated by the productivity and systematicity of thought. Saying that we are capable of entertaining an unbounded number of distinct thoughts implies that we can entertain an unbounded number of thoughts with distinct intentional and cognitive contents. Saying that certain thoughts exhibit systematicity implies that our ability to have thoughts with certain intentional and cognitive contents carries with it the ability to entertain other thoughts with distinct cognitive and intentional contents. Thus, the compositionality desideratum carries with it two component requirements: intentional-content compositionality and cognitive-content compositionality.[5]

1.2.7 Publicity

The final desideratum is publicity. Concepts must be capable of being shared by different individuals and by one individual at different times. This requirement has been emphasized by many (e.g., Rey 1983, Peacocke 1992, Fodor 1998). It must be satisfied if concepts are to play some of their most important explanatory roles. Two of these roles stand out (Fodor and Lepore 1992). First, it is almost universally assumed that concepts play a pivotal role in linguistic communication. According to the standard picture, people understand each other's words in virtue of the fact that they associate the same (or quite nearly the same) concepts with those words. If no two people associate the same concepts with their words, then communication is impossible. Therefore, concepts must be sharable.

A second reason for thinking concepts are public is that concepts are implicated in intentional explanations of behavior. An intentional explanation of behavior is one that explains what a person does by appeal to her mental states. For example, Mary opened the liquor cabinet because she desired a glass of scotch and believed that she could find some there. As this example illustrates, typical intentional explanations make reference to propositional attitudes, and attitudes are composed of concepts. Perhaps the most striking feature of intentional explanations is their apparent generality. A single intentional explanation can subsume many different people. Felix, Hugo, and Greta might all open their respective liquor cabinets for precisely the same reason that Mary did. But, actions can be motivated by the same attitudes only if those attitudes are composed of the same concepts. If intentional explanations generalize, concepts must be sharable.

As with compositionality, the publicity requirement must be explicated along two dimensions. Concepts must be sharable in both intentional content and in cognitive content. Explaining communication clearly requires that intentional contents be sharable. To understand what someone is saying, we must know what their words and thoughts refer to. For this, their concepts and ours must refer to the same things. It would be a mistake to assume that we can satisfy the publicity requirement by merely establishing that people can have coreferential concepts. It is equally important to show that concepts can share their cognitive contents.

For example, consider Twin Earth cases. There is a strong intuition that I share something with my doppelgänger on Twin Earth when he and I think about the stuff in our respective rivers and lakes. My concept refers to H_2O and his refers to XYZ, but these concepts can arguably be subsumed by some of the same psychological laws. My desire to drink the stuff I call "water" disposes me to the same behaviors as his desire to drink the stuff he calls "water." Thus, there is reason to think that concepts can be importantly alike despite differences in intentional content. Shared cognitive contents provide the best explanation.

Second, consider interpersonal versions of Frege cases (see Aydede 1998). Standard Frege cases involve one person with two coreferential concepts. Interpersonal versions involve two or more people both of whom possess the same pair of coreferential concepts. For example, the ancient Greeks falsely believed that the morning star (Hesperus) is different from the evening star (Phosphorus). They had two different concepts, and their beliefs involving those concepts can be subsumed under the same generalizations. For example, anyone who wanted to see Phosphorus would go outside in the evening, and not in the morning. These common behaviors cannot be explained by shared intentional contents, because that would obscure the fact that other behaviors with the same intentional contents lead to different behaviors. In particular the desire to see Hesperus makes people go out in the morning. Once again, the relevant kind of concept sharing involves shared cognitive contents. Thus, the publicity desideratum demands that both cognitive content and intentional content be potentially sharable.

The issue of concept sharing raises many thorny questions. There is considerable debate about whether children share concepts with adults (see, e.g., Carey 1985), whether people with radically different beliefs share concepts (Kuhn 1962), whether people with healthy minds share concepts with people who have damaged minds (Stich 1983), and whether humans share concepts with other animals (Sterelny 1990). I do not address these questions here. Even if they are all answered in the negative, there remains ample evidence that concept sharing is possible in ordinary cases. The exotic cases just mentioned are exactly the cases in which the arguments from communication and intentional explanation are least persuasive. For example, it is highly contentious to claim that we truly communicate or fall under the same psychological laws with nonhuman animals. In less exotic cases, we have every reason to believe that concept sharing occurs. This is the claim that an adequate theory of concepts must accommodate.

1.3   Do We Need Language Desiderata?

In laying out these desiderata, I mentioned relations between concepts and language several times. For example, I said that conceptual differences might underwrite the informativeness of linguistically expressed identities, and I said that conceptual publicity is needed to explain linguistic communication. Such remarks raise the question, How exactly are concepts related to language? There are two questions of special interest here. First, we might ask how concepts are related to linguistic meanings. Second, we might wonder whether one can have concepts without language. I address these in turn.[6]

It is widely assumed that concepts should figure into a theory of linguistic meaning. Some consider this a desideratum on a theory of concepts (e.g., Rey 1983). In the strongest form of this desideratum, one might say that concepts simply *are* the meanings of words. Call this the meaning desideratum. I already hinted at my reasons for leaving the meaning desideratum off the list. I noted that some recent semantic theories restrict meaning to reference. On such reference-based theories, the Fregean and Putnamian data that motivate the intentional-content desideratum should not be taken as evidence that meaning outstrips reference. These data only show that our ways of understanding words outstrip reference. Ways of understanding arguably belong to psychology rather than semantics.

On reference-based theories, concepts may play some role in a full theory of language. First, they may play a role in linguistic epistemology. In this capacity, a theory of concepts may be said to contribute to a theory of how we understand language or how we select linguistic forms in the service of communication. Even though the meaning of a word is exhausted by its referent, our understanding of the word depends on our understanding of its referent. And our understanding of referents is mediated by concepts. Likewise, in communication we typically choose words that refer to the objects or facts that we would like to express. Our knowledge of those objects and facts is, again, mediated by concepts.

Second, concepts may play a role in determining linguistic reference. My utterances of the word "dog" may refer to dogs virtue of being associated with a concept of mine that refers to dogs. This does not mean that the concept itself constitutes the meaning of the word, much less that the concept contributes *all* of its content to linguistic meaning. In particular, the cognitive content of a concept may have nothing to do with meaning. On this view, concepts merely contribute their referents.

All this suggests that it may be inappropriate to saddle a theory of concepts with the responsibility of providing a theory of meaning.

Concepts may play a role in semantic theories, but saying that concepts *are* meanings is not necessarily motivated in light of recent developments in semantic theory.

Of course, reference-based semantics have not gone unchallenged. One worry is that reference-based semantics cannot explain apparent semantic differences between distinct vacuous terms; "unicorn" and "centaur" both refer to the same thing, namely nothing, but they seem to have different meanings. Reference-based theories also offer no easy explanation of apparent restrictions on substitutivity. It is beyond the scope of this discussion to evaluate the success of such objections. It is enough to point out that reference-based semantics are both highly popular and incompatible with the meaning desideratum.

I turn now to the second question about concepts and language. Some philosophers have been tempted to say that public language is necessary for the possession of concepts. To those outside of philosophy the claim may sound absurd. Surely, we know that nonhuman animals engage in behavior that is sophisticated enough to warrant ascriptions of concepts. We know that human infants, chimps, and even parrots can categorize objects. They can identify which things go together. Even more dramatically, aphasics, who suffer serious linguistic deficits, do not exhibit more general cognitive impairments. Their behavior seems entirely appropriate to the situations that confront them, including manifest frustration with their linguistic deficits. Doesn't this show there can be concept possession without linguistic mastery? Another argument against the thesis that concepts depend on language owes to Fodor (1975). He argues that we need concepts to acquire language in the first place. How do we learn a word if not by mapping it onto a previously attained concept?

Despite such obvious motivations for attributing concepts to infraverbal creatures and persons, some philosophers have been tempted to defend the radical view that such attributions are inappropriate. One reason for this odd-sounding claim can be extracted from the philosophy of Wittgenstein (1953). Here is an argument loosely drawn from Wittgenstein's critique of private language. According to Wittgenstein, concepts can be individuated by how they are used. Having a concept is being able to follow a rule for using that concept. For something to count as a rule, there must be criteria for correctness. Merely thinking that one is following a rule is not the same as following a rule. If rules were private rather than public, there would be no way to confirm that you were conforming to them. If I on one occasion stipulate that I will always use a private concept in some particular way and then use that concept on a subsequent occasion, I will have no way to be sure that I am using it in the same way. I may misremember my initial rule, and there will be no one to correct me, no one to keep me honest. There can be no private criteria for correctness. Correctness and rules only have application in public contexts. Thus, if concepts are individuated by how they are used, the use that matters must be public. Concepts are publicly used in language. Thus, there can be no concepts without language.

If this argument is right, attribution of concepts to infraverbal creatures and persons must be taken with a grain of salt. Such attributions show only that there are some superficial similarities between them and us. An infraverbal creature can appear to possess a concept by, say, sorting things in some way, but there can be no criteria for correctness. If a parrot groups together a bunch of triangles and then includes a square, we cannot say that it made a mistake. Fodor's argument can also be answered. The early language learner may be acquiring words by mapping them onto mental states, but those mental states are not bona fide concepts, because they are not governed by criteria of correctness. Only when a word is in place and anchored to communally determined rules for correct application can the child be said to have a concept. Perhaps we need to have the ability to sort things in order to learn a concept, but sorting only becomes subject to correction, and hence conceptual, when brought under linguistic labels. If these Wittgensteinian considerations are right, then we might want to introduce another desideratum: a theory of concepts must ensure that concept possession requires language.

This brief treatment cannot do justice to Wittgenstein's philosophical outlook. I wish only to show where his position may be vulnerable. Wittgenstein's claim that there can be no private criteria for correctness can be challenged in various ways. First, a number of recent philosophers have proposed "naturalized" theories of error (see chapter 9 for an example). These theories purport to show that correctness need not depend on public policies. Some views explain correctness in terms of conformity to laws, rather than rules, and others explain correctness in terms of conformity to evolved or designed functions (Fodor 1990, Millikan 1984). If these accounts pan out, Wittgenstein's claim will be refuted.

Second, Wittgenstein's opposition to private criteria for correctness turns in part on considerations about how difficult it would be for an individual to confirm that she was conforming to a private rule. This reasoning is flawed. The fact that a person cannot tell if she is following a rule does not prove that she is not following (or failing to follow) that rule. A criterion for correctness can simply be a correct way of conforming to a rule rather than a method of verifying that one is conforming. Wittgenstein intentionally conflates conformity with knowledge of conformity. The reason for this may stem from the view that rules involve a normative dimension. If someone fails to conform, she can be held accountable. If there is no way for a person to determine whether she is conforming or failing to conform, such accountability is threatened. In response, one might opt for a reliabilist measure of accountability. One might say that a person is justified in thinking that she is following a rule just in case the mechanism by which she reapplies the rule is reliable. For example, if memory systems work reliably, applying a rule from memory is a reliable process. A person can be held accountable for trying to apply a rule using an unreliable process.

A third worry about Wittgenstein's argument is that he may have an inflated picture of how correctness criteria work in public language. What does it mean to say that there are correct and incorrect uses of public words. One possibility, suggested by Chomsky (1991), is that public rules have more to do with authority than correctness. To say that there is a right way to use a word amounts to the claim that some language users use it in that way and will penalize those who do not. Misuse of language can be punished by public correction, social marginalization, and failure of communication. In the private case, there can be no serious threat of penalty. If I have a private rule and threaten to punish myself if I fail to conform, I know that it is within my power to refrain from carrying out that threat. If the difference between public and private rules amounts to the applicability of punishment, it would seem odd to say that public rules are privileged. After all, public rules do not have a special relationship to justification or accountability on this picture. Moreover, even though I cannot threaten myself, misapplied rules could lead to costly mistakes that serve as punishments. If I misidentify a poisonous plant as another instance of a familiar nutritious plant, I will pay the consequences. If normativity amounts to threat of penalty, apparent differences between public and private criteria for correctness may be exaggerated.

Though not decisive, all these considerations show that the Wittgensteinian argument may be vulnerable. If Wittgensteinian arguments do not go through, many of the remarkable cognitive abilities exhibited by infraverbals can be taken as evidence for conceptual abilities. I assume that infraverbal creatures can have concepts.

Saying that one can possess concepts without language does not imply that language plays no role in our conceptual abilities. Language is, first of all, a dominant means of learning new concepts. People direct each other to new concepts by description, explicit definition, verbal pointing, and so forth. Moreover, concepts that get lexicalized are often more salient and easier to learn. Language also aids in using concepts. Highly complex concepts can be expressed using a single word. Those words can serve as conceptual placeholders in working memory to avoid the burden of processing the corresponding concepts in their full complexity. For linguistic creatures, some concepts may even be constituted by words. The best examples are concepts known only by deference to experts. A person ignorant of physics might arguably be said to possess a QUARK concept by possessing the word "quark" and being disposed to consult physicists about its use (Putnam 1975, Burge 1979).

I leave all of these as open possibilities. I am only committing to the assumption that concept possession can occur without language. All the theories of concepts that I consider have proponents who share this assumption. This does not entail that a complete theory of concepts can be developed without mentioning language. It does suggest, however, that one can present a theory of what concepts are without mentioning language. If some concepts depend on language, then this precept may have to be violated to accommodate the scope desideratum. I allow such violations, but I regard language-dependent concepts as the exceptions.

For this reason, language has a limited role in the chapters that follow. I part ways with those who think that a theory of concepts is motivated primarily in the context of a theory of language. Fortunately, mine is not a renegade position. Many researchers investigate concepts under the assumption that they are language-independent. The omission of a language desideratum in my list reflects a general, if tacit, bias in concepts research. It has been the burden of this section to show that this bias rests on a stable foundation.

1.4 Preview

In the following chapters, I use the desiderata presented above to measure the comparative success of various theories of concepts. Most of these theories claim that typical lexical concepts decompose into representations of features. A lexical concept is a concept expressed by a single word (e.g., BIRD, CAR, JUSTICE). A feature representation, or just "feature" for short, is a representation of some attribute possessed or condition met by objects falling under a concept. Thus, a BIRD concept may decompose into features such as FLIES, HAS WINGS, and so forth. Features are generally construed as concepts in their own right, some of which decompose into further features, and some of which do not (the "primitive" features). Most of the debates between competing theories of concepts concern the nature of features. Three questions can be distinguished. First, one can ask what the features constituting our concepts represent. Different theories claim that concepts decompose into features representing different kinds of attributes. They disagree about what kind of information a typical lexical concept contains about the category it represents. Second, one can ask which features are primitive. At one extreme are researchers who say that primitives are restricted to features representing perceivable properties; at the other extreme are those who say that primitives are roughly word-sized units. On the latter view, lexical concepts cannot be decomposed into more primitive features. The third question concerns the "mental medium" in which our concepts are couched. Are concepts like mental images, mental word lists, or something else? Most theories of concepts focus on the first of these questions, but all are important.

Chapters 2 through 4 evaluate the leading theories of concepts. None of these theories ends up with a perfect score. They each stumble on one desideratum or another. Such widespread failings are likely to invite a degree of skepticism. If none of the top theories of concepts can satisfy all the desiderata, perhaps the list is too demanding. Perhaps concepts cannot do all the things we want them to do.

I combat this skepticism by proposing a theory of concepts that is informed by the strengths and weaknesses of these other theories. That is the task of chapters 5 through 11. Readers familiar with prevailing theories and convinced of their shortcomings are invited to begin with chapter 5. There I define concept empiricism and offer preliminary arguments in its defense. In chapter 6, I describe how the empiricism I endorse differs from its historical ancestors. I also begin to show that this brand of empiricism can accommodate the desiderata by examining publicity and categorization. In chapter 7, I address scope, showing that perceptual representations have far greater expressive breadth than ordinarily appreciated. Acquisition is the subject of chapter 8, where I challenge received opinion that many of our concepts are innate. In chapter 9, I defend a theory of intentional content, building on causal and informational semantic theories. In chapter 10, I suggest an alternative to leading "narrow content" approaches to cognitive content. This leaves only compositionality, which I take up in the final chapter.

Together these chapters form an extended plea for recidivism. The theory that I defend is modern in that it avails itself of contemporary cognitive science and appropriates many insights from recent theories of concepts. However, it also harks back to more traditional accounts that sought to blur the boundary between conception and perception. When brought up to date, such accounts show tremendous promise. We can move forward by glancing backward and embracing the idea that concepts have a perceptual basis.

2

Traditional Philosophical Accounts

Two theories of concepts stand out in the history in philosophy. According to one, concepts are perceptually derived mental images. According to the other, concepts are enduring definitions that specify essential conditions for category membership. Image-based accounts enjoy little support today. The definitional view has also come under attack, but it retains a loyal following in some circles. In this chapter, I explore definitional and image-based theories of concepts, highlighting their virtues and recalling their major flaws.

2.1 Imagism

Most people form images when they think about the categories that inhabit the world. Consequently, it is natural to assign images a central role in our theories of concepts. It is unsurprising, then, that image-based theories have been around since antiquity. Aristotle remarked, "The soul never thinks without an image" (1961, 431a8). This sentiment is echoed by Epicurus, Lucretius, and others in the ancient world, and by the British empiricists.

Locke (1690) argues that all concepts (or "ideas") have a basis in externally directed perception or inner perception of our own mental states. It is natural to interpret Locke as holding the view that ideas are mental images (see, e.g., Ayers 1991). This interpretation has been controversial because Locke also insisted that a single idea could abstract away from the details of any particular object. An idea could represent triangularity without depicting any particular kind of triangle. Berkeley (1710) argues against this possibility on the grounds that it is incompatible with the view that ideas are images. It is far from clear how a mental image could represent triangularity as such. The puzzlement is especially pronounced if one assumes that mental images are like pictures. Pictures cannot abstract away from certain details. A picture of a triangle is always either isosceles, equilateral, or scalene. Berkeley can be interpreted as adopting the view that ideas are picturelike images (at least when visually derived) of the particular objects and properties that we encounter in experience. This view is known as "imagism." Hume (1739) enthusiastically supported Berkeley's critique of Locke and explicitly identifies ideas with images as well. He too is often interpreted as an imagist.

The belief that thoughts consist of images remained popular into the early part of the twentieth century. Introspectionist psychologists such as Titchener (1910) recorded detailed descriptions of the images that come to mind while thinking. Considerable energy was spent debating the possibility of imageless thought and trying to explain how we get by without abstract ideas. Prominent philosophers also embraced image-based theories (Russell 1921; see also Price 1953).

Imagism is the view that concepts are derived from conscious perceptual states (called "impressions" by Hume). When we encounter an object, it produces a conscious state in our sensory systems. That state leaves a memory trace, which, though less "vivacious" than the original, can later be called up to represent either the object that caused it or the category to which the object belongs. Imagists also assume that we can generate concepts by reflecting on our mental states. For example, we can form a concept of ANGER by attending to that emotional state when it arises within us. Finally, one can acquire a concept by combining concepts previously acquired by sensation or reflection. Hume (1748, sec. II, p. 19) gives the example of a GOLDEN MOUNTAIN concept formed by merging a mountain image with an image of gold.

Imagism has its advantages. First and foremost, imagism incorporates a theory of ontogenetic acquisition of concepts. As we just saw, concepts are acquired by storing perceptual states in memory. Since the postulation of perceptual states are independently motivated to explain perception, they provide an inexpensive resource for building a theory of concepts. If most concepts are identified with complex perceptual experiences or imaginative combinations of stored percepts, then most concepts turn out to be learned on this view. This lightens the explanatory load by avoiding commitments to strong forms of nativism. Of course, imagists generally embrace a set of primitive perceptual concepts, which may be regarded as innate (Hume 1748, sec. II). Alternatively, one might adopt the view that there is an innately specified similarity space, or way of judging the similarity of percepts. These concessions to nativism are comparatively cheap because perceptual primitives and similarity spaces are independently motivated to explain how we perceive the world. In other words, imagism is a parsimonious theory. It delimits the number of mental media by building concepts from representations used in perception.

The imagist also has an advantage in explaining phylogenetic acquisition. If we can come up with a plausible account of how perceptual systems evolved, then all we need is an account of how perceptual states came to be stored in memory and used as concepts. In contrast, if concepts were not derived from perceptual states, then it would be more difficult to explain how they evolved. It is generally easier to explain how evolution puts an existing tool to new uses than to explain how new tools evolve.

Imagism also offers an account of cognitive content. One might explain the fact that the identity between the morning star and the evening star can be informative by pointing out that one can form two different images corresponding to these distinct descriptions. Conversely, one might explain the commonality between my concept of water and my doppelgänger's concept of twin water by saying that both comprise images of a clear, tasteless liquid.

Imagism can also be used to explain certain kinds of categorization. Category identification often involves the recognition of objects encountered in perception. Imagism simplifies this task by claiming that concepts are qualitatively similar to percepts. The perceptual state caused by seeing a dog can be compared directly to a DOG concept because that concept is a copy of a perceptual state caused by a previous encounter with a dog. Category production can be explained by our ability to "read information off" images. We describe dogs as furry and as having tails because such features are apparent in our dog images. The typicality effects mentioned in the preceding chapter can be explained by the fact that some members of a category are perceptually more salient and therefore more likely to be represented in images. A percept caused by seeing an atypical dog is less like the image constituting my DOG concept than the percept caused by a typical dog.

Some experimental results also suggest an imagistic explanation of basic-level categorization. Rosch et al. (1976) demonstrate that basic-level categories can be represented by a single mental image. In one test for this hypothesis, they gave subjects category names at different levels of categorization followed by briefly presented, degraded pictures of members of those categories. They found that subordinate and basic-level category names increased picture recognition more than superordinate names. Rosch at al. conclude that the basic level is the highest level of abstraction that can be captured by mental images. Superior performance at this level might be taken as evidence that concepts comprise images, as the imagists maintain.

Despite these apparent strengths, imagism has fallen on hard times. It is the only account I consider that does not have a broad base of support within contemporary cognitive science. One complaint is that imagism does not satisfy the scope requirement. It is highly unlikely that there could be an image corresponding to each of the concepts we possess. Some concepts are hard to image because they designate nonperceptible entities or properties. For example, there seem to be no images corresponding to virtue, truth, or prime number. Other concepts are hard to image because they abstract away from perceptual differences. This is Berkeley's point in insisting that every image of a triangle is either scalene, equilateral, or isosceles. Berkeley's observation was intended to show that Locke should embrace imagism more fully, but it can also be used to argue for the opposite conclusion. If concepts were images and images cannot represent triangularity, then there would be no way to form a concept of triangularity. Of course, we do posses such a concept, so imagism must be wrong.

Berkeley responds to this objection by showing that an image of a particular object can be used to represent a class of objects. He notes that particular triangles are often drawn to support geometric proofs about all triangles. Hume shared this view, and it may have been Locke's actual position as well. The difficulty is that none of these authors offer an adequate theory of use. How do we use a particular image to represent a class? A natural suggestion is that we ignore those features that make it unique. The suggestion works in the triangle case. A geometer's proof might exploit the fact that her triangle figure has three interior angles, while ignoring the fact that those angles have some specific measurements. The problem is that this strategy cannot work for all cases. How do we form an image of justice? Perhaps we form an image of a particular just act and ignore those features that make it unique. But what features remain? What part of the image of a just act can stand in for all instances of justice? Berkeley's proposal for capturing abstract ideas without abstraction may work for triangularity, but it does not lend itself to concepts whose instances lack perceivable similarities. By seeking a thoroughgoing imagism, Berkeley and Hume seem to have also discovered a reductio ad absurdum of empiricism.

Problems also plague the imagist account of categorization. On closer analysis, imagism does not predict the basic-level advantage. The basic level lies at an intermediate level of abstraction. We more readily categorize something as a dog than as a rottweiler or an animal. Likewise, we more readily categorize an object as a triangle than as a scalene triangle or as a polygon. This finding is at odds with imagism. Berkeley's critique of Locke demonstrates that the intermediate level is more abstract than most images. Insofar as images are like pictures, they generally cannot depict something as a dog without also providing information that would indicate its variety, and they cannot depict something as a triangle without providing information about the relative sizes of its interior angles. If it is easier to form images of things at this level of specificity, then it should also be easier to imagistically categorize things at this level of specificity. Therefore, imagistic theories of concepts incorrectly predict optimal categorization performance at too low a level of abstraction. Shape similarities at the basic level might facilitate basic-level categorization and explain Rosch et al.'s experimental results on an imagist account, but subordinate-level categorization should be easier.

The specificity of images also leads to a problem with publicity. If my concepts are constituted by my images of the objects I have experienced, they differ from your concepts for the simple reason that we have experienced different objects. If my DOG concept was generated by perceptual encounters with rottweilers and yours was generated by perceptual encounters with chihuahuas, our concepts consist of very different images. To satisfy the publicity requirement, it seems that concepts must abstract away from the differences between particular category members. Images, as imagists traditionally conceive them, do not do that.

A further problem is that images are ambiguous. All images resemble many different things. An image resembling a man ascending a hill also resembles a man descending a hill (Wittgenstein 1953), an image resembling dogs also resemble wolves (Price 1953), and an image resembling a person with a distended belly also resembles a pregnant person (Fodor 1975). These ambiguities raise problems concerning intentional content. Imagists generally presume that images refer by resemblance. Russell writes, "The 'meaning' of images is the simplest kind of meaning, because images resemble what they mean" (1921). If imagists adopt resemblance theories of intentionality, then ambiguous images refer ambiguously. Thus, images are less specific than concepts. A concept can refer to dogs and only dogs, but an image resembling dogs also resembles, and hence refers to, wolves. This raises serious doubts about attempts to provide resemblance-based theories of intentionality.

The imagists account of intentional content is plagued by further problems. Following Descartes (1637), Berkeley (1710) argues that mental images and the extramental world might be so radically different that resemblance between the two is impossible. This worry poses an equal threat to dualists and materialists, who assert an identity between mental states and brain states (or causal roles filled by brain states). Brain states do not seem to resemble the extramental world. Berkeley resolves this problem by concluding the world is really made up of ideas. Resemblance between mind and world is secured by idealism.

A materialist can respond to Berkeley's challenge by appeal to structural isomorphism (Russell 1927, see also Palmer 1978). Isomorphism requires only a one-to-one mapping between features of our brain's representational systems and features of the world. Brain states need not look like their referents in order to be isomorphic with them. More interestingly, there is now evidence that certain brain states do resemble their referents. By staining monkey brains, researchers have discovered retinotopically organized maps in visual areas of the brain (Tootell, Silverman, Switkes, and De Valois 1982). Like pictures, adjacent neural populations in these areas corresponds to adjacent boundaries or surface points in the objects they represent.

One problem with this response is that many areas of cortex are not organized into retinotopic (or other kinds of topographic) maps. Another problem is that brain-world resemblances are still vulnerable to an objection presented above: any given brain state is structurally isomorphic with many different things.

Goodman (1976) advances other objections to the resemblance theory of intentionality. He argues that resemblance, unlike reference, is symmetric. A person resembles her portrait as much as that portrait resembles her. Nevertheless, a person does not refer to her portrait. This also shows that resemblance cannot be sufficient for reference. Indeed, any two objects resemble each other in one way or another, but this does not mean that every object refers to everything else.

Once we have admitted the insufficiency of resemblance in explaining intentionality, Goodman then argues that resemblance plays no role at all. Assume that my mental image of a dog cannot represent a dog solely in virtue of resembling one. To explain its intentionality, we might supplement the resemblance story by saying that my dog image is a perceptual state that was initially caused by my seeing a dog. Once we have introduced this causal story, the fact my dog image resembles a dog seems to do no explanatory work. If my mental image was caused by a dog but does not resemble one (*per impossible*, given the ubiquity of resemblance), it might still represent one (consider a very abstract painting).

The final problem I consider involves compositionality. As I indicate above, empiricists believe that images combinable. Hume's golden mountain is an example. Trained artists learn to combine simple pictorial elements in countless ways. A simple pattern for painting a tree can be reproduced at different scales and at different places on a canvas. Patterns for drawing human body parts can be recombined to depict people in different positions. Piecing together drawings of different animals can generate chimeras. One can construct a diagrammatic system in which pictures of building components (walls, columns, windows, etc.) plus rules for combination allow one to generate complex architectural drawings compositionally (Mitchell 1990). All this suggests that the imagist should be somewhat optimistic about explaining compositionality.

Such optimism is quickly extinguished. First, there is often no systematic way to build complex images from simpler ones. Someone who can picture a carnivorous organism and a plant is necessarily able to form an accurate image of a carnivorous plant. Second, images of complex things often cannot be decomposed into obvious components. Someone who can picture a carnivorous plant cannot necessarily picture other carnivorous organisms or other plants. The way carnivorousness or planthood are depicted might vary from one context to the next. Concepts, in contrast, have to be the kinds of things that can be recombined productively.

One can conclude that imagism, as traditionally conceived, cannot succeed. In later chapters I argue that a modernized descendent of imagism may fare considerably better, but I first evaluate a variety of other theories.

2.2   Definitionism

According to a theory that can also be traced back to the ancient world, concepts are definitions. This approach was once so widespread that it has been dubbed the Classical Theory of concepts by psychologists (Smith and Medin 1981). According to definitionists (as I call them), concepts can be identified with sets of individually necessary and jointly sufficient features or conditions. Definitionism seems to work well for certain taxonomic and kinship terms. To take some hackneyed examples, the concept BACHELOR is traditionally identified with the features UN-MARRIED, ADULT, MALE, and HUMAN BEING; a VIXEN is a FEMALE FOX; and a MOTHER is a FEMALE PARENT. Mathematical and theoretical terms are also often definable. An EVEN NUMBER is A NUMBER DIVISIBLE BY TWO WITHOUT REMAINDER, and a TRIANGLE is A CLOSED POLYGON WITH

THREE INTERIOR ANGLES. Definitionism also does a reasonably good job with certain artifact concepts. For example, an AXEL is a ROD CONNECTING TWO WHEELS, and, more controversially, a COMPUTER is an AUTOMATIC INTERPRETED FORMAL SYSTEM (Haugeland 1985). This last example illustrates the fact that some definitions can be discovered only through careful investigation and analysis. Philosophers have suggested, and subsequently criticized, the proposals that TRUTH is CORRESPONDANCE WITH A FACT and KNOWLEDGE is JUSTIFIED TRUE BELIEF. Much of philosophy concerns itself with the search for such definitions. This activity is dubbed "conceptual analysis," and its practitioners typically assume that concepts can be identified with their successful analyses. Definitionism is the view that concepts can be analyzed into sets of defining conditions.

Plato was the seminal definitionist. Many of his dialogues try to arrive at definitions of important concepts, such as LOVE, GOOD, and PIETY. According to Plato, we dwell in an abstract realm before birth. That realm is occupied by ideal "Forms," which are timeless, abstract objects that capture the essences of the things found in terrestrial life. They constitute the defining conditions in virtue of which dogs are dogs and good things are good. After birth, tacit memories of the Forms allow us to categorize concrete, real-world objects. We can make our tacit knowledge explicit by a process of "recollection," which is facilitated by philosophical analysis and dialogue. For Plato, the Forms serve as concepts. They are the entities by whose acquaintance we are able to think about the world.

Definitionism remained popular long after Plato. Descartes's (1637) ontological argument infers the existence of God from the definition of the concept GOD, and Kant (1783) introduces the notion of analyticity to describes judgments in which one concept is contained in the definition constituting another. The judgment that sisters are siblings might be a case in point. The notion of conceptual containment is a bit obscure, but some notion of analyticity is now widely recognized as an important presupposition of the definitionist position. If concepts consist of necessary features, then we should be able to read off necessary truths from our concepts. Analyticity is now more frequently construed as a property of sentences rather than of judgments. A sentence is analytically true if it is true in virtue of what its terms mean (where meanings are presumed to be concepts). Synthetic truths, in contrast, are true in virtue of how the world is.

Frege also articulates a version of definitionism. He explicitly seeks definitions for mathematical concepts with the hope of reducing arithmetic to logic. Definitionism may also lie behind Frege's notion of sense. His claim that the sense of a term determines its referent is often interpreted as the claim that senses consist of defining conditions that objects must satisfy to fall under the corresponding terms. If we identify concepts with senses so construed, we arrive at the view that a concept is a set of necessary and sufficient conditions. Like Plato, Frege believes that senses are abstract objects, but he also says they are constituents of thoughts. The apparent conflict between these views is eliminated by the fact that thoughts are also abstract objects for Frege. Thoughts and the senses that compose them can nevertheless be grasped psychologically. It is by grasping senses that linguistic expressions come to have cognitive significance for us.

Definitionism of the kind endorsed by Plato and Frege differs markedly from imagism, but the two views need not be opposed. Many philosophers have argued that definitionism can be improved by joining forces with imagism or some other brand of empiricism. Without this alliance, definitionism faces a problem. All definitions must be built up from a foundation of concepts that are themselves undefined. If each defining feature of a concept were itself a concept that must be defined by still other concepts, we would enter into a regress. One attempt to avoid this regress is to say that concepts are entangled in a kind of web. That may have been Wittgenstein's view in the *Tractatus*. But if all concepts are understood in terms of other concepts, we are still trapped in a circle. Wittgenstein accepted this conclusion. He embraced a semantic solipsism according to which an individual's world is, in some sense, exhausted by a network of interlinked concepts and propositions.

Those who want to break out of the circle generally conjecture that all concepts ultimately decompose into undefined primitives that do not require further analysis. But which concepts are primitive? What kinds of concepts can be understood without analysis? Historically, the most popular answer has been that the primitives are perceptual. The simplest version of the view, sometimes attributed to Hume, is that primitive concepts are simple mental images, and all complex concepts are definitional composites of them.

A more recent marriage of definitionism and empiricism came out of Vienna. Logical positivists believed that concepts can be defined in terms of observable verification conditions. These definitions were specified linguistically with a vocabulary of observation terms, which designate observable conditions or sense-data. In providing definitions, logical positivists tended to focus on terms found in scientific theories. They were concerned with stipulating definitions that could be scientifically useful rather than describing the definitions that were naturally deployed in thought. In this sense, their brand of imagist definitionism was normative, whereas the older tradition had been a form of descriptive psychology.

Positivism and imagist definitionism waned in the 1950s. It is extremely hard to come up with definitions that reduce concepts to sensory states. For example, suppose KILL can be defined as CAUSE TO DIE. How can we reduce CAUSE TO DIE to sensory states? We might be able to find concepts that characterize what causing someone to die typically looks like, but having those typical looks is not a necessary condition for being an instance of killing. Therefore, if we really want concepts to be *definitions* and not, say, representations of typical appearances, the empiricist project must be abandoned. Nonsensory states must be admitted into our conceptual repertoires. The logical positivists thought that we must define concepts by appeal to observable verification conditions in order to facilitate scientific communication. Critics rebuffed by noting that scientists chronically postulate unobservable entities and regard observable tests for such entities to be contingent. If two labs use a different test for detecting the presence of electrons, they do not mean different things by "electron."

Definitionism outlived logical positivism. Early cognitive psychologists presumed that some form of definitionism is true (Bruner, Goodnow, and Austin 1956). Researchers interested in linguistics also jumped on the bandwagon. In a theory inspired by Chomsky's seminal work in syntax, Katz and Fodor (1963) argue that all concepts have definitions that are organized in branching-tree structures (like syntactic trees) and stored in the mental equivalent of a dictionary. This tradition is continued by current work in lexical semantics. Unlike positivists, lexical semanticists do not shy away from innate nonsensory concepts such as CAUSE and DIE (Jackendoff 1983).

Peacocke (1992) advances another recent incarnation of definitionism. He argues that concepts should be individuated by possession conditions. Possession conditions are sets of inferences that a person must master to possess a concept. For instance, the concept of CONJUNCTION is possessed by someone who finds inferences from "A" and "B" to "A & B" and from "A & B" to "A" or "B" primitively compelling. While not committed to empiricism, Peacocke does think that certain concepts can be related to perception. The possession conditions for observational concepts include finding it compelling to make certain judgments under certain observational conditions. For example, one can be said to possess the concept SQUARE only if one finds it compelling to judge "That is square" when visually confronted with square objects. The compulsion rests, in turn, on having the ability to recognize, be means of nonconceptual representations, the presence of lines, right angles, and certain kinds of symmetries.

In addition to possession conditions, each concept has what Peacocke calls a determination theory, which determines its semantic content. The determination theory explains how possession conditions, together with the world, determine semantic content. The concept CONJUNCTION designates the conjunction relation in virtue of the fact that its determination theory specifies that CONJUNCTION designates the relation that makes the inferences forming its possession conditions truth-preserving. SQUARE designates squares because the determination theory specifies that SQUARE pick out those objects that satisfy the conditions under which we judge something to be square in accordance with the possession conditions of SQUARE. Very roughly, the idea can be summarized by saying that each concept is individuated by a set of inferences, and each concept refers to whatever makes those inferences true (or truth-preserving). Possessing a concept is a matter of knowing what conditions need to be satisfied for something to fall under that concept. This is a definitionist thesis.

For Peacocke, like Plato and Frege, concepts are abstract objects. For lexical semanticists and imagist-definitionists, concepts are mental representations. At first glance, these two ontological perspectives may appear markedly different. One places concepts in the Platonic heavens, and the other places them in the head. This difference does not matter for the purposes at hand. Definitionists who deny that concepts are mental representations still insist that they are mentally accessed. Platonic Forms, senses, and possession conditions can be recollected, grasped, or learned. Plato, Frege, and Peacocke also insist that concepts underwrite various cognitive abilities, such as categorization and inference. To make sense of this, concepts that are construed as abstracta must have mental counterparts. Conversely, concepts construed as mental representations have abstract counterparts. While tokens of mental representations are concrete entities existing in people's minds, mental-representation *types* are abstract (compare: individual cows are concrete objects, but the property of being a cow is abstract). One can reconcile the two species of definitionism by proposing that concept types are abstract objects, and concept tokens are mental representations of those abstracta.

One advantage of definitionism is that it offers an ostensibly promising explanation of intentionality. Rather than appealing to the problematic notion of resemblance, definitions appeal to satisfaction. Definitions consist of necessary and sufficient conditions, and concepts refer to whatever satisfies those conditions (as with Peacocke's determination theories). UNCLE, for example, refers to all and only male siblings of parents. Satisfying a definition, unlike resembling an image, is sufficient for reference, and because definitions can pick out very exact groups of things, the definition view avoids the problems that plagued imagism.

The apparent success of definitions in accounting for intentionality also contributes to an attractive account of intentional compositionality. The intentional content of a thought or compound concept must be determined by the intentional content of its constituent concepts together with combination rules. Consider the concept WOODEN CHAIR. On a definition theory, the constituents of this compound might be defined as follows: x is WOODEN if and only if x is made of the material that constitutes the trunks and branches of trees and bushes, and x is a chair if and only if x is a portable seat for one. In addition, there might be a combination rule that says x is an ADJECTIVE-NOUN if and only if x is a member of the intersection of the intentional contents of ADJECTIVE and NOUN. When this rule is applied to the present example, it entails that x is a WOODEN CHAIR just in case x is a portable seat for one made of the material that constitutes the trunks and branches of bushes and trees. Similar rules can be used to derive contents for WOODEN HOUSE or WOODEN SPOON, on the one hand, and PLASTIC CHAIR or ROCKING CHAIR, on the other. The compounds inherit their intentional contents from their parts.

Definitions are alleged to satisfy the cognitive-content requirement. Frege's posits sense for just that purpose. Like images, two definitions that pick out the same intentional content can be different. Compare: x is the MORNING STAR if and only if x is the largest visible celestial body other than the Sun and the Moon in the morning, and x is the EVENING STAR if and only if x is the largest visible celestial body other than the Sun and the Moon in the evening. These distinct sets of conditions converge on a single object, the planet Venus. We have distinct cognitive contents with a common referent. Twin Earth cases get a similar treatment. My Twin Earth doppelgänger and I can have a WATER concept that is defined as the clear liquid in rivers and streams.[1] These refer to different substances on our respective planets, but the concepts are alike.

Definitionists also seem to do well with the publicity requirement. They are aided here by their endorsement of an analytic/synthetic distinction. This distinction allows one to draw a sharp line separating features that are definitive for a concept and features that are not. If such a distinction obtains, we can say that, among the many features we associate with members of a category, only a small subset defines the concept for that category. Without an analytic/synthetic distinction, all features associated with a concept, or at least all necessary features, could be candidates for conceptual constituents. Suppose that I have the true belief that all bachelors have 46 chromosomes and you, having slept through your biology class, disagree. Does this mean we have different BACHELOR concepts? Are we talking past each other when we use the word "bachelor"? By selecting a restricted set of defining features, definitionists can constrain concept size and increase chances of sharing.

Despite these apparent virtues, definitionism suffers from some serious flaws. One problem involves the primitives from which definitions are built. As we saw, imagist definitionists claim that those primitives are sensory. This is an appealing idea because primitive concepts are often presumed to be innate, and it does not strain intuitions to suppose that we are innately equipped with sensory capacities. Nevertheless, imagist definitionism is now regarded as implausible. Definitionists must now say what the primitives are. One strategy for answering this first question is to analyze concepts into their parts until we arrive at features that seem to be undefined. For example, BACHELOR may reduce to UNMARRIED MAN, and UNMARRIED may reduce to NOT and MARRIED, but its hard to see how the feature MARRIED can be further reduced. If MARRIED is primitive and primitives are innate, then MARRIED is innate. This seems implausible because marriage is a social practice that postdates the evolution of our genome. We cannot improve situations by further decomposing MARRIED because candidate features fall prey to the same problem. Perhaps MARRIED means HAVING BEEN BOUND BY A RITUAL THAT BINDS TWO PEOPLE INTO A CONTRACT THAT CONFERS THE RESPONSIBILITY OF MUTUAL LOYALTY AND SUPPORT. Are we to presume that RITUAL, CONTRACT, and RESPONSIBILITY are innate? Even if this were plausible, it would deprive definitionism of its motivation. Concepts are presumed to decompose into defining features that are basic in some sense (e.g., universally shared, simple to understand, used to build many concepts, etc.). The features that one comes up with in providing definitions often appear at least as complex as the concepts they purport to define (Armstrong, Gleitman, and Gleitman 1983). Once empiricist projects are abandoned, hope for a set of basic building blocks seems to wane.

One can also raise concerns about the definitionists' account of intentionality. According that account, a concept refers to those things that satisfy its defining conditions. Suppose that VIXEN refers to all and only things that satisfy FEMALE and FOX. Now we must say what it is to satisfy these conditions. In virtue of what does something satisfy FOX? Perhaps it is in virtue of satisfying some further conditions. This simply pushes the problem of reference back a level. Eventually we must come to a set of primitive concepts. Suppose that FOX is primitive. To say that FOX refers to things that satisfy it tells us absolutely nothing, because "satisfaction" is a synonym for "reference." A theory of intentionality must say why certain things and not others satisfy the concepts that they do. The satisfaction theory appears helpful because we can think of definitions as referring to things that satisfy each item on a checklist of conditions, but when we consider one item at a time, we realize that definitionists provide no theory of what it is to satisfy a condition. They postpone the problem of intentionality rather than solving it.

Another difficulty stems from Wittgenstein's (1953) well-known discussion of concepts like GAME. The features we use to identify something as a game are not necessary for falling in that category. For example, games do not all involve two or more sides (consider solitaire), and they do not all have a winner (consider catch). Wittgenstein concludes that there is no set of common features uniting all and only games. Instead, games are unified by a family resemblance: any pair of games share some features in virtue of which they both count as games, but different pairs share different features.

In response to cases like this, definitionists can argue that family-resemblance concepts have disjunctive definitions. Perhaps something is a game if and only if it has at least three of the following features: having two sides *or* having a winner *or* being a source of amusement *or* having a set of rules *or* involving a ball. This is a definition, but it departs from traditional definitionism, which is characterized by the view that concepts consist of conditions that are individually necessary.

Another problem stems from Quine's (1951) critique of analyticity, which can be briefly summarized as follows. First, Quine argues that standard definitions of analyticity are circular. They define analyticity in terms or meaning, semantic necessity, or some other construct that presupposes a clear division between the analytic and the synthetic. Second and more important, he argues that prevailing accounts of analyticity are committed to a false theory of belief confirmation. Analytic truths are presumed to be invulnerable to empirical revision. Quine claims that no truths have this status. Confirmation is a holistic process. When confronted with an unexpected piece of evidence, we consider how our entire set of beliefs can be adjusted with minimal disruption. For example, suppose my uncle gets a sex change. I can conclude that he is no longer my uncle, or I can conclude that not all uncles are male. The latter alternative is a live option even though it involves a change in a belief taken to be analytic on traditional accounts. Every belief is answerable to experience.

Critics of Quine can try to answer his challenge be dissociating analyticity and empirical immunity. But this is easier said than done. If all beliefs are equally revisable, why think that any have a special semantic status? Anyone who believes in definitions has the burden of explaining what distinguishes defining features from nondefining features. This challenge is serious, because it threatens to undermine the definitionists' ability to satisfy the publicity requirement. If there is no principled way to distinguish analytic beliefs from collateral knowledge, definitions devolve into unwieldy, holistic bundles. The sum of my beliefs about uncles or bachelors surely differs from yours. Thus, until definitionists provide a principled analytic/synthetic distinction, they have difficulty explaining how concepts can be shared.

Definitionism is most seriously threatened by the scope requirement. It is extremely difficult to find concepts that have plausible definitions (Fodor, Garrett, Walker, and Parkes 1980; Fodor 1981). Throughout the history of philosophy and psychology, there have been attempts to defend versions of the definition theory, and each generation has had to rediscover that most of the concepts we use are impossible to define. Any attempt to specify the necessary and sufficient conditions for membership in a category is vulnerable to counterexamples. Even the concepts that seem easiest to define lack airtight definitions. For example, intuitions suggest that a Catholic priest is an unmarried man, but not a bachelor; a children's swing is a portable seat for one, but it is not a chair; a sperm donor is a male progenitor, but not a father.

Defenders of reference-based semantic theories, mentioned in chapter 1 (Putnam 1975, Kripke 1980), emphasize a related problem. They argue that ordinary language users do not rely on definitions in their understanding of proper names and natural-kind terms. Instead, people use descriptions that merely fix reference by appeal to contingent features. One might identify Plato as the author of *The Republic*, but he was Plato prior to writing that work and would still have been Plato had he never written a word. Therefore, being the author of *The Republic* cannot be essential to the meaning of the word "Plato." Likewise, we identify gold by its shinny yellow color, but a shinny yellow color is neither necessary nor sufficient for being gold. Fool's gold is not gold, but it is shiny and yellow, while tarnished pink gold is gold, but is neither shinny nor yellow. There may be features that are essential to being gold (an atomic number) or being Plato (a genetic description), but most people have no cognitive access to such information. Most people possess concepts without knowing the necessary and sufficient conditions for falling under those concepts.

Definitionism also fails to provide an adequate account of concept acquisition. Allen and Brooks (1991) experimentally demonstrate that definitions are not easy to learn by observation. Subjects are shown a group of pictures of creatures that fall into two distinct categories, which can be distinguished by a simple rule. After viewing these examples, they are asked to categorize a group of pictures of other instances of the same two categories. Subjects who were not told the categorization rule frequently misclassified pictures of creatures that satisfied the rule for one category but resembled a previously viewed picture of creatures from the other category. This shows that rules are hard to learn by observation. More surprising, subjects who are explicitly taught the rule during training make the same kinds of errors, though not as frequently. These findings seriously jeopardize the definition theory. Most of our concepts are not learned by explicit rule instruction. When instruction occurs, it often takes the form of ostensive definition (e.g., "That is an elephant," said while pointing). The results of Allen and Brooks suggest that we do not learn definitions under such conditions. And when definitions are explicitly taught, these results suggest that this knowledge is subverted by reliance on observed similarities between instances.

Definitionism is also ill equipped to explain certain facts about categorization. First, it fails to explain basic-level categorization (Rosch et al. 1976, Smith and Medin 1981). Definitionism does not predict that categorization will be easiest at an intermediate level of abstraction, because there is no reason to think that definitions at that level are qualitatively different from other levels. In fact, definitionism sometimes predicts an advantage for the more abstract superordinate level because superordinate concepts can be included in the definitions of basic-level concepts. For example, a definition of TRIANGLE might include the feature POLYGON, and a definition of DOG might include the feature ANIMAL. This means that someone has to identify something as a polygon or as an animal before identifying it as a triangle or a dog, respectively. If so, superordinate categorization should be faster.

Definitionism is equally unable to explain or predict typicality effects (Rosch 1975, Rosch and Mervis 1975). In a definition, all defining features are treated equally; each places a necessary condition on falling under the defined concept. There is no reason why some features should be identified faster than others or used to identify category members more readily. Moreover, Hampton (1979) finds that typicality effects often occur for features that are not necessary for category membership. Something counts as a typical bird and is identified more readily if it flies, even though flight is not a necessary condition for being a bird. Subjects do not categorize on the basis of features presumed to be shared by all category members. Such observations led to the demise of definitionism in psychology.

The evidence suggests that definitions are not psychologically real. In response the definitionist might consider two strategies. The first is to claim that definitions are not the bread and butter of cognition, but deep underlying knowledge that takes considerable training to elicit. Definitions are in the head, but they are hidden from view. The cases that seem to support this contention most closely are the ones that keep philosophers in business. Philosophers spend many hard hours trying to draw out definitions of such lofty notions as the good, the true, and the beautiful. When definitions for such concepts are proposed, we seem to have strong intuitions about which ones are plausible and which ones are not. The availability of such intuitions might suggest that deep down we really know definitions for the good, the true, and the beautiful. They are psychologically real structures, which come to the surface given enough effort and intuition probing.

This conception of what goes on in philosophical analysis is alluring, but not obligatory. When good definitions are attained through analysis, it is not necessarily by tapping into some preexisting mental structure. An alternative possibility is that we mentally store a bunch of paradigm cases for familiar categories and subsequently devise sets of conditions that unite them. For example, there may be a bunch of facts that I take myself to *know*. My reasons for grouping these together as instances of KNOWLEDGE rather than mere conjecture may stem from some relatively superficial fact. Perhaps they are beliefs that I feel especially disinclined to give up. In searching for a definition, I may discover that the beliefs that I am least likely to give up are also true, justified, and grounded in reasons that are not accidental. This does not mean that my concept KNOWLEDGE was tacitly associated with a mental structure consisting of the features NONACCIDENTALLY JUSTIFIED, TRUE, and BELIEF.

Consider a second example. I may believe that it is good to give to Oxfam, and that it is good to save a child from a burning house. Perhaps I group these together on the basis of the fact that both tend to generate gratitude. I subsequently speculate about other unifying properties: both tend to increase net happiness, I would want both to be universal laws, both exemplify the character trait of kindness, and so on. Such discoveries do not imply that I always possessed the definitions of THE GOOD proposed by utilitarians, Kantians, and virtue theorists. Philosophical analysis does not expose concepts hidden away within our conceptual systems; it provides principled ways of grouping together category instances that had initially been assembled by some rough and ready means.[2] A proposed definition strikes us as "intuitive" when it gets the grouping right, not when it awakens tacit knowledge. The latter idea may be a philosophical myth left over from Plato's doctrine of recollection.

Definitionists can also respond to arguments against the psychological reality of definitions by conceding the point. This strategy has been advocated by Rey (1983, 1985). Like Plato, Frege, and Peacocke, Rey believes that concepts are definitions, but he also concedes that in some cases the definition making up a concept is unknown to the possessor of that concept. In these cases, Rey says that concepts consist of "external definitions." A definition is a specification of the metaphysical conditions that are necessary and sufficient for belonging to a category. For example, the concept DOG consists of the conditions that something must satisfy to be a dog. Such conditions on membership are unknown to most of us. Indeed, they are often unknown to the scientific community and must await further empirical investigation. But this does not mean there is no definition of doghood. That definition is external: it is a fact about the world, not a mental state of those who possess the concept DOG. The definition of doghood awaits scientific discovery.

Rey's theory of external definitions escapes a number of the objections that face other definitionists. Most of those objections attempt to establish that definitions lack psychological reality. Definitions are very hard to come by. People generally do not know them, have trouble learning them, and once they have learned them, find them difficult to apply. These observations suggest that many of our concepts are not mentally represented by definitions. If so, we have reason to reject any form of definitionism that assumes that the definitions of the concepts we possess are psychologically real. Rey's theory has an apparent advantage because it rejects this assumption. If definitions are unknown, the results that undermine other forms of definitionism pose no threat.

In effect, Rey has insulated his theory against standard attacks by flouting the acquisition, categorization, and cognitive-content desiderata as I have formulated them. He admits that concepts are difficult to learn and that categorization and ordinary thoughts about categories are mediated by superficial features that are neither necessary nor sufficient. We think about dogs using such contingent features as barking and tail wagging. He calls these features conceptions rather than concepts (Rey 1985). Concept researchers have been led astray by failing to keep these apart. Conceptions explain epistemological facts (e.g., how we judge that something is a dog), while concepts explain metaphysical facts (e.g., what makes something a dog).

But why do concepts explain metaphysics rather than epistemology? Rey's answer is that identifying concepts with the structures that underwrite our epistemological abilities would jeopardize the publicity requirement. People can identify dogs in any number of different ways, but what makes a dog a dog remains constant. Thus, the principles underwriting dog metaphysics are better suited than the principles we use to identify dogs for explaining how people share concepts.

To evaluate Rey's theory, one must keep in mind that concepts are theoretical entities postulated to serve certain explanatory purposes. Most often, they are postulated to play a role in the explanation of behavior.

Concepts are the ingredients of thoughts, and thoughts are the things we advert to in explaining how people act. This explanatory goal is hardly anomalous. It is the prevailing motive behind concept research in cognitive science. Once we recognize this goal, Rey's external-definition approach is not very satisfying. If definitions are unknown or deeply hidden entities that do not guide our ordinary cognitive practices, their ascription cannot explain ordinary behavior. Suppose we say that Jones got charcoal because she wanted to ignite the grill and believed that charcoal is flammable. Does her behavior depend on her knowing exactly what makes something charcoal or on what fire really is? It would seem not. Her behavior depends on her knowing how to recognize charcoal and her believing that real instances of it possess certain properties, which she can also recognize and which serve her current desires. The successful procurement and utilization of charcoal, which is the behavior we want to explain, does not hinge on definitional knowledge. Likewise for the overwhelming majority of what we do.

Rey (1985) replies to a related objection. Smith, Medin, and Rips (1984) argue that Rey's theory is irrelevant to psychology because it identifies concepts with definitions that are not mentally represented. In response, Rey insists that even when definitions are unknown, they are psychologically relevant. This comes out most typically in modal contexts. We do not know what makes a dog a dog, but we do know that something could still be a dog if it did not bark or wag its tail. In other words, we know that the features we use to identify dogs are contingent and that some definition of doghood exists. If we want a theory of concepts to explain ordinary cognitive abilities, it should explain our modal judgments. The external-definition account does just that.

Rey's reply touches on an important point. We do know that the metaphysical conditions of category membership go beyond the conditions that we typically use to categorize. But this basic maxim is all that we need to explain our modal intuitions. The definitions themselves, in all their detail, still do no psychological work. Therefore, when Rey identifies the concept DOG with a definition, he identifies it with an entity that cannot explain the myriad ordinary cognitively mediated actions that a theory of concepts should explain (including the modal judgments that he uses to defend his theory).

Another problem faces Rey's account. Definitionists who endorse the psychological-reality assumption have a plausible theory of concept possession; in particular, they can say that we possess a concept when we have mentally represented the definition that constitutes it. On Rey's view, concepts must come to be possessed in some other way. He proposes that we come to possess concepts by becoming causally "locked on to" the properties defining them. To a first approximation, we possess the concept DOG, which is a metaphysical definition, by becoming reliable dog detectors. We detect dogs using contingent features such as barking and tail wagging, and this endows us with the ability to refer to dogs. Once we have states that refer to dogs (i.e., states that have doghood as their intentional content), we can be said to "possess" the DOG concept, which specifies what doghood is. In this sense, Rey's theory of natural-kind concepts is really a hybrid of definitionism and informational atomism, which I discuss in chapter 4. He provides a definitionist theory of concept identity and an informationalist (i.e., reliable-detector) theory of concept possession.

This account of concept possession may be worth considering, but it undercuts a major motivation behind Rey's definitionism. Rey thinks that identifying concepts with external definitions is the only way to satisfy the publicity desideratum. This motivation is undermined by his account of concept possession. People possess concepts, on his view, not by mentally representing definitions but by becoming locked onto the same properties. Why not explain publicity the same way? Two people can be said to share a concept by being locked onto the same property. In other words, we can explain the commonality across individuals with different inner psychological states by appeal to the referents of those states. There is no need to appeal to common definitions.

Rey is unsatisfied with this reply. He thinks there are certain cases for which publicity cannot be explained by appeals to common referents. These are the cases where concepts necessarily lack referents. As examples, Rey (personal communication) cites such concepts as SOUL, FREE WILL, and MONSTER. He thinks there are no possible worlds in which these concepts refer. At the same time, he thinks they can be shared. If so, not all cases of concept sharing can be explained by appeal to shared referents.

3
Similarity-Based Accounts

In the preceding chapter, I reviewed two theories of concepts that have been important to philosophers. Support for imagism has waned, but definitionism retains a loyal following in some philosophical circles. Definitionism cannot boast such enduring popularity in psychology. A battery of inventive experiments led cognitive and developmental psychologists to conclude that definitions are not psychologically real. Most of this evidence comes from studies of categorization, where it was found that people often group objects together on the basis of similarity judgments. This discovery was thought to have important implications for the nature of conceptual structure, and it led to the emergence of two new theories of concepts in the 1970s. I critically examine these similarity-based theories in this chapter.

3.1 Prototype Theory

In the late 1960s, Posner and Keele (1968) performed a series of experiments in which they showed subjects patterns formed out of small dots. In the training phase of the experiment, subjects practiced sorting a number of different dot patterns into four categories. In the test phase, they were given a second set of patterns to sort into the original categories. Some patterns were drawn from the training set and some were new. Among the new patterns were ones that captured the average of each of the four groups of patterns in the training set. Subjects were generally worse at sorting the new patterns, but they sorted the new average patterns as well as the old patterns. A natural explanation of this result is that subjects computed and internally represented an average dot pattern during the original training session, and that this average pattern had been stored in memory.

About the same time, anthropologically oriented psychologists were assessing the Sapir-Whorf hypothesis, according to which linguistic differences determine mental differences. To refute this hypothesis, psychologists showed that people from different cultures organize their color concepts around the same focal values (Berlin and Kay 1969, Heider 1972). Despite differences in the size and nature of color vocabularies, people generally agree on the major divisions between colors (red, yellow, etc.) and on the best instances within those divisions. In cultures with very impoverished color vocabularies, people still exhibit robust sensitivity to these best instances. Similar results were obtained when members of isolated cultures were exposed to geometric shapes for the first time. They showed a preference for perfect triangles even after they had been trained on distorted triangles.

These results suggest that we store information about categories by forming representations of what we take to be their best instances. In the case of the dot patterns, the best instance is an average of several different displays. In the color case, the best instances are presumably determined by focal color values in our visual systems. In the case of geometric shapes, straight lines prevail over irregular lines.

The hypothesis that memory and categorization exploit representations of best instances was developed into a full-fledged theory of concepts over the course of the 1970s. Eleanor Rosch and Carolyn Mervis give its seminal defense (Rosch and Mervis 1975; see also Rosch 1973; Rosch 1975; Smith, Shoben, and Rips 1974; Hampton 1979). They observe that many categories are associated with small sets of "typical" features. Typical features are ones that are diagnostic, statistically frequent, or salient. Unlike defining features, they are often contingent for category membership. Rosch and Mervis also observe that category instances judged to be best are the ones that exhibit the maximum number of typical features. They called these best instances "prototypes" and, appropriating a term from Wittgenstein, said that prototypes maximize family resemblance. Many psychologists adopted the view that concepts are mental representations of these best instances, and they used the term "prototype" to refer to such representations.[1]

Table 3.1
A prototype represented with an attribute-value frame

BIRD	
BODY PARTS (0.5)	BEAK (0.5)
	WINGS (0.4)
	TWO LEGS (0.1)
LOCOMOTION (0.3)	FLIES (0.8)
	WALKS (0.1)
	PADDLES (0.1)
HABITAT (0.1)	TREES (0.9)
	LAKES (0.2)
DIET (0.1)	WORMS (0.4)
	SEEDS (0.4)
	FISH (0.2)

Adapted from Smith 1989, figure 13.1, with permission.

There are a number of ways to make prototype theory more precise, corresponding to different ways in which one can mentally represent the best instance of a category. For example, a prototype might be a point in a multidimensional space, a mental image of some real or idealized category instance, or a set of feature representations (see Smith and Medin 1981). The last option is the most popular and can be further subdivided. On the simplest version, prototypes are just lists of binary features.[2] The concept bird may be represented by HAS WINGS, FLIES, HAS FEATHERS, HAS A BEAK, EATS WORMS. Alternatively, each feature can be assigned weights corresponding to its subjective importance. HAS WINGS may be given a higher value than EATS WORMS. An even more sophisticated version divides features into attributes and values (table 3.1). Rather than simply listing the features above, each of these is represented as a highly weighted item in a range of values along an attribute dimension. For example, a BIRD prototype may have a LOCOMOTION dimension that includes the values FLIES, WALKS, and PADDLES ON WATER, with FLIES having a high weight. In addition, the dimensions themselves can be weighted, so, for example, LOCOMOTION may be treated as more important in our BIRD prototype than a DIET dimension. Attribute dimensions add representational power to prototypes (Barsalou and Hale

1992). They allow concepts to be aligned for focused comparisons. For example, if one wants to compare the diet of several different creatures, one has only to align their DIET attribute dimensions, rather than searching through every feature for the relevant information.

Prototypes were initially postulated to explain typicality effects and basic-level categories. It is therefore unsurprising that prototype theory does an admirable job in satisfying the categorization desideratum. On feature versions, which will be my focus, categorization works as follows. When an object is encountered, its features are mentally represented and compared to prototype representations. This is done by using some kind of similarity metric. In the simplest case, the similarity between an object and a prototype is just the sum of their shared features. On weighted-feature versions, the similarity value contributed by each shared feature depends on its weight. More formally, the similarity between a category instance and a prototype can be measured by equation 3.1:

$$\text{Sim}(I, P) = \sum_{i \in I \cap P} w_i \tag{3.1}$$

Here I and P are the feature sets of the compared instance and prototype. The function sums the weights for each feature i that is in both I and P.

Some similarity metrics, such as Tversky's contrast rule, also compute information about nonshared features (Tversky 1977; adopted in Smith and Osherson 1989 and Hampton 1992). Here similarity is a function of the number of features common to an instance and a prototype minus the number of features unique to each. The idea is captured by the following formula:

$$\text{Sim}(I, P) = (I \cap P) - (I - P) - (P - I) \tag{3.2}$$

Here "$I \cap P$" is shorthand for the number of features common to I and P, while "$I - P$" and "$P - I$" represent the number of features unique to I and unique to P, respectively. This formula can be modified to accommodate feature weights (as in equation 3.1) and attention effects.

Prototype theory also requires a threshold function that specifies how much similarity is required to make a positive categorization (Hampton 1992). If an instance exceeds the critical threshold for just one proto-

Table 3.2
Typicality as measured in a prototype model

ROBIN	EAGLE	CHICKEN	BIRD
Yes	No	No	Small size (0.5)
Yes	Yes	No	Flies (0.8)
Yes	Yes	Yes	Walks (0.8)
Yes	Yes	Yes	Feathered (1.0)
3.1	2.6	1.8	Threshold 1.5

type, it is identified as a member of the category represented by that prototype. Alternatively, one might say that an instance is categorized under the prototype for which it achieves the highest similarity score, even if it is over the threshold for others as well.

Prototype theory is tailored for explaining typicality effects. Category instances are rated as more typical than others when they have a greater number of prototypical features. An illustration of this is given in table 3.2. Several concepts denoting different kinds of birds are compared to the BIRD prototype, which is represented as a weighted-feature list with a categorization threshold of 1.5. Similarities are computed using equation 3.1. All instances are over the threshold, but they vary in the number of features they share with the prototype. This variation is proportional to their intuitive typicality rankings. This explanation has been experimentally corroborated by the fact that typicality ratings are well correlated with the degree of feature overlap (Rosch and Mervis 1975). When one group of subjects lists features associated with a concept and another group rates the typicality of instances, the typicality judgments coincide with the number of features those instances possess from the first subjects' feature lists.

Explanations of why we categorize typical instances fastest vary, depending on one's processing model. One possibility is that when there are many overlapping features, there are fewer differences to tally up in computing similarity. Feature-listing preferences can also be explained. When subjects are asked to describe a category, the features they list are those constituting the prototype, and within that list, the most heavily weighted are listed first.

Prototype theory is equally adept at explaining basic-level categorization (Rosch et al. 1976). According to one explanation, basic-level categories have two significant features. On the one hand, their members share many of their most salient features with each other. On the other hand, their salient features differ substantially from the salient features of sibling categories.[3] In other words, the basic level of categorization is one that maximizes both intracategory similarities and intercategory differences in salient features. A related explanation is that the basic level results from the drive to maximize both intracategory similarity and abstractness. Given these two constraints, the basic level is the highest level at which category members still share salient features. These explanations accurately predict that CAR, TRIANGLE, APPLE, and DOG are basic-level concepts. The intracategory-similarity condition rules out concepts such as VEHICLE, SHAPE, FRUIT, and ANIMAL, and the abstractness and intercategory-difference constraints rule out concepts such as LUXURY SEDAN, ISOCELES TRIANGLE, MACINTOSH APPLE, and ROTTWEILER. Prototype theory also predicts exceptions to the basic-level phenomenon. For example, prototype theorists predict that ostriches will not be categorized at the basic level (i.e., as BIRDS) because ostriches are much more similar to the ostrich prototype than to the BIRD prototype. This is exactly what occurs (Joliceur, Gluck, and Kosslyn 1984).

Prototype theory can also boast a plausible account of concept acquisition. Casual observation of category members is rarely sufficient for discovering a unifying definition, but it is sufficient for abstracting a prototype. Prototypes capture statistical frequencies and saliencies among observable features. Consequently, the most natural way to acquire a prototype is to observe category members. Ostension is the forte of prototype theory. Some experimental support for the ease of prototype acquisition comes from Posner and Keele's (1968) results. Further support comes from the fact that simple, two-layered artificial neural networks can abstract prototypes. The appreciably more complex neural networks in our brains are surely up to the task.

Prototypes also yield a promising account of cognitive content. Informative identities are explained by the fact that prototypes of the same object can differ. For example, the morning star and the evening star correspond to distinct prototypes because one is typically observed in the morning and the other is typically observed in the evening. This distinguishing feature, time of visibility, is a paradigmatic case of a prototype feature: it is contingent but diagnostic.

Now consider Twin Earth cases. The similarity between my WATER concept and my doppelgänger's Twin Earth WATER concept is explained by the fact that they are both comprised of the same prototypical features (e.g., thirst-quenching, clear, liquid). This is exactly the kind of explanation Putnam offered, using the term "stereotype" instead of "prototype," when he introduced Twin Earth (Putnam 1975).

There is fascinating evidence supporting a prototype theory of conceptual combination. In a series of experiments, Hampton (1988) obtained what initially appeared to be violations of compositionality. Consider the conjunctive concept TOOL THAT IS ALSO A WEAPON. Intuitively, everything that falls under this concept should be both a tool and a weapon. Subjects in Hampton's experiment judged differently. For example, they said that a screwdriver is a tool that is also a weapon, but denied that a screwdriver is a weapon! Hampton argues that prototypes are capable of explaining this fact. To simplify, imagine that an object must have more than half of the features represented by a prototype to be included in the category corresponding to that prototype. Suppose that the TOOL prototype consists of features f_1, f_2, and f_3, while the WEAPON prototype consists of features f_4, f_5, and f_6. Suppose further, that two prototypes are conjoined by pooling all their features together. This rule is perfectly compositional because it guarantees that compounds inherit their features from their constituent prototypes. For example, this rule equates TOOL THAT IS ALSO A WEAPON with features f_1 to f_6. Now consider an object possessing just f_1, f_2, f_3, and f_4. Such an object would be identified as a TOOL and as a TOOL THAT IS ALSO A WEAPON, but it would not have enough features to pass the threshold of the WEAPON prototype (see table 3.3). This toy example illustrates how prototypes can be combined compositionally while explaining apparent violations of compositionality.[4]

Unlike images and definitions, prototypes are pervasive. This gives them an advantage when it comes to scope. All kinds of concepts exhibit typicality effects that can be explained by postulating prototypes. Typicality effects are found for concepts of ordinary middle-sized objects such as BIRD and CHAIR (Rosch 1978); abstract concepts such as ART, SCIENCE,

Table 3.3
How prototypes produce conjunctive overextensions

TOOL	WEAPON	TOOL & WEAPON	SCREWDRIVER
f_1		f_1	f_1
f_2		f_2	f_2
f_3		f_3	f_3
	f_4	f_4	f_4
	f_5	f_5	
	f_6	f_6	

and WORK (Hampton 1981); goal-derived concepts such as THINGS TO TAKE ON A VACATION or THINGS TO TAKE FROM ONE'S HOME WHEN ITS BURNING (Barsalou 1983, 1991); social concepts such as INTROVERT and EXTROVERT (Cantor and Mischel 1979); verbal concepts such as CAUSE (Lakoff 1987); and spatial relations (Huttenlocher, Hedges, and Duncan 1991). Even concepts that have good definitions, such as ODD NUMBER, FEMALE, and GRANDMOTHER, exhibit typicality effects (Armstrong, Gleitman, and Gleitman 1983). For example, subjects say 7 is a better example of an *odd number* than 23, a ballerina is a better example of a *female* than a policewoman, and a gray-haired, brownie-dispensing, woman is a better example of a *grandmother* than Zsa Zsa Gabor.

There are, of course, concepts about which we know virtually nothing. For example, someone who does not know anything about sassafras can wonder what sassafras is (Komatsu 1992). One needs to possess some sort of SASSAFRAS concept to wonder about it. If one can have a SASSAFRAS concept without having a SASSAFRAS prototype or any other information about sassafras, then concepts cannot all be prototypes. This objection can be met by interpreting thoughts about sassafras as metalinguistic. Wondering what sassafras is amounts to wondering what "sassafras" refers to.

The evidence that prototypes are pervasive can also be used to criticize prototype theory. Armstrong et al. (1983) object as follows. Subjects make graded typicality judgments even when they know that the concept has a good definition. Subjects know that a number is odd just in case it is not divisible by 2 without a remainder, but they still think some odd numbers are better examples of oddness than others. This shows that we should be reluctant to infer that concepts are constituted by prototypes from the presence of typicality effects. Those effects suggest that prototypes are used in making certain kinds of judgments, but they do not prove that concepts *are exhausted by* or even *partially identifiable with* prototypes. Instead, prototypes might be mere heuristic devices that accompany concepts and aid in categorization.

Armstrong et al. also argue that prototype theory faces a version of the primitive-feature problem discussed in the preceding chapter. The features alleged to compose prototypes often seem no more primitive than the prototypes they compose. For example, the prototypical snake is dangerous, the prototypical chocolate cake has many calories, and the prototypical yacht is expensive. Explaining how we come to have the concept DANGEROUS seems more difficult than explaining how we come to have the concept SNAKE. Prototype theorists typically give no reason for thinking the features they name in describing the contents of prototypes are primitive or reducible to primitives. They offer no theory of what the primitives are or how they are acquired. Thus, their theory of acquisition is inadequate.

Further concerns involves intentionality. Proponents of prototype theory sometimes assume that prototypes refer on the basis of the same features by which they categorize. This assumption is implicit in the claim, made by some prototype theorists, that a prototype reference is graded. For example, it is sometimes suggested that the BIRD prototype refers to sparrows more than it refers to ostriches. More contentiously, prototype theory is sometimes believed to entail that the sentence "Sparrows are birds" is true to a greater degree than "Ostriches are birds" (Lakoff 1972, Rosch and Mervis 1975). Critics (e.g., Rey 1983) have argued that this is untenable. The fact that ostriches are less typical birds does not mean that they are birds to a lesser degree. Being an unusual member of a kind simply does not diminish an object's membership. This is obviously true for such natural kinds as birds, but it is also true for artifacts and other kinds of concepts. Forklifts are atypical vehicles, but they are vehicles to the same degree as cars. Breuer's Wassily chair is an atypical chair, but it is no less a chair than a standard La-Z-Boy recliner. This is not to say that reference is never graded. (Is a raft as much of a boat as a schooner is? Is a teepee as much of a tent as the "big top" over the circus?) The point is that atypicality does not always coincide with graded membership.

One might reply by suggesting that prototypes refer equally to all those things that possess a sufficient percentage of the features they contain. On this proposal, being above some critical similarity threshold is sufficient for full category membership. This allows one to say that prototypicality is graded, but membership is not.

The threshold proposal is unsuccessful. Surpassing the similarity threshold for a prototype is neither necessary nor sufficient for reference. For example, eels are fish, but they are utterly dissimilar to the FISH prototype. Thus, being above the threshold for the fish prototype is not necessary for being a fish. Conversely, eels are very much like snakes in appearance and likely exceed the threshold for the SNAKE prototype. But this does not make eels snakes. Being over the threshold for the snake prototype is not sufficient for being a snake. Likewise, dolphins are much more like typical fish than eels, but they are not fish. Prototypes cannot determine reference, because they are constructed from features that are superficial, whereas reference depends on category divisions that are not skin-deep. Prototypes do badly with oddballs and decoys. To presume that prototype similarity determines reference is a mistake.

This is not to say that prototypes could never determine reference. Kamp and Partee point out that certain kinds of concepts might work this way (Kamp and Partee 1995). For example, they have us consider sensory concepts, such as RED, and personality concepts, such as BULLY. Kamp and Partee recognize that these examples are quite controversial. Colors might be real properties of the world (e.g., reflectance triples). If so, something can be red without matching our RED prototype. BULLY faces similar problems. A passive aggressive individual with a superficially sweet and mild-mannered persona might qualify as a bully without exceeding the BULLY prototype threshold. The prototypes for personality traits do not always coincide with the deeper features on the basis of which we make informed personality judgments. Perhaps the only cases where prototypes determine reference are such trivial ones as the concept PROTOTYPICALLY RED or PROTOTYPICALLY BULLYISH or PROTOTYPICALLY BIRDLIKE. Even if more substantive cases do exist, they do not pose a

(a)   **(b)**

Figure 3.1
A raccoon (a) before and (b) after transformation. Reproduced from Keil 1989, figure 8.2, with permission.

threat to the claim that most prototypes do not determine reference. This is enough to show that prototype theorists lack an adequate explanation of intentionality.

A more serious embarrassment is that prototype theorists encounter problems explaining categorization, the area billed as their greatest strength. Here is an example from the research of Frank Keil (1989). Subjects are shown a picture of an ordinary raccoon (figure 3.1a) and asked to imagine that scientists paint the depicted animal black with a white stripe down the back and affix to it a sac that releases a foul smell. Subjects are shown a picture of the result, which looks like an ordinary skunk (figure 3.1b). After the transformation, the animal resembles a prototypical skunk more than a prototypical raccoon, but from about fourth grade on, subjects insist that it is still a raccoon. Prototype theorists make the opposite prediction. If categorization depends solely on similarity to a prototype, then subjects should say the animal has been turned into a skunk. Clearly, we are capable of ignoring prototype similarity when we make categorization judgments.

The troubles do not end there. Prototype researchers often assume that different people form the same prototypes. Suppose I learned my DOG concept by encountering huskies, chihuahuas, and rottweilers, and you learned your DOG concept by experiencing poodles, boxers, and labradors. We might both converge on a prototype comprising the same features (e.g., short fur, barks, and medium height), and we might both rate a golden retriever as more typical than a dachshund or sheep dog. Since prototypes represent the central tendency of a category, it is possible, in principle, for two people to have the same prototype despite the fact that they have had different experiences. In practice, this does not seem to occur. Larry Barsalou (1987) discovered that typicality judgments vary considerably. When different people are asked to make typicality judgments about category instances, only about a .5 agreement is found. Even more striking, when a single individual is asked to rate the typicality of category instances on one occasion and then asked to rate the typicality of the same instances one month later, that individual's responses change. There is only a .8 correlation between an individual's typicality judgments from one occasion to the next. Baraslou (1989, 1993) also discovered that the features listed by people in describing categories vary considerably. Typicality judgments and feature lists are presumed to reveal the structure of prototypes. If they are unstable, then prototypes are presumably unstable as well. If prototypes vary from person to person and moment to moment, then they apparently fail to satisfy the publicity requirement.

Prototypes have come under attack for failing to provide an adequate account of compositionality as well. Prototype theory trivially fails to explain intentional compositionality because it cannot explain intentionality. It also fails to accommodate cognitive compositionality, despite a good showing with the screwdriver example above. To count as cognitively compositional, the cognitive content of a compound prototype has to be a function of the cognitive content of its constituents. This is not always the case. When subjects are asked to list features typical of the category designated by a compound concept, they often include features that are not rated as typical of the categories designated by its constituent concepts (Osherson and Smith 1981; Rey 1983; Murphy 1988; Medin and Shoben 1988; Kunda, Miller, and Claire 1990; Fodor and Lepore 1996). For example, pet fish typically live in bowls, but neither pets nor fish typically live in bowls; large spoons are typically made of wood, even though the same is not true of large things or spoons; and, finally, carpenters with Harvard degrees are typically nonmaterialistic, even though the same is not true of carpenters or Harvard graduates. In a word, prototypical features of phrasal concepts are often *emergent*; they are not inherited from their constituents. If this is right, then prototypes are not compositional.

To escape this problem, Osherson and Smith (1981) recommend a hybrid theory of concepts. Prototypes, they suggest, are mere identification procedures for rough-and-ready categorization. In addition to prototypes, concepts have deeper, core features, which are closer to definitions (see also Smith and Medin 1981; Armstrong, Gleitman, and Gleitman 1983). When concepts are combined, they contribute their cores, not their prototypes. Cores, like definitions, can combine compositionally. They are the true constituents of thoughts, and thus the currency of high-level cognition. The hybrid view can also help with other problems, such as Keil's raccoon example and Armstrong et al.'s observation that well-defined concepts exhibit typicality effects. Core features may also be used to explain publicity, because they can remain stable as prototypes change (Medin and Ortony 1989). For these reasons, the hybrid view has been a frequent refuge for those who want to preserve a role for prototypes.

There is reason, however, to resist this hybrid. First, people do not seem to differentiate between core and prototype features (Hampton 1979). Second, proponents of cores face a dilemma. If cores are construed as defining features, they can be rejected on the grounds that few concepts have definitions. If cores are nondefining, they, like prototypes, probably fail to combine compositionally. Third, there is good reason to think that prototypes are not merely used as identification procedures. Biases based on prototype similarity have been found in studies of probabilistic reasoning and inductive inference (Sloman 1993). Thus, the cores are not the primary currency of higher cognitive tasks.

I conclude that prototype theory is inadequate as it stands, and that it cannot be saved by simply supplementing prototypes with cores.

3.2 Exemplar Theory

Prototypes, like definitions, are "summary representations" (Smith and Medin 1981). They contain a relatively concise set of features corresponding to properties exhibited by many category members. They abstract away from the idiosyncrasies of individual category members to capture a central tendency. In so doing, prototypes can sometimes bring together features that are never coinstantiated in actual category instances. Imagine a species of tropical fish in which adults have blue scales and juveniles have yellow fins, but very few have both. Because of the prevalence of these two features, a person might abstract a prototype for this species that included both blue scales and yellow fins, even if she had never seen an actual instance with both features. Now suppose, after forming the prototype in this way, that a person finally sees one of the rare instances that actually conforms to the prototype. Prototype theory predicts that she will be able to identify this rare prototypical instance more readily than the nonprototypical instances that she had actually experienced. Ideal cases can outperform less typical familiar cases.

This prediction is not always borne out. Under certain circumstances, similarity to previously experienced category instances is a better (or equal) predictor of speed than similarity to a representation that summarizes the central tendency of a category. This has led a number of authors to conclude that people store information about previously experienced category instances and use that information to make their categorization judgments. Individual category instances are called "exemplars," and the theory that concepts are constituted by collections of representations of exemplars is called *exemplar theory* (Medin and Schaffer 1978, Brooks 1978, Medin and Schwanenflugel 1981, Nosofsky 1986, Estes 1994). For terminological clarity, I use the term "instance" to refer to an actual category member and "exemplar" to refer to mental representations of category members.

As with prototype theory, exemplar theory comes in several varieties. Exemplar theorists disagree about how instances are represented. Like prototypes, exemplars may be images, points in a multidimensional space, or sets of features. There is also a question of whether exemplars are represented as entire objects or in small clusters or correlated features (or "fragments"). Fragmentary views have been recommended for exemplar-based theories of grammar acquisition. Studies of artificial-grammar acquisition suggest that it is useful to store representations of small phrases as well as entire sentences (Perruchet and Pacteau 1990). Exemplar theorists also disagree about whether there is any need for abstract, summary representations. On the most extreme version of exemplar theory, people do not generate any representations that summarize the features of distinct exemplars. On more liberal versions, both summary representations and exemplar representations are formed (Smith and Medin 1981).

According to exemplar theory, categorization is accomplished by comparing a target object to sets of stored exemplars. Medin and Schaffer (1978) introduced a very influential model of exemplar-based categorization. On their model, context can determine what feature dimensions, and hence what exemplars, contribute to categorization. The probability that an instance will be identified as falling under a given category is a function of its perceived similarity to the contextually selected set of exemplars of that category relative to its perceived similarity to the stored exemplars of other categories under consideration. The context model computes the similarity between exemplars and instances using a multiplicative rule rather than an additive rule, the kind of rule favored by prototype theorists. Rather than summing shared features, it multiplies numerical values corresponding to the degree to which each feature is shared. The multiplicative rule introduces a bias in favor of cases in which an instance closely matches a specific exemplar in a category over cases where it is moderately similar to many.

For example, consider the case illustrated in table 3.4. A concept comprising two exemplar representations is compared against two instances. The first instance shares 50% of the features of each exemplar. The second instance has 75% of the features of one exemplar and 25% of the features of the other exemplar. Assume that features that are not shared are rated as shared to a degree of 0.5. To compute similarity between an instance and a concept, one sums the similarity of that instance to each exemplar making up the concept. To compute the similarity between an instance and an exemplar, one multiplies the values corresponding to the degree to which each feature is shared. If this latter function were additive, the two instances in table 3.4 would be rated equally similar to the concept. With a multiplicative rule, the instance that is highly similar to one exemplar gets a higher rating than the instance that is relatively similar to both. In this way, exemplar theory can explain cases in which atypical instances outperform prototypical instances.

Table 3.4
An example of similarity assessment on an exemplar model

Concept				
Exemplar 1	Short legs	Red fur	Long claws	Sharp teeth
Exemplar 2	Long legs	Blue fur	Short claws	Dull teeth
Instances				
Instance 1	Short legs	Blue fur	Long claws	Dull teeth
Instance 2	Long legs	Red fur	Long claws	Sharp teeth

Similarity calculations
Sim(Instance 1, CONCEPT)
    = Sim(Instance 1, Exemplar 1) + Sim(Instance 1, Exemplar 2)
    = $(1 \times 0.5 \times 1 \times 0.5) + (0.5 \times 1 \times 0.5 \times 1) = 0.5$
Sim(Instance 2, CONCEPT)
    = Sim(Instance 2, Exemplar 1) + Sim(Instance 2, Exemplar 2)
    = $(0.5 \times 1 \times 1 \times 1) + (1 \times 0.5 \times 0.5 \times 0.5) = 0.625$

Exemplar theory rivals prototype theory in its ability to explain typicality effects. Comparison with a set of exemplars behaves like comparison with a prototype because prototypes are averages abstracted from multiple instances. In cases where an instance does not closely match a stored exemplar, categorization speed can be predicted by similarity to the central tendency. Graded typicality ratings can be explained by the fact that some instances are more similar to a set of exemplars than others. Thus, exemplar theory simultaneously accommodates prototype effects and exemplar effects (i.e., our proficiency with familiar, but atypical, instances).

Exemplar theory also tends to do better than prototype theory when it comes to superordinate categories, such as furniture, clothing, or vehicles. Typically, members of a superordinate category differ significantly from one another (e.g., compare a chair and an armoire or a motorcycle and a sailboat). It is hard to imagine how a single prototype representation could summarize such disparate objects. Superordinates are much easier to represent using a group of exemplar representations.

Exemplar representations outperform prototypes on the acquisition desideratum as well. Like prototypes, they can be easily learned by neural networks (Kruschke 1992). But exemplar representations are somewhat easier to learn because the central tendency of a category does not need to be computed during acquisition. In addition, exemplar theory predicts that we should have no difficulty learning concepts representing categories that are not linearly separable. A category is not linearly separable when it is impossible to draw a straight line between members and nonmembers on a graph showing its membership distribution. Categories with exclusive disjunctions in their membership criteria are not linearly separable. Prototype theory predicts that linearly separable categories will be easier to learn. The evidence supports the prediction of exemplar theory (Medin and Schwanenflugel 1981).

Exemplar theory can go beyond categorization. It fits in very nicely with some theories of reasoning. There is considerable evidence that we often reason by applying information about particular cases we have experienced to novel situations (e.g., Hammond 1989). This kind of "case-based reasoning" would not be possible if we did not store information about exemplars. Similarly, Holyoak and Glass (1975) point out that we often use knowledge of specific exemplars when we reason by counterexample. One might reject the claim that all rottweilers are vicious by recalling a friendly rottweiler encountered on a previous occasion. Johnson-Laird's (1983) theory of reasoning based on mental models also affords a role to a certain kind of exemplar representations. He suggests that we represent quantified sentences in syllogisms by forming representations of particular situations or objects. If these theories are correct, they show that reasoning often involves representations of unique category instances. This does not force us to identify concepts with exemplars, but lends support to such a hypothesis by showing that such representations play central roles in cognition.

Brooks (1978) argues that certain circumstances encourage the acquisition of exemplar representations. Time pressure might prevent us from abstracting a prototype, goals might require specific exemplar knowledge, and repeated encounters with a single individual might cause us to store specific information about that individual. If such circumstances practically force us to acquire exemplar knowledge, there is every reason to think that we can use such knowledge in categorization and other conceptual tasks. Brooks also notes that storage of exemplars contributes to flexibility. If concepts are constituted by many exemplar representations, as opposed to a single prototype, they can be applied in different ways as dictated by context. We have the option of using knowledge of specific exemplars *and* computing summary representations to meet particular demands. If exemplar knowledge is simply discarded, we lose this option.

Some critics of exemplar theory have worried about storage and processing costs. If we retain memories of each exemplar we experience, we place an enormous burden on our storage capacities. And if we categorize by comparing objects to all stored exemplar representations, we place enormous demands on our processing capacities. As remarked, it is easier to acquire exemplar representations than prototypes because prototypes need to be computed. But, the cost of computing prototypes seems to yield tremendous savings in storage and subsequent processing. Furthermore, exemplar theory seems to carry the unlikely prediction that it should take more time or energy to confirm that something falls under a very familiar category than under a less familiar one because there are more memory traces to compare it to.

The storage and processing worries may be answerable. There is evidence that we are capable of storing a staggering number of specific experiences. Studies of picture memory, for example, have shown that a person can be shown 10,000 pictures for 5 seconds each and subsequently identify the overwhelming majority of them (Standing 1973). If our memory for pictures is that good, our memory for category exemplars may be as well.

Exemplar theorists can address the concern about processing time by denying that categorization requires explicit comparison to all stored exemplars. Perhaps, when we experience an object, the representation produced is capable of calling up similar representations without going through an exhaustive search procedure. If a close match is found, the instance is categorized as belonging to the same kind. When an instance of a familiar category is experienced, there is greater likelihood that one will have a highly similar stored exemplar. This would facilitate categorization rather than slowing it down.

Our ability to recall familiar category instances may also contribute to an explanation of concept combination. I remarked above that combining concepts can result in emergent features. On a prototype theory, these features seem to appear ex nihilo, which suggests that prototypes do not combine compositionally. On an exemplar theory, some of these emergent features can be easily explained. Consider the feature WOODEN that emerges from the compound LARGE SPOON. For a prototype theorist, this is mysterious because WOODEN is not part of the prototype of either LARGE THING or SPOON. Exemplar theorists explain this case by observing that the actual instances of large spoons that people encounter are typically made of wood. This feature is stored among the exemplar representations that constitute a concept; it does not emerge ex nihilo. Likewise, PET FISH produces the feature LIVES IN A BOWL because most of the pet fish exemplars we encounter live in bowls, and YELLOW JACKET produces the feature MADE OUT OF VINYL because of our familiarity with raincoats. If these proposals are right, some emergent features do not violate compositionality. If concepts consist of exemplar representations, and emergent features come from exemplar representations, then the cognitive content of conceptual compounds does not need to go beyond the content of their constituents. The reason why features seem to emerge is explained by the fact that we retrieve different exemplars when asked to describe a concept in isolation and in combination. Exemplar theory already assumes that we are capable of calling on different exemplars in different contexts. That is what makes exemplar theory so flexible. Perhaps this flexibility can be harnessed and exploited by a theory of conceptual combination.

The exemplar-theoretic approach to conceptual combination runs into some problems, however. Exemplar theory cannot explain intentional compositionality, because, like prototype theory, it offers no account of intentionality. The account of cognitive compositionality just mentioned is also extremely limited. It is not clear how exemplar representations can be used to capture the cognitive content of novel combinations (Hampton 1997). LARGE SPOON is easily accommodated within an exemplar framework because large spoons are familiar objects. Conceptually representing them is a simple matter of memory retrieval. But what about novel combinations, such as PET WALRUS? Without having experienced pet walruses, how can we represent them? Presumably, we perform some kind of combination operation on the exemplar representations of the constituent concepts. But which exemplar representations are chosen?

Do we factor in all of the exemplars for PET and WALRUS, or just some subset? And once the relevant exemplars are chosen, how they are combined? Do we first combine the set of PET exemplars and the set of WALRUS exemplars separately to form two single representations and then combine those two to form one, or do we combine all these exemplars together at once? If all at once, is the result a single representation or a set of representations? Novel compounds may also generate emergent features. Perhaps pet walruses are presumed to live in swimming pools. How can exemplar knowledge explain this if no familiar pets or walruses live in pools?

A related problem is that exemplar theorists have difficulty explaining our ability to possess concepts referring to categories whose instances we have not experienced (Rips 1995). These include fictional kind concepts, such as UNICORN, and the many concepts that are learned by description rather than acquaintance. Obviously, these concepts cannot be represented by memories of instances. It is possible that these concepts are derived by combining exemplar representations, in which case the problem with concepts whose instances have not been experienced collapses into the problem of novel compounds. Both of these problems highlight an important point. The exemplar theory cannot generalize. As long as we can represent unexperienced concepts and novel compounds, some concepts cannot consist solely of exemplar representations. The exemplar theory does not satisfy the scope requirement. It is, at best, a partial theory of concepts.

Exemplar theorists also have difficulty satisfying the publicity requirement. Each of us has experienced different exemplars. If our concepts are constituted by memories of those exemplars, each of us has different concepts. This consequence echoes one of the failings of imagism. With prototypes, there is at least the possibility that two people will abstract the same summary representation from distinct experiences. On exemplar and imagistic models, true concept sharing becomes all but impossible.

The claim that exemplar theory outperforms prototype theory can also be challenged on other grounds. Exemplar theory is very much like prototype theory in that both explain categorization on the basis of similarity judgments. As a result, exemplar theory inherits some flaws of prototype theory. For example, exemplar theory falsely predicts that Keil's painted raccoon would be categorized as a skunk, because it looks like familiar instances of that category.

The primary advantage of exemplar theory over prototype theory is presumed to stem from the ability of exemplar theory to explain the "exemplar effects" in categorization, described at the beginning of this subsection. This may be a red herring. Barsalou (1990) shows that prototype representations that include information about feature correlations perform in ways that are equivalent to collections of exemplar representations. On standard models, prototypes are merely lists of typical features, but such lists could easily be extended to include information about the frequency with which those features co-occur. On this model, the prototype for the tropical fish species described above would have a very low association between yellow fins and blue scales, which would bias categorization against such cases. Such a representation would still count as a prototype because it would be a summary built up from typical features rather than a family of separate memory traces of instances. Thus, exemplar theory does not undermine prototype theory; it only motivates some enrichments.

Barsalou's argument shows that it can be extremely difficult to decide experimentally between prototype and exemplar models. In response, exemplar theorists can appeal to the fact that people have rich memories of category instances. Even if both models predict the same categorization results, the independent evidence for exemplar memories favors exemplar theory. However, it is not enough to show that such memories exist. If summary representations are to be ruled out, one must show that categorization invariably exploits such memories.

There is some neuropsychological evidence against the hypothesis that categorization always depends on exemplar memories. Knowlton and her colleagues study the categorization performance of patients with amnesia using dot patterns of the kind used by Posner and Keele (Knowlton and Squire 1993, Knowlton 1997). After training, these patients are quite adept at *categorizing* dot patterns, including prototypical patterns that they have never seen before. At the same time, they are unable to *recognize* the patterns that were used during training. None of the patterns seem familiar. The most natural explanation of this result is that such subjects abstract prototypes during training without storing knowledge of exemplars. If so, their performance cannot be explained by appeal to use of multiple exemplars during categorization. Their success in categorization may rely on summary representations. If brain-damaged subjects use such representations, normal subjects probably do so as well.

There is also an a priori complaint against extreme versions of exemplar theory. Despite some claims to the contrary, exemplar theory cannot completely dispense with abstract representations. Hampton (1997) remarks that similarity assessments depend on abstractions. One assesses the similarity between a perceived instance and an exemplar stored in memory by picking out shared features. It is generally assumed that to do this, features must be represented either explicitly or in the form of dimensions on a multidimensional space. Feature representations cannot themselves be exemplars. They are abstract in two senses. First, they abstract away from other information. To represent a given feature of an object as such, other features of the object must be separated from it. Second, to establish that two things share a feature, one must use representations of the same type. The way a given feature is represented in a currently perceived category instance and in a stored exemplar must be the same. Otherwise, no match can be made. This is another form of abstractness. In other words, exemplar representations might represent unique instances, but they consist of features that are not unique, because they can be repeated in representations of distinct instances. Exemplars cannot go all the way down. An exemplar theorist needs to provide an account of how features are represented. Once again, there is an unanswered demand for a theory of primitives. There can be no complete account of how exemplar representations are acquired without an account of how their building blocks are acquired.

3.3   Conclusions

The debate between exemplar theorists and prototype theorists rages on in the literature. At first blush, exemplar theory looks preferable because it explains certain categorization results not predicted by prototype theory. Closer analysis, however, reveals that prototype theory has some advantages over exemplar theory. Prototypes have greater scope than exemplars because we can form a prototype of objects we have not seen, provided that its typical features are described to us. Prototypes also may be more efficient to store and process than exemplars. Moreover, some versions of prototype theory can accommodate the exemplar-categorization effects (Barsalou 1990).

Perhaps the best conclusion, however, is that both kinds of representations exist. We certainly store memories of specific instances, and there is good reason to believe that we store summary information as well (see Knowlton's amnesia studies). Further evidence comes from an ingenious set of studies by Marsolek (1995). As with Posner and Keele, subjects were first trained on one group of patterns and then asked to categorize a second group containing previously viewed patterns, novel patterns, and prototypes abstracted from the original group. The difference is that the subjects were allowed to see the patterns with only one visual field during the categorization task. Subjects who saw the patterns in their right visual fields (and hence used their left cerebral hemispheres) performed optimally on the prototypical patterns. Subjects who saw the patterns in their left visual fields (and used their right hemispheres) performed optimally on previously viewed patterns. This strongly suggests that the brain stores both prototype and exemplar representations in the visual system, and that there are hemispheric differences in the proficiency with which such representations are formed.

Even if both prototypes and exemplars exist, the arguments in this chapter challenge any attempt to identify them with concepts. Neither theory has the resources to accommodate all the desiderata from chapter 1. Both of them account for certain categorization results, but even on this desideratum, success is incomplete. When categorization goes beyond appearances, as with Keil's painted raccoon, both theories predict the wrong results. Prototype and exemplar theories face even more serious problems with intentionality and compositionality.

In the face of such difficulties, one might be inclined to abandon prototypes and exemplars altogether. This would be hasty. Typicality effects and other experimental results suggest that prototype and exemplar theorists have discovered something important. The theory of concepts that I ultimately defend actually encompasses exemplars and something like prototypes. Consequently, I have to answer a number of the objections surveyed in this chapter. That cannot be done without exploiting lessons from two other theories of concepts, which have gained popularity as support for similarity-based accounts has waned. I take up these theories in the next chapter.

4

Maximal and Minimal Accounts

Similarity-based theories of concepts dominated psychology during the 1970s and early 1980s. Since then, psychologists have begun to question the role of similarity and to develop new theories of categorization. According to these theories, much more knowledge is brought to bear in conceptual tasks than prototype and exemplar theories had recognized. Concepts must incorporate that knowledge. In philosophy, an account that had been emerging at the same time as prototype theory offered a diametrically different perspective. Rather than packing more knowledge into concepts, it identifies concepts with unstructured word-like entities. On the first approach, concepts embody a wealth of beliefs about the world. On the second, they embody none. One maximizes the information in concepts, and the other minimizes the information in concepts. Despite this radical difference, the two approaches have some common ground. Both depart from similarity-based accounts, and both have emphasized the fact that category membership is not determined by superficial appearances.

4.1 The Theory Theory

Prototype theory and exemplar theory are close cousins. Their defenders believe that categorization is based on judgments of superficial similarity to representations of idealized or actual category members. They tend to ignore or downplay the role of knowledge and reasoning in concept formation and application. On these views, concepts simply capture the most salient features in objects. In stark contrast, many psychologists now say that concepts encompass beliefs about causal mechanisms, teleological purposes, hidden features, and fundamental divisions in ontology. On this view, conceptual processing is not restricted to mere feature matching and frequency tabulation; it is often more like problem solving. In short, concepts are construed as mini theories of the categories they represent. This approach is known as the theory theory (seminal defenses include Murphy and Medin 1985, Carey 1985, Keil 1989).

The term "theory" is taken quite literally by theory theorists. Comparisons have been drawn between the way lay people and scientists conceptualize the world. Gopnik and Meltzoff (1996) are admirably explicit in developing the analogy. They distinguish structural, functional, and dynamic features of theories. Structurally, theories are systems of abstract entities and laws. They are abstract insofar as they postulate things and relations that transcend experience, and they are lawful insofar as they provide counterfactual supporting causal principles underlying superficial regularities. Functionally, theories are in the business of making predictions, providing interpretations, and offering explanations concerning observable phenomena. Dynamic features of theories include the accumulation of counterevidence, an initial tendency to deny theory violations, ad hoc theory adjustments, and, finally, theory change. Gopnik and Meltzoff believe that these features can be found in science and conceptual development. Another important component of the theory theory is the idea that individual concepts belong to larger bodies of knowledge pertaining to specific domains. Like scientific disciplines, the mind divides into distinct sets of explanatory principles for making sense of different aspects of the world. We have naive theories of biological kinds, of human-made artifacts, of mechanical relations between concrete objects, of psychology, and so on.

Some theory theorists have been less explicit than Gopnik and Meltzoff in saying what theories are, but they generally make claims that are consistent with Gopnik and Meltzoff's analysis. They draw our attention to "theoretical" facts that are known to concept users but neglected by defenders of similarity-based accounts. Four of these are discussed most frequently. First, theory theorists argue that concepts encode information about explanatory relations between features. This criticism incorporates one of Gopnik and Meltzoff's structural features (theories provide causal laws) and one of Gopnik and Meltzoff's functional features (those laws explain observable phenomena). Second, theory theorists argue that concepts encode and give priority to information about features that are unobservable or "hidden." This idea ties into the structural feature of being abstract. Third, theory theorists criticize similarity-based accounts for failing to appreciate the fact that different concepts are informed by different overarching principles. This echoes the idea that the mind is parceled into domains. Finally, theory theorists argue that concepts go through developmental changes that parallel theoretical changes. This incorporates Gopnik and Meltzoff's dynamic features. I consider some evidence for each of these claims.

Prototypes and exemplar representations are often thought to represent features without encoding information about how those features are related. In particular, they omit *causal and explanatory relations*: relations that offer explanations of why the possession of one feature co-occurs with the possession of another. For example, the fact that wings enable flight explains why having wings co-occurs with the ability to fly. The BIRD prototype includes the features HAS WINGS and FLIES, but it does not represent the enabling relation that unites these features. Theory theorists argue that this is a serious omission because explanatory beliefs influence categorization (Murphy and Medin 1985).

Medin and Shoben (1988) demonstrate the point by showing that explanatory beliefs can override beliefs about typicality. Subjects rate the feature of BEING CURVED to be equally typical for both boomerangs and bananas. Prototype theorists would therefore predict that this feature would be equally weighted in BOOMERANG and BANANA concepts. Apparently, this is not the case. Subjects believe that a straight object is much more likely to be a banana than a boomerang. BEING CURVED is equally typical but unequally criterial in making categorization judgments. The explanation suggested by Medin and Shoben involves explanatory/relational structure. Both boomerangs and bananas are curved, but in the case of boomerangs, curvature is presumed to enable another feature, namely, the ability to return to the thrower when thrown. As a result, the curvature of boomerangs seems obligatory. It is (erroneously) believed that if there is no curvature, an object cannot behave as a boomerang. In contrast, the curvature of bananas has no strong explanatory ties with other features. Therefore, even though curvature is universal in bananas, it has less impact on categorization. This result is not predicted by prototype theory, which is driven by statistical frequency.

In a similar experiment, Rips (1989) has subjects imagine a circular object three inches in diameter and decide whether it is more similar to a quarter or a pizza. Because of its size, subjects say that it is more similar to a quarter. Then he asks them to decide whether it is more likely to *be* a quarter or a pizza. They say it is more likely to be a pizza because, despite its similarity to a quarter, quarters must have a uniform size. Quarters are machine made and regulated by the Federal Government. Both pizzas and quarters *tend* to be uniform in size, but our background knowledge dictates that only quarters *must* be. Background knowledge transforms a statistical probability into a necessity by establishing an explanatory relation between features (size and means of manufacture). Rips concludes that similarity cannot be the basis of categorization because subjects are willing to identify an object with the member of a pair of things with which it is less similar.

The theory theory also helps solve another problem. Because it does not include explanatory relations between features, prototype theory seems unconstrained (Smith and Medin 1981). In forming concepts, we represent only a few of the myriad features that objects possess. How do we select these features? One answer is that we pick features that are rendered salient by previous knowledge and interests, and that these features are held together by the fact that they form a coherent, interdependent whole (Murphy and Medin 1985).

The second kind of information emphasized by theory theorists is nicely illustrated by Keil's case of the painted raccoon (Keil 1989). As we saw in chapter 3, an animal that begins as a raccoon continues to be identified as a raccoon even if its appearance is transformed so that it looks like a skunk (figure 3.1). Superficial appearances are not sufficient for being a skunk. The true essence of skunkhood lies deeper. Subjects believe that such essential features can be "hidden" in at least two senses. First, the essence of a thing can include features that are not readily observed. Even if the observable features change, the essence can remain constant. This is a departure from prototype theory, which emphasizes features that are readily observed and known to be contingent. Second, essences can be unknown to concept possessors. Sometimes we know the essence of a category. For example, we know that what makes something water is not its clarity or its presence in rivers, but the fact that it is composed of H_2O molecules. But for many other categories, most of us cannot specify the essential features, even though we presume that such features exist. We know the trivial fact that, say, raccoons have raccoon essences, but we cannot specify what such an essence is in any complete or noncircular way. The claim that concept users have faith in hidden essences is called *psychological essentialism* (Medin and Ortony 1989; Gelman, Coley, and Gottfried 1994).

The third kind of information that theory theorists emphasize is the division of concepts into separate domains. These domains often correspond to very broad ontological kinds. For example, subjects are sensitive to a distinction between natural kinds (e.g., raccoons, flowers, rocks) and artifacts (e.g., screwdrivers, lamps, coffeepots). Among natural kinds, subjects also distinguish living things from nonliving things, and among living things they distinguish plants and animals (Keil 1979). Each domain is governed by its own set of core beliefs.

Theory theorists argue that the essence associated with a concept depends on the domain in which it is placed. In support of this, Keil shows that judgments about the effects of superficial transformations vary according to basic ontological categories. Natural-kind concepts behave like RACCOON: superficial changes do not alter category membership. Artifact concepts, such as SCREWDRIVER, behave differently. If a screwdriver's appearance is significantly modified, subjects say that it looses its identity as a screwdriver. This does not mean purely superficial features dictate artifact categorization, as some similarity-based accounts suppose. Instead, the essence of an artifact is presumed to be the function that it is intended to serve, and functionality often depends on observable features. A screwdriver that is transformed to lack a flat tip would not serve its intended function. Keil attributes his findings to a mental division between a theory of biological kinds and a theory about artifacts.

The fourth fact emphasized by theory theorists involves conceptual change. It can also be illustrated by considering beliefs about essences.

In modern industrialized cultures, adults generally assume that animal essences depend on heredity and genes. By the time they are in fourth grade, children in such cultures make parallel assumptions. Something counts as a horse if it has horse parents and horse "innards" (Keil 1989, Carey 1985). Natural substances are presumed to depend on chemical constitution, while artifacts depend on function. Younger children behave somewhat differently. Keil shows that there is a developmental shift from an emphasis on "characteristic" features to "defining" features (see also Keil and Batterman 1984). Young children tend to categorize on the basis of superficial appearances before becoming sensitive to deeper essences. When a horse is transformed to take on the characteristics of a zebra, they think it has become a zebra.

At first blush, the characteristic-to-defining shift gives the impression that concepts are not driven by theories of ontological categories during early stages of development. Keil calls this hypothesis the "Original Sim" because it says we begin life categorizing on the basis of similarity. If this analysis were correct, the characteristic-to-defining shift would not be an example of theoretical change. It would be a case of going from atheoretical knowledge to theoretical knowledge. Closer analysis leads Keil to reject the Original Sim hypothesis. He argues that categorization is never completely similarity-based. To support this claim, he shows that very young children do not categorize by similarity when they consider transformations that cross basic ontological categories. For example, when an artifact is transformed to look and act like an animal, they insist that it is still an artifact. This suggests that our concepts are driven by ontological categories from the start. Development is marked, not by the sudden emergence of essentialist theories, but by theory change. When young children categorize on the basis of characteristic features, this shows only that their theories erroneously take such features to be essential.

Evidence that concepts are driven by beliefs about ontology from the start can be also found in studies of language acquisition in very young children. When learning nouns, children focus on different kinds of features according to the stimuli they are shown (Landau, Smith, and Jones 1988; Soja, Carey, and Spelke 1991). When presented with solid objects, children typically focus on shape, and when presented with nonsolid substances, children are more likely to focus on things like texture. Because shape and texture are superficial features, this tendency seems to favor similarity-based accounts of categorization. However, attention to distinct superficial features may actually reveal a sensitivity to differences in general ontological categories (Soja, Carey, and Spelke 1991). In particular, prelinguistic children seem to distinguish objects from substances.

In sum, theory theorists show that categorization judgments are not uniform across ontological genera, as similarity-based accounts predict. Categorization depends on beliefs about essential features, which depend, in turn, on ontological categories and our evolving beliefs about such categories. This is not to say that superficial features play no role in categorizing natural kinds. They can serve as rough-and-ready "identification procedures" when knowledge of deeper features is absent. Theory theorists are willing to admit that the superficial features stressed by similarity-based accounts are used in categorization, but they insist that concepts contain a wealth of other information.

These remarks clarify the position advocated by theory theorists, but some vagaries remain. Theory theorists often say that concepts are *embedded* in theories, that theories and concepts are *inseparable*, and that concepts *incorporate* theoretical information. According to Murphy and Medin (1985), concepts and theories "live in harmony," and Keil (1989) proposes that concepts "inhabit" theories. Such metaphors leave the exact nature of the relationship between concepts and theories obscure.

The simplest way to explicate the relationship between concepts and theories is to propose an identity. Earlier I said that concepts are simply mini theories, according to the theory theorists. An immediate problem arises from this proposal. Theories are generally thought to consist of concepts. If concepts are theories and theories are made from concepts, we get entangled in a circle. Murphy and Medin (1985) anticipate this objection. In response, they retreat from the claim that concepts *are* theories, and suggest instead that concepts are *affected* by theories. This allows them to claim that theories consist of concepts without any circularity. The problem is that this move leaves us without any account of what concepts *are*. If theory theorists do not identify concepts with theories, then they still owe us an account of conceptual structure.

There is a better way to reconstruct the theory theorists' conception of the concept-theory relation. We can begin by noting that definitionism and prototype theory face a problem that parallels the one confronting the theory theory. Like theories, definitions and prototypes are built up from conceptlike units or features. This invites a regress. As we have seen, definitionists and prototype theorists are forced to escape the regress by postulating a level of primitive features. Definitions and prototypes cannot go all the way down. Theory theorists can say the same thing. The difference between the theory theory, definitionism, and prototype theory can be seen primarily as a difference in the kinds of features that enter into our concepts. Unlike the features constituting prototypes, the features constituting mini theories may represent hidden essences and explanatory relations, and they may be selected on the basis of background beliefs rather than perceptual salience and statistical frequency. Unlike definitions, the features constituting mini theories include placeholders for essences rather than explicitly representing necessary and sufficient conditions for membership (Medin and Ortony 1989), and they might be more vulnerable to empirical revision (Gelman and Coley 1991).

On this reconstruction, concepts can be related to theories in three different ways. First, many concepts are mini theories. The theories consist of features that embody a set of beliefs about the essence and explanatory structure of categories. Second, some concepts are constituents of theories. For example, the primitive concepts making up mini theories qualify as theory constituents. Finally, concepts can be affected by theories. The features that get included in one mini theory can be affected by another mini theory. For instance, our mini theory of substances might specify that if something is nonsolid, it can be identified by its texture. When constructing a mini theory of a particular substance, the mini theory of substances causes one to encode information about its texture. Likewise, a mini theory of aviation might cause one to include the hypothesis that wings enable flight in our mini bird theories. This reconstruction shows that concepts can be related to theories in numerous ways without introducing any circularity. For most of the remaining discussion, I assume that this is what theory theorists have in mind.

The greatest asset of the theory theory is its account of categorization. As we have seen, beliefs about explanatory relations and hidden essences influence feature selection, correlation, and weighting. This, in turn, influences the way we categorize. The theory theory has wide scope as well. Background knowledge about domains, feature relations, and essences can influence any conceptual judgment. The theory theory also has a story to tell about cognitive content. Informative identities can be explained by the fact that two theories can converge on the same thing, and Twin Earth cases can be explained by the fact that parallel theories can pick out different things in different environments. The theory theory can contribute to a theory of compositionality by providing an explanation of how certain features emerge during concept combination. For example, Kunda et al. (1990) explain the emergence of the feature NON-MATERIALISTIC from the compound HARVARD CARPENTER by appeal to naive sociological theories. We know that Harvard graduates can be very successful financially and that carpenters do not earn high incomes, and we reason that a carpenter with a Harvard degree must have voluntarily chosen not to pursue a lucrative career. Such a person, we conclude, must be nonmaterialistic.

Unfortunately, these four advantages are overshadowed by problems. First, it turns out that the theory theory may get some of our categorization judgments wrong. Hampton (1995) performed a variant of Keil's transformation experiments. For example, subjects were asked to consider an animal that is born to horse parents but, after being given a special experimental diet, begins to look and behave just like a zebra. Contrary to Keil's studies, only a third of the subjects said that the animal remained a horse after the transformation. Here, superficial similarity seems to trump theoretical beliefs about the importance of heredity.

Smith and Sloman (1994) performed a study that employed a variant of Rips's materials. Rips found that subjects judge a three-inch disk to be more similar to a quarter but more likely to be a pizza. This revealed a dissociation between similarity judgments and categorization. Smith and Sloman argue that the result is a consequence of the fact that Rips provides his subjects with very sparse descriptions. They modified his experiment by asking subjects to imagine a three-inch disk that is silver

A more serious problem is that the theory theory fails to provide an adequate account of intentional content. How do theories refer to categories? What makes a tiger theory a theory of tigers? A natural proposal is to think of theories as definite descriptions that refer by listing features that their referents uniquely possess. This does not work. Unlike definitions, our mini theories do not specify necessary and sufficient conditions for category membership. First, they typically fail to explicitly represent essential features. A mini theory cannot descriptively pick out all and only tigers if it does not specify what conditions are essential to being a tiger. If there were a distinct species that looked just like tigers, our theories would be insufficiently rich to tell them apart. Worse still, mini theories sometimes specify such essences circularly. Tigers are identified as those creatures with tiger innards or tiger parents. This description defines tigers by reference to tigers. If we try to resolve the circularity by replacing the term "tiger" with a variable, the description fails to distinguish tigers from other animals. Any animal X has X innards and X parents. Finally, mini theories often contain false information. I might believe that blowholes in whales serve an excretory function when in fact they really serve a respiratory function. If satisfying all the components of our theories were necessary for reference, my WHALE concept would be vacuous. The theory theory must be supplemented if it is to satisfy the intentionality requirement.

The failure of the theory theory to satisfy the intentionality requirement obviously entails that it is not able to explain intentional compositionality. More surprising is a major deficiency in theory theorists' account of cognitive compositionality. Suppose that concepts are mini theories and that NONMATERIALISTIC emerges from the compound HARVARD CARPENTERS as a theoretical inference. This does not make its emergence compositional. NONMATERIALISTIC is not a constituent feature of our mini theory of Harvard graduates or our mini theory of carpenters; it is introduced to resolve a conflict between those theories. The compositionality requirement demands that the constituents of compounds be *inherited* directly from their components, at least some of the time. To explain the productivity of thought, it must be possible to compute the cognitive contents of compounds from their constituent concepts alone. Theory theories never explain how this is achieved.

Theories, in all their cumbersome complexity, are not the kinds of things that can be easily combined.

The theory theory also fails to satisfy the publicity requirement. It is very unlikely that any two people have exactly the same theories of the categories they represent. The problem is exacerbated by the fact that it is difficult to find a principled way to distinguish the beliefs that belong to a given theory from those that do not. This is more intractable than the analyticity problem that definitionists face because theories are presumed to include information that is contingent or false, empirically learned, and empirically revisable. Consequently, the theory theorist has a harder time showing that one class of beliefs about a category is privileged. Theories mushroom out to include all our beliefs about a category. Such large beliefs sets inevitably differ from person to person.

Theory theorists might think that they can prevent theories from mushrooming out too far. There is a natural proposal for distinguishing theoretical beliefs from other beliefs. One can say that theories include just beliefs about ontological category membership, essence, and explanatory structure. But with this restriction, theory attribution is poorly suited for explaining the kind of convergence between individuals that motivates the publicity requirement. Suppose that you and I have radically different bird theories. You think they are robots, you think they melt when they burn, you think they were created by mad scientists on another planet, and you think they fly because they hang from thin threads connected to spaceships that orbit the earth. Still, we have much in common. We both call the same things "birds," we agree that most birds eat seeds, we both know that birds sing. Your bizarre beliefs do not impair your ability to communicate with others about birds. Similarly, most of the psychological laws describing my interactions with birds subsume yours as well. Contrast this case with that of two people who share bird theories but disagree about the more superficial properties. Suppose that you and I believe that birds are animals descended from dinosaurs that do not gestate their young. But suppose also that you do not know that birds have wings, feathers, and beaks. Despite similarities in our theories, most of our everyday behaviors involving birds differ. You cannot identify birds in the park. We have in common only our responses to certain unusual theoretical questions about birds.

If we identify theories with beliefs about ontology, essence, and causal structure, the most mundane commonalties in our behavior cannot be explained by theory attribution. Mundane commonalties are just what explanations of concept sharing are intended to explain.

In sum, theory theorists cannot explain publicity even if a principled distinction between theory components and noncomponents can be found. However restricted theories are, they can vary wildly because the theories that people form are influenced by their background beliefs and training. Two people exposed to the same category instances might form dramatically different theories of them. If I believe that forests are enchanted, I see every tree and tuber as cognizant; if my theory of aviation has been formed by observing hot-air balloons, I might think that birds fly by filling their lungs with hot air and expelling it through tiny abdominal holes; if I have never seen the hook on the back of a hammer pull out a nail, I might believe hammer hooks are intended for hanging up hammers after use. Does this mean that I do not share the concepts TREE, BIRD, and HAMMER with the majority of my linguistic community? An affirmative answer would entail that we are simply talking past each other when we discuss the nature and function of these things. There must be some kind of commonality across disparate beliefs to ensure communication and psychological generalization. This is not to say that most people have radically distinct theories. It is only to point out that commonalties in ordinary behavior can occur despite radical differences in theories.

In response, theory theorists could stipulate that beliefs about superficial properties are components of our theories along with more overtly theoretical beliefs. Then they could point out that ordinary commonalities can be explained by *similarities* rather than strict identities between theories. Perhaps you and I act the same way around birds because our disparate bird theories share *some* of the same features, namely, those pertaining to bird behavior and appearance. The problem with this proposal is that the features doing the explanatory work are not the kinds of features that theory theorists emphasize. They are the features emphasized by defenders of prototype theory, which the theory theory was designed to replace. If theory theorists can explain commonalities in

mundane behaviors only by assuming that concepts incorporate prototypes, then perhaps we should just stick with prototype theory.

Like the other accounts that I have considered, the theory theory is
unable to satisfy several important desiderata on a theory of concepts.
This is not to deny that we have beliefs about hidden essences and
explanatory structure, or that such beliefs are important in cognition.
The moral is that we should not be too quick to conclude that this information is contained within our concepts. A theory of concepts should
consider all the things we know about categories and decide which pieces
of information, if any, should count as conceptual constituents. That
decision should be made with the desiderata in mind. Conceptual constituents should help explain the kinds of things we want a theory of
concepts to explain. The kinds of features emphasized by theory theorists do not always serve this purpose.

4.2   Informational Atomism

The next theory of concepts I consider is diametrically opposed to the
theory theory. Theory theorists pack much more information into concepts than do defenders of similarity-based accounts. This strategy runs
into difficulties. If concepts are overly complex, concept combination and
publicity become difficult to achieve. Informational atomism, a theory
pioneered by Jerry Fodor, takes another course. It deprives concepts of
any complexity or structure. More specifically, informational atomism is
the view that (almost) all lexical concepts are unstructured symbols—
hence, atomism—that obtain their identity, in part, by carrying information about aspects of the environment—hence, informational.[1]

A symbol is unstructured when it has no components that are semantically interpretable. The smallest semantically interpretable part of a
concept is the concept itself. Lexical concepts do not decompose into features. "Carrying information" refers to a particular approach to intentionality, which I discuss at length in chapter 9. For present purposes, a
concept C carries information about a property P if C is under the nomological control of P (Fodor 1990, Fodor 1994; see also Dretske 1981).
To say that C is under the nomological control of P means, to a first

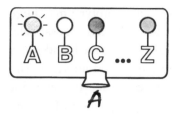

Figure 4.1
A letter-detecting machine.

decomposed into parts that represent letter parts. Nevertheless, the lights *represent* letters because they are reliably caused by letters. Likewise, if concepts obtain their content informationally, they need not be structured. They can be conceived as little lights that go off in the head when properties are detected in the world.

As in a letter detector, there may be semantically structured mechanisms mediating the causal relationship between our inner lights and the properties they detect, but the lights themselves are atomic. To introduce a distinction, one might say that these mechanisms are detectors because they actually do the detecting, while the lights they switch on are indicators because they merely indicate that something has been detected. For Fodor, concepts are indicators.

One might be tempted to identify concepts with detectors rather than indicators. If this were right, concepts would be structured entities, like letter templates. They would be the mechanisms that mediate content-conferring causal relations. Fodor has argued against this suggestion (1991, 1998). First, it is likely that we use many different mechanisms to detect the same properties. These mechanisms vary from person to person, context to context, and time to time. In fact, just about everything we know about a property can potentially contribute to detecting it. With so much complexity and diversity, it is unlikely that detection mechanisms are capable of satisfying the publicity requirement. Second, Fodor believes that detection mechanisms are not compositional. For example, the optimal mechanism for detecting red and the optimal mechanism for detecting hair do not combine to form the optimal mechanisms for detecting red hair (see Fodor 2000). Therefore, identifying concepts with detection mechanisms would undercut two desiderata.

Fodor thinks we can avoid these problems if we adopt an atomistic account, which identifies concepts with indicators. Informational atomism accommodates publicity because it individuates concepts by their intentional contents. Two people have the same concept just in case they have inner lights that indicate the same properties. It does not matter if those properties are detected in different ways because Fodor does not identify concepts with detection mechanisms. To take a simple example, I might detect dogs by listening to their barks, and you might detect them by watching for wagging tails. If these two methods both lead to reliable dog detection, if they both reliably flash an inner light when dogs are present, you and I have the same concept. People with very different beliefs can share concepts, provided those beliefs detect the same properties.

To see how Fodor's atomism handles compositionality, we can shift from an inner-light analogy to an analogy that Fodor prefers. Imagine a device that flashes individual words rather than inner lights. Imagine further that this device has the ability to string those words together into sequences, much as words can be strung together into sentences. Fodor views concepts as languagelike in just this sense. They are unstructured symbols that can be strung together to form more complex representations or thoughts. Just like words, concepts contribute roughly the same things to each of the strings into which they enter. Words contribute two things when they combine with other words: content and form. The content of a word is its meaning, and the form of a word is its shape (or its sound if it is a spoken word). Words retain their meanings and forms in different sentential contexts. The content of a concept is the property that it reliably indicates, and the form of a concept is, metaphorically, the shape of the mental representation that plays that indicating role. Of course, concepts do not literally have shapes, but Fodor presumes that they have some comparable nonsemantic characteristics that recur whenever they enter into different thoughts.

I mention this business about form because it plays a pivotal role in informational atomism. Form, Fodor (1998) has claimed, can play the role of cognitive content. My potential failure to recognize that Cicero is Tully is a consequence of the fact that my concepts corresponding to the names "Ciccro" and "Tully" are formally distinct. They are different symbol types in my language of thought.

By equating cognitive content with form, the informational atomist also delivers an ostensibly attractive explanation of cognitive compositionality. If form is cognitive content, and the form of a compound concept is inherited from the forms of its constituent concepts, then cognitive content is compositional.

Informational atomism also has a distinct advantage when it comes to scope. Some concepts cannot be imaged, some concepts cannot be defined, some concepts have no exemplars or prototypes, and, perhaps, some have no correlated theories. In contrast, any concept can be represented by a single unstructured symbol. The expressive breadth of unstructured symbols is nowhere more evident than in languages. Words can represent any number of things. They are equally suited for naming abstract kinds, concrete kinds, and fictional kinds. They can designate classes, properties, individuals, relations, events, and actions. If we assume that concepts are structured, a question quickly arises about whether any one kind of structure is suitable for all kinds of contents. If concepts are unstructured, the question does not arise. If concepts are structurally uniform (or uniformly unstructured), a uniform theory of concepts is easier to achieve.

The first hurdle that atomists encounter involves acquisition. Concept acquisition, Fodor observes, is generally explained in terms of hypothesis testing and confirmation. When we encounter members of a category for the first time, we generate, and ultimately confirm, a hypothesis about what it takes to fall in that category. For instance, one might see a bunch of triangles for the first time and hypothesize that they are all POLYGONS WITH THREE INTERIOR ANGLES. Once confirmed, this hypothesis constitutes a TRIANGLE concept. The fact that TRIANGLE is learned consists in the fact that it is a new combination of previously existing concepts. Of course, this process has to bottom out somewhere. Certain concepts, the primitives, do not decompose into more basic concepts. If learning always involves forming hypotheses in terms of more basic concepts, primitives must be unlearned. If primitives are unlearned, then, suggests Fodor, they must be innate. Some of the theories that we have considered assume that we can reduce all lexical concepts to a *small* set of primitives that are intuitively good candidates for being innate (notably, basic sensory concepts). Atomists say that this assumption is hopeless because most lexical concepts cannot be decomposed into more primitive concepts.

Fodor's argument can be posed as a dilemma. Lexical concepts cannot be decomposed into defining features because good definitions are frightfully scarce, and they cannot be decomposed into nondefining features, such as prototypes, because those do not combine compositionally. It follows that almost all lexical concepts are primitive. But if most lexical concepts are primitive and primitive concepts are innate, then most lexical concepts are innate (Fodor 1975, 1981).

It would be charitable to say that Fodor has satisfied the acquisition desideratum. Instead, he skirts the issue by saying that most concepts are not acquired. This would be acceptable if the case for radical nativism could be sustained. In chapter 8, I argue that it cannot. In the interim, I only remark that Fodor's nativism is immensely controversial and is regarded as a point of great vulnerability. I ultimately argue that his nativism is not as radical as it appears, but that argument opens the door for a more thoroughgoing critique of his theory of concepts.

The difficulties with atomism do not end with acquisition. By giving up conceptual structure, the atomist also loses explanatory resources that are essential for accommodating other desiderata. First consider the cognitive-content requirement. As noted, Fodor thinks that concepts have both intentional contents and forms. He calls on the latter to explain the some of the phenomena that motivate cognitive content. Notably, he believes that a person's failure to recognize that a pair of coreferring concepts corefer stems from the fact that the concepts in this pair have distinct forms.[2] This proposal has several problems.

Some of the problems can best be seen by comparison with language. Frege is sometimes interpreted as saying that senses, his candidate for cognitive content, map one-to-one onto words. "Cicero" has just one sense and "Tully" has another. More recently, it has become clear that this one-to-one mapping is untenable. First, senses are more fine-grained than words. This is nicely illustrated by a case that Kripke (1979) presents. Consider this variant. Sally fails to realize that Farrakhan the violinist and Farrakhan the leader of the Nation of Islam are one and the same person. She possesses two beliefs *with different cognitive contents* that she would express by the sentence, "Farrakhan likes to perform for an audience." Since this sentence has one form and she has two corresponding beliefs, senses cannot map one-to-one onto words. Conversely, senses can also be more coarse-grained than words. Consider translation. Ollie has a belief that he would express as, "Austria is beautiful," and Otto has a belief that he would express by, "Österreich ist schön." These two beliefs can be subsumed under many of the same psychological laws. They lead to similar behavior. This suggests that they have the same cognitive content. In Frege's terms, distinct words can have the same sense.

The moral of these considerations has to do with the relationship between cognitive content and linguistic expression. You cannot individuate cognitive contents by word forms. This does not *entail* a parallel conclusion about the relationship between cognitive contents and the forms of mental representations, but it does raise some concerns. The ease with which we can demonstrate the failure of a one-to-one mapping between cognitive contents and words suggests that there is something fundamentally wrong with thinking of cognitive content as a purely formal property. We usually describe differences in cognitive content by appeal to epistemic differences, i.e., differences in beliefs. For example, Sally may distinguish her two Farrakhan concepts by thinking of one as a musician and the other as an orator. Ollie and Otto may be said to have the same concepts corresponding to "Austria" and "Österreich" in virtue of sharing a core of common beliefs about Austria. If epistemic differences and similarities play such a central role in verifying our attributions of cognitive content and formal differences do not, then cognitive contents must be epistemic in nature. Such differences must derive from the semantically interpretable features of concepts, rather than the purely formal properties of concepts. If cognitive content is defined in a way that does not involve constituent features, it cannot offer the kind of explanation that the cases devised by Frege and Kripke demand.

The second problem brought out by Kripke's cases and the translation example is that we do not have a clear handle on what forms are. When philosophers appeal to the formal properties of a concept, it is not always clear what they are talking about (Aydede 1998; see also Stich 1983). One possibility is that formal properties are physical properties. On this view, two concept tokens are identical in cognitive content just in case they are tokens of the same physical type. Unless the type-identity theory is right, which it almost certainly is not, this renders it virtually impossible for the same concept to be tokened twice. Publicity would be unachievable. A second possibility is that tokens are formally identical if they have the same intentional content. This account does not help Fodor, because Fodor's explanation of Frege's cases depends on the supposition that concepts with the same intentional content can be formally distinct.

The third answer, which Fodor actually endorses, is that two concepts are formally identical if they play the same functional role. But, as Aydede (1998) argues, this proposal also does violence to the publicity requirement. Fodor himself has argued that it is virtually impossible for two people or two time slices of the same person to have concepts that play the same functional role. The main reason is that there is no way to draw a principled distinction between the portion of a concept's functional role that is relevant for individuation and the portion that is not. Functional roles are ineluctably holistic. Two people could have concepts with the same cognitive contents, on this interpretation, only if those concepts played exactly the same roles. Such convergence never occurs. In chapter 1, I argued that publicity demands the possibility of shared cognitive contents. Because of its tacit holism, Fodor's theory of cognitive content undermines that possibility.

In sum, cognitive content cannot be equated with form. First, it fails to cohere with our practice of distinguishing cognitive contents by appeal to semantically interpretable differences in mental states. Second, it renders publicity impossible. The major alternative to formal accounts of cognitive contents is to say that cognitive contents are sets of beliefs or features (e.g., senses, stereotypes, definitions, prototypes, etc.). Adopting this view is tantamount to adopting the view that concepts are structured. Fodor rejects structured concepts because he thinks they render publicity and compositionality impossible. We have now seen that his own view of cognitive content raises publicity problems. It turns out that Fodor's atomism also introduces difficulties for compositionality.

One of the remarkable facts about human concept combination is that we can readily produce lists of features to describe the things designated by our phrasal concepts. Sometimes the features we come up with are obviously emergent. These may reflect a noncompositional process that introduces information not contained in the concepts being combined. But often our descriptions of compounds do seem to reflect the information associated with their constituents.

The simplest cases involve feature inheritance. The characteristic feature HAS LONG EARS is inherited from the concept BUNNY in the novel compound RUBBER BUNNY. Other cases involve feature deletion. Bunnies, but not rubber bunnies, are said to be furry, to be animals, and to make good pets. An attractive explanation of this phenomenon is that these features are eliminated through some kind of consistency-checking procedure in the compound RUBBER BUNNY (see Hampton 1991). We are able to generate features for completely unfamiliar compounds (rubber bunny, ten legged yak, tin foil sofa, green flamingo), and these features bear some relation to the features we list for their constituents. This suggests that the features associated with compounds are, to some degree at least, a function of the features associated with their constituents. In a word, it suggests that features are generated in part by a compositional process. Although we do not have an adequate theory of how this compositional process works, we have good reason to assume it exists (namely, the productivity of feature listing for unfamiliar compounds).

Fodor could concede this point but simply insist that the compositional mechanisms that correlate features with compounds are *external* to concepts. Concepts, construed as atoms, might nevertheless have features associated with them, and those features might combine in systematic ways when concepts combine. To preserve his atomism, Fodor needs only to insist that these associated features are not constituents of the concepts with which they are associated. But this reply misses the point. One of the main motivations for atomism is Fodor's claim that (nondefinitional) structured representations cannot combine compositionally. The fact that we productively generate features when combining concepts provides strong prima facie evidence that this claim is false. Productive feature generation suggests that there is a compositional process underlying the combination of structured representations. This undermines a central motivation for atomism. A more complete argument to this effect, one that explains emergent features and offers an informal model of concept combination, is presented in chapter 11.

The greatest shortcoming of atomism involves categorization. Unstructured mental representations simply cannot explain how we categorize. First, consider category production. If concepts are structured, the properties named in describing a category can be associated with features contained in the concept representing that category. If concepts have no constituent features, our ability to produce such descriptions must be explained by information that is not contained in our concepts. Now consider category identification. On most views, our ability to identify the category of an object depends, again, on features contained in the concept for that category. For the atomist, identifying the category of an object depends on a set of detection mechanisms that are external to the concept for that category. The atomist says that an explanation of categorization is not within the explanatory jurisdiction of a theory of concepts.

This is a major shortcoming. Most psychologists regard the categorization desideratum as the main motivation for postulating concepts. They tend to implicitly define "concepts" as the mechanisms by which we categorize. To say the concepts do not contribute to categorization is almost incoherent from this perspective.

It might be argued that Fodor and psychologists are just talking at cross-purposes. Fodor begins with the assumption that concepts constitute propositional attitudes, and he argues that the things that do so must be unstructured. An opponent of Fodor might begin with the assumption that concepts explain categorization and argue that the things that do so cannot constitute attitudes. Perhaps Fodor and this opponent are simply using the term "concept" differently, and their theories are compatible. More interesting is the debate between Fodor and those of his opponents who share his initial assumption. One might agree that concepts are the constituents of attitudes and still insist that they contribute

5

Empiricism Reconsidered

5.1 Introduction

In the last three chapters, I surveyed the theories of concepts that have dominated discussion in philosophy and psychology. Each theory has its strengths, but none satisfies all of the desiderata presented in chapter 1. Confronted with this fact, one can either abandon some of those desiderata or try to devise a theory that satisfies them all. In the following chapters, I pursue the latter course.

The theory I propose appropriates elements from almost all of the theories that I reviewed, but it shares most, in spirit, with imagism. Imagism complies with untutored intuitions. When we introspect during thought, all we find are mental images, including auditory images of natural-language sentences (subvocal speech). With no phenomenal traces of nonsensory representations, it is tempting to conclude that all thought is couched in perceptual imagery.

This is not a sufficient reason for being an imagist. Introspection is very limited. There are good theoretical reasons for postulating representations that exist outside of consciousness. Moreover, imagism has been subjected to numerous objections, and some of these are insurmountable. I want to suggest, however, that imagism is less wrong than is often assumed, that classical empiricists had things importantly right. The brand of empiricism I arrive at in the following chapters differs from traditional imagism, but it follows that tradition in attempting to ground conception in perception.

Resuscitating empiricism is not a new idea. The history of Western philosophy has been punctuated by empiricist revivals. In the first half of the twentieth century, British philosophers such as Russell (1919, 1921) and Price (1953) carried the torch for Hume and Locke, who were defending views that hark back to ancient Greece. Twentieth-century British empiricists updated these older traditions by adding logic to the expressive toolkit of their representational systems and by their increased interest in language analysis. Outside of Britain, the Viennese logical positivists began an empiricist revival of their own. Like Russell, they had been impressed by Frege's attempt to reduce mathematics to logic and even more impressed by the young Wittgenstein's attempt to initiate a similar reduction for all of language. The members of the Vienna Circle recast Wittgenstein's reductive program in an empiricist light by restricting the reduction base to sentences that can be tested through publicly observable verification conditions. Talk that does not meet this verification principle, including much of ordinary language, was deemed unintelligible.

The biggest difference between British and Viennese empiricists was that the Viennese became enamored with behaviorism. Members of the Vienna Circle, such as Carnap and Hempel, sought to define mental vocabulary in terms of behavior rather than introspective experience, because experiences fail the test for public verifiability. These authors were also inspired by Frege, who denounced attempts to identify meanings with images on the grounds the images are unsharable. In resuscitating empiricism, they did not want to resuscitate imagism.

The behaviorism of the Viennese positivists proved to be more enduring than their verification principle. Quine's post-positivist empiricism is deeply behavioristic. Quine does not attempt to define mental terms by listing behaviors, but this is a consequence of his distaste for definitions. Quine (1960) regards appeals to inner mental states as methodologically suspect and applauds the learning theory developed by psychological behaviorists. The former sentiment is also defended by ordinary language philosophers, such as Ryle and the later Wittgenstein. Wittgenstein denies being a behaviorist, but he claims that mental terms cannot refer to private, inner states. For Wittgenstein, mental terms have behavioral criteria for application. This constitutes a form of behaviorism.

Psychology had empiricist leanings from the very beginning, and these saw expression in introspectionism around the turn of the twentieth century. Introspectionists sought to understand the mind by describing the mental images that people form under various conditions. This methodology proved exasperatingly unreliable at a time in which psychologists were hoping to make their field scientifically rigorous. In its place, American psychologists, led by J. B. Watson, began to advocate behaviorist techniques, which neither probed not postulated inner mental states. B. F. Skinner argued that such inner states were both scientifically intractable and explanatorily superfluous for explaining behavior.[1]

Behaviorism usurped introspectionism with its more rigorous methodology and effectively silenced much theorizing about inner mental states in the United States. The departure from imagist introspectionism was not a departure from empiricism. The idea that psychology has its basis in experience was simply reconceived as the view that external stimuli and reinforcement histories were the basis of intelligent behavior. The idea that the mind begins as a *tabula rasa*, molded entirely by experience, receives its most extreme endorsement from the behaviorists.[2]

Cognitive science emerged in this climate. George Miller began exploring the capacity limitations of short-term memory storage, Herbert Simon and Alan Newell began developing machines that could prove theorems and play chess by means of internal programs, and Noam Chomsky began arguing that internal rules and representations formed the basis of our language capacity. Inner mental life was exonerated. By this time, empiricism was so deeply associated with behaviorism that they were destined to fall together. Those who could recall a prior history of empiricism were likely to think of the introspectionists, whose methodological difficulties fueled the emergence of behaviorism. Early cognitive psychologists did not revive the claim that thought is couched in images. Indeed, most avoided studies of mental imagery altogether. Researchers in artificial intelligence focused on tasks that were far removed from experience, and tackled these tasks using languagelike programming codes rather than imagelike representations. Linguists argued that humans are born with highly specific innate principles, which were incompatible with the prevailing empiricist theories of learning. In rejecting behaviorism, many cognitive scientists rejected the whole empiricist tradition.

Empiricist views are now reemerging in cognitive science. Attempts to blur the boundary between perception and cognition can be found in the work of psychologists (Mandler 1992, Tomasello 1992, Glenberg 1997), neuroscientists (Edelman 1992, Damasio 1994), linguists (Talmy 1983; Fauconnier 1985; Johnson 1987; Lakoff 1987; Langacker 1987, 1991), and roboticists (Stein 1994). Despite many differences, all these authors agree that our conceptual capacities utilize perceptual resources. At the same time, many of these authors would resist being called empiricists. A more thoroughgoing defense of traditional empiricist claims can be found in the recent work of Lawrence Barsalou and his colleagues (Barsalou 1993; Barsalou, Yeh, Luka, Olseth, Mix, and Wu 1993; Olseth and Barsalou 1995; Barsalou and Prinz 1997; Goldstone and Barsalou 1998; Barsalou, Solomon, and Wu 1999; Prinz and Barsalou 2001). The position I defend extends these efforts.

Despite its allure, longevity, and recent resurgence, empiricism is still unpopular. It is easy to find philosophers, psychologists, and linguists who think empiricist theories are completely hopeless. Some of this reputation may derive from guilt by association with logical positivism, behaviorism, and introspectionism, but empiricist theories also face a number of daunting objections. In the chapters that follow, I respond to those objections and argue that a viable empiricism must be distinguished from traditional imagism. In this chapter I define empiricism, offer a methodological argument and several empirical considerations in its defense, and address one important objection.

5.2   What Is Concept Empiricism?

5.2.1   Concept Empiricism Defined
The empiricism I want to defend is, of course, an empiricism about the nature of concepts. According to a traditional formulation, concept empiricists endorse the following claim:

The Perceptual-Priority Hypothesis   Nothing is in the intellect that is not first in the senses (*nihil est in intellectu quod non fuerit in sensu*).

This stands in need of some clarification. One might wonder about the nature of the implied priority. In saying that concepts are in the senses *first*, does one mean that sensation is logically prior to cognition, metaphysically prior, or merely causally prior?[3]

The first option, that the senses are logically prior to concepts, does not seem plausible. If the sensory were logically prior to the conceptual, then it would be a logical truth that concepts have a sensory basis. To make this case, one would have to provide a conceptual analysis of the concept CONCEPT and then establish that the analysis entails this logical truth. Neither task is promising. First, "concept" is a theoretical term. It picks out a class of entities postulated to do certain explanatory work, which may vary across and within disciplines. On the strategy I advocate, the desiderata used to introduce the term "concept" do not qualify as an analysis if by "analysis" one means a set of necessary conditions. The entities that deserve to be called "concepts" at the end of inquiry may fail to explain some of the phenomena for which they were originally postulated. If "concept" is a theoretical term, it may be impossible to find *logical* entailments of the concept CONCEPT beyond, possibly, the general claim that concepts ought to explain some proportion of their current explanatory desiderata. This weak requirement would establish a logical link between the conceptual and the sensory only if some indispensable members of that group of desiderata logically implicated the senses, but that is not the case. None of the desiderata in chapter 1, at any rate, logically implicate the senses in any obvious way.

Perhaps the Perceptual-Priority Hypothesis involves a metaphysical priority. Independent of what the term "concept" means, one might advance the thesis that *being* a concept ineluctably depends on having a certain kind of connection to the senses. To see this, first suppose that being a concept depends on being intentional. Second, suppose that intentionality is metaphysically tied to conscious experience; suppose, more specifically, that a creature without conscious experience could not have intentional states. I do not think this claim is plausible, but it has been defended by certain philosophers (Searle 1992). Finally, suppose that, in all metaphysically possible worlds, all conscious states are sensory. In sum, one could argue that it is metaphysically necessary that (a) concepts are intentional, (b) intentionality depends on conscious states, and (c) conscious states are sensory. Together, these could yield a metaphysical link between the perceptual and the conceptual.

Arguments for a metaphysical priority provide an interesting option for the empiricist, but the classical empiricist tradition seems to be committed to something weaker. The empiricists of Britain, at least, seem to argue for a causal priority. As far as Locke says, for example, it could have turned out that empiricism is false. Indeed, it could be that it is false for some other creatures. His theory of the sensory origin of ideas is presented as an empirical conjecture about how human minds work.[4]

What are we to make of the alleged causal priority? Viewed as an evolutionary claim, it may seem relatively uncontroversial. Creatures capable of sensation may have evolved before creatures capable of forming concepts. For classical empiricists, however, the causal priority claim is intended ontogenetically. They defend the view that, as a matter of fact, the concepts that humans use in thought are copied or built up from sensory states. In Hume's words, "We shall always find that every idea which we examine is copied from a similar impression" (1748, II). In more modern dress, Hume's formulation of the empiricist credo would be stated using the term "concept" in place of "idea" and "perceptual representations" in place of "impressions."[5] Empiricists believe that perceptual representations serve as a causal preconditions for concepts: concepts would not come into existence if the perceptual representations were not available to be copied or assembled. This interpretation of the Perceptual-Priority Hypothesis can be restated as the following thesis:

Concept Empiricism   All (human) concepts are copies or combinations of copies of perceptual representations.

This definition of concept empiricism offers a more perspicuous statement of the view expressed by the Perceptual-Priority Hypothesis. It states that the priority of perception stems from the fact that concepts are "copies." Copying is properly conceived as a causal process. The term may sound hopelessly metaphorical, but it is possible that copying literally occurs in the mind. One proposal is that representations produced in perceptual systems are duplicated in other systems. Imagine, for example, that a visual percept is a pattern of neural activity in a topographic map corresponding to the visual field. A stored copy of that percept might be a similar pattern in a topographic map stored elsewhere in the brain. An alternative possibility is that representations in perceptual systems leave behind records in other systems that allow those representations to be regenerated in their original perceptual systems on subsequent occasions. Imagine that a stimulus causes a state in the visual system, and then some other system stores a record that can cause the visual system to generate a state of the same kind when the stimulus is no longer there. Stored records themselves are not copies, on this proposal; rather they are instructions for producing copies. On both proposals, an active token of a concept qualifies as a copy of a perceptual representation.

Concept empiricism underscores a point that is only implicit in the Perceptual-Priority Hypothesis: concept empiricism is a thesis about the nature of mental representations or the *vehicles* of thought. In this, concept empiricism differs from other forms of empiricism. First, concept empiricism is very different from epistemological forms of empiricism. It makes no mention of conditions for justification. There is no assumption that knowledge claims must be grounded in incorrigible sensory experience. Nor is concept empiricism a semantic empiricism. There is no claim that meanings must be reducible to perceptual verification conditions. The thesis says that concepts, construed as a class of mental representations, have a perceptual origin, but nothing has yet been said about how such representations attain meaning. Concept empiricists are also not to be mistaken with behaviorists, who also claim to be empiricists. The views are incompatible because behaviorists repudiate internal representations. Throughout this treatment, I often use the term "empiricism" to mean "concept empiricism," but it is important not to confuse this thesis with some of the other forms of empiricism.

A more complicated question concerns the relationship between concept empiricism and the thesis that concepts are not innate, which is often associated with the empiricist tradition. As formulated, concept empiricism is compatible with nativism. But historically, concept empiricism has been closely tied to an antinativist stance. The primary motivation for embracing empiricism has often rested on arguments against nativism. For example, Locke presents his perceptual theory of concepts just after a detailed attack on nativism in the first book of his *Essay* (1690). Having argued that beliefs and their constituent concepts are not innate, Locke is compelled to provide an alternative story about how they are attained. Locke concludes that concepts (or ideas) are built up from perceptual representations.

Yet it is important to see that concept empiricism is not identical to an antinativist thesis. The second book of Locke's *Essay* may be motivated by the negative arguments in the first, but it presents a positive theory of the mind that can be evaluated on his own merits. There is some comfort in this. Antinativist arguments are not very convincing to contemporary readers. Cognitive scientists frequently postulate innate rules and representations. Most cognitive scientists think that strong forms of nativism are not only tenable, but also ineluctable. They are not gripped by Lockean intuition that there is a pressing need to find an alternative to nativism. Without the antinativist sentiment, one might wonder why concept empiricism is worth considering.

I do not think the case for concept empiricism depends on arguments against nativism. One can motivate empiricism by focusing on a positive claim about the nature of conceptual representations. This is the task of section 5.3 below. If arguments can be marshaled in favor of the claim that concepts consist of perceptually derived representations, support for concept empiricism will no longer be seen as depending on the highly controversial denial of nativism. That would be a significant advance. Of course, it might turn out that concept empiricists are committed to *some* form of antinativism. Chapter 8 determines whether this is the case, and if so, whether such antinativism can be defended.

5.2.2 Perceptual Representations

According to the definition of concept empiricism, concepts derive from perceptual representations, but what, one might wonder, are these? What makes a representation count as perceptual? What distinguishes perceptual representations from other kinds of representations? I consider various possibilities.

One possibility is that perceptual representations can be distinguished by their syntactic properties. Consider, first, syntactic density, a property identified by Goodman (1976) in his analysis of symbol systems used in the arts. A symbol system is syntactically dense if, between any two symbols in that system, there is a third. This is true in painting. Between any two paint strokes, there is a possible third, intermediate in length, shape, or color. Density is not restricted to spatial arts. In music there is always a third note between any two, though not all are named in musical notation. This seems like a feature that might apply equally well to mental representations in different senses. Visual images, auditory images, and even gustatory images seem to be dense. Could density be a criterial feature of perceptual representations?

Unfortunately not. As we will see, some empirically supported theories of human perception rest on the assumption that certain perceptual representations are not syntactically dense (see, e.g., Biederman 1987). Moreover, syntactic density is not sufficient for being perceptual. Any artificial neural network whose nodes can take values along a continuum is syntactically dense, but it would be misleading to say any neural network is therefore perceptual. Being dense and being perceptual are independent.

Another syntactic proposal for identifying perceptual representations takes its inspiration from discussions of what philosophers call non-conceptual content. Those who believe in this category typically use it to capture the contents of mental states that are perceptual. Perhaps defining characteristics of nonconceptual contents can be appropriated to capture perceptual representations. One suggestion stresses combinatoric properties (see Evans 1982 and Davies 1989). Nonconceptual representations are sometimes thought to lack "generality." A system of representations has generality if having a predicative representation F and two nominal concepts a and b endows one with the ability to form the representation Fa and the representation Fb. Perhaps perceptual representational systems lack this property. Perhaps one's ability to perceptually represent various features does not necessarily carry with it the ability to represent other combinations of those features by recombining them.

An immediate problem is that cognitive scientists often assume that perceptual systems use recombinable primitive symbols that exhibit generality (Marr 1982, Biederman 1987). More important, it would be self-defeating for concept empiricists to say that perceptual representations cannot be readily combined. First, they are committed to the possibility of concepts emerging through the process of combining perceptual representations. Second, if perceptual representations are not combinable, their copies are unlikely to be readily combinable. If combinability is necessary for being a concept (as I conceded in endorsing the compositionality desideratum in chapter 1), then it would turn out that copies of perceptual representations are not concepts. The idea of nonconceptual content is also awkward for the empiricist. If conceptual representations are copies of perceptual representations, then the latter are better viewed as *pre*conceptual than *non*conceptual. "Nonconceptual" implies a too sharp a distinction between the perceptual and the conceptual.

According to another proposal for distinguishing perceptual representations, perceptual representations are spatial, whereas nonperceptual representations are not. In presenting his theory of mental imagery, Kosslyn (1980) provides a useful account of what it is to be a spatial representation. He says that two parts of a spatial representation are adjacent to each other (or function as if they were adjacent) just in case they represent adjacent parts of an object. Some perceptual relations undoubtedly have this property (e.g., topographic visual states), but others presumably do not (e.g., gustatory representations).

Being a spatial representation is a property that straddles syntax and semantics. A similar proposal is that perceptual representations are isomorphic with the things the represent. In cases of isomorphism, there is a one-to-one mapping between properties of representations and properties of the things they represent. For example, if A is larger than B and B is larger than C, a perceptual representation of A bears some transitive relation to a perceptual representation of B that B also bears to the representation of C.[6] Perhaps isomorphic mappings are distinctive to perceptual representations.

The problem with this proposal is that representations that are not obviously perceptual can be isomorphic with the things they represent. Wittgenstein (1919) notes that there is an abstract isomorphism between true sentences and the world. If there were a language of thought, utterly removed from perception, it could have this property.[7]

According to a purely semantic proposal, perceptual representations are those mental states that represent *perceivable* properties. The problem here is that the question of which properties are perceivable is steeped in controversy. Classical empiricists claim we can only perceive simple primary properties, such as shape and solidity, and secondary properties, such as colors and smell. New Look psychologists claim we can come to perceive causes and neutrinos. Gibsonians claim that we can perceive possibilities for bodily interaction.

It is not worth adjudicating these debates. For one thing, representing a perceivable property may be a necessary condition for being a perceptual representation, but it certainly is not sufficient; presumably, the non-perceptual representations envisioned by opponents of empiricism can represent perceivable properties too. Furthermore, if there is a principled difference between features that are perceivable and features that are not, it is likely to hinge on facts about our perceptual input systems. Something counts as perceivable for us when our input systems can pick it up. Perceivability is defined in terms of our input systems. A perceivable property is one that can be detected using perceptual machinery. This platitude brings us to the conclusion that a perceptual representation is just a representation indigenous to our senses. If so, the most direct path to distinguishing perceptual representations from concepts is not to isolate privileged semantic properties but to distinguish the senses from other cognitive faculties.

The last observation points toward a more traditional method of defining perceptual representations. In a word, one should appeal to *faculties*. The Perceptual-Priority Hypothesis exemplifies faculty talk in mentioning the *intellect* and the *senses*. Perhaps perceptual representations are simply representations that have their origins in the senses. If we can say what the senses are, we can say what perceptual representations are. This can be done contrastively by explaining the difference between the senses and the intellect. If there is no difference between the senses and the intellect, it is incoherent to assert that one is prior to the other.

What makes something count as a sense?[8] One answer is that sensory systems, unlike the intellect, are modular (Fodor 1983). Modular systems are fast, domain specific, associated with specific neural architectures, and informationally encapsulated. Saying that perceptual systems are informationally encapsulated means that processing in perceptual systems cannot be influenced by information contained in other systems. This hypothesis is sometimes defended on evolutionary grounds: perceptual systems are able to respond to stimuli more quickly and efficiently if they are insulated from central cognitive systems, which store all of our beliefs about the world. The evolutionary argument fails, as can be seen by a simple analogy. We are designed to flinch, without intervention from central systems, when we see an object looming toward us, but that encapsulated response does not show that we cannot also move our facial muscles by an act of will. Evolution might have designed perceptual systems to be capable of stimulus-driven responses without restricting them to such responses.

Some have used empirical considerations to argue that perceptual systems are not informationally encapsulated, and hence not modular (e.g., Churchland 1988). Well-known phenomena such as phoneme restoration (in which we hear speech sounds that are not actually articulated) and interpretation of fragmented pictures (which sometimes calls on knowledge of what they represent) provide evidence that beliefs, expectations, and high-level interpretations can affect what we perceive. Further support for a nonmodular picture comes from the fact that there are massive efferent pathways from high-level brain regions into perceptual regions. Admittedly, few pathways directly connect high-level systems with the lowest-level perceptual subsystems. This provides some evidence that these lowest levels are modular, which may explain why, e.g., certain optical illusions continue to work even when we know, in our central systems, that they are illusory. But low-level modularity does not entail modularity all the way up. Even if most levels of perceptual processing were encapsulated, the existence of a single level that is not encapsulated would show that modularity is not necessary for being a sense modality.

Modularity may also be insufficient for being a sense modality. There is growing suspicion that central cognitive systems are divided into modules (see Samuels, Stich, and Nichols 1999). Some researches believe that concepts and various modes of reasoning are divided into informationally encapsulated domains. Selective deficits in specialized cognitive abilities cannot be remedied by preserved knowledge in other domains. A full treatment of these proposals would require a lengthy discussion, but mere mention is enough to raise concerns about using modularity to distinguish the senses from the intellect.

Another proposal for characterizing the senses points to the primary function they serve. Sensory systems are in the business of receiving inputs from the extramental environment, including one's own body. A popular version of this proposal is found in the Kantian suggestion that the senses are "receptive," passively receiving stimulations from the environment, while the intellect is "spontaneous," actively generating novel representations under the executive control of the organism.

This suggestion encounters some problems. The first is that the intellect is not always spontaneous. It presumably also engages in exogenously controlled reception of inputs, albeit at a later stage in processing. When one sees a familiar object, it is likely to cause activity from transducers all the way up to the level of judgments. If one sees a cat, for example, no act of will can prevent one from judging that there is a cat. The idea that the senses are purely receptive has also hit upon hard times. It is widely believed that we transform, reconstruct, and interpret signals from very early stages on, reducing noise, filling in gaps, utilizing prior knowledge and expectations. The senses can also be used to actively seek out objects, as in cases of visual search, and they can issue commands to motor systems, as when we saccade to a bright light or recoil from a hot grill. Finally, leading theories of mental imagery have it that we can form mental images by willfully reactivating our input systems. Such a view is especially important to empiricists who want to say that the senses can underwrite performance of conceptual tasks. If receptivity implies passivity, the proposal that senses are merely receptive seems importantly wrong.

Despite these difficulties, the modularity and receptivity proposals have kernels of truth. The receptivity proposal is right to say that the senses serve the function of responding to inputs. The modularity proposal is right to say that the senses serve functions that are domain-specific. If we put these ideas together, the senses can be regarded as systems that respond to particular classes of inputs. This does not mean the senses are passive or impenetrable. Instead, it means that each retains a crucial degree of independence, processing its own preferred stimuli in its own preferred way. The idea can be summarized by saying that the senses are *dedicated input systems*.

In saying that the senses are *systems*, I want to emphasize the fact that they each consist of their own sets of operations and representations, housed in separate neural pathways. Distinguishing separate neural pathways is crucial. To see why, consider an alternative view according to which we can individuate the senses by external "sense organs." One problem with this alternative is that we can imagine creatures that have two organs serving a single sense modality. Interoception may be a case in point. Internal bodily organs are surely distinct, but they provide inputs to the sensory system that monitors internal feelings. Another problem is that the same organ can serve two senses. For example, the skin serves in heat and pressure detection, which may be distinct senses. More dramatically, people with synesthesia report having sensations in one modality caused by stimulation of an organ associated with another (Keeley, forthcoming). A further problem is that organ individuation pre-supposes modality individuation. Is the ear a single sense organ? Despite lessons learned on mother's knee, the answer seems to be "no," because the ear contributes to both audition and proprioception; proprioception uses semicircular canals and vestibular sacs, which extend from the cochlea. To individuate sense organs, we must begin with the sense before we can properly identify the organs that supply it with inputs.

One might think that one can avoid these difficulties by switching emphasis from organs to receptor types. Different senses have different kinds of receptors, and these play an important role in individuating the senses. It would be a mistake to stop with the receptors, however. We can imagine creatures that have numerous receptor types outside the brain but only a single processing system within the brain—an extreme version of Lashley's (1950) equipotentiality proposal. True sensory systems can be distinguished internally. The internal divisions can be functional rather than anatomical, though in our own brains these two often coincide. Brodmann's cytoarchitectonic regions often play distinct functional roles. This is unsurprising, because neural populations that work in tandem are likely to group together. To say that senses are systems means that they can be divided up internally, in our case, by distinct collections of cooperative neural populations.

In saying that senses are *input* systems, I mean that they are systems that receive inputs from outside of the brain. These may stem from the external environment (as with audition, sight, and the pheromone system) or from within the body (as with proprioception, interoception, hunger, and thirst). Some components of a sense system lie far from the transducers that first receive input signals, but to count as a sense, there must be inputs somewhere, and the components must contribute to the processing of those inputs. Functional neuroimaging has given great insight into how input systems are differentiated. One can see which areas are concurrently active when the body receives sensory inputs. This indicates the anatomical boundaries of systems involved in processing such inputs.

Finally, in saying that senses are *dedicated*, I mean that each sense responds to a proprietary input class.[9] Psychophysicists point out that different senses are specially tuned to different kinds of physical magnitudes. For example, vision responds to wavelengths of light, audition responds to frequency of molecular motion, and smell responds to molecular shapes. Notice that I talk of "responding" rather than "representing." As mentioned above, there is considerable controversy about what the modalities represent. As cell recordings suggest, neurons in the visual system represent things such as lines or shapes, but it is able to do so by responding to patterns of light. The claim is not that different modalities necessarily represent different things, only that they represent by responding to different kinds of magnitudes. This gets around some of the worries associated with the perceivable-properties proposal above.

Also tied to the notion of dedication is the assumption that modalities use different kinds of representations. This claim is a bit harder to establish. A familiar tradition favored by rationalists is that all mental systems share a "common code" (see Leibniz 1765, Pylyshyn 1978).[10] On this view, perceptual modalities all use the same kinds of symbols as each other and as the more central systems associated with high-level cognition. Call this "common-code rationalism." In contrast, empiricists traditionally conceive of the mind as a multimedia system because they presume that the senses use distinct kinds of representations.

The supposition that the senses use different kinds of representations is supported by the fact that they have proprietary inputs and specialize in different kinds of information processing. As Kosslyn (1980) has emphasized, different kinds of representations may be better suited for different tasks. The representations ideally suited for deriving information from light are not ideal for deriving information from sound. Those who theorize about processing in different modalities postulate distinct representational primitives. It would be difficult to adapt, say, Marr's theory of vision to audition. The assumption that sensory modalities are relatively independent systems also lends some support to the hypothesis that they use different kinds of representations. It is believed that different sensory systems have different evolutionary histories. This is reflected in the fact that they show different patterns of development and maturation. If they evolved separately, the different selectional forces that shaped them may have resulted in different kinds of representations.

Further support for disparate representations comes from introspection. Phenomenal awareness is mediated by mental representations. An auditory experience of an object as being to the left feels different from a visual experience of an object as being to the left. This provides prima facie evidence that different representations are involved.

Finally, attempts to explain processing within perceptual systems using representations that have a nonproprietary character have met with mixed results. Anderson (1978) showed that one could simulate the performance of visual-image rotation using propositional representations. Propositional representations are the kinds of things that current defenders of the common-code hypothesis tend to envision. They are structured like symbols in formal logic. Anderson's proof seems to support the common-code hypothesis, but it also exposes a flaw. If visual-image rotation uses a spatial medium of the kind Kosslyn envisions, then images must traverse intermediate positions when they rotate from one position to another. The propositional system can be designed represent intermediate positions during rotation, but that is not obligatory. If we assume that a spatial medium is used for imagery, we can predict the response latencies of mental-rotation tasks; if we assume a common propositional code throughout the mind, we can only match those results by introducing post hoc constraints. Assuming disparate codes is more predictive and explanatory.

All this evidence seems to shift the burden onto the common-code camp. What reasons are there for thinking modalities use the same kinds of mental representations? One answer comes from the a priori assumption that a common code would be more efficient. We can easily transfer information from one sensory modality to another if they use the same codes.

This kind of argument is undercut by the argument that multiple codes may add efficiency. Gains in the ability to transfer information from one modality to another may carry costs in the ability to process information efficiently within modalities. Thus, one cannot assume a net efficiency gain from a common code. Moreover, empirically motivated theories of perception already support multiple representation types *within* sense modalities. Vision, most notably, is widely conceived as a series of representational levels, each with different properties. The characteristics of neural populations in the lateral geniculate nucleus of the thalamus (response properties, receptive field sizes, firing patterns, etc.) seem to differ from the characteristics of neural populations within the visual areas of inferotemporal cortex, for example. It is conceivable that the former functions like a bitmap graphics program (in which primitives are pixels representing local points of light) and the latter like a vector graphics program (in which primitives include whole shapes). Intramodal diversity casts doubt on intermodal uniformity. Transfer of information between systems provides little reason to suppose that different sense modalities use the same kinds of representations (though I revisit the issue below).

I have now argued that perceptual representations are representations in dedicated input systems and that dedicated input systems use disparate kinds of mental representations. According to concept empiricism, concepts are copies or combinations copies of perceptual representations. Taken together, these hypotheses entail a corollary of concept empiricism:

The Modal-Specificity Hypothesis   Concepts are couched in representational codes that are specific to our perceptual systems.

The Modal-Specificity Hypothesis is inconsistent with common-code rationalism. Like common-code rationalists, defenders of modal specificity say that perception and cognition use the same mental codes, but they believe that these codes are fundamentally sensory and that they vary from sense to sense. Modal specificity also rules out another form of rationalism. Some rationalists agree with empiricists that perceptual modalities use disparate media, while insisting that thought is couched in a different medium entirely. On this view thought is couched in a code not shared by any modality. Call this "central-code rationalism." If modal specificity is true, central-code rationalism is false. There is no lingua franca of the mind. This sentiment captures an important component of traditional empiricism, which can be overlooked when one simply states that concepts are perceptually derived.

5.2.3   Perception Broadly Construed

Concept empiricists use the term "perception" broadly (Hume 1748, Barsalou 1993). The analysis of sense modalities offered above readily accommodates both externally directed senses (e.g., vision) and internally directed senses (e.g., proprioception). All of these senses belong to dedicated input systems. They coincide with the states that Hume calls "sensations." Hume argues that not all impressions are sensations, however. In addition, there are "impressions of reflexion." These include, most notably, emotional states or passions. Fear, pain, anger, joy, and perhaps a handful of other affective states seem to be among our most basic experiences. It is not yet clear whether reflective states fit into the definition of perceptual representations that I have proposed.

Are concept empiricists really entitled to include such reflective states as emotions in their repertoire? Do these really count as perceptual representations? Intuitively, the answer is negative. Emotions do not seem to be tied to specific input systems. The same emotion can be caused by a visual experience, an auditory experience, or even a smell. Moreover, emotions do not seem to be representations. Anger may be caused by an event, but it does not represent that event. It is just a reaction.

The empiricist can respond to this worry. There is a long tradition beginning with James (1884) and Lange (1885) of treating emotions as perceptual states. Researchers in this tradition believe that emotions are perceptions of various bodily states, including facial expressions, and various changes brought on by our autonomic nervous systems (e.g., heart rate) and endocrine systems (hormone levels). To paraphrase James, we do not tremble because we are afraid; we are afraid because we tremble. When perceived, a predator may cause trembling, a racing heart, a white palor, and perspiration. Fear is the experience of these bodily states.

The James-Lange theory is controversial, but it enjoys some experimental support. Researchers have found that certain emotions are associated with specific bodily states and that entering those states by nonemotional means can cause emotional reactions. For example, when subjects are instructed to move their facial muscles into positions that coincide with emotional expressions, they feel the correlated emotions (Levenson, Ekman, and Friesen 1990). It has also been found that severed-spinal-cord patients who can no longer detect crucial bodily states often experience diminished emotions (Montoya and Shandry 1994). Damasio (1994) employs a version of the James-Lange theory to explain the behavior of patients with frontal-lobe damage, who fail to show either autonomic or emotional responses to emotionally provocative stimuli. (A recent philosophical defense of the James-Lange theory can be found in Prinz, forthcoming.) If the James-Lange theory is correct, then emotions qualify as perceptions. They reside in systems that are dedicated to bodily inputs.[11]

Another class of problematic states requires a minor amendment of the concept-empiricism and modal-specificity hypotheses. Researchers interested in "situated cognition" emphasize the role of physical skills in our understanding of the world. Our knowledge of objects, for example, often includes knowledge about how we physically interact with them. Knowing what a hammer is involves knowing what to do with it, and knowing what to do with it involves knowing a sequence of motor movements. Developmental psychologists, such as Piaget, have argued that motor abilities play a foundational role as infants learn to manipulate their bodies and their environments.

Motor abilities are representational. They include commands to move body parts in various ways. Motor abilities are also housed in dedicated systems. Areas of frontal cortex and basal ganglia are highly involved in various aspects of motor control. But these motor areas do not qualify as *input* systems. They are predominantly concerned with outputs. Therefore, they do not qualify as perceptual representations on the definition that I offered.

To compensate for this shortcoming, I could reformulate concept empiricism and modal specificity to explicitly mention motor representations. For expository convenience, I will simply use the terms "perceptual representations" and "perceptual systems" as elliptical for "perceptual and/or motor representations" and "perceptual and/or motor systems." Admitting motor representations does nothing to vitiate the spirit of concept empiricism. Classical empiricists surely would not have denied that motor systems are among our innate faculties, and including motor representations in the empiricist repertoire carries no commitment to a common or central code.

In sum, concept empiricism interprets perception in a fairly inclusive way. It is the view that concepts are derived from a broad class of states including emotions, motor commands, and sensations.

5.3   Why Empiricism?

5.3.1   Indicators and Detectors

Why think that concept empiricism has any hope of being true? The traditional answer is that empiricism is the best remedy for untenable forms of nativism, but other answers can be given as well. Some of these other answers were presented in the discussion of imagism in chapter 2. Empiricist theories can be defended by appeal to methodological parsimony. Once we have postulated a certain class of representations for a theory of perception, it is cost effective to see whether those same representations can be used in a theory of cognition. We should try to make use of what we already have rather than overpopulating the mind with other kinds of mental representations.

I think parsimony considerations give us a reason for preferring empiricist theories over nonempiricist theories, all other things being equal. This parsimony argument is not decisive, because it does not explain why perceptual representations are good candidates for being conceptual building blocks. Obviously, perceptual representations are well motivated for explaining perception, but why think representations of this type have anything to do with concepts? Without independently establishing a link between concepts and percepts, the attempt to reduce the former to the latter seems precariously undermotivated. Needed is a strengthened argument that draws a direct link between perceptual representations and concepts. In this section, I offer such an argument.

The survey of competing theories of concepts in the preceding chapters ended with a discussion informational atomism. In some ways, atomism is the oddest contender because it is the only theory that does not take concepts to be decomposable into meaningful parts. This is a serious shortcoming. It prevents the atomist from providing satisfying accounts of acquisition, cognitive content, cognitive compositionality, cognitive publicity, and categorization. By giving up structure, the atomist gives up many of the explanatory goals that theories of concepts have traditionally sought to achieve. Atomism does have a major virtue, however. It offers an attractive account of intentionality.

The intentional-content desideratum was an Achilles heel for most of the accounts that I surveyed. Imagism, prototype theory, and exemplar theory all presuppose resemblance or similarity-based accounts of intentionality, which cannot work, because similarity is neither necessary nor sufficient for reference. The theory theory did no better, because mini theories of categories are incomplete and inaccurate. Definitions determine intentional contents by picking out the objects that satisfy their necessary and sufficient conditions, but definitionists owe an explanation of the satisfaction relation. Informational atomism gets over the problem of intentionality by proposing that concepts refer in virtue of standing in nomological relations to their referents. Informational theories are the best available strategy for explaining intentionality.

Informational atomism is in a funny position. Its informational component constitutes the most promising account of intentionality, but its atomistic component sacrifices structure, which is needed to accommodate most of the other desiderata. There is an obvious solution. Perhaps we can accommodate all of the desiderata if we combine the informational component of informational atomism with a nonatomistic theory of conceptual structure. On this approach, concepts would be identified with semantically structured entities that get their intentional contents through informational relations.

This proposal faces two challenging questions. What kind of structured representations can be reconciled with an informational semantics? And can such structured representations overcome objections to the nonatomistic theories of concepts reviewed in earlier chapters?

To address the first question, it is useful to recall the distinction between indicators and detectors, introduced in the previous chapter. An indicator is an unstructured entity that falls under the nomological control of some property (e.g., a light that is flashed when a particular letter is presented to a letter-detecting device). A detector is a mechanism that mediates the relation between an indicator and the property it indicates (e.g., a template that causes a red light to be flashed when *As* are presented). Both indicators and detectors carry information. Detectors carry information when they are successfully engaged. A letter template, for example, carries information that its corresponding letter is present when it is successfully matched to the input representation of that letter, because such successful matching reliably covaries with the presence of that letter. A letter indicator carries the information that a particular letter is present when it is "switched on" by a detector, because its being switched on reliably covaries with the presence of that letter. What counts as being "successfully engaged" or "switched on" depends on the device.

Detectors, unlike indicators, are often structured. Their parts detect parts of the things that cause them to be engaged. A detector for the letter *R* might have one part that detects straight lines, one part that detects semicircles, and a third that detects angles. An indicator for the letter *R* has no interpretable parts. If one hopes to find structured entities that are compatible with an informational semantic theory, detectors are the obvious choice. They are structured entities that enter into nomological relations with properties, and they do so in virtue of their structure.

If concepts were identified with structured detectors, we would be able to combine the benefits of informational approaches to intentionality with the benefits of structure. Call this the detector proposal. By identifying concepts with structured entities, the detector proposal provides a resource for accommodating desiderata such as cognitive content and categorization. The detector proposal is also more economical that informational atomism. Both approaches require detectors, but atomism goes on to postulate a set of internal indicators, which are unnecessary if concepts are identified with detectors. Moreover, detectors, unlike indicators, directly participate in establishing content-conferring causal relations with properties. Detectors actually do the detecting, while indicators merely indicate that something has been detected. If concepts are detectors, how a concept gets its intentional content is determined in part by things *intrinsic* to it. This allows concepts to play a role in determining their intentional contents, rather than merely being determined by their intentional contents, as the atomist would have it. Finally, detectors are less arbitrary than indicators. In a letter-detecting device, a light of any color could be used to indicate any letter, and similarities between lights are semantically irrelevant. An *R*-indicating light need not be more like a *B*-indicating light than an *O*-indicating light. Detectors are more constrained, and similarities between them can reveal facts about the world. An *R* detector is generally more like a *B* detector than an *O* detector because they detect common letter components. If concepts are detection mechanisms, we can predict similarities in objects by studying similarities in the concepts that refer to them.

Adding structure clearly increases the range of phenomena that concepts can explain. All things being equal, we should accept the detector proposal. We arrived at this conclusion by a kind of parsimony argument. If detectors are needed to confer content to concepts, why suppose that concepts are anything above and beyond detectors? But this is not *just* a parsimony argument. It is not just an argument that proliferating internal representations is extravagant. The point is also that detectors have explanatory properties above and beyond the arbitrary symbols that function as indicators. Those explanatory properties are just the sorts of things we would like to see in a theory of concepts.

We have now arrived at a strengthened parsimony argument for the conclusion that concepts are internally structured detection mechanisms. Unfortunately, the benefits of structure come at a price. Fodor would argue against the detector proposal on two grounds. First, Fodor thinks that the detector proposal generates problems for publicity; the mechanisms that people use for detection vary widely, and they can include all the beliefs that a person associates with a category. Second, Fodor thinks that detection mechanisms cannot be combined compositionally; the best mechanism for detecting pet fishes is not formed from the best mechanisms for detecting pets and fishes. I argued that Fodor's atomistic account too has problems satisfying these desiderata, but this response is just a tu quoque. An adequate response would have to show that structured representations can overcome Fodor's objections. I respond to the publicity objection in chapter 6, and to the compositionality objection in chapter 11.

For the moment, I simply assume that Fodor's objections can be met. If they can, we have the makings of a viable new argument for concept empiricism. The argument goes like this. In order for detection mechanisms to establish content-conferring causal-relation concepts and the external properties that concepts denote, they must be perceptual. Causal relations between our inner states and external properties are mediated by the senses. If I have a DOG concept that refers to dogs in virtue of being reliably caused by dogs, I must have stored perceptual representations that reliably match the perceptual representations caused by dog encounters. In adopting an informational semantics, Fodor commits himself to the view that concepts are correlated with detection mechanisms, and those mechanisms presumably do their detection perceptually. But once one admits that concepts are correlated with perceptual detection mechanisms, parsimony considerations encourage one to replace the correlation claim with an identity claim. One can dispense with an extra layer of representations by saying that concepts *just are* perceptual detection mechanisms. The appeal to parsimony gains strength when coupled with the observation that such an identity would also endow concepts with explanatory properties that they would lack if they were not identified with such detection mechanisms. Thus, there is a direct road from Fodor's theory of concepts to concept empiricism. When one adopts informational semantics, empiricism becomes quite attractive.

This argument for concept empiricism is an advance over some of its historical counterparts. First, it does not depend on arguments against nativism. Second, it bolsters appeals to parsimony with appeals to the explanatory power afforded by structure. Third, it avoids phenomenalism, which has tempted many empiricists, e.g., Berkeley (1710), Mill (1843), Ayer (1940). Phenomenalists believe that concepts refer to possible experiences rather than to a mind-external world. The present argument for empiricism escapes this trap by incorporating a commitment to informational semantics.

Most important, the present argument motivates the definitive perceptual component of empiricism. The reason why perceptual representations are good candidates for the building blocks of concepts is not just that they are independently motivated by theories of perception but also that they play an indispensable content-conferring role in our best theories of concepts. Perceptual representations must be associated with concepts if concepts attain content by reliable detection. The link between concepts and perceptual representations is forced on us by the best theory of how concepts get their intentional contents. Empiricism is not just a strategy for budget-conscious postulators of mental representations; it can be defended with considerations of the semantic relations by which concepts attain their identities.

5.3.2 Empirical Considerations

Empirical evidence also lends support to concept empiricism. A number of findings from psychology and cognitive neuroscience are consistent with the hypothesis that concepts are perceptually based.

One line of empirical evidence comes from studies of individuals whose conceptual abilities have been selectively impaired. Of particular interest are category-specific deficits (McCarthy and Warrington 1990). Patients with focal brain lesions sometimes selectively lose their ability to identify and verbally characterize categories in a single conceptual domain. For example, some patients exhibit impairments with abstract concepts but not with concrete concepts. Within concrete concepts, some show impairments with various object concepts but not with animal concepts. Within man-made-object concepts, some show impairments with small manipulable artifacts (e.g., forks) but not with large artifacts (e.g., buses).

Even more interesting than the deficits themselves is the explanation that McCarthy and Warrington offer for them. They suggest that concepts consist of modality-specific perceptual information, and that selective impairments can be explained by differences in how different category types are perceptually represented. For example, they speculate that the dissociation between abstract and concrete concepts arises because abstract concepts tend to be encoded using more emotional and verbal information, which can be selectively destroyed or spared. Concepts of animals can be dissociated from concepts of other kinds of objects because the latter contain more information about function and context of use. Finally, concepts of small manipulable objects are vulnerable to selective impairment because they encode more proprioceptive or motor information than concepts of large objects.

The modal-specificity interpretation of category deficits enjoys considerable support. For example, neuroimaging studies show greater activation in visual regions of the brain when subjects think about living things, as opposed to nonliving things (e.g., Thompson-Schill, Aguirre, D'Esposito, and Farah 1999). Neuroimaging and lesion studies also show that deficits in tool categorization involve left premotor regions, which are associated with hand movements (Damasio, Grabowski, Tranel, Hichwa, and Damasio 1996). Such studies suggest that a perceptually based theory of concepts can account for the ontological divisions in categorization that theory theorists have emphasized. Different ontological taxa are represented with different kinds of perceptual features. Cognitive domains may emerge as a result of these perceptual differences.

Support for concept empiricism also comes from Damasio's (1989) theory of convergence zones. A convergence zone is a neural record of activity in perceptual areas of the brain (including sensory and emotional centers). When simultaneous activity occurs in perceptual areas during perception, convergence zones are formed. Convergence zones are hierarchically organized. First-order convergence zones store records of co-occurring perceptual features, and higher-order convergence zones store records of lower-order convergence zones. By first binding together features and then binding together collections of bound features, convergence zones can scale up to store records of complex event sequences. Convergence zones are not merely records. They can also be used to "retroactivate" the perceptual states from which they came. This is essential to the role they play in cognition. For example, we make plans by using convergence zones to retroactivate the perceptual states that would arise if those plans were executed. For convergence zones to be of any use, they must be able to retroactivate modality-specific perceptual states in this way. Thinking works by perceptual reenactment.

According to Damasio, perceptual regions of the brain are actively used in cognition. A compatible possibility is that brain regions outside of perceptual systems store and manipulate modality-specific copies of perceptual representations. Support for this possibility comes from work on monkeys. Goldman-Rakic (1998) presents evidence that areas of prefrontal cortex associated with working memory, but not traditionally identified as perceptual, are divided into parts that correspond to the dorsal and ventral divisions in the visual system. Perceptual organization is recapitulated in working memory regions. Human neuroimaging studies have also shown that different frontal regions are activated when subjects are asked to memorize different kinds of stimuli (e.g., McDermott, Buckner, Peterson, Kelly, and Sanders 1999). This is consistent with the hypothesis that modality-specific representations are used outside the areas that initially process inputs. Thinking may use modality-specific states both in and outside of perceptual systems. Both possibilities accord with concept empiricism.

Further evidence comes from cognitive psychology. Barsalou and his colleagues have performed a number of studies that support a perceptually based theory of concepts (reviewed in Barsalou 1999). An illustrative example of these studies tested for the spontaneous use of perceptual information in feature listing (Wu 1995). One group of subjects was asked to construct and describe mental images of various concepts, and another group of subjects was simply asked to list typical features of those concepts. A perceptually based theory of concepts predicts that subjects should list the same kinds of features in both of these conditions. Wu also manipulated the instructions: half of the subjects in each group were given single noun concepts (e.g., WATERMELON, FACE), and half were given noun concepts with modifiers that reveal internal parts (e.g., HALF WATERMELON, SMILING FACE). A perceptually based theory of concepts predicts that subjects will list more internal features in the revealing-modifier condition. Perceptual representations generally represent the surfaces of objects. When revealing modifiers are used, those representations should be altered to reveal features lying beneath the surface. If perceptual representations are not used, internal features should be accessible under both conditions. Wu's results confirmed both predictions of the perceptually based theory: Imagery instructions do not effect listed features, and revealing modifiers cause subjects to list internal features.

Psychological studies of discourse analysis are also consistent with concept empiricism. Morrow, Greenspan, and Bower (1987) demonstrate that people form spatially organized representations when reading texts. They first ask subjects to study the floor plan of a multiroom interior with a number of objects in it. They then remove the floor plan and asked subjects to read short passages that describe the movements of a protagonist through that interior, beginning in one room (the source), passing through another (the path), and arriving at a third (the destination). After reading the passages, subjects are asked to confirm whether a particular object is in the same room as the protagonist. Responses to these questions are fastest for objects in the destination room, a bit longer for objects in the path room, and longer still for objects in the source room. Locations farther away from the current focal area of the text take longer to access. This suggests that subjects are visualizing the room currently occupied by the protagonist and tracing backward through the imagined interior when they do not find the sought object in the currently occupied room. These results support the view that thinking involves perceptual simulation.

Some psychologists have resisted the hypothesis that cognition is couched in modality-specific codes. One line of criticism stems from work on rebus sentences. A rebus sentences is a sentence that has one or more words replaced by a corresponding image. Potter, Knoll, Yachzel, Carpenter, and Sherman (1986) find that rebus sentences are comprehended as quickly as ordinary sentences. If thought were couched in visual images, they should be comprehended faster, and if thought were couched words, they should be slower. Comparable comprehension speed suggests that both pictures and words are translated into a central code during comprehension.

I am not convinced. Empiricists should not predict a temporal advantage for rebus sentences. Picture interpretation is not a trivial process. A picture must be converted into the code used by the visual system and then matched against visual memory to find a stored category representation. The move from a written word to an image of its referent may be a faster process. After all, we are far more practiced at reading words than naming pictures. The fact that there is no temporal advantage for rebus sentences may result from the fact that rebus sentences are unusual. A common-code theory predicts rebus sentences to be interpreted more slowly than ordinary sentences because we have so much more experience with the latter. The fact that rebus sentences are not interpreted more slowly suggests that the pictures they contain compensate for our inexperience by facilitating processing. This supports empiricism.

One can support this interpretation using a test that does not require rebus sentences. If images facilitate sentence comprehension, one should find that comprehension is faster when sentences contain words that are easier to image. This is exactly what has been found. Sentences containing concrete words are comprehended faster than sentences abstract containing words (Schwanenflugel 1991).

The "concreteness effect" suggests that concrete words and abstract words are represented differently. According to the dual-code model developed by Paivio (1986), the mind contains two functionally distinct representational systems: one uses associative networks of words, and the other uses sensory images. Postulating a verbal network does not conflict with empiricism, because words are perceivable objects, and they can be stored in associative networks as a result of experience. Paivio speculates that the comprehension of abstract words often depends on the verbal system. Our understanding of some abstract words may consist largely in knowing how they are used in language. We know how to use concrete words in language, but we can also form images of what they represent. Thus, both abstract and concrete sentences activate the verbal system, but concrete sentences also activate the imagery system. Sentences containing concrete words are understood faster because they can be processed by two systems.

Paivio presumes that imageability has an additive effect on comprehension speed and therefore predicts that the concreteness effect will remain when sentences containing concrete words are situated in paragraphs. This prediction is wrong. When placed in paragraphs, abstract sentences are comprehended as quickly as concrete sentences (Schwanenflugel 1991). Consequently, Schwanenflugel rejects the dual-code model and offers an alternative explanation of concreteness effects, called the context-availability model. According to this model, abstract words are generally processed more slowly than concrete words because abstract words require more contextual information to retrieve the knowledge essential for their interpretation. When abstract words are situated in paragraphs, the effect disappears, because the surrounding verbal information provides a rich context that facilitates processing.

Pace Paivio and Schwanenflugel, I think the dual-code model makes the correct prediction. On the dual-code model, abstract word comprehension relies on verbal information. As a result, processing speed for abstract words should increase when more verbal information is provided. When single sentences are presented, concrete words are understood faster than abstract words because there is minimal verbal information. When a full paragraph is provided, the effect disappears. The dual-code interpretation is consistent with the context-availability model because it says that abstract words are processed faster when more information is available. It predicts that abstract words need a richer verbal context for rapid retrieval.[12] The dual-code model also predicts that there will be no comparable improvement in performance on concrete words because performance is already near ceiling levels when concrete words are presented in isolation. The referent of a concrete word can be readily imagined even when no verbal context is provided.

The empirical evidence suggests that cognition makes extensive use of perceptual representations. This is what concept empiricism and modal specificity predict. There remains one body of evidence for an amodal code that may seem incontrovertible. I turn to that now.

5.3.3   The Intermodal Transfer Objection

The most famous argument against modal specificity pivots around a problem that Molyneux posed for Locke regarding communication between the senses, or intermodal transfer. Molyneux asked whether a congenitally blind person with restored vision would be able to recognize a sphere by sight alone (Locke 1690, II.ix.8). With Locke, he speculated that the answer would be negative. Associations between the senses were presumed to be learned. Despite ample tactile familiarity with spheres, a blind person with restored vision would have no way to guess what spheres look like. Our own ability to infer appearances from touch, and vice versa, rely on prior experiences in which both senses were used to explore the same objects at the same time. This view presupposes modal specificity. Locke thought the senses use different kinds of representations and that there is no amodal system of representation into which those representations are translated in thought. In the terminology introduced above, he denied both the common-code theory and the central-code theory. Rationalists make the opposite prediction concerning Molyneux's case. For example, Leibniz (1765, II.ix.8) reasoned that one should be able to make inferences across the senses without the benefit of learned associations, because the mind uses codes that are amodal. Tactilely exploring a square can produce the very same representations as seeing it, so when seen for the first time, the sphere should be identifiable.

Leibniz's prediction has a qualification. He astutely anticipates that there might be an initial period in which individuals with restored vision would be so "dazzled" by their new experiences that visual identification would be impossible. Several cases of restored vision have been recorded in the time since the original debate about Molyneux's problem, but Leibnizian bedazzlement and other confounds make interpretation difficult (Senden 1932). Without immediate postoperative reports of intermodal transfer, it is difficult to determine which prediction is right.

Fortunately, there is a developmental analogue of Molyneux's problem that does not depend on exotic cases of restored vision. If the senses use or have access to an amodal code and that code is available at birth, then transfer between the senses should be possible at birth. If we are only born with modality-specific codes, then one might predict a learning period before which intermodal transfer is impossible.[13]

There is now considerable evidence bearing on the developmental version of Molyneux's problem. For example, Wertheimer (1961) found that 10-minute-old newborns shift eye gaze toward clicking sounds made next to either ear. Still, this case does not quite get at Molyneux's problem, because visually orienting toward sources of sound is not the same as object recognition across modalities. Developmentalists have probed more sophisticated mental capacities of preverbal infants by exploiting a host of new techniques. They explore infants' preferences by recording sucking, touching, and staring patterns. Coupled with carefully devised stimuli, training, and test conditions, these simple behaviors reveal fascinating facts about how very young minds organize the world.[14] These methods have been used to show that extremely young infants can transfer information between the senses, which supports the rationalist prediction that this ability does not require learned associations.

Several examples illustrate. First, Streri, Spelke, and Rameix (1993) observed 4-month-old infants as they handled pairs of rings connected either by a rigid bar or by a string. The ring pairs were hidden beneath a cloth so that the infants could not see them as they explored them with their hands. The infants were then presented with visual displays of rigidly connected and unconnected objects. The infants who handled the rigid objects stared preferentially at the rigid object displays, and those who handled the nonrigid objects stared preferentially at the uncon- nected object displays. This suggests that infants transfer information between haptic experience (exploratory touch) and visual experience. One might think that 4 months is too old to test between innate abili- ties and learned associations. Younger infants have limited control over their limbs, so one must observe their oral exploration, instead of their hand exploration. Meltzoff and Borton (1979) gave 1-month-old infants pacifiers with shaped tips and then displayed visual images of shapes. The infants stared preferentially at the visual shapes that match the shapes of their pacifiers. Kaye and Bower (1994) found the same behav- ior in 12-hour-old newborns! This provides very strong support for the claim that intermodal object recognition (or similarity assessment) is pos- sible at birth.

Equally impressive evidence stems from a series of studies on infant imitation. Meltzoff and Moore (1983) found that infants have a ten- dency to imitate facial expressions, which is already exhibited in the first day of life. After viewing adults sticking out their tongues or opening their mouths, infants do the same. This demonstrates an ability to transfer visual information to a corresponding pattern of motor commands.

Locke was evidently wrong to think that associations between the senses (or between the senses and motor systems) must be learned through association. Does this mean that concept empiricism is wrong? This conclusion would threaten if innate intermodal-transfer abilities demonstrated that the modal-specificity hypothesis is false. That is not the case. It is a non sequitur to infer a common amodal code from intermodal transfer abilities, because there is a competing explanation. We may be born with a set of rules that directly map modality-specific representation in one sense onto modality-specific representations in another. This would explain transfer without requiring an amodal code. This explanation may even be more parsimonious. If there were an amodal code mediating intermodal transfer, our brains would have to convert representations from one sense into that code and then convert that code into the other sense. This is a bit like translating English into French by translating both into German. If mapping rules directly correlate representations in different modalities, no middle step is needed.

A rationalist might respond to this argument by proposing that all the senses use the same kinds of representations, i.e., by endorsing what I have called the common-code theory. This move can be blocked. Kellman and Arterberry (1998) argue that the evidence for intermodal transfer in infants provides indirect support for the claim that perceptual modalities use different kinds of mental representations. As we just saw, infants show a preference for pairs of *matching* stimuli when given intermodal transfer tests. For instance, they stare longer at the image that matches the shape that is orally presented. In contrast, infants show a preference for *novelty* in experiments that investigate responses to stimuli within a single modality. For example, when shown a series of visual displays of one object, they prefer a subsequent display of a different object over a subsequent display of the same object. This discrepancy supports the conclusion that the senses use different codes. If the senses used the same codes, then we would expect infant performance on intermodal tests to be just like their performance on intramodal tests. This is not what happens.

To make the intermodal-transfer objection work, the rationalist needs to adopt the central-code theory, according to which the senses use distinct codes but central processing uses a single amodal code. If intermodal transfer depends on a central code and intermodal transfer is innate, then the central code is innate. If the central code is innate, then the medium of thought is not perceptually derived, as concept empiricists maintain.

There is some prima facie evidence for a central-code explanation of intermodal-transfer abilities. Neurophysiological studies suggest that some neurons fire in ways that are not specific to individual modalities. For example, certain neurons in somatosensory cortex respond to both tactile stimulation and visual experience of the same bodily locations (Graziano and Gross 1995). Other cells, in the superior colliculus, are maximally responsive when both an auditory signal and a visual signal originate from the same location (Stein and Meredith 1993). Stein and Meredith have argued that cells like this contribute to intermodal transfer. One might conclude that the mind is furnished with an innate amodal code. This would undermine concept empiricism.

A few responses are available. First, one can argue that, despite appearance, the cells in question are actually modality-specific. A moment ago I suggested that transfer might be explained by a direct mapping between the senses. Consider how a direct mapping would work. Suppose that two separate modalities contain cells that respond to a common feature of the environment, such as a location in space. To communicate, externally induced activation of space cells in one modality might cause activation of the corresponding space cells in the other modality. With this configuration, there would be cells within each modality that responded to stimulation from that modality, from the other modality, and, maximally, to simultaneous stimulation in the two modalities. This corresponds to the firing profile of the cells described. Of course, it would take extra work to show that these cells were properly regarded as modality-specific. One would have to show, for instance, that they were located in an anatomical network that was more strongly associated with one of the two modalities to which they respond, or that they gave rise to phenomenal experience associated with a single modality.

A second response strategy requires less work. The empiricist might point out that the cells is question are bimodal, rather than amodal. They respond to concurrent inputs from two modalities. In the cases mentioned, the cells are contained within anatomical regions that are regarded as sensory. Somatosensory cortex is largely dedicated to somatosensory processing, and the superior colliculus is a subcortical relay station for the senses. Bimodal cells in these regions do not show that there is an amodal central code, as the rationalist picture suggests.

Rather, they show that dedicated input systems include some bridge cells that facilitate communication.

As a rejoinder, rationalist might point out that more anterior regions of the brain's cortex, associated with higher cognitive functions, also use cells that are not unique to individual modalities. In fact, some of these cells are alleged to be responsive to inputs from *multiple* sense modalities, rather than just two. Perhaps these cells truly deserve to be called "amodal."

This argument can also be challenged. Cells that appear to be amodal might serve as convergence zones (Damasio 1989). As we saw, convergence zones are cell populations that record simultaneous activity in sensory areas and serve to reactivate those areas during cognition. Damasio's theory predicts, and is partially based on, the existence of cells that cannot be associated with a single modality. At the same time, it is consistent with the empiricist view because occurrent cognitive activity and conceptual performance rely on activity within the modalities. Convergence zones may qualify as amodal, but they contain sensory records, and they are not the actual vehicles of thought. Convergence zones merely serve to initiate and orchestrate cognitive activity in modality-specific areas. In opposition to the rationalist view, the convergence-zone theory assumes that thought is couched in modality-specific codes. If an amodal code exists, it works on credit rather than serving as the primary currency of thought. On this interpretation, amodal cells actually support the modal-specificity hypothesis.

In sum, Locke may have been wrong to assume that mappings between the senses are learned, but he was equally wrong to assume that the contrary view threatens concept empiricism by undermining modal specificity. Evidence for the innateness of intermodal-transfer abilities leaves both hypotheses in tact.

5.4 Conclusion

This chapter offers a preliminary defense of concept empiricism. The strengthened argument from parsimony supports the conclusion that concepts are couched in modality-specific codes. This is consistent with psychological findings that suggest that perceptual resources are exploited in performing conceptual tasks. It is also consistent with lessons from neuroscience that, despite evidence for amodal cells, suggest that the brain uses modality-specific codes at the highest levels of processing. When viewed as a whole, the evidence shows that empiricist theories deserve to be taken seriously.

A complete defense of concept empiricism must also prove that copies of perceptual representations can satisfy the desiderata on a theory of concepts. That challenge is taken up in the following chapters.

6

Proxytype Theory

In the preceding chapter, I argued that concept empiricism is worthy of consideration, but I said little about the specifics. Traditionally, concept empiricists have been imagists. They identify concepts with conscious picturelike entities that resemble their referents. In chapter 2, I reviewed reasons for thinking imagism is inadequate. To bring concept empiricism up to date, one must abandon the view that concepts are conscious pictures. Contemporary cognitive science helps in this endeavor by identifying a rich variety of highly structured, unconscious perceptual representations. In this chapter I argue that such representations can be used to form concepts.

6.1 From Percepts to Proxytypes

6.1.1 Visual Representations

Contemporary empiricists can avail themselves of rich representational resources found in current theories of perception. To illustrate these resources, I will examine recent research on vision because it has been studied most thoroughly.

Vision is believed to involve a hierarchy of processing levels that are subdivided into functionally specialized components. Vision begins outside the brain, with the retina, which consists of more that 10^7 light-sensitive cells (rods and cones). During visual perception, these cells form a two-dimensional array not unlike a snapshot of a perceived scene. This information is sent through the optic nerve and the thalamus to primary visual cortex (V1). Cells in this region are arranged retinotopically and respond to such local features as lines and edges. Edge information may be extracted by a filtering process that identifies discontinuities in luminance coming in from the retina (Marr 1982).

After this "low-level" of visual processing, information is passed into extrastriate cortical areas, where intermediate-level processing begins. Here anatomically separate regions process information about color, motion, and form (Zeki 1992).

According to Ungerleider and Mishkin (1982), high-level visual processing divides into two streams. A dorsal stream in posterior parietal cortex is used to determine the location of objects, and a ventral stream in inferotemporal cortex is used to recognize the identity of objects.[1] There is some debate about how objects are visually recognized. Behavior studies have been used to defend two competing theories. According to one, recognition is achieved using mental representations that are viewpoint-invariant, in that the same representation would be produced when an object is perceived at different orientations (Marr 1982, Biederman 1987). On these theories, invariant recognition is achieved by decomposing perceived objects into representations consisting of simple volumetric primitives that can be identified from many vantage points. Biederman calls these "geons" (from "geometric ions"). Geons do not encode metric information such as specific sizes of angles making up shapes. They can be combined using a handful of simple relations: vertical position (above, below, beside), join type (end-to-end, end-to-middle centered, end-to-middle off-centered), relative size (larger, smaller, equal to), and relative orientation (parallel, orthogonal, oblique). Biederman (1990) shows that, with a vocabulary of 24 geons and these combination relations, one can generate an indefinite number of models (see figure 6.1).

According to the competing theory of visual recognition, we identify objects by means of representations specific to particular viewpoints. Discrepancies between the view-specific representation produced by a perceived object and one stored in memory can be resolved by rotating one to align with the other (Tarr and Pinker 1989).

Electrophysiological studies of monkey inferior temporal cortex (IT) may help to resolve the debate. Cells in different parts of IT have different response properties. Some respond to two-dimensional forms,

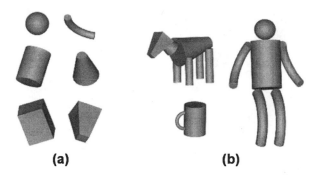

(a) **(b)**

Figure 6.1
(a) Some geons. (b) Models built from those geons. Adapted from Biederman 1990, figure 2.4, with permission.

while others respond to three-dimensional forms (Janssen, Vogels, and Orban 2000). Some respond to whole objects, while others respond to object parts (Buckley, Gaffan, and Murray 1997). And some respond to objects from a particular viewpoint, while others respond to objects from a range of viewpoints (Booth and Rolls 1998). These cells may work together in the following way. First, object parts are represented using both two-dimensional and three-dimensional representations that are viewpoint-specific. Whole objects are then represented via collections of part representations or individual cells that are responsive to such collections. Cells that are responsive to several collections of viewpoint-specific part representations are viewpoint invariant. These may be introduced for very familiar objects.

On this story, viewpoint-invariant representations comprise only a small portion of the cells used in recognition. However, recognition may make extensive use of viewpoint-specific representations built up from simple volumetric parts. These can be regarded as two-dimensional analogues of Biederman's geon models. Hereafter, I use the generic term "object model" to subsume these viewpoint-specific representations as well as the viewpoint-invariant representations that Biederman defends.

According to Marr (1982), object models can be highly structured. Imagine approaching a gorilla from a distance. Your visual system first represents the basic arrangements of its torso and extremities. As you

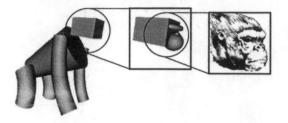

Figure 6.2
A hierarchical representation.

draw near, you discern the parts making up its limbs and head. A closer look reveals its surface detail, such as facial features, wrinkles, and fur. Marr speculates that such perceptual states can be grouped together into a hierarchical representation (figure 6.2). Different kinds of cells in IT may be especially adept at representing different hierarchical levels. Cells representing three-dimensional forms may be adapt at representing gross body parts, for example, while two-dimensional cells are adept at representing surface details.

Object models may be grouped to form representations of scenes. For example, if one perceives a person standing next to a dog, one can form a person model and a dog model simultaneously. The relation "next to" can be captured using the resources for representing location found in Ungerleider and Mishkin's "where" system. Cells in that system may be responsive to adjacency relations regardless of what objects are occupying those relations. Similar ideas have been suggested without appeals to physiology (see Talmy 1983, Langacker 1987, Barsalou and Prinz 1997).

The visual system can also accommodate dynamic representations. When we have perceptual encounters with moving objects, we produce a sequence of distinct perceptual representations. By abstracting away from extraneous details, we can perceptually represent an action, pattern of movements, or event (Marr and Nishihara 1978, Hogg 1983, Vaina 1983, Langacker 1987, Biederman 1987, Barsalou 1993). For example, by attending to the sequence of positions of a bird's wings in flight, we can form a perceptual representation of a bird flying (figure 6.3). Complex scenarios can be represented using a sequence of scene representations.

Figure 6.3
A dynamic representation of a bird in flight.

I have been focusing on vision, but an equally impressive range of representations can also be found in other sense modalities. For example, somatosensory area of the brain can discriminate weight, texture, and bodily location. Primary somatosensory cortex may represent highly specific features, such as a texture of a particular grain size, while secondary somatosensory cortex represents more abstract features, such as texture types within a broad range of grain sizes (Jiang, Tremblay, and Chapman 1997). Similarly, auditory cortical areas begin processing simple features like frequencies and sound "edges" produced by frequency changes, and then go on to represent more complex features such as sound movement and conspecific vocalizations (Merzenich 1998). These examples suggest that sense modalities are generally organized into hierarchical processing levels. Each modality furnishes the mind with a multitude of representations tuned to various aspects of the environment.

The representations postulated by contemporary accounts of perceptual processing are quite different from the simple images postulated by traditional empiricists (see also Barsalou and Prinz 1997, Barsalou 1999). First, by postulating multiple levels of processing and multiple cell types, current theories of perception arm the contemporary empiricist with a range of representations to work with. This marks a significant advance over classical empiricists, who typically envisioned only one kind of perceptual representation in each modality.

Second, unlike the perceptual states of classical empiricism, only some of the representations in contemporary theories are thought to be conscious. Recent research strongly suggests that conscious perceptual images be identified with intermediate-level perceptual representations (Jackendoff 1987, Tye 1991, Kosslyn 1994, Prinz 2000b). The highest level of perceptual representation may reside entirely outside of consciousness.

Other differences stem from the specific characteristics of high-level representations. The representations postulated by contemporary theories are more schematic than those described by some more traditional imagists. They can abstract away from details of position, scale, metric proportion, and viewpoint. High-level representations are also highly structured. They can be built up from simple parts arranged hierarchically. Traditional empiricists often talk about images combining, but they do not explain how individual representations of objects decompose into coherent manipulable parts. Nor do traditional accounts explain how we can represent dynamic forms and spatial relations. In sum, the perceptual representations available to contemporary concept empiricists provide a more powerful foundation than representations invoked by earlier theories. Perceptual representations are not simple pictures in the head.

6.1.2   Long-Term Memory Networks

Once we have experienced an object and perceptually represented it, the perceptual representation can be stored in long-term memory. Otherwise, recognition would be impossible. Stored perceptual representations can be modified and updated over time. As we experience more objects that produce similar representations, we refine those that have already been stored. One important form of fine-tuning involves the adjustments of feature weights. Marr and Biederman assume that perceptual matching requires simply congruence in the parts of two visual models. But some parts may be more important than others. One might notice in observing gorillas, for example, that there is greater variation in torso girth than relative arm length. Some gorillas are fatter than others. Thus, arm length is more diagnostic in gorilla identification. Therefore, the arm portion of a gorilla model may, over time, be assigned higher diagnosticity weights than the torso portion.

Sometimes refinements in weights are insufficient. To adequately represent variation within a category, collections of perceptual representations must be grouped together. The evidence on the basis of which we group representations together may be called a "link principle," and the particular way in which two representations are grouped can be called a "link type." Link types can be distinguished by their functional roles. To illustrate, first consider hierarchical representations. The link type connecting components of a hierarchical representation can be called a *hierarchy* link. A hierarchy link causes a person to exchange one perceptual representation into another when using the mental operation of zooming. When we zoom in on a model of a gorilla's body, we exchange the body representation with a representation of its head, or whatever other body part we happen to zoom in on. The link principle is coinstantiation during an approach. When one approaches a gorilla from a distance, one forms different representations at different distances and recognizes that these are coinstantiated in a single object.

Coinstantiation can be used to establish other kinds of links as well. First, objects sometimes change as we are observing them. For example, a gorilla might beat its chest. Because the same object was observed both standing still and beating its chest, the perceptual representations corresponding to these two states get grouped together. Call this a *transformation* link, because each is stored as a permissible transformation of the other. Second, perceptual representations formed in different modalities may also be grouped together on the basis of coinstantiation. If I hear a sound as a gorilla beats its chest, I may store a record of the sound along with the visual representation of arm movements because the two are coinstantiated. One might call this a *binding* link. Finally, we sometimes observe scenes, props, or other things that co-occur with an object of interest, even though they are not physically bound to that object. We might see a gorilla eating a banana, for example. Call this a *situational* link.

Other representations can be grouped in other ways. For example imagine seeing a gorilla that produces a representation that is similar, but not identical, to a stored gorilla representation. After this encounter, the new representation may be stored together with the old. The representations are stored together because they are quite similar. Call this the matching principle. How they are connected can be called a *predicative* link. To a first approximation, a predicative link occurs when there is a disposition to transfer features linked to one representation though hierarchy, transformation, or binding to another representation. A stored

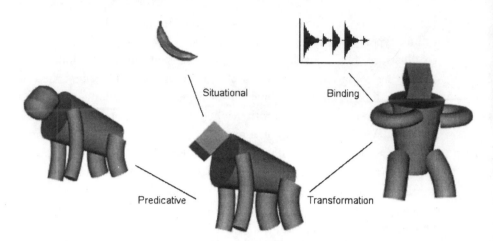

Figure 6.4
A long-term-memory network of perceptual representations. The labels on the links correspond to functional relations described in the text.

group of linked perceptual representations can be called a "long-term memory network." Figure 6.4 depicts an example.

Long-term memory networks can come to store various kinds of information about commonly encountered categories. To switch examples, consider the information we store about dogs. We know a great deal about dogs, including all the kinds of things emphasized by leading psychological theories of concepts. We know about prototypical dogs, dog breeds, dog exemplars, casual/explanatory facts involving dogs, dog behaviors, and various verbal facts pertaining to dogs. Examples of this information are summarized in table 6.1.

The crucial question for the empiricist is whether perceptual representations can capture all this information. In some cases, the answer is obviously affirmative. Prototypical features such as furriness, having four legs, and barking can surely be captured by perceptual representations. Furriness can be a captured by visual and tactile texture representations. Having four legs can be represented within a model of dogs (see figure 6.1b). Barking can be captured by auditory representations, dynamically bound to a visual model of a dog's moving mouth. Dog breeds and exemplars can be represented by adding details corresponding to their unique

Table 6.1
Various kinds of information stored about dogs

Information type	Examples	Link type
Prototypical	Fur, four legs, bark	Binding
Breeds	Retrievers, boxers, pugs	Predicative
Exemplars	Fido, Rover, Spot	Predicative
Causal/explanatory	Dogs have hidden essences; dogs wag tails when happy	Hierarchy, binding, transformation
Behavioral	Fetching, begging, petting	Transformation, situational
Verbal	Called "dogs"; respond to "sit" and "roll over"	Situational

proportions, colors, and sounds. Dog behaviors can be stored as dynamic multimedia event sequences, such as a tactile-kinesthetic-motor representation of stick throwing, followed by a visual representation of a dog fetching it. Dog related words can be stored as auditory representations of, for example, dog commands linked to visual representations of the behaviors elicited by those commands.

The belief that dogs wag their tails when they are happy is more complex, but not intractable. It may involve a disposition to attribute happiness to dogs when we perceive their tails wagging. Attributing happiness to dogs can, perhaps, be achieved by imaginatively projecting our own mental states (see chapter 8, Gordon 1986, Goldman 1989). We know what it is like to experience happiness, and we can imagine that dogs are in the same kind of state when they wag their tails. This furnishes us with a piece of knowledge that contributes to interpretations, explanations, and predictions. For example, if one believes that dogs enjoy playing fetch, one may form the prediction that a dog will wag its tail while playing fetch, even if that has not been noticed in the past.

Other kinds of causal/explanatory beliefs, which have been emphasized by theory theorists, are more challenging to accommodate using perceptual representations. How does one represent the fact that happiness is *causally* related to tail wagging? How does one represent the fact that dogs have essences? A complete answer to these questions must wait. In chapter 8, I say something about the perceptual basis of essentialist beliefs, and in chapter 7, I discuss representations of causality and other things that seem to resist perceptual representation. I argue that the failure to see how certain properties can be perceptually represented is almost always a failure of imagination. Although my examples here are highly simplified, I hope that I have convinced the reader that perceptual representations can capture the full range of facts that we store about categories.

6.1.3 Proxytypes

If the foregoing speculations are correct, perceptually derived long-term memory networks encode all the information emphasized by leading psychological theories of concepts. But how can we decide which aspects of this information count as conceptually constitutive? How can we adjudicate the debate between leading psychological theories? One hint is given by the suggestion defended in chapter 5. I proposed there that concepts are mechanisms of detection. To answer the questions at hand, we must ask, What information in our memory networks can contribute to detection? The obvious answer is "All of it." Under different circumstances, any item of dog knowledge, for example, can help us identify something as a dog. Therefore, it is tempting to identify concepts with entire long-term memory networks.

This proposal is problematic. Barsalou (1987) argues that concepts cannot be identified with the totality of category knowledge stored in long-term memory, because it is difficult to determine where knowledge of one category begins and that of another category ends. Does my knowledge that dogs make good pets belong to my DOG concept or my PET concept? This worry may be surmountable. There is no reason to insist that boundaries between concepts must be sharp. Different concepts can encode some of the same knowledge.

A more recalcitrant concern stems form the claim that concepts are constituents of thoughts. It is important to distinguish between a thought and a piece of standing knowledge. Standing knowledge is knowledge that I possess even when I am not thinking about it. I know that dogs bark even when I am thinking about the weather. Thoughts are occurrent states. One cannot have a thought about dogs without activating a dog representation.[2] Standing knowledge is stored in long-term memory, and thoughts are stored, for their brief duration, in working memory. Concepts cannot be identified with long-term-memory networks, because working memory does not have the capacity to activate an entire network. If I entertain the thought that dogs wag their tails, I cannot call up all of my dog knowledge (similar concerns were raised in chapter 4).

The natural solution, recommended by Barsalou (1987), is to identify concepts with the temporary representations of categories formed in working memory. I think this is a good proposal, but it requires a minor revision. It seems odd to say that a concept used in working memory ceases to be a concept when it is inactively stored in long-term memory. Unlike thoughts, concepts can be possessed when they are not currently being entertained. Therefore, it would be better to say that concepts are mental representations of categories that are or *can be* activated in working memory. I call these representations "proxytypes," because they stand in as proxies for the categories they represent.

To put this all together, the claim that concepts are detection mechanisms can be reconciled with the daunting observation that everything in our long-term-memory networks contributes to detection by saying that long-term-memory networks contain (and produce) a multitude of concepts. On the proposal I am recommending, concepts are proxytypes, where proxytypes are perceptually derived representations that can be recruited by working memory to represent a category.

A proxytype can be a detailed multimodal representation, a single visual model, or even a mental representation of a word (e.g., an auditory image of the word "dog"). Every long-term-memory network of perceptual representations contains many overlapping proxytypes. Just about any concise subset from such a network can do the job. Context determines what proxytype is used in working memory on any given occasion. If one is looking for dogs in the arctic tundra, one can call up a representation of a typical sled dog. If one is looking for a guard dog, one can use a representation of a more ferocious breed. Sometimes these proxytypes already exist in long-term memory, and sometimes they must be constructed. If one reads a news report about a dog that is 5 feet tall, one probably constructs a new representation on the fly (see Barsalou 1987). This flexibility makes proxytypes ideal for tracking things.

If concepts are proxytypes, thinking is a simulation process (Barsalou 1999). Tokening a proxytype is generally tantamount to entering a perceptual state of the kind one would be in if one were to experience the thing it represents. One can simulate the manipulation of real objects by manipulating proxytypes of them in their absence. The term "proxytype" conveys the idea that perceptually derived representations function as proxies in such simulations. They are like the scale models that stand in for objects during courtroom reenactments. They allow us to reexperience past events or anticipate future events. Possessing a concept, on this view, involves having an ability to engage in such a simulation, what Barsalou calls a "simulation competence."

A few notes about simulation are in order. First, as on nonempiricist theories, the simulation account allows different kinds of propositional attitudes to be distinguished by differences in functional roles (e.g., Fodor 1987). Beliefs are simulations that we take to match the world, and desires are simulations that dispose us to pursue the realization of a matching situation. Second, some simulations may be purely verbal. Rather than representing what a situation looks like, we sometimes use verbal descriptions. In these cases, we are simulating the experience of hearing someone talk about a situation rather than the situation itself. Third, because many simulations are not verbal, the words used to report them often correspond imperfectly or incompletely to the simulation, like captions on a picture. A simulation that one might report as a "belief that dinner is on the table" may involve representations of plates, flatware, chairs, and a table of a particular shape.

The construct of a mental simulation raises questions about proxytype individuation. Suppose that Boris forms the desire to hunt a fat gnu, and this desire consists of a perceptual simulation of a person with a rifle pursuing a gnu-shaped animal with an oversized belly. Is there a component of this simulation that counts as the GNU proxytype? Can it be distinguished from the FAT proxytype? Or the HUNTING proxytype?

In some cases, one may be able to distinguish parts of a simulation by intrinsic features. Different bound shape representations, for example, may constitute distinct proxytypes. Perhaps the gnu-shaped representation can be distinguished from the person-shaped representation and the rifle-shaped representation in this way. But there is no separate representation for hunting or for fatness. These are built up from or into the bound shape representations. If there is no distinct proxytype for hunting or for fatness in this simulation, how can we say it is a token of a desire to hunt a fat gnu? The answer may lie in the origin of the simulation. Mental representations of hunting and fatness are used when the simulation is initially formed. Boris's memory network for hunting may consist of schematic representations of pursuits, together with some stored records of paradigm cases (duck hunting, deer hunting, a hunting lion, etc.), and representations of instruments used in hunting (rifles, bows, teeth, etc.). This information is used to arrange the shape representations in the hunting scenario and to equip the hunting figure with a rifle representation. Likewise, Boris's memory network for fatness may include representations of various creatures with bellies (and other features) that are larger in diameter than in the most typical cases. These representations are used to extrude the belly shape in one's gnu representation when forming the hunting simulation. While one cannot separate out the representations of hunting or of fatness, one can identify the contributions that Boris's knowledge of these things make to his simulation. There is a sense in which proxytypes for HUNTING and FAT are contained in the simulation, but they meld with other proxytypes. Consequently, one can say that these concepts are tokened, but one cannot use shape boundaries to identify them. Individuating proxytypes in a thought is tricky but not impossible.

The picture that I have been defending differs significantly from orthodox theories of thinking in cognitive science. According to the orthodoxy, inspired by classical computing, thinking occurs in a symbolic medium, whose representations have subject-predicate structure and are manipulated by logical rules. Thoughts are more like verbal descriptions than reenactments.[3] It is often presumed that thought must be couched in an amodal medium, carried our in a central processing system that functions independently of input systems. This bias is so ingrained that cognitive scientists are immediately suspicious of alternatives. The suspicion lacks foundation. After all, thoughts are internal representations of the outer world, and the outer world is not linguistically structured (see McGinn 1989). The outer world consists largely of physical inter-actions between three-dimensional objects. Perceptual representations and simulations are ideally suited to represent such things. Some of our less concrete thoughts pose a challenge to the empiricist, but the plethora of concrete thoughts that occupy our minds present a contrasting chal-lenge for the proponent of amodal symbols. Why would a naturally evolved cognitive system use amodal symbols to represent concrete inter-actions when it could use the very perceptual states that are caused by those interactions?

The proxytype theory of concepts follows the work of Barsalou in several ways. It follows his (1987) suggestion that concepts can be tem-porary constructions in working memory. It follows his (1993) sugges-tion that concepts consist of perceptual representations that are stored in networks. And it follows his (1999) suggestion that using concepts can be regarded as a form of simulation. The term "proxytype" can be regarded as a synonym for Barsalou's term "perceptual symbol."[4] Barsalou has not shown that perceptual symbols can satisfy each of the desiderata outlined in chapter 1, though he has made useful sugges-tions. That is the goal of the remainder of this monograph. Proxytype theory extends Barsalou's efforts by addressing such issues as publicity, intentionality, and innateness. Continuing faith in amodal representa-tions is implicitly grounded in the presumption that perceptually derived representations cannot serve as concepts. By showing that proxytypes can satisfy all of the desiderata, this skepticism can be quelled.

6.2   Publicity

6.2.1   Default Proxytypes
Long-term-memory networks often contain a huge number of proxy-types and are capable of generating many more to meet contextual demands. Moreover, the range of proxytypes that different people possess vary considerably. Different experiences and explanatory beliefs lead to differences in long-term-memory networks. If each proxytype that can be derived from a network of dog representations qualifies as a DOG concept, then we all have countless DOG concepts, including many that are not shared by other individuals. If concepts are proxytypes, then

it is hard to see how concepts are shared. Proxytype theory does not seem to meet the publicity requirement.

The publicity requirement must be satisfied to explain successful psychological generalizations and communication. If no two people had the same DOG concepts, it would be impossible to predict similarities in their dog-directed behaviors. Likewise, if people always assigned different concepts to the word "dog," communication would be impossible.

Proxytype theorists must show that our proxytypes can be and often are shared. In some cases, one can explain sharing by appeal to intentional contents. Two different proxytypes may represent the same category. If the DOG proxytype I form on an occasion differs from the one you form, we may still be able to communicate in virtue of the fact that we are both thinking about the same class of things. Appeals to intentional content do not explain all cases of concept sharing, however. As I argue in chapter 1, there is a sense in which I share a "water" concept with my doppelgänger on Twin Earth despite the fact that the concepts we express using that word pick out different intentional contents. To explain this kind of concept sharing, the proxytype theorists must try another strategy.

Ostensibly, the primary obstacle to proxytype sharing is their context sensitivity. The way one represents a dog depends on whether one is thinking about the arctic tundra or Central Park. The way one represents an elephant depends on whether one is at a circus, in a zoo, or on a safari. The way one represents a fish depends on whether one is in a restaurant or scuba diving. With such variability it is hard to see how proxytypes can be shared.

This concern can be assuaged in two ways. First, contextual variability may actually facilitate proxytype sharing. Contexts often place strong constraints on proxytypes. When people think of fish in a restaurant, for example, they are likely to use proxytypes corresponding to the appearance of a fish filleted on a plate rather than swimming by a coral reef. Contextual sensitivity only tends to impede communication when would-be communicators are in different contexts. This is unusual, and when it occurs, difficulties in communication come as no surprise.

Second, variability across some contexts does not entail variability across all contexts. There is reason to believe that we have default proxytypes. A default proxytype is the representation that one would token if one were asked to consider a category without being given a context. When no context is specified, we use representations of the kind that figure most frequently in our interactions with category members. I speculate that default proxytypes are relatively stable, widely shared, and frequently responsible for guiding ordinary category-directed behavior. If I am right, then default proxytypes may play an important role in explaining publicity.

It is difficult to find an independent measure for predicting what information gets included in our default proxytypes. An initially tempting proposal appeals to "cue validity." Cue validity is the subjective probability that a given object belongs to a particular category given that it has a particular feature (Brunswik 1956, Rosch et al. 1976, Rosch 1978). Highly cue-valid features are the ones that are most diagnostic. As mentioned, features making up the representations in our memory networks are weighted for diagnosticity. Perhaps default proxytypes contain just those features that have high diagnosticity weights, i.e., features that are highly cue-valid.

This proposal cannot be right. Some highly cue-valid features are not sufficiently accessible to enter into the most ordinary interactions with categories. For example, being H_2O is maximally cue-valid for being water, but our ordinary water interactions and water thoughts do not depend on knowledge of chemical constitution. Similarly, having a long, curved, pink neck is highly cue-valid for being a bird because it is highly cue-valid for being a pink flamingo and pink flamingos are birds. But thinking about birds rarely employs long-neck representations because most birds have short necks. Conversely, some features that are low in cue validity seem to be integral to our default proxytypes. Being quadrupedal, for example, is not very cue-valid for being a dog, because numerous other creatures have four legs. Knowing that something is quadrupedal does not greatly increase the subjective probability that it is a dog. Nevertheless, our default DOG proxytypes presumably represent them as quadrupedal.

A second proposal is that default proxytypes contain features that are high in "category validity." This is the subjective probability that an object has a particular feature given that it belongs to a particular category (Smith and Medin 1981, Murphy and Medin 1985). This proposal could explain why default DOG proxytypes contain the feature QUADRUPEDAL; if something is a dog, it is highly probable that it has four legs. It can also explain why LONG PINK NECKS are not included in default BIRD proxytypes; long pink necks are a rare, and hence improbable, feature of birds. But the water problem remains. If something is water, it is maximally probable that it is (largely) H_2O, but this knowledge rarely figures in water thoughts. Likewise, having a spleen is highly category-valid for dogs, but it does not figure into dog thoughts. Chemical constitutions and internal organs are not good candidates for default proxytype features because they are not readily perceived, and they are not relevant to our most typical interactions with objects. Therefore, being highly category-valid is not sufficient.

One might try to fix this problem by proposing that default proxytypes contain features that are highly category-valid *and* readily perceived. Even this combined condition is insufficient. One problem is that theoretical beliefs sometimes cause us to neglect features that are both highly perceivable and cue-valid. For example, it might be that every boomerang I have ever seen is made out of wood. Nevertheless, this feature does not figure into my default proxytype, because I believe that being wood is inessential to being a boomerang. Being curved, in contrast, is part of my default proxytype because I think curvature is what makes boomerangs return to their throwers (see Medin and Shoben 1988). That particular belief about boomerang mechanics may not be included in my default proxytype, but it influences which features are included.

What ultimately determines whether a feature is included in a default proxytype is how frequently one represents a category as having that feature. The factors just considered are not irrelevant, however. The frequency with which a feature is used can be affected by its cue validity, category validity, perceptual salience, or conformity to theories. Even if none of these factors can perfectly predict which features get included in our default proxytypes, they can all exert some influence.

There is an obvious kinship between default proxytypes and prototypes. The features that constitute a default prototype, like the features that constitute a prototype, generally capture the central tendency of the corresponding category. Default features are also likely to be superficial and contingent rather than deep and defining, because hidden features do not figure into our most common interactions with category members. This kinship allows the proxytype theorist to capitalize on some of the explanatory virtues of prototype theory.

At the same time, there are some differences between the default proxytypes and prototypes as they are usually construed. One difference is that default proxytypes can contain features that are derived from theories rather than passive abstraction. Prototype theorists often exclude or ignore such features. Default proxytypes are also likely to include representations of category names (e.g., the word "dog"), since such names are frequently used in identification and communication. Prototypes are not presumed to contain linguistic information.

Another difference is that proxytype theory is committed to the claim that concepts derive from perceptual primitives. Prototype theorists generally offer no theory of primitives. The choice of primitives gives the proxytype theorist an unexpected advantage. Prototypes are often criticized for their failure to represent relations between the features that compose them. They do not represent simple spatial relations (e.g., the fact that the beak of a bird protrudes from a different part than its wings) or more complex explanatory relations (e.g., the fact that having wings is responsible for being capable of flight). In contrast, proxytypes typically encode a considerable amount of relational information. The spatial relation between beaks and wings is inevitably represented in BIRD proxytypes as a consequence of the fact that they are built up from perceptual representations, such as visual object models. The relationship between having wings and being capable of flight is also inevitably represented because being capable of flight is represented by the sequence of wing movements.

Finally, proxytype theory incorporates an informational theory of intentionality (see chapter 9). Prototype theorists often assume that prototypes refer to anything that exceeds their similarity thresholds. As we saw in chapter 3, this assigns the wrong intentional contents to our concepts. By adopting an informational theory of intentionality, proxytype theory explains why we mentally represent prototypical features in the first place. Such features are chosen because they are the most reliable detectors, and by reliably detecting, they allow our thoughts to designate real categories in the world.

6.2.2 Sharing Defaults

We depart from default proxytypes only when contextual information demands an alternative representation. Since some contexts introduce strong constraints, we should expect considerable overlap in our non-default proxytypes. In circumstances where contexts do not introduce strong constraints, we use our default proxytypes. Such circumstances may be common. I hypothesized that default proxytypes are used most of the time. To show that concepts are widely shared, we must establish that default proxytypes are widely shared.

If defaults are widely shared, successful communication can be explained even in cases where interlocutors happen to employ divergent, nondefault representations in the course of a conversation. Suppose that you say that birds are really robots. I might think that you just mean something different by the word "birds." To disabuse me of this suspicion, you may say that by "birds" you mean to refer to those small, feathered, flying creatures with beaks and two legs. Since this coincides with my default proxytype, I recognize that you do mean birds by "birds."

But why think default prototypes are shared? One preliminary piece of evidence is that they are comparatively resilient to change. If I learn that walruses have kidneys, this fact might enter permanently into my knowledge of walruses, but it is unlikely to enter my default WALRUS proxytype. Knowledge of kidney possession is not relevant to ordinary interactions with walruses. Memory networks are in constant flux because they are updated whenever we store new information, but there is no reason to think that this regularly impacts our default representations in a significant way.

This example shows how default proxytypes can remain relatively stable as we acquire knowledge, but it does not show how we achieve publicity. We must also show that different people end up with the same features in their default proxytypes. Evidence for feature convergence can be found by considering some of the factors that influence what gets included in default proxytypes. As mentioned, default proxytypes often contain features that are cue-valid, category-valid, and salient. These are all subjective measures, but they are grounded in objective fact. Features that are cue-valid, category-valid, and salient for me are likely to be cue-valid, category-valid, and salient for you. Traits are generally cue-valid if they are distinctive of a category, category-valid if they occur in most existing instances of a category, and salient if they are readily perceived by the perceptual faculties common to our species. Because of these common factors, our default proxytypes tend to contain common features.

One might object by pointing out that theoretical knowledge can influence default proxytypes. Theoretical knowledge can vary from person to person, which poses a threat to publicity. Furthermore, there is empirical support for the claim that conceptual representations are not perfectly shared. As discussed in chapter 3, Barsalou found that typicality judgments vary both interpersonally and within individuals over time. This may suggest that default proxytypes are unshared.

This concern can be met by relaxing the publicity requirement. Rather than demanding strict identity between default proxytypes, we can settle for similarity. If you and I agree about the most conspicuous walrus features, then we understand each other when we use the word "walrus," and we engage in similar walrus-directed behaviors. If the publicity desideratum is intended to explain such examples of coordination, a theory that predicts considerable conceptual similarity will suffice.

Because of the more objective factors influencing feature selection, default proxytypes are likely to overlap considerably. The differences brought on by theoretical knowledge and other variable factors may be minimal. This claim is supported by Barsalou's results. He found a 0.5 overlap between individuals' proxytypes and a 0.8 agreement within individuals' proxytypes, which is fairly impressive considering the overall diversity of our beliefs. A subsequent unpublished analysis by Hampton (personal communication) found even greater stability for judgments about highly typical category instances. The comparative instability of atypical instances may owe to the fact that they are more likely to tap into knowledge that lies outside of our default proxytypes. Some of the variance found by Barsalou may derive from the intrusion of nondefault features. The features in our default proxytypes may be more stable than his numbers suggest.

Fodor and Lepore (1992) have cautioned those who appeal to similarity, rather than strict identity, between concepts. They note that such appeals depend on having an account of what it is for two concepts to be similar. Similarity is generally defined in terms of partial identity. Two concepts are said to be partially identical if a proper subset of their features are identical. To show that similarity is possible, on this account, one must show that distinct concepts can have identical features. They argue that certain theories of concepts, such as those defended by some connectionists, fail on exactly this point because they give holistic criteria for feature individuation. One can circumvent the problem by providing a nonholistic account of feature individuation. I offer such an account in chapter 10.

Relaxing the publicity requirement bears valuable explanatory fruit. Communication is often imperfect. People generally manage to refer to the same objects and to associate many of the same features with those objects, but they do not necessarily associate all of the same features. My default proxytype for snakes may represent them as dangerous while yours represents them as harmless. My failure to understand why you do not flinch when I say there is a snake by your foot can be regarded as a very localized communication failure. Likewise, if we want to explain behavior by appeal to concepts, we often find situations where congruence is close but imperfect. I cower near snakes, and you do not. These minor discrepancies can be explained by saying that our concepts are similar but not exactly alike. Publicity does a better job of explaining communication and behavioral congruence if it admits of degrees.

Two people can come to have very different default proxytypes under anomalous circumstances. This need not bother us, however, because those are precisely the cases where we would expect communication and psychological generalizations to break down. If the information that you and I most frequently access in thinking of walruses were radically different, our walrus-directed thoughts and behaviors would differ significantly.

This account of concept sharing raises an important question. In ordinary parlance we sometimes use the definite article in talking about concepts; we say "*the* concept of X." Proxytype theory claims that concepts are highly variable. Each of us can generate many concepts corresponding to a given familiar category. Do any of these deserve to be called *the* concept of X? Or must we dispense with that idea entirely?

It should be noted that we only use the definite article for certain kinds of concepts. We say "the concept of justice," "the concept of reincarnation," or "the concept of gravity." We rarely say "the concept of dogs," "the concept of string beans," or "the concept of screwdrivers." The definite article is typically reserved for cases where concepts refer to things that are highly theoretical. These concepts are often culturally transmitted in the form of explicit theories. The ability to use them depends on knowledge possessed by experts in our communities. We ask gurus about reincarnation, physicists about gravity, and philosophers about justice.[5] Such theoretical concepts take on a normative dimension. By appealing to authorities, we imply that there is some particular way that we *should* think about these things. Here use of a definite article reveals more about sociology than cognitive science.

We generally do not talk about concepts like DOG, STRING BEAN, and SCREWDRIVER at all. When we do refer to these concepts, definite articles are avoided. We may say, "Martha has a concept of screwdrivers that differs from mine," or "Hector and I conceive of dogs in the same way," or "When little Billy first acquired a concept of string beans, he though they were all puréed." Nevertheless, I think there is some license in using a definite article for these mundane concepts. In many cases, there is a canonical way of thinking about things. Despite differences, we are all capable of representing dogs as furry barking quadrupeds, string beans as long (usually) green vegetables, and screwdrivers as tools with metal rods, flat tips, and cylindrical handles. Someone who failed to attribute these properties would have a very different way of conceiving these categories. These are just the sorts of properties that we represent with our default proxytypes. Therefore, if there is any sense in using the definite article for talk about the concepts of familiar categories, it should be used when referring to default proxytypes. *The* concept of dogs is just the kind of representation that most of us form by default when thinking about dogs.

The arguments in this subsection suggest that proxytype theory can satisfy the publicity desideratum. There is likely to be considerable similarity in the proxytypes we form. The degree of similarity in increased by the presence of default proxytypes, which, like prototypes, conform to the common central tendencies underlying differences in individual knowledge. Proxytype theory allows for a balance of stability and contextually sensitive variability. Publicity is satisfied without adopting the unrealistic assumption that the features used in conceptual representations remain perfectly fixed.

6.3 Categorization

Default proxytypes play an important role in explaining publicity. They also contribute to an explanation of categorization. In particular, they aid in what I call category production (see chapter 1). When asked to describe members of a category, we generally name features in our default proxytypes. For example, when asked to describe dogs, we are more likely to mention their wagging tails than their spleens. This observation is almost trivial because a default proxytype can be operationally defined in terms of the features we represent when asked to consider a category without being given information about context.

This is not to say that we name every feature in a default proxytype when performing category-production tasks. Pragmatic factors may prevent us from naming features that are hard to verbalize (such as a specific shape) or insufficiently distinctive (such as having a torso). Nor is it to say that feature listing always exploits default proxytypes. Contextual effects can cause one to access features that would not have been represented by default. To repeat an earlier example, if one is asked to describe properties of fish while at a restaurant, one names different features than if one is asked to perform the same task at a scuba site. In such cases, nondefault proxytypes are likely generated.

In chapter 1, I distinguished category production from category identification. Category identification often depends on nondefault information contained in our long-term memory networks. Here is a plausible story. When an object is perceived (or named or described), we represent it using a set of features. Those features are matched with features in our memory networks. The similarity between a perceived object and a memory network is measured by summing the diagnostic weights of all features that match a representation in that network. An object is recognized as falling under the category whose memory network contains a representation with which it has the highest similarity (provided that the similarity rating exceeds a critical threshold). For example, if a perceived object is more to similar to a representation in a DOG network than to any other representation, it gets identified as a dog.

This proposal explains the effects that motivate the exemplar theory. We can categorize objects on the basis of atypical features because we have access to our memory networks for category identification. When a familiar but atypical category instance is experienced, it calls up a corresponding exemplar representation in a memory network and is identified on that basis. If the match is close, the identification can be quite fast.

The examples that motivate the theory theory are a bit more complex. Consider Keil's painted raccoon. We see an animal that looks like a skunk but learn that it began as a raccoon and was painted to give it its present appearance. To represent this fact, we engage in a mental simulation that begins with a representation predicatively linked to a RACCOON proxytype. We then imagine it being covered with paint. Our RACCOON network is connected to networks that store knowledge about animals. We know that animals have hidden essences. Therefore, the imagined transformation does not cause us to break the predicative link. The painted raccoon is not identified as a skunk, because it remains linked to a RACCOON proxytype.

The evidence that motivates prototype theory is easier to explain. First consider typicality effects. Forming typicality judgments is a category-production task. It requires that we call up a representation of a category. As with feature listing, we generally call up default proxytypes. The judged typicality of a category instance is a function of its similarity to a default proxytype for the category to which it belongs. Typicality effects in category identification can also be explained. We identify typical instances more quickly than unfamiliar atypical instances because they closely match default proxytypes, which are stored in memory networks and highly accessible.

Proxytype theory offers an attractive account of basic-level categorization. The basic level generally lies at an intermediate level of abstraction. We learn concepts for such categories earliest and are most likely to apply those concepts in category-identification tasks. In their pioneering work on the basic level, Rosch et al. (1976) demonstrate that the basic level is the highest level of abstraction at which category instances have similar shapes (see also Jolicoeur, Gluck, and Kosslyn 1984; Tversky and Hemenway 1985; Biederman 1987). Superimposed pictures of dogs, cars, and screwdrivers overlap much more than superimposed pictures of animals, vehicles, and tools. This suggests that shape similarity confers an advantage in learning and categorization. Proxytype theory predicts this because proxytypes are perceptually derived and shape plays a very dominant role in object perception (Biederman and Ju 1988). The basic level is the highest level at which the perceptual representations in our memory networks are similar in shape.

The superordinate level may be built up from multiple basic-level files (see Hampton 1992 for a similar suggestion). For example, the vehicle file may consist of files representing cars, boats, planes, and so on. Proxytype theory predicts that superordinate categories will often be represented thus because it is difficult to represent them more concisely with perceptually derived representations. That would explain why basic-level concepts are acquired before superordinates. It would also explain why we are faster at basic-level categorization. If superordinate representations consist of basic-level representations, something can only be identified at the superordinate level if it is identified at the basic level first.[6]

Proxytype theory also predicts the advantage of basic-level categorization over the subordinate level. The shape representations that we generate in perception are often highly schematic. They exclude information that would facilitate categorization at the subordinate level. A single visual object model, for example, captures the shape of rottweilers, beagles, and huskies. To capture their differences, that model must be supplemented by representations of color, texture, and distinguishing features, such as ears. These representations require closer inspection than the more schematic shape representation. Identifying something at the subordinate level is more difficult than identifying it at the basic level because our perceptual systems discern gross shapes faster than fine details.

In sum, proxytype theory does an admirable job of explaining categorization. It explains more categorization results than any theory I have considered because proxytypes can encode a broad range of information.

6.4   Conclusion

Proxytype theory integrates the best features of other theories. It borrows the view that concepts are perceptually based from imagism. It borrows a theory of intentional content from informational atomism. It borrows the use of instance information and essentialist beliefs from exemplar theory and the theory theory. It borrows idealized summary representations from prototype theory. Proxytype theory is a hybrid, but its many facets can be unified under a single overarching idea: concepts are mechanisms that allow us to enter into perceptually mediated, intentionality-conferring, causal relations with categories in the world. Put differently, proxytype theory is like informational atomism without the atomism. Atomists have no adequate theory of vehicles, no adequate theory of detection mechanisms, and no ability to handle several important desiderata. Proxytype theory remedies all of these problems by identifying concepts with perceptual representations that are used as detection mechanisms and sufficiently structured to explain many aspects of our behavior. In this chapter I argued that proxytype theory provides explanations of categorization and publicity. In the chapters that follow, I address the remaining desiderata.

7

The Perceptual Basis

7.1 The Scope Trial

In the last chapter, I presented a version of concept empiricism called proxytype theory. Satisfying the scope desideratum is often regarded as the greatest challenge facing any empiricist theory of concepts. It is widely believed that there are many concepts that cannot be identified with perceptually derived representations. This point has become an antiempiricist dogma. Many believe that empiricism faces obvious counterexamples. A random sampling of those who voice this opinion includes Geach (1957), Alston (1964), Bennett (1971), Cummins (1989), Gauker (1994), and Rey (1994). If these authors are right, the expressive scope of proxytype theory is severely limited. Some concepts just do not lend themselves to such a treatment.

7.1.1 Hard Cases

Ironically, some of the alleged counterexamples have come from the empiricists themselves in an effort to advance skeptical claims about the limits of human understanding. Empiricists have a standard elimination argument that can be schematized as follows: concepts are perceptually derived; concept C cannot be perceptually derived; therefore, we do not have concept C. This kind of skepticism has its place. Empiricism can play a valuable role by weeding out nonsensical concepts. That has been one of the selling points of empiricism in the twentieth century. Positivists, for example, used a verificationist form of the elimination argument to dispose of what they called "metaphysical" concepts. Unfortunately, the range of concepts that are vulnerable to the empiricist's knife is enormous. If all of these constitute legitimate counterexamples, then empiricist pruning will be forced to cut the forest of meaningful concepts down to a few sorry shrubs.

A few of the cases that were once deemed difficult are relatively easy to accommodate with contemporary theories of perception. With Marr's theory of high-level vision, for example, it is easy to see that we could have a visual representation of a triangle without specifying whether it is scalene, isosceles, or equilateral (see Berkeley 1710). Likewise, Wittgenstein's (1953) ambiguous man on a hill could be transformed by using dynamic visual representations into a representation of a man ascending (as opposed to descending backwards). Unfortunately, this is just the tip of the iceberg, as the following catalog suggests.

First, there are of concepts designating unobservables. These include concepts of hidden relations, such as CAUSATION, and concepts designating things that exist but are too small to perceive, such as ELECTRON. If such things are truly unobservable, there seems to be no way of representing them using perceptually derived representations.

Equally popular are lofty and intangible concepts, such as TRUTH, VIRTUE, and DEMOCRACY. These concepts strike many as too complex and too abstract to be represented using a simple collection of percepts. They are not the kinds of things whose instances can be recognized by simply looking. Instead, they are deeply nested in a theoretical background.

The concepts adverted to in formal systems are also frequently cited as counterexamples to empiricism. One class of formal concepts derives from logic. It is far from obvious how a perceptually derived concept could represent QUANTIFICATION, DISJUNCTION, or NEGATION. Another class of formal concepts derives from mathematics. These include concepts for individual numbers and concepts used in performing calculations. Mathematical concepts are so abstract that they seem to resist representation within perceptual media.

Examples can be multiplied. If none of these concepts can be captured by perceptually derived representations, and that is all our minds have at their disposal, then these concepts lie beyond our grasp. This conclusion is surely unacceptable.

7.1.2 Sharing the Burden

Before facing these putative counterexamples head-on, I want to give some reasons for thinking that there *must* be ways to handle them. I believe their insolubility would spell trouble for empiricists and antiempiricists alike. If I am right, antiempiricists and empiricists should join forces in showing that the concepts under consideration can be perceptually represented.

To arrive at this conclusion, it is useful to begin by asking how these concepts would be represented on nonempiricist accounts. Consider, for example, the concept DEMOCRACY. There is a general presumption that mentally representing such intangibles poses a particular problem for the empiricist. I think this presumption is wrong. It rests on the intuition that modality-specific representations are not suited for representing concepts at this level of abstraction because their referents cannot be directly experienced in perception. We cannot see, hear, smell, or taste a DEMOCRACY. To presume that we could strikes many as a category error. Amodal representations, in contrast, are thought to be ideally suited for representing intangibles, precisely because they are not bound to any particular kind of experience. The difficulty arises when ones asks how such amodal representations represent. Consider the belief that France is a democracy. An antiempiricist may say that this representation is composed of a group of amodal symbols, including one that stands for the property of being a democracy. By calling it a "democracy symbol," we give the impression that it gets it semantics for free.

This is a cheat. Merely calling something a democracy symbol does nothing to endow it with meaning. Somehow, an amodal representation must come to represent the property of being a democracy. How can it do that? One answer appeals to other symbols. Something is a democracy just in case it is a government whose policies are determined by consent of the governed. But what do these other symbols, such as "government," mean? If the answer is yet other symbols, we will end up in a hermeneutic circle, i.e., a collection of uninterpreted symbols that never get grounded in the external world to which they purportedly refer.

The best solution for the amodalist is to break out of the circle causally. There are two standard proposals for doing this. Etiological theories invoke a causal chain dating back to an initial baptism. On this approach, a democracy symbol refers to democracies in virtue of being introduced in the presence of a demonstratively presented democracy. Informational theories invoke lawlike causal relations between symbols and things. Here a democracy symbol refers to democracies in virtue of being reliably caused by them. Alternatively, one can say that the democracy symbol decomposes into other symbols that get their meaning in one of these causal ways.

The adoption of a causal semantics plays into the hands of the empiricist. First consider etiological theories. If one can demonstratively present a democracy, then it must be the kind of thing you can point to. If you can point to it, you must be able to perceive it, or its manifestations. In chapter 5, I made a parallel point about informational semantics. If democracy symbols get their meaning by reliably detecting democracies, then democracies must be perceptually detectable. Causal semantic theories entail that the property of being a democracy can be perceptually represented. That does not necessarily mean we can have a mental picture of what a democracy is, but it means we can have perceptual representations that, for whatever reason, allow us to track or point to democracies. In sum, an amodalist's best option for escaping the fate of vacuous symbols is to adopt a semantic theory that is implicitly committed to the possibility of perceptually representing the properties designated by those symbols. If amodalists can explain how we represent intangible properties in this way, they will have furnished the empiricist with an explanation along the way.

The amodalist might still hold out hope that a few of the putative counterexamples will work. For example, Fodor (1990) thinks that informational semantics can handle DEMOCRACY but not logical concepts. Some other theory is needed for these. In particular, Fodor says that we are forced to appeal to functional roles. I account for logical concepts below. At this point in the game, however, there is already a moral victory. Scores of other concepts that are widely thought to topple empiricism must be amenable to perceptual representation on pain of vacuity. Amodalists who appeal to *those* cases will only embarrass themselves. Empiricists and amodalists who embrace causal approaches to semantics are in the same boat.

This observation is not completely comforting. Since I am both an empiricist and a proponent of causal semantics, the success of putative counterexamples would mean double jeopardy for me. Perhaps we need a radically new semantic theory that magically establishes mind-world relations without causal interaction. Fortunately, we can avoid that dire conclusion. With a little creativity, we can begin to imagine how our least concrete ideas could have a perceptual grounding.

7.2   Countering Counterexamples

7.2.1   Response Strategies

There are several promising strategies for responding to putative counterexamples. By using some combination of these, I think concept empiricism can be vindicated. I briefly describe some strategies in this subsection and suggest how they might be applied to specific cases in the next subsection.

Some traditional empiricist theories got into trouble because they assumed that concepts are definitions. If concepts are definitions and concepts consist of perceptual representations, then the referents of concepts must have perceivable essences. Most of the strategies for handling hard cases exploit a feature of causal theories of reference. On causal theories, to have a concept of Xs, one does not need to have exhaustive knowledge of what it is to be an X; one only needs to know enough to enter into the right kind of causal relations with them. To enter into the right kind of causal relation, one can mentally represent features that are reliably, but contingently, correlated with a category. Categories whose essential conditions are impossible to perceive are often contingently correlated with perceivable features. These features can serve as signs for that category. Representing such categories by detecting contingently correlated perceivable features can be called "sign tracking."

One kind of sign tracking uses superficial appearances. Consider the concept HUMAN BEING. The necessary and sufficient conditions for being human lie beneath the surface, coded in the human genome. Humanlike appearances are only contingently coupled with those defining conditions, but the coupling is highly reliable. The genome will ordinarily produce such appearances, and few other things will. Therefore, if we have a perceptually derived representation of human appearances, it can be used as a reliable human-being tracker.[1]

Another kind of sign tracking is closely related to appearance tracking. Some unperceivable properties have perceivable instantiations. For example, the property of being humorous does not look like anything, but it is instantiated in various perceivable things: jokes, New Yorker cartoons, garish makeup, and so on. These are not appearances of humor as human forms are appearances of humanity, but they are perceivable manifestations of a property. We can track properties by their instantiations.

A third kind of tracking uses scientific instruments. For example, we may be able to refer to the planet Neptune, which is imperceptible to the naked eye, by tracking its image in telescopes. Instrument tracking is like appearance tracking, but the appearances in question depend on the mediation of special tools.

Finally, one can track objects with words in natural languages (Millikan 1998). In some cases it is easier for an individual to track words than directly to track the objects that those words designate. Forming representations of words can permit one indirectly to enter into a content-conferring relation with the things those words designate, provided some other mechanism is in place to connect words with things. Most often this works by exploiting experts in our linguistic communities (Putnam 1975, Fodor 1994). I can refer to Neptune by using the word "Neptune," which is used by experts who can identity Neptune through telescopes. Tracking by appearances, instantiations, instruments, and words greatly extends the expressive power of our concepts.

Word tracking is related to another strategy. Most of our concepts are associated with representations of words. As is often noted, these words are stored in associative networks. Words frequently heard together get linked in memory. But mere association is not the only way to store verbal knowledge. We learn specific facts about how words are related. We often know which words can be derived from which others, which words can be related to together in identifying statements, which words can be used in various linguistic contexts, and so on. We have a variety of linguistic skills. As I said above, one cannot explain the possession of a concept solely on the basis of interrelated words. That would trap us in a hermeneutic circle. But there is a role for such verbal skills. While they may not be sufficient to link our concepts with their referents in the world (as with sign tracking), they can contribute to cognitive content by giving us a way to grasp and reason about properties that are otherwise intangible.

A very different defense strategy for the empiricist is to identify certain hard cases with mental *operations* rather than concepts. Mental operations include the rules used in combining concepts and the processes used to adjust feature weights. The hard cases listed above are all presumed to name concepts. The inability to figure out how they can be represented using proxytypes leads one to conclude that proxytype theory is unworkable. Closer analysis reveals that we are sometimes looking in the wrong place. Some of the cases in question should be identified with rules, not representations. Proxytype theory is not committed to saying that rules consist of perceptual states.

I mention one final strategy for handling hard cases, one that has been developed by members of the cognitive-grammar movement. Cognitive grammarians try to explain our linguistic abilities by appeal to general cognitive resources. Some cognitive grammarians argue that many of our more abstract concepts are understood by "metaphorical projection" from a small number of more basic mental representations that have a direct link to experience (e.g., Lakoff and Johnson 1980, Lakoff 1987, Johnson 1987, Gibbs 1994). For example, some have claimed that certain abstract concepts can be metaphorically grounded in our experience of forces (see also Talmy 1988). From a very young age, we experience things acting on our bodies (e.g., light, gravity, wind, etc.), and soon we come to experience ourselves acting on things (e.g., toys, tools, and our own bodies). These experiences give rise to a concept of FORCE, which can form the basis of other, less experiential concepts. Our understanding of moral obligation is one example. We understand the meaning of "ought" in terms of the force that values have on us. Values *compel* us toward certain actions (Johnson 1987). Virtue is a property of those who *are swayed* by their beliefs.

The problem with this strategy is that metaphors leave remainders. When one says that two things are alike, one implies that there are various things they have in common, but one also implies that there are differences. Otherwise, the comparison would be an identity. To say that the force in moral obligation is like the force of pushing and pulling explains certain phrases used in moral discourse. But moral obligations cannot literally pull and push in the same way that physical forces do. The difference between moral obligations and physical forces is that the former are moral rather than physical. This, of course, is exactly what makes the concept of MORAL OBLIGATION difficult. The metaphor leaves out the meat. Likewise, Jackendoff (1990) criticizes cognitive grammarians for trying to explain the concept of ownership by appeal to metaphors of spatial proximity. Spatial prepositions are used in ownership talk (I can give an object *to* you and take one *from* you), but this does not explain what makes ownership and mere proximity distinct. The remainder in the comparison is exactly what makes ownership count as ownership; it is proximity (in some cases) plus the property of being owned.

This is not to say that the metaphor strategy should be abandoned. Verbal examples produced by cognitive grammarians provide an impressive case for thinking that metaphors play an important role in thought. In particular, metaphors may help organize knowledge of abstract concepts by capitalizing on structures that have been erected within more tangible domains. Metaphors neither fully exhaust our understanding of abstract concepts nor explain how they get linked to their referents in the world, but they do tell us something about how we grasp and reason with such concepts. Like the verbal-skill strategy, the metaphor strategy can tell us something about cognitive content.

Others have extensively explored the metaphor strategy. In discussing hard cases, I focus on sign tracking, verbal skills, and operations. These strategies provide rich resources for handling counterexamples.

7.2.2   Applications

In this subsection I explore how the concept empiricist can accommodate the examples in 7.1.1. The proposals I make are sketchy and speculative. One cannot provide a priori specifications of how particular concepts are mentally represented. Any proposal about how a concept is represented must be tested experimentally. My goal is to illustrate the kinds of tools that concept empiricists have at their disposal, not to provide correct or complete conceptual analyses.

First, consider concepts designating unobservables. Concepts such as ELECTRON are understood through verbal skills. We know that "electrons are negatively charged particles." But this does not explain how ELEC-TRON connects to its referents. For that, many of us rely on word tracking. We track electrons by deferring to experts who use the word "electron" professionally. Some experts ground their ELECTRON concepts by tracking the appearances electrons produce on scientific instruments. Notably, experts can use photographs to track traces left by electrons as they pass through bubble chambers. Their electron proxytypes include perceptual representations produced by studying trace photographs. These, in turn, are reliably caused by electrons.[2]

This last proposal faces a problem. I said that experts' ELECTRON concepts track electrons by using photographs to track electron traces. But TRACE PHOTOGRAPH concepts also track electrons by tracking electron traces. What distinguishes an ELECTRON concept from a TRACE PHOTO-GRAPH concept?

The response depends on details of the theory of intentionality developed in chapter 9, but the basic idea can be presented here. What distinguished an ELECTRON concept from a TRACE PHOTOGRAPH concept is their counterfactual behavior. TRACE PHOTOGRAPH concepts track photographic traces in every world. An ELECTRON concept would be different in a world where electrons were detected with some other technique. An ELECTRON concept is one that picks out electrons. In this world, some of our ELECTRON concepts pick out electrons by tracking traces in photographs. In another world, this might not be the case. So ELECTRON concepts vary counterfactually. Representations of trace photographs can serve as ELECTRON concepts if one is disposed to revise, modify, or replace it as better electron-detecting techniques are developed.

Now consider the concept of CAUSATION. Hume (1748) kindled philosophical worries about causation by noticing a gap between perception and metaphysics. We often presume that causes necessitate their effects and that they do so in virtue of possessing casual powers or forces. But there is a problem if we assume that concepts are perceptually based. As

Hume noted, we only see contiguity and succession when we perceive causal events between two physical objects. We see one billiard ball make contact with a second, and then we see the second move. Contiguity and succession are weaker relations than causation; contiguous and successive events can lack a necessary connection. This generates an epistemological worry: how can one be justified in inferring a necessary connection from contiguity and succession? More relevantly, it generates a representational worry: how can one mentally represent causal relations if one is limited to perceptually representations? If necessary connections and causal powers transcend experience, how can one possess the concept of CAUSATION?

This objection can be tackled in various ways. First, one might apply the appearance-tracking strategy. A mental representation of contiguity and succession can be used to reliably detect instances of a deeper causal relation even if the latter is not directly perceivable. One can detect instances of causal relations between billiard balls by means of a dynamic representation of one billiard ball contacting another, followed by the other moving. If reliable detection is sufficient for reference, then this representation refers to a causal relation. A collection of causal-relation detectors could qualify as a CAUSATION concept. In this vein, some contemporary psychologists have suggested that we conceptualize causation by tracking observable-movement patterns (see Mandler 1992).

This proposal may be inadequate. If our concept of causation tracks causal relations by contiguity and succession, then two visual events with the same contiguity and succession relations should be interpreted in the same way. This may not be the case. Some years ago Michotte (1946/1963) found that subjects interpret certain displays as causal events. Imagine a film clip of one ball rolling onto the screen from the right, striking a second ball situated in middle of the screen, followed by the second ball rolling off the screen to the left (figure 7.1). If you watch such a film, you experience the first ball as having caused the movement of the second. Now imagine seeing a film clip of the same event with a brief delay between the time the first ball strikes and the time the second ball moves. The delay removes the appearance of a causal relation. This confirms Hume's view about how we conceptualize causation because the two film clips show different relations of succes-

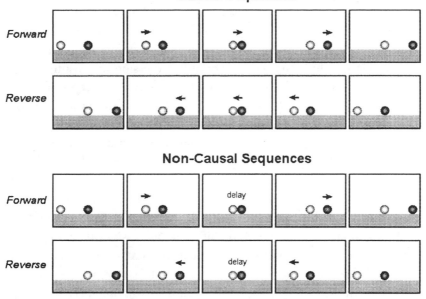

Figure 7.1
Leslie and Keeble's causation displays. Adapted from Leslie and Keeble 1987, figure 2, with permission from Elsevier Science.

sion. In the first clip the movement of the second ball immediately succeeds the movement of the first; in the second clip it does not. But now imagine seeing a third film clip, which is just a copy of the first film clip played in reverse. Now a ball moves in from the right, strikes a ball in the middle, and causes it to roll off to the left. Aside from the direction of movement, this third clip has exactly the same contiguity and succession relations as the first. Just like the first film clip, we see this clip as causal. The change in direction makes an important difference, however. In the first clip, we perceive the ball on the left as the causal agent. We assign to it a causal power, which is transferred to the ball in the center of the screen. In the third clip, the ball on the right is the causal agent.

Leslie and Keeble (1987) showed film clips like these to 6-month-old infants and found that they were sensitive to this difference as well. When infants watch the second clip, played first forward and then in reverse, they do not get very excited by the reversal. When they see the first clip played forward and then in reverse (like the third clip), they get very excited by the reversal. The first reversal is perceived as a change in the locus of causal power, but the second reversal is not thus perceived. Leslie and Keeble conclude that continuity and succession are insufficient to explain how we think about causation. In addition to concepts of spatial and temporal properties, we have a concept of CAUSAL POWER. Spatial and temporal properties are guides to attributing causal powers, but they are not constitutive of causal powers. The Humean account leaves out this component of causal understanding, which is already in place at 6 months.

Leslie and Keeble do not take this conclusion to undermine the claim that we can perceive causation, but rationalists might use their findings to do just that. We perceive contiguity and succession, they might say, but these merely occasion the deployment of a CAUSATION concept that transcends the perceivable. The idea of CAUSAL POWER, which underlies our concept of CAUSATION, cannot be identified with any perceptual representation. To overcome this objection, one must explain the attribution of causal powers without calling on representational resources that lie outside of perceptual systems.

I think empiricists can tell a reasonable story about how causal powers are attributed. Infants are frequently both sources and recipients of causal forces. They manipulate objects and, more often, feel the pushings and pullings of objects that make contact with them. In these situations, characteristic experiences are presumably felt. There are kinesthetic experiences produced by handling things and somatosensory experiences produced by being handled. It is conceivable that infants use such experiences to ground an early notion of CAUSAL POWERS. They may project such properties onto perceived objects. The patterns of contiguity and succession that they see when billiard balls collide are relevantly similar to the patterns produced by seeing their own interactions with objects. In this way infants may acquire a method of representing causation that transcends mere visual-movement patterns. Adults may inherit their concepts of CAUSAL POWERS from infants. We may project a representation of force derived through somatosensory and kinesthetic experience onto inanimate objects when they act as causes. If so, our representation of causation does go beyond contiguity and succession, but it does not require any nonperceptual representations.

Hume (1748, vii) considers the possibility that we come to understand the idea of causal powers by perceiving the affects of our will on our bodies. He concludes that this proposal is vulnerable to the same problems that arise when we restrict ourselves to ideas based on contiguity and succession. When a state of will causes a bodily movement, we cannot directly perceive the necessity of the connection. Why does the will cause the particular movements that it does? Why can't the will cause every part of the body to move with equal control? How does something mental cause a physical change? The fact that such questions arise suggests that we form knowledge of the link between states of the will and physical actions by observing regular co-occurrence. Experiences of willed bodily changes cannot supplement the ideas of CONTIGUITY and SUCCESSION if it depends on those ideas.

In explaining concepts of CAUSATION, this argument does not undermine my appeal to bodily knowledge. In appealing to bodily knowledge, I was not trying to explain how we come to believe that causes necessitate their effects. The sense of necessity may derive from a strong sense of expectation brought on by frequent co-occurrence, as Hume suspected. Bodily knowledge explains how we conceptualize causal powers. Cause attribution involves both an expectation of subsequent movement (owing to familiar patterns of contiguity and succession) and projection of the properties we experience through kinesthesia and other bodily senses. The expectations explain our idea of causal necessity, and the bodily states explain our idea of causal power. These two components, which Hume tended to run together, can both be explained using resources available to perceptual systems.

I turn now to lofty intangible concepts.[3] Consider TRUTH first. While we occasionally talk of dreams "coming true" and pictures that are "true to life," truth is generally regarded as a property of sentences. We say that sentences are true. Mastery of TRUTH, as applied to sentences, may require mastery of certain verbal rules or language games for deploying the word "true" and its cognates (for example, we learn that "*S* is true" is a special way of saying *S*). But "truth" often also has built into it an idea of CORRESPONDENCE, which is a feature that we can recognize in

moral concepts though ensembles of words, emotions, operations, and representations of paradigm cases.

The concept of DEMOCRACY, another lofty concept, is grasped in part through verbal skills. If you ask someone what a democracy is, she may say that it is a form of government in which policies are determined by consent of the governed. As we saw in section 7.1.2, this does not get us very far. The notions of GOVERNMENT, CONSENT, and POLICIES are still highly abstract. In some cases, people associate concrete images with democracy: they may imagine lines at a voting both or a ballet box. Such images may help us perceptually identify democratic scenarios, but they are sadly superficial. A somewhat deeper notion is CONSENSUS. People may think about consensus using notions related to empathy and impartiality, considered a moment ago. As we probe subjects about their DEMOCRACY concepts, we may eventually arrive at simpler concepts that can be pinned down in experience. One might be able to sit a subject down in an experimental setting and say, "What is a democracy?" and then ask parallel questions for each term that the subject offers in response. Perhaps this method would arrive at some simpler, more tangible features. This is a good method for finding perceptual foundations of abstract concepts that experimentalists should keep in mind. We may be surprised at how quickly people end up referring to concrete scenarios.

But we may also find that many people end up in circles, defining terms using other terms, and then defining those other terms using the first ones. Concepts like this are slaves to our lexical networks. They are purely verbal. But this kind of circularity may not be pernicious. The words in our circular definitions can be used to track words used by other members of our communities. Some of the words and phrases we use to understand what democracies are may be grounded in highly complex and socially distributed practices for tracking democracies. We can avoid hermeneutic circles by combining verbal skills with word tracking. If our verbal skills are coordinated with social practices that ultimately circumscribe the properties designated by our concepts, those skills can help secure reference. Language games can be a route to reference.[6]

I turn now to logical concepts. Here we must be careful to distinguish between our concepts of logical operations and the psychological analogs of those operations themselves. This is the difference between thoughts about logical operations and thoughts governed by logical operations. We must distinguish a thought about disjunction from a disjunctive thought. In thinking about logical operations, emotional representations may play a role. For example, thinking about disjunction might involve representing the feelings of hesitation (Russell 1940, Price 1953). This would put such concepts in line with evaluative concepts like VIRTUE. Of course, this is only a marginal way in which logic enters our thoughts.

A disjunctive thought is a thought governed by the definition of disjunction given in formal logic or something related to that definition. If concept empiricism cannot explain our ability to form thoughts governed by logical principles, it will lack an important tool for explaining how we reason. Many traditional empiricists are associationists. They argue that the central operation of the mind is that of associating ideas together. The problem with associationism is that thought transformations governed by mere associations do not preserve semantic properties. If one starts with true thoughts and uses them to call up associated thoughts, the associated thoughts have an arbitrary chance of being true. Rules of logic, in contrast, are truth-preserving. The empiricist does not need to say that reasoning conforms to the logical rules that we learn in the classroom. But we should hope that the mind is furnished with rules that combine and manipulate thoughts in a way that can, in some situations, be fairly reliable in preserving truth. To support such rules, thoughts must have something like logical form. They must have a structure that allows them to be manipulated in ways that are sensitive to the truth of their components rather than the frequency with which their components have been associated.

The empiricist must show that analogs of logical rules can operate on perceptually derived representations. There is no reason to think this cannot be done. Let us start with negation. Consider the thought that goats are animals. A situation confirms this thought if our representation of that situation is sufficiently similar to our representation of the thought to count as matching (see my discussion of TRUTH). Negation may work by inverting the matching function. For example, the thought that rocks are not animals is matched if experience fails to match the thought that rocks are animals. Matching a negated thought works by failing to match the thought in its unnegated form. On this approach, there is no constituent of the thought that rocks are not animals that corresponds to the word "not." Negated and nonnegated versions of a thought have *exactly* the same constituents. What differs is how those constituents are compared to the world. Negated thoughts are confirmed by counterevidence.

The proposal can be formalized by using a rule for similarity assessment. As we saw in chapter 3, one popular tool for modeling similarity assessments is Tversky's contrast rule:

$$\text{Sim}(A, B) = (A \cap B) - (A - B) - (A - B)$$

This formula measures the similarity between sets of features by subtracting their differences from their commonalities. It can be used to define a second formula for negation. When a concept is negated, similarity can be measured as follows:

$$\text{Simnegation}(A, \text{not-}B) = 2 \times \text{Threshold}(B) - \text{Sim}(A, B)$$

Here we begin by measuring the similarity of B (not negated) to A. We then subtract this measurement from the threshold of B multiplied by 2.

Consider the thought that rocks are not animals. If we want to assess this thought, we begin by comparing a ROCK representation to an ANIMAL representation. This comparison will have a very low score, well below the threshold needed to confirm that rocks are animals. Assume that the similarity between ROCK and ANIMAL is 0.1, while the threshold for being sufficiently similar to ANIMAL to qualify as falling under that concept is 0.5. To achieve a negation, we must invert that score. We want to assign a similarity score that is as high above the threshold has the original comparison was below the threshold. We do this by doubling the threshold, getting 1.0, and subtracting the original similarity score, 0.1, which yields a score of 0.9. As a result, "Rocks are not animals" is as obviously true as "Rocks are animals" is obviously false.

Notice that this proposal is not committed to the view that negation is graded. Simnegation delivers the degree to which something typifies noninstances of a category. A rock is a very good example of a nonanimal, and a teddy bear is a very bad example. But as long as these both come in below a critical threshold, they are both similar enough to the nonanimal category to qualify equally well for membership.

This formula for dealing with negation is only one suggestion, but it illustrates a promising strategy. Rather than thinking of negation as something that must be embodied in its own perceptual representation, we can think of it as an operation, a special way of measuring similarity between sets of features. The existence of a negation operation, even if it is innate, poses no threat to the claim that *concepts* are perceptually represented in modality-specific codes. Negation, on this approach, is not a concept.

Other logic cases may be handled in similar ways. A disjunctive thought may be composed of two separate components and a special similarity function that confirms matches to the whole thought just in case at least one of its components is confirmed. I will forgo the formalization.

Disjunctive operations may be built into some of our concepts. Consider the concept BESIDE. On a perceptual view, one might wonder how one could possibly represent this spatial relation instead of the more specific relations LEFT-OF or RIGHT-OF. The solution may be that BESIDE consists of a disjunction of these two relations. In assessing whether one thing is beside another, we check whether it is either RIGHT-OF or LEFT-OF. This example shows how some concepts may be logically constructed from perceptual representations.

To handle quantification, one might follow a proposal developed by Johnson-Laird (1983). He explains quantification by appeal to methods of introducing objects into mental models. A mental model of a set of sentences (e.g., the premises of an argument) is a representation of a situation in which those sentences are true. According to Johnson-Laird, we represent a universally quantified sentence of the form "All *A*s are *B*" by introducing representations of an arbitrary number of *A*s into our model and representing all of them as having property *B*. "Some *A*s are *B*" can be represented by introducing a few *A*s and representing some of them as *B* and some of them as not *B*. We confirm inferences based on the model by constructing alternative models that are compatible with the same premises. In this way, we can reason fairly successfully using quantified premises. This method is compatible with concept empiricism because the representations introduced into a model can be images in one of our sensory modalities, as Johnson-Laird sometimes suggests, or proxytypes. Quantifiers are not explicitly represented. They are mental operations.

There are alternatives to Johnson-Laird's theory of how we reason with quantifiers that are equally consistent with concept empiricism. For example, some have suggested that people use mental analogues of Venn diagrams or Euler circles to understand syllogisms involving quantification (see Johnson-Laird 1996). These techniques qualify as perceptual because mental representations of diagrams can be perceptually acquired. A diagrammatic technique for solving syllogisms involving disjunctions is described by Bauer and Johnson-Laird (1993). The sentence "Julie is in Atlanta or Tacoma" can be represented using one shape labeled "Julie" and two other shapes labeled "Atlanta" and "Tacoma" with recesses in the form of the "Julie" shape carved into them. One can conceptualize the disjunction of possibilities by recognizing that the shape standing in for Julie can fit into either of the two recesses. The diagrams in these examples are all learned through explicit instruction, but people may come up with their owns ways of "visualizing" logical relations.

Mathematical concepts are regarded as especially challenging for empiricists. How can something as abstract as math be conceptualized using mental representations derived from experience? One answer to these question stems from the formalist tradition in the philosophy of mathematics. Hilbert (1964) argues that mathematical concepts can be explained in terms of the forms of mathematical expressions. Since these are perceivable, they can provide an account of mathematical concepts that is consistent with concept empiricism.[7] One can deny that formalism is a correct theory of mathematical ontology (i.e., mathematical objects may not be identifiable with physical marks), while claiming that it is a plausible approach to the psychology of mathematics. Many of us think of numbers in terms of numerals and perform mathematical operations by applying memorized rules of symbol manipulation.

Some empirical support for this formalist proposal comes from recent work by Dehaene and his colleagues. Dehaene (1997) argues that people perform certain mathematical calculations using the symbols and words for numbers that we learn in our natural languages. Languages or cultures with more efficient ways of representing numbers allow for more efficient calculation. Chinese, for example, has a more efficient way of naming numbers than European languages, and as a result, Chinese speakers are faster at mental calculation. Dehaene, Spelke, Pinel, Stanescu, and Tsivkin (1999) confirmed the role of language in calculation using functional magnetic resonance imaging (fMRI). They found that arithmetic uses parts of the brain that are normally involved in verbal memory. Mathematical concepts used in arithmetic are apparently grasped through verbal skills that track real mathematical relations.

This verbal approach captures aspects of mathematical reasoning that are book-learned or memorized by rote. But evidence from Dehaene and others suggests that some other mathematical abilities have a different origin. Dehaene, Dehaene-Lambertz, and Cohen (1998) review evidence that preverbal infants and various nonhuman animals are able to identify quantities, compare quantities, and sum small quantities. In one experimental paradigm used to test for these abilities, subjects are presented with groups of stimuli through distinct sensory modalities. For example, evidence for numerical abilities in infants can be provided by seeing whether an infant will show increased interest to a visually presented group of dots after the hearing the same number of drum beats. Because infants lack language, their success cannot be explained by verbal skills.

Some mathematical abilities in adults are also independent of language. For example, in quantity discrimination tasks (which quantity is bigger?), adults are slower with quantities that are closer together than quantities that are farther apart, regardless of whether those quantities are presented as dots, Arabic numerals, or number words. Dehaene et al. (1998, 358) conclude that numbers are translated into a continuous analog format regardless of presentation format. Support for this hypothesis comes from fMRI studies in which Dehaene et al. (1999) find that mathematical tasks involving approximate quantities activate areas involved in spatial reasoning rather than verbal memory centers.

The studies of nonverbal mathematical skills lead Dehaene et al. (1998) to conclude that humans and other animals are born with a cognitive domain specialized for basic mathematical reasoning about quantities. This conclusion is not obligatory. To say that there is an innate math domain implies that there is a system of rules and representations beyond those necessary for explaining perception. An alternative is that our preverbal math abilities derive from operations on representations found in our senses.

Consider, first, preverbal infants' ability to identify small quantities across modalities. If an infant recognizes a similarity between three dots and three drum beats, she does not necessarily have an amodal representation of the number three. Instead, she may have the ability to map representations in one modality onto another. This is a mathematical ability, in some sense, but not one that requires extrasensory machinery. I argue in chapter 5 that empiricists should embrace innate machinery for mapping representations from one sense onto another. Empiricists should also admit that we are born with mechanisms of attention. Attention mechanisms can track multiple objects. If we combine attention mechanisms with intermodal transfer mechanisms, we get the ability to bind features perceived across more than one sense modality for more than one object at the same time. Infants can presumably attend to a growling wolf and a chirping bird simultaneously. This is a quantitative ability. It requires matching a certain number of sounds with a certain number of visual images. If an infant heard both a growl and a chirp but only saw a bird, she had better look for the source of the growl. Saying we can keep track of quantities in this way explains quantitative performance, but it requires little more than multiobject attention mechanisms, intermodal transfer, and modality-specific perceptual representations. No specialized domain containing mathematical rules and representations is required.

The ability to discriminate between quantities can also be explained in a way that is consistent with concept empiricism. On Dehaene's theory, quantity discrimination depends on an analog representation of a number line implemented in areas of the brain associated with spatial reasoning. Empiricists can welcome this proposal and say that the number line is a modality-specific (e.g., visual) representation.

Number lines can be regarded as metaphors for quantities. Larger quantities are not literally farther along a line than smaller quantities. It is possible that our use of number lines is learned, like our use of Venn diagrams. Infants and nonhuman animals may compare quantities in some other way. Notably, they may form mental images of groups of objects and then mentally scan them to see which is larger. This method of quantity discrimination is not metaphorical. It is a case of appearance tracking. Larger sets of objects give rise to larger appearances. This does not mean that larger sets must take up more of the visual field to be identified as larger. High-level visual representations abstract away from size in visual space. Using high-level representations, groups of objects can be scanned from size differences stemming from the number of members they contain rather than their visual volume.

In sum, our ability to understand mathematics rests on a combination of abilities. We master verbal skills, we use spatial representations metaphorically, we use attention and transfer operations to map multiple objects across our senses, and we use scanning operations to detect size differences in mental images of groups. None of these approaches to mathematical cognition requires representations outside of our perceptual systems. Like the other hard cases, mathematical concepts pose an interesting challenge, but not an unmeetable one.

7.3   Conclusion

My analyses of the putative counterexamples to empiricism are incomplete, and some may be refuted by empirical investigation. Their purpose is to provide grounds for optimism and directions for research. Even if all of my analyses are wrong, they show that it is premature to dismiss concept empiricism. Proxytype theory uses a rich assortment of perceptual representations and avails itself of modern causal semantic theories. Representations of words, emotions, and other perceptual states conspire with causal theories to track properties in the world. The range of properties that can be perceptually tracked far exceeds the range of properties that can be directly perceived. This gives proxytypes considerable expressive breadth. Those things that cannot be represented using proxytypes may be identified with operations on proxytypes. Together, these strategies insulate proxytype theory from charges that empiricism cannot satisfy the scope desideratum. Antiempiricists have yet to produce a decisive counterexample. If such a counterexample is produced, it may threaten antiempiricists and empiricists alike.

8

Overcoming Concept Nativism

In the last three chapters, I examined the idea that thinking is a matter of redeploying perceptual representation off-line. This view is consistent with those defended by the classical British empiricists. One difference is that their positive proposals are partially motivated by the arguments against nativism presented by Locke. Their attempt to ground cognition in perception is, in part, an attempt to show that concepts and principles can be acquired though experience rather than being present at birth. As a result of the classical empiricist tradition, it is often thought that empiricism presupposes a strong opposition to nativism.

Cognitive science was born out of arguments for nativism. The behaviorists, who dominated American psychology in the first half of the twentieth century, considered themselves empiricists. Chomsky's seminal attack on behaviorism simultaneously inaugurated cognitive science and laid the groundwork for a self-consciously rationalist reinstatement of the hypothesis that we are born with highly specific innate knowledge structures. Arguments in favor of nativism continue to abound. There is a widespread assumption among cognitive scientists that no cognitive ability can be explained without postulating a rich innate basis. It is also widely assumed that empiricists must be categorically opposed to nativism. Together, these two assumptions constitute a refutation of empiricism. The goal of this chapter is to assess whether either assumption is true.

8.1   Stances on Nativism

8.1.1   What Is Nativism?

A nativist about a trait says that the trait is innate. It is not clear, however, what it means to claim that a trait is innate. Many proposed definitions of innateness turn out to be unacceptable. If innateness cannot be given a satisfactory definition, the debate between nativists and their opponents is incoherent. I try to avoid that conclusion.

A common first stab defines innate traits as those that are present at birth. This is not sufficient for innateness, however, because some learning may take place in utero. Nor is it necessary, because many allegedly innate traits are not present at birth.

What distinguishes innate traits that appear after birth from noninnate traits that appear after birth? It is tempting to propose that innate traits are independent of the environment; they appear as a result of factors wholly internal to the organism. This will not work. There are two kinds of innate traits that appear after birth. Triggered innate traits are ones that require triggers for their expression. A trigger is a special environmental condition that causes the trait to appear. For example, macaques are said to be innately afraid of snakes, but evidence suggests that they will only manifest this attribute if they experience, during a critical period, a conspecific displaying an aversive reaction to snakes (Mineka, Davidson, Cook, and Keir 1984). In contrast, a maturational innate trait is one emerges without the contribution of special environmental conditions. Secondary sex characteristics are often presented as an example. However, maturational innate traits still depend on the environment. At a minimum, they depend on adequate nutrition.

If both innate and noninnate traits depend on the environment, there must be another way to distinguish them. Some researches have argued that innate traits are ones that are canalized (Waddington 1940, Ariew 1996). A canalized trait is one that would appear over a wide range of environmental variations. Being robust across environments may lie behind intuitions supporting the proposal that innate traits are independent of the environment.

Canalization is not necessary for innateness, because it does not subsume triggered traits. Triggered traits require highly specific environmental conditions for their manifestation and are thus unlikely to occur over different environmental variations. Triggering conditions can be highly specific and even rare. In this regard, certain learned traits have much in common with triggered traits. For example, one will not develop a fear of handguns without being in an environment where handguns exist and are known to be dangerous. Certain other fears, like those constituting phobias, may require traumatic episodes. What makes the fear of snakes innate, while these other fears are learned? Canalization provides no answer to this question, because all these fears require conditions that are highly specific. Canalization is also insufficient for innateness. Certain learned traits, such as the belief that the sun is bright, qualify as canalized because they arise in a very large range of environments.

Cowie (1998) tries to identify what leading nativists in cognitive science mean by the word "innate." She comes up with one definition, namely, that innate psychological traits are those whose presence cannot be explained using the explanatory resources of psychology (see also Samuels, forthcoming). If we had a psychological story to explain how a trait came into existence, we would be able to conclude that the trait is learned (in some broad sense). If no psychological story is available, the trait is unlearned, and hence innate. Cowie calls this the metapsychological view of innateness and attributes it to Fodor.

One difficulty with the metapsychological view is that it must count psychological traits that are acquired by, say, whacking someone on the head, as innate (Samuels, forthcoming).[1] If a closed head injury leads me to believe that I am Napoleon, that belief is acquired in a way that cannot be explained at the level of psychology. Should we say that the belief is innate? Another problem with the metapsychological view is that it is hard to identify the explanatory jurisdiction of psychology. The boundaries of academic disciplines change. These days, psychology is incorporating more and more tools from neuroscience and evolutionary biology. What is metapsychological today may be a branch of psychology tomorrow. The claim that talk of genes and neurons are outside of the proper domain of psychology is a statement about current academic sociology, rather than a reflection of some deeper fact. Another problem is that the metapsychological definition of innateness does not generalize to innate traits that are not mental. For example, the metapsychological definition cannot be used to explain what it means to say that the standard morphology of human feet is innate while the shape of feet that have been deformed through foot binding is not innate.

There might be a fix. Rather than saying that innate traits are those that cannot be explained by psychology, one might say that innate traits are those that can be explained by a branch of biology, namely genetics. Genetics does not suffer from the disciplinary boundary worries that psychology does, because it can be circumscribed by its subject matter: genes. Genetics handles the head-whacking example because states caused by head whacks are not genetic. Genetics also handles triggering cases nicely. The canalization proposal makes triggered innate traits, like snake phobias, difficult to accommodate. The genetic account even generalizes. Genetic explanations can subsume both innate psychological traits and foot morphology. Finally, the genetic account connects up nicely with our (scientifically informed) intuitions. Innate traits are coded in the genes.

One objection to the genetic account is that it could not be what philosophers historically meant by "innateness." The term belongs to a debate that predates the discovery of genes. This objection can be answered if we regard "innateness" as a natural-kind term. In past centuries, the property of being innate was picked out by approximate reference-fixing descriptions and paradigm cases. Science has now discovered the underlying property to which past authors were pointing.

Another worry about the genetic account is that it is not clear what it means for a trait to be genetic. It is too weak to say that genetic traits depend on information in our genes. Learned traits also depend on our genes, because they depend on learning abilities that are genetically specified. One might respond by proposing that genetic traits are ones that can be fully explained by genetics. But this is too strong. As already observed, even innate traits depend on certain environmental conditions to be expressed. A third proposal is that a trait counts as genetic if there is a gene for it. This locution does not necessarily mean that the gene is sufficient for the expression of that trait (unlike the last condition), only that there is a gene that has the evolved functional role of producing that trait within certain environments (Sterelny, Smith, and Dickenson 1996).

It is also a bit stronger than a mere dependency claim because it correlates innate traits with specific genes.

The gene-for-X condition may be sufficient for innateness, but it is not necessary. In many cases, gene-to-trait mapping is much more complex. Requiring a gene for each innate trait would be unfair to the nativist. To get around this worry, one might simply substitute the phrase "gene(s)-for-X." It may be that certain gene complexes co-evolved because they collectively produced a phenotypic trait. One does not need to find a single gene for a psychological trait to show that it is genetic. Critics may still worry. Perhaps genes code for chemical chains and not for traits. Perhaps genes are not the only replicators, in which case genetic traits do not differ in principle from other kinds of traits. Perhaps mutated genes could result in traits that are genetic but not innate because they do not correspond to an evolved function of genes. More work would have to be done to support a genetic theory of innateness.

That work can be left to another occasion. I think a genetic account of innateness can be made to float, but in the interim, one can identify innateness operationally. Various tests for innateness have been suggested throughout the history of discussions of innateness. Some of these tests can be rejected. For example, Locke successfully debunked the proposal that we can identify innate traits with those that are universal. Universality is neither sufficient for innateness (the belief that the sun is bright is universal but not innate) nor necessary (eye color is innate but not universal). But other tests for innateness may fair better. For example, it is hard to dispute the viability of poverty-of-the-stimulus arguments. Very roughly, if nothing in an organism's past experience could explain how it attained a trait, one must conclude that the trait is innate. This is the central test for innateness used by Chomsky. Other nativists have devised equally plausible tests for innateness. One might construe such tests as attempts to define innateness (see, e.g., Cowie 1998 on poverty of the stimulus), but they are equally often used as reference fixers. On this construal, innateness cannot be defined as "acquired despite impoverished stimuli," but it can be diagnosed that way. Innateness is a real property of the world that we do not fully understand, but we can pick out examples of innateness via poverty-of-the-stimulus arguments and various other tests. We do not need to know the essence of innateness if we can point to it. Even if the genetic account fails, we have provisional ways to discuss innateness and to assess arguments for innate traits.

8.1.2   Must Empiricists Oppose Nativism?

Naive expositors may be inclined to saddle the empiricist with the absurd view that *nothing* is innate. How could a simple hunk of tissue learn anything if this were the case? Surely some innate machinery must be in place if learning is possible at all. Locke's (1690, I.i.15) pronouncement that the mind begins as an empty cabinet should not be taken too literally. Just as the mind is not really a cabinet, for Locke it is not really empty.

Moving into the realm of plausibility, the naive expositor might attribute to empiricists the view that the mind is only innately furnished with a single learning rule. This supposition derives from classical associationism. In the eighteenth century, empiricists began to claim that all learning occurs by association. Belief in a single association-based learning rule has since been endorsed by some behaviorists and connectionists, both frequently regarded as heirs to classical empiricism.[2]

Despite the allure of parsimonious learning rules, they are not obligatory for the empiricist. It is often forgotten that Locke (1690, II.xxxiii) is critical of association-based learning. Associations from experience are a valuable source of knowledge, but we must also exercise caution when associating things whose connection may be highly contingent. Locke also implies that there are a variety of learning rules when he endorses innate faculties. The faculties of discerning and abstracting are distinct ways of acquiring information from the senses. One might also expect diversity of learning rules across the senses. Rules that attain information from light waves may differ from rules that obtain information from sound waves. Even within modalities, distinct and specific learning rules may be in place. There might be one set of rules for deriving information from stereoscopic disparity and another for deriving information from collinear edges. Different ways of deriving information contribute to different learning rules in the trivial sense that leaning involves the formation and subsequent retention of representations.

A third possibility is that empiricists deny the existence of innate representations. Some empiricists may hold this view, but it is needlessly strict. Concept empiricists say that concepts are copied from perceptual representations. This thesis is totally neutral about how perceptual representations are acquired. It is consistent with concept empiricism that perceptual systems come equipped with representations, such as primitive shape or color detectors in the visual system.

Elman, Bates, Johnson, Karmiloff-Smith, Parsi, and Plunkett (1996) argue that it is unlikely that the brain has innate representations. Representations are construed by patterns of neural activation. Innate representations would depend on innately determined patterns of neural connectivity, which would be costly to determine genetically and inconsonant with the evidence for significant neural plasticity. These points may not completely rule out innate representations. First, some cell types at or near the level of transduction, such as cone cells in the retina, are innate. If one can make a case for their activity being both mental and representations, then mental representations are certainly innate. Second, it may be a mistake to identify representations with patterns of activation across connected neurons. By this criterion, it could turn out that no two people share any representations. Instead, what matters is having neurons or neural populations that are innately wired to detect the same things. Two different firing patterns can both detect edges. If brains are prewired with edge detectors in place, there are innate edge detectors, even if they differ at the cellular level from person to person. Concept empiricism can tolerate these kinds of innate representations.

The kind of nativism relevant to concept empiricism is nativism about concepts. Innate representations that do not qualify as concepts pose no threat. In contrast, one might suppose that the concept empiricist must deny the existence of innate concepts. On this interpretation, concept empiricists are committed to the following:

Strong Antinativism about Concepts   No concepts are innate.

Strong antinativism about concepts is not the only stance available to the concept empiricist. Concept empiricism says that all concepts are copies (or combinations of copies) of perceptual representations. Now suppose that perceptual representations can qualify as concepts in their own right. This would allow the concept empiricist to adopt with the following view:

Weak Antinativism about Concepts   All innate concepts are perceptual representations.

Hume (1748, II) explicitly admits that basic sensory concepts are innate, and Locke should not be unhappy with this claim.[3] Locke's campaign against nativism is primarily directed against innate *principles*, such as, "Whatsoever is, is" and " 'Tis impossible for the same thing to be, and not to be." He briefly criticizes the postulation of innate concepts (see Locke 1690, I.iv.17), but here his focus is on highly abstract concepts, and he denies their innateness only to challenge the alleged innateness of the principles that contain them. To say that some perceptual concepts are innate is broadly consistent with Locke's antinativist stance.

Following Locke, one might assume that empiricists must reject innate principles. Even this is not obligatory. If concept empiricism admits innate perceptual representations and innate perceptual concepts, it might also admit innate principles, provided they consist of entities of these two kinds. Admitting innate principles is a problem only in cases where those principles involve concepts that are not perceptual representations. Locke's opposition to innate principles *tout court* extends beyond his empiricist theory of concepts.

To summarize, concept empiricists are entitled to endorse either a weak or a strong opposition to nativism. Both views are compatible with the existence of innate perceptual representations and innate principles. The weak antinativist position also allows some innate concepts. Before leaving this section, I want to consider some of the issues that might decide between these two alternatives. If both strong and weak antinativists agree that some perceptual representations are innate, then the division between them involves the status of those representations. To choose between strong and weak antinativism, one must determine whether any innate perceptual representations qualify as concepts. To do this, one must first ask what makes a representation count as a concept.

In chapter 5, I considered proposals for distinguishing the senses from the intellect. According to a proposal that I rejected, the senses are receptive and the intellect is spontaneous. The problem with this proposal is that the senses are often active and the intellect is often passive. The receptivity/spontaneity distinction does provide, however, an excellent method of distinguishing mere perceptual representations from concepts. I suggest that concepts are spontaneous: they are representations that can come under the endogenous control of the organism. Mere perceptual representations are receptive: they are controlled solely by exogenous stimuli. Or more accurately, mere perceptual representations are representations that can be caused by environmental stimulation along with mechanisms within input systems, as opposed to mechanisms that are endogenous but outside of the input systems. By adding the qualifier "mere," I leave open the possibility that some perceptual representations count as concepts. These are the perceptual representations that can be controlled by the organism.

The present proposal captures the intuition that concepts can be freely deployed in thinking, while certain perceptual representations are under environmental control. It also allows empiricists to draw a boundary between concept and perceptual representations without making that boundary exclusive. It even provides an empiricist definition of concept acquisition. A mere perceptual representation *becomes* a concept when it comes under endogenous control. In some cases, perceptual representations come under endogenous control as soon as they are formed, but in other cases, it is a slow developmental process.

This way of distinguishing mere perceptual representations from perceptual representations that qualify as concepts provides a way to adjudicate between empiricists who endorse strong antinativism about concepts and those who endorse weak antinativism about concepts. The former are right if all innate perceptual representations are under exogenous control, and the latter are right if some innate perceptual representations can also be controlled endogenously.

In the following sections, I will not try to decide between strong and weak antinativism. I argue that both can survive arguments widely believed to undermine any antinativist position. If this defense succeeds, it is evidence for the claim that concept empiricism can satisfy the acquisition desideratum.

8.2   Arguments for Innateness

Arguments for nativism can be found in every branch of cognitive science. The most significant arguments span three disciplines. Linguists argue that grammatical rules are innate, psychologists argue that folk theories are innate, and one philosopher argues that all lexical concepts are innate. All of these arguments are said to threaten empiricism. I address them in turn.

8.2.1   The Language Organ

I cannot do justice to the vast topic of language here, nor can I ignore it. Contemporary discussions of innateness have focused more on language than any other domain. This can be credited to the monumental influence of Chomsky. Before Chomsky, it was fashionable to minimize the mind's innate endowment. Since Chomsky, it has been fashionable to assume that the mind is preequipped with highly specific mechanisms. The tide changed when Chomsky argued that language learning requires an innate set of rules and representations, a language-acquisition device.

Arguments for linguistic nativism rest on at a number of observations. Various facts are hard to explain without postulating an innate language faculty. Here are ten of the most important observations:

1. **Early acquisition**   Languages are acquired early in life, before many other cognitive abilities are fully developed.

2. **Independence of intelligence**   Differences in general intelligence do not come with corresponding differences in linguistic competence.

3. **Language areas**   Language abilities are associated with particular regions of the brain, most famously, Broca's and Wernicke's areas, damage to which can occur without affecting other cognitive abilities.

4. **Species specificity**   Nonhuman animals, including great apes, lack humanlike language abilities.

5. **The critical period**   Evidence from recovered aphasics and people who were deprived of language during childhood suggests that a first language can be acquired only during a critical period that ends around puberty.

6. Structure-sensitive rules   Linguistic rules are structure-sensitive, and thus often not the simplest generalizations of the primary linguistic data.

7. Arbitrary rules   Some linguistic rules seem arbitrary or idiosyncratic.

8. Incomplete data   The primary linguistic data used in language acquisition lack certain constructions that children come to form correctly.

9. No negative data   Children make mistakes that go uncorrected, but go on to learn to learn the correct rules anyway.

10. The birds and the bees   Many nonhuman animals have innate systems of communication.

Observations (1) through (5) provide support for the claim that language is a separate domain, learned via language-specific rules rather than general rules or central cognitive systems. Observations (6) through (10) provide more direct support for the innateness of rules used in language acquisition.

As noted, the existence of highly specific innate learning mechanisms in and of itself does not pose a threat to concept empiricism. Nor would arguments for linguistic nativism pose a threat if they showed only that we have innate mental representations. The arguments would pose a threat only if they demonstrated the existence of innate, nonperceptual concepts. Demonstrating the existence of innate concepts would refute strong antinativism, and demonstrating the existence of nonperceptual concepts would refute concept empiricism. At first blush, the arguments may appear to do both of these things.

Chomsky and his followers conceive innate grammars as sets of rules. Statements of these rules use terms that designate grammatical categories. For example, in his Government Binding Theory, Chomsky (1986) postulates an innate parameter that determines the location of heads in phrases. One might suspect that this parameter contains the concepts HEAD and PHRASE. One might also suspect that these concepts do not qualify as perceptual representations. After all, sentences can come in different media: sound, ink marks, bumps on a page, hand gestures, and so on. These can be experienced though audition, vision, touch, and kinesthesia. It seems wrong to assume that concepts designating grammatical categories belong to a single modality. If innate grammatical rules contain amodal concepts, empiricists can start playing taps.

There is room for an empiricist response. First, consider the supposition that representations making up grammatical rules are conceptual. It is an open possibility that when these rules are first exercised, they fail to satisfy the condition on concepthood introduced above: they may not be under endogenous control. It is often noticed that language-comprehension skills develop at a faster rate than production skills. Perhaps early grammatical rules are stimulus driven and come under control of the organism only after a certain amount of time and exposure. If language begins under exogenous control, it will have the character of a nonconceptual system.

This may be cold comfort to the empiricist. Even if language skills are initially outside of organismic control, there is still the worry that they are underwritten by representations that are nonperceptual. Once these amodal representations came to function as concepts, they would refute the modal-specificity hypothesis.

One can challenge the supposition that the rules constituting our innate grammatical abilities are nonperceptual. The simplest strategy is to argue that the language faculty qualifies as a perceptual modality in its own right. The language faculty appears to be a dedicated input system. It processes inputs, occupies its own neural circuitry, and uses its own kinds of rules and representations.[4] Viewed thus, language is like vision, audition, and touch. It is a sense. We have developed a special faculty attuned to grammatical structures, which other creatures fail to detect.

The language-sense proposal assumes that there is an innate faculty dedicated to language. One can also deny this. A more radical possibility is to argue that language abilities emerge from other faculties, including perceptual and motor systems. To defend this possibility, one must take on the arguments for linguistic nativism. I will briefly consider how empiricists might begin to address observations (1) through (10). There is emerging opposition to the view that the evidence for linguistic nativism is decisive. Researchers have critically reassessed nativist arguments and have developed powerful learning models that do not incorporate innate, language-specific rules. Detailed treatments can be found in the work of Elman et al. (1996) and Cowie (1998). What I offer is highly abridged and programmatic.

First consider early acquisition, (1), and independence of intelligence, (2). These observations are sometimes challenged on their own terms. We learn language early, but not that early. Full mastery takes a number of years. Likewise, language is not completely independent of intelligence. A standard argument for independence of intelligence appeals to subjects with specific language impairments (SLI), who make frequent grammatical errors despite allegedly normal intelligence. In actual fact, when IQ tests where given to affected and unaffected members of a family with high incidence of SLI, affected members had scores that averaged 18–19 points below unaffected members (Vargha-Khadem, Watkins, Alcock, Fletcher, and Passingham 1995). Better evidence for independence of intelligence comes from subjects with Williams Syndrome and many autistics who demonstrate good language skills despite having low IQ scores. Language skills in these populations are not exactly normal (Williams subjects have unusual vocabularies and autistic subjects exhibit defective pragmatics), but grammatical abilities are very good. This suggests that basic mastery of syntax is unlike basic mastery of quantum theory in its insensitivity to differences in intelligence.

Nevertheless, independence of intelligence cannot be taken as decisive evidence for the domain specificity of language. Language acquisition may piggyback on perceptual and motor systems, rather than systems of general intelligence. For example, language may depend on picking up subtle statistics in the primary linguistic data, using perceptual pattern detectors. It is known that infants attend to maternal speech and that they use various properties to determine where boundaries within those sounds occur (DeCasper and Spence 1986, Jusczyk 1997). Shi, Werker, and Morgan (1999) have shown that 1-to-3-day-old infants can categorically discriminate lexical and grammatical words in maternal speech. Speech sounds contains a wealth of information that our intellectual faculties tend to overlook. Giving the task over to perceptual systems may be the key to bootstrapping into language.

Two kinds of pattern-detection mechanisms may be especially valuable in linguistic-pattern detection. First, we can process very rapid transitions in auditory signals. Subjects with specific language impairments have difficulty processing rapid auditory transitions as well as rapidly sequenced stimuli in other modalities (Nagarajan, Mahncke, Salz, Tallal, Roberts, and Merzenich 1999; Johnston 1997). Second, we can replicate and rehearse complex movement sequences with our orofacial muscles. Vargha-Khadem et al. (1995) demonstrate that SLI subjects exhibit orofacial praxic impairments. SLI is passed on through a particular gene. Some believe that this is a gene *for* grammar because it correlates with a grammatical deficit. If that interpretation were correct, it would prove that grammar is innate by the genetic definition of innateness. Vargha-Khadem et al. offer an alternative hypothesis. The so-called grammar gene may really be a gene for fine-tuned orofacial control (or rapid sequence processing), the absence of which happens to hinder language acquisition.

These proposals clearly weaken arguments from independence of intelligence. If language acquisition depends on perceptual systems rather than high-level cognitive systems, we should not expect cognitive deficits to have much impact on language. The proposals also help debunk early-acquisition arguments. In normal subjects, perceptual and motor systems develop early. Language acquisition may occur faster and more effortlessly than some other aspects of cognitive function precisely because it exploits such systems. Early-acquisition and intelligence-independence arguments actually support empiricist accounts, rather than counting against them. One can only threaten empiricism by showing that domain-general perceptual and motor systems are not sufficient for acquiring language, which these argument, taken alone, do not show. The case against empiricism must rest on other arguments.

The existence of language areas, (3), looks like direct evidence for an innate language faculty. Why, one might wonder, are specific brain regions associated with linguistic abilities? If language acquisition is just a matter of perceptual-pattern recognition, shouldn't every perceptual area of the brain be equally capable of underwriting language skills? In response, one should first note that localization claims are exaggerated; numerous brain areas in both hemispheres have been seen to participate in language (Elman et al. 1996, Poeppel 1996). One can also question whether the standard language areas, Wernicke's and Broca's, are language-specific. Perhaps these areas are specialized for acoustic properties and motor sequences that happen to coincide with properties of linguistic inputs and outputs.

More specifically, the traditional language areas may be especially sensitive to subtle sequenced patterns. Broca's area may be especially adept at directing very fine patterns in orofacial movements, and Wernicke's area may be adept at picking out rapid auditory transitions. Because few general cognitive abilities depend on such fine auditory and muscular sequencing, language deficits leave general cognitive abilities intact. At the same time, this hypothesis predicts that linguistic deficits will be comorbid with dysfunctions in fine sequencing that are not related to language. This is exactly what has been found (Vargha-Khadem et al. 1995). Bates (1999) points out that that no one has been able to establish that language areas only participate in language processing. She cites a neuroimaging study by Erhard, Kato, Strick, and Ugurbil (1996) in which each proposed part of Broca's area was shown to be active during nonlinguistic tasks. This undercuts arguments that focus on the existence of language areas and adds further support to the claim that linguistic abilities are acquired by domain-general perceptual systems.

Now consider the argument based on species specificity, (4). Many creatures have perceptual systems very much like ours. Indeed, macaque monkeys are outstanding models for studying the human visual system (though see Preuss 2000). At the same time, other creatures are utterly incapable of acquiring language. Any approach that tries to explain linguistic skills by appeal to faculties that are not specific to language must explain why our linguistic abilities are so far advanced.

There is some debate about how to characterize the linguistic differences between us and other species. Great apes, especially bonobo chimps, have shown impressive abilities to learn languages (Savage-Rumbaugh 1991). They can acquire sizable vocabularies, form sentences, and understand novel, even bizarre, verbal commands. There are limits to these abilities, however. For example, bonobos do not form inflections or embedded clauses, and their sentences are very short and often contain repeated words. Apes master only those linguistic skills that could be mastered by humans who are language-deprived before the end of their critical periods (Jackendoff 1995). Perhaps these are the only linguistic skills that can be acquired without a specialized language faculty. Alternatively, apes may get this far only by having a more primitive specialized language faculty, perhaps inherited from a common genetic ancestor. This could explain why monkeys and other creatures are incapable of learning humanlike languages. In sum, language-learning experiments with great apes have often tended to support linguistic innateness by highlighting how unique we are or by pointing to an evolutionary ancestor of the language faculty in our closest species.

The opponent of linguistic nativism must explain the differences between linguistically normal humans and other creatures. Trying to explain such differences by appeal to perceptual systems is difficult because our perceptual systems are quite similar to those of creatures that cannot learn language. This does not refute the perceptual hypothesis, however. One possibility is that there is a difference in degree. Anatomically, we humans have considerably larger brains for our body weights (Passingham 1973). With larger brains, our perceptual and motor systems may develop greater abilities than those of our simian cousins. It is known, for instance, that humans can make more facial expressions than chimps or other primates. Perhaps, with greater control of our facial muscles, we developed greater abilities to rehearse the complex articulatory sequences used for language. Likewise, our ability to process rapid acoustic sequences may have increased with greater encephalization. Other primates have homologues of Broca's and Wernicke's areas, but ours may be better at responding to subtle patterns.

Another intriguing possibility is that the difference between humans and other primates involves differences in systems that interact with perceptual and motor systems. Most plausibly, a big difference may involve an increased working-memory capacity. With a larger brain, human working memory may have increased as well. In fact, some believe that the frontal lobes, which house working-memory systems, grew more than any other part of the brain (Deacon 1997; though see Semendeferi, Damasio, Frank, and Van Hoesen 1997).

How could a mere increase in working memory capacity support language abilities? Newport (1990) and Elman (1991) propose an intriguing answer. They claim that the key is not just a larger working-memory capacity, but a working memory that increases its capacity during development. It is an advantage to start out with a small working memory. A small working memory forces us to focus on very local patterns, such as two-word pairings, found in the primary linguistic data. Entire sentences can be quite complex. If a toddler had to monitor all the patterns found in speech strings, she would be overwhelmed. With gradual increases, she can build on simple patterns and come to handle full grammatical complexity.

To test this idea, Elman trained artificial neural networks on sentences with embedded clauses (e.g., "The boy who the dogs chase sees the girl"). The networks were designed to predict the next word in such sentences. To succeed, the networks must choose verbs that agree with nouns occurring earlier in the sentences; they must achieve long-distance binding. This is a complex grammatical ability that has not been convincingly demonstrated in nonhuman primates. Elman used recurrent networks with a set of context units that functioned as a working memory for previous words as the network made its way through a sentence. Initially, he used a network with a large number of context units, simulating a large working-memory capacity. In this condition, the network performed poorly. Like real children, it was exposed to numerous sentences, many of which were complex. This complexity overwhelmed the network, which lead to many errors. Elman trained another network that began with a small number of context units, which slowly increased over time. The new network was extremely successful in achieving binding agreements in sentences with embedded clauses.

A gradually increasing working-memory size, housed in a large frontal lobe may mark an important difference between normal humans and nonhuman primates. We may do better than apes because our working memories increase to a greater extent. Apes may do better than other primates and animals because of a significant, but less extreme, difference in working-memory size. These results show how a qualitative difference in language ability can result from a quantitative difference in memory, a faculty not specialized for language.

This idea can also be used to explain the critical period for language acquisition, (5). Newport (1990) conjectures that people cannot learn languages successfully after the critical period because their working memories have grown too large by that time. Without significant resource limitations, language learning is unmanageably complex. This is exactly what Elman's networks show. When they begin with large working memories, acquisition of structure-sensitive rules becomes difficult.

These considerations also weaken arguments from structure-sensitive rules, (6), to linguistic nativism. In effect, Elman shows that a dumb pattern detector can pick up on structural relations. Critics may be dissatisfied. Merely showing that a neural network can achieve something that looks like distance binding does not show that it has attained fully structured representations of language. Fortunately, the empiricist does not need to say that all of our success in generating structured representations comes from dumb pattern recognition. I have already noted (in chapter 6) that perceptual systems traffic in highly structured representations. The ability to do this may be innate as far as the empiricist is concerned. Complex, hierarchical representations may also be required for an adequate theory of motor sequence control. Unlike Elman's simple networks, the pattern detectors in the brain's perceptual and motor systems exploit structured representations. The high degree of structure achieved in language may be a consequence of the fact that linguistic data is processed and stored by such perceptual processors.

This suggestion helps formulate a response to the objection from arbitrary rules, (7). Proponents of an innate language faculty often assert that their opponents are unable to explain why some of our linguistic rules seem idiosyncratic or arbitrary. This arbitrariness may be an artifact of the perceptual origins of language. When a system is applied to a purpose for which it was not evolved, it may end up with some behavior that seems arbitrary. No one expects a perfect fit when borrowing a suit tailored for someone else. Conversely, if a system was evolved for language, one might expect less arbitrariness. Linguistic idiosyncrasies are better evidence for perceptual piggybacking than for an innate language faculty.

Some of the most arbitrary-seeming rules in language may turn out to be even easier to explain. Consider the subjeceny principle, which has long been paraded as a rule that demands a language-specific explanation. Subjacency says that phrases cannot be moved too far, when shifting location from one place in a sentence to another, as in the formation of questions. We can go from "Sally learned that the French eat slugs" to "What did Sally learn that the French eat?" But we cannot go from "Sally learned that fact that the French eat slugs" to "What did Sally learn the fact that the French eat?" According to Chomskyan linguists, the latter question is ungrammatical because the noun ("slugs") is converted to a question word ("what") that must leap over two bounding categories (a sentence and a noun phrase) as it makes its way to the beginning of the sentence. This, they say, is forbidden by a setting on an innate grammatical rule.

Ellefson and Christiansen (2000) set out to refute this interpretation using an experiment with simple computer models. They devised two artificial languages, one of which conformed to subjacency and the other of which did not. They then exposed two groups of artificial neural networks to sentences in one of these two languages. The networks began with no language-specific information, and their goal was to extrapolate from sentences entered during learning to new sentences that were consistent with the grammar. More specifically, when a new sentence was entered one word at a time, the networks had to predict the next word in a way that conformed with the grammar of the training corpus. In turned out that the networks made fewer errors in learning the grammar that conformed to subjacency than in learning the grammar that did not. Simple associative networks that learn by "hearing" various sentences in a language find that language easier to learn if it does not allow words to move too far. Subjacency, on this view, is not an innate grammatical principle but a bias that emerges from domain-general systems that rely on sequential learning. Other seemingly arbitrary rules might be explained in similar ways, or they might be accidental by-products of constraints on systems that have evolved from nonlinguistic tasks.

Of course, the devil is in the details. One example using simplified linguistic inputs and addressing a single alleged idiosyncrasy of language hardly qualifies as a refutation of Chomsky. Much more work needs to be done. Serious attempts to explain language skills by appeal to the mechanisms underlying other faculties are still in their infancy. Several decades of research within the Chomskyan tradition have produced impressive theories, but little resolution or consensus. Newer traditions, such as cognitive grammar and some connectionist theories, explore relations between language and other mental faculties. These approaches are still working with incomplete theories of cognition and a limited understanding of the actual neural systems involved in linguistic performance. Within time, domain-general theories may offer detailed explanations of a wide range of linguistic idiosyncrasies. Work by Ellefson and Christiansen (2000) and others shows that we must not draw a priori conclusions about which rules demand language-specific mechanisms.

The next observation used to support linguistic nativism appeals to the incompleteness of the data used in language acquisition, (8). Children use rules that outstrip the primary linguistic data. Some of these rules are not the simplest possible inductions from sentences that children observe. No general method of abductive inference from surface ordering could arrive at them. Chomsky (1975) gives the following example. Children hear declarative sentences such as "The man is tall," as well as interrogatives such as "Is the man tall?" Together, these sentences form evidence for a rule that specifies how to transform declaratives into interrogatives. But what rule is that? The simplest rule would say, Take the first "is" and move it to the front of the sentence. But this simple rule is wrong. It converts more complex sentences, such as "The man who is tall is in the room," into ungrammatical monstrosities, such as "Is the man who tall is in the room?" The correct rule for forming an interrogative is structure-sensitive. It has us move the "is" that follows the highest noun phrase in the phrase-structure tree for the sentence. Children get this rule right. They correctly form complex interrogatives even if they have only been exposed to simple interrogatives. They instinctively adopt the structure-sensitive rule instead of the simplest rule. Chomsky concludes that the child must be using innate, language-specific mechanisms.

This conclusion is hasty. The structure-insensitive rule may not be simpler than the other rule. Ostensibly, it looks simpler. Moving the first "is" seems to involve less work than moving the "is" after the highest noun phrase. Moving the "is" after the highest noun phrase also looks harder because one has to be able to identify noun phrases. But now look at the two sentences from a dumb statistical perspective. Consider the sentence "The man who is tall is in the room." If a child recognizes that one "is" must move to form an interrogative, moving the second "is" may appear simpler for statistical reasons. Suppose the child considers her options by considering small groups of words at a time and assessing the consequences of moving the "is." Removing the "is" from the phrase "man who is tall" leaves the statistically bizarre phrase "man who tall." Removing the "is" from "is in the room" leaves a perfectly familiar phrase, "in the room." Removing either "is" from the statistically uncommon "is tall is in" leaves an equally uncommon word string. Only the first case involves a net loss in statistical probability. Moving the first "is" would not be the ideal choice for a system that worked by repeating familiar patterns.

Nativists might retort by citing even more dramatic evidence of language learners going beyond the data. Pinker (1994) cites evidence that children can acquire grammars that have considerably more structure than those of the adults from which they learn. Of particular interests is a case study by Singleton and Newport (in press), in which a deaf child was found to acquire American Sign Language from parents whose signing abilities were quite imperfect. The child seemed to impose rules even where his parents obeyed none. Similar claims are made by Bickerton (1990) regarding the transition from pidgin languages to creoles. A pidgin is hybrid of several languages, improvised by people of different nationalities who wish to communicate. Pidgins often fail to obey systematic rules. Creoles are the languages that derive from these, and they obey systematic rules. Bickerton says that the children of pidgin speakers can spontaneously arrive at a creole in a single generation. Like the sign-language case study, this shows that learners can impose order on chaos, which is a serious embarrassment for statistical-learning theories.

Closer scrutiny allows friends of statistical learning to breath a sigh of relief. Singleton and Newport's study, it turns out, does not illustrate the emergence of rules ex nihilo. To the contrary, the deaf child whom they studied only arrived at a consistent rule in his sign language when his parents obeyed that rule a significant percentage of the time. In cases where the parents were insufficiently consistent, his signs too were generally inconsistent. This does not show that a child can impose structure where there is none; it only shows that a child can turn a moderate statistical regularity into a consistently applied rule.[5] We can derive a parallel moral from creolization. Pace Bickerton, there is evidence that creoles generally take a long time to emerge and that the rules they obey can be attributed to one of the language (or a compromise between languages) that contributed to the original pidgin (Mufwene 2001). Creoles siphon out the order hidden in disorder; they do not impose order where there was none.

None of this is intended to show that children never acquire structure-sensitive rules or never violate statistics. Statistical regularities may ultimately give rise to structure-sensitive rules. And once acquired, those rules can be enforced in cases where pure statistics would not suffice (as when we construct novel sentences). The point is that some accomplishments in language acquisition may appear to go beyond the data without actually doing so.

Now consider the dearth of negative data, (9). Children are rarely told when they make mistakes, and when they are told, they often fail to correct themselves. Gold (1967) develops a formal proof to show that negative data is necessary for arriving at correct rules. The space of possible grammars is too massive to select from without information about which grammars are wrong. Our ability to arrive at a single grammar without much negative data convinces many linguists that we are born with innate constraints on the space of possible grammars.

To my mind, Cowie (1999) has effectively addressed this argument, and I will only gesture at one of her replies. Cowie shows that language learners may have access to more negative data than we might think. One source of negative data can come from prediction. Suppose that children, like some recurrent connectionist networks, make predictions about what sentences or words they will hear while listening to adults. A failed prediction could be used as evidence that the rule underlying that prediction was wrong. If learners make predictions of this kind, they have a rich source of negative data without ever being corrected or responsive to correction. Cowie goes on to describe other sources of negative data, raising more than a reasonable doubt about the assumptions built into arguments from the Chomskyan tradition.

The final argument for nativism that I consider rests on the fact that other creatures have innate communication capacities, (10). If bees are innately wired to dance and birds are innately wired to sing, why not think that human beings are innately wired to bind and inflect words?

This is an argument for plausibility. As such, it is not that strong. Linguists will be the first to admit that human language abilities differ from other forms of communication in nature. Our languages are structurally much more complex, expressively much richer, and cross-culturally much more variable. If human language differs fundamentally from the communication systems of other creatures, the innateness of the latter offers little support for the innateness of the former. Also note that communication in other creatures is probably underwritten by modality-specific codes. Bees may represent nectar locations visually and represent dance instructions in their motor systems. Translation from nectar location to dance movements and back again can be achieved by intermodal transfer rules without amodal intervention. Our primitive communication systems using, e.g., gestures, cries, and facial expressions can also be explained by modality-specific codes. Evidence from the birds and the bees may show that these are innate, but that does not imperil empiricism.

Much more would need to be said to make this case against linguistic nativism stick. We are far away from having domain-general explanations of language acquisition. My goal here has been to show that arguments for linguistic nativism are not demonstrative. Linguists tend to view young children as miniature college students who learn by explicit instruction or conscious induction. Language cannot be learned thus on the evidence available, and so, linguists conclude, language must be innate. If it turns out that children are statistical learners who pick up subtle patterns by monitoring frequencies and making unconscious predictions, then all bets are off. We do not currently have a full understanding of what statistical learning mechanisms can achieve or what kinds of constraints they require in order to pick out the sound segments, phrase boundaries, grammatical categories, and rules that make up language. Connectionist models are beginning to reveal the wealth of information hidden in linguistic inputs, but this is just a start. Most connectionist networks can master only one limited task. The antinativist position assumes that language processing requires cognitive moonlighting. Ideally, we should first construct neurally plausible computational models of systems involved in motor sequencing, rapid auditory response, and working memory, and then use those models to process linguistic inputs. We may discover that these systems can discern rules in the seemingly impoverished data from which children learn. In the interim, concept empiricism is less imperiled by arguments for linguistic nativism than many have assumed.

8.2.2   The Infant University

Another attack on concept empiricism comes from psychology. As we saw in the discussion of the theory theory, recent psychological evidence has been used to support the contention that we are born with mini theories of basic ontological domains, such as psychology, mathematics, and biology. I will call mini theories of ontological domains "folk theories" to distinguish them from other mini theories also postulated by theory theorists. On the folk-theory view, the infant's mind is like a little university, divided into separate departments.[6] Each of these departments has its own subject matter, and its own general principles for making sense of that subject matter. Innate principles are often presumed to require innate concepts. Thus, the alleged innateness of folk theories, like linguistic innateness, presents a challenge for concept empiricists.

Consider an example. Spelke (1990) has argued that infants have a specialized set of principles composing a rudimentary domain of physical knowledge, a kind of folk mechanics. Infants are alleged to know facts like the following:

1. Objects move as connected wholes.
2. Objects move separately from one another.
3. Objects maintain their size and shape.
4. Objects act on each other only on contact.

These principles seem to contain a number of concepts, most obviously, the concept OBJECT. To show that such principles are innate, Spelke and her colleagues study infant preferences. The basic assumption is that if an infant mentally represents a particular physical principle, the infant will expect it to be obeyed by physical objects, and if it fails to be obeyed, the infant will exhibit behavior that shows surprise or interest. When infants experience events consistent with their physical expectations, they

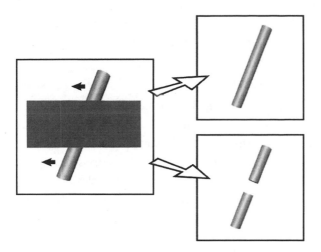

Figure 8.1
A bar moving behind an occluder with two test trials. Adapted from Kellman and Spelke 1983, figure 3, with permission from Academic Press.

will be less interested. Infants act surprised when principles (1) to (4) are violated.

A study by Kellman and Spelke (1983) can illustrate. They repeatedly show 4-month-old infants a display in which a bar moves back and forth behind another object, which occludes its central portion (figure 8.1). In accordance with principle 1, adults expect to see a connection between the two visible portions of the bar when the occluder is removed. If the occluder is removed to reveal two separate bars that happen to move in sync, adults are surprised. To test for these expectations in infants, Kellman and Spelke followed the occluder displays with one of two test trials. In the first, the occluder is removed to reveal a single bar; in the second, it is removed two reveal two separate bars. In the second condition, 4-month-old infants stare at the display significantly longer. Like adults, they assume that segments moving together constitute whole objects (though see Bogartz and Shinskey 1998).

Together with other experiments, this supports the conclusion that infants are in possession of an innate folk mechanics. The existence of such folk theories is often presumed to constitute a refutation of empiricism. This can be encapsulated in the following argument:

P1   If there are innate folk theories, there are innate concepts.

P2   If there are innate concepts, concept empiricism is false.

P3   There are innate folk theories.

C   Therefore, concept empiricism is false.

Each of these premises can be challenged. I consider them in turn.

One can defend P1 in two ways. First, one can argue that innate folk theories consist of innate principles, and innate principles consist of innate concepts. Second, one can say that innate folk theories simply are concepts. On this latter view, the set of mechanical principles governing physical knowledge actually constitutes the concept OBJECT (Xu and Carey 1996). In either case, the move from innate folk theories to innate concepts looks sound.

The soundness is illusory. By the criterion introduced earlier, something qualifies as a concept only if it can be controlled endogenously by the organism. To show that folk theories constitute or consist of concepts, one needs to show that this criterion is met. As far as I have seen, this has not been done. The experiments do not show that innate principles are encoded in a way that allows infants to freely deploy them off-line. For example, infants may be surprised to see that synchronized line segments are not connected, but there is no evidence that they can freely think about connectedness or objecthood. The Kellman and Spelke experiment does not even show evidence that infants can generate representations of line segments without seeing the right stimuli. Without evidence for endogenous control, experiments on infants cannot license the inference from innate folk theories to innate concepts.

P2 can also be rejected. Concept empiricists are welcome to endorse weak antinativism about concepts. This is sufficient to show that P2 is false. Proving that there are innate concepts would undermine strong antinativism about concepts, but it would not necessarily undermine weak antinativism.

In response to this complaint, a nativist might try to salvage P2 by revising it to say this:

P2′   If there are innate *nonperceptual* concepts, concept empiricism is false.

To preserve the validity of the argument, P1 would have to follow suit:

P1′ If there are innate folk theories, there are innate *nonperceptual* concepts.

I just argued that the evidence for innate folk theories fails to show that there are innate concepts, because it fails to show that innate folk theories can be endogenously controlled. Suppose that new evidence firmly establishes the endogenous control of innate folk theories, thereby establishing the existence of innate concepts. Alternatively, suppose that one comes to the same conclusion by producing arguments against the endogenous-control criterion. Should we conclude that the innate concepts forming our innate folk theories are nonperceptual? I think not.

The evidence for the existence of innate folk theories rests on infants' responses to perceived stimuli. Those responses are naturally interpreted as having a basis in perception. Infants expect to have certain kinds of experiences and are surprised when other experiences arise. There is no reason why the principles underlying such expectations could not be contained within perceptual input systems (see Haith 1999).

For example, the principle that causes infants to see two moving line segments as part of a whole may be built into the visual system. As we have seen, the visual system contains subsystems responsive to different visual features. MT processes motion information, and V3 processes shape. In both of these regions, adjacent cell populations have adjacent visual fields, corresponding to neighboring portions of perceived space. Perhaps MT obeys the following rule: when two nonadjacent receptive fields register motion along the same trajectory, a signal is sent to V3, which causes the cells between the nonadjacent shape detectors in that region to "fill in" the area that divides them. If this rule is obeyed, the initial display used in the Kellman and Spelke study causes MT to generate a representation of a unified shape in V3. This embodies something like the whole-object principle that Spelke attributes to infants, but it does so using perceptual representations. Other physical principles evidenced by infants' responses to perceived displays may also reflect rules built into infant perceptual systems. A resourceful empiricist may be able to provide this kind of explanation for all principles attributed to innate folk theories. Thus, even if one has some inclination to call such folk theories conceptual, there is reason to suspect that their constitutive concepts have a perceptual basis. This means that P1′ is untenable. Without P1′, P2′ is impotent. P2 is false without revision and potentially impotent when revised to be true.

Now consider P3. Theory theorists generally assume that at least some of our folk theories are innate. Keil (1989) is among many who have been explicit about this. He supports nativism about folk theories by contrasting nativist accounts with an alternative view associated with empiricism. According to this alternative, we begin life classifying by pure perceptual similarities and only acquire folk theories later on in development (Quine 1969). We encountered this view in chapter 4, which Keil calls "Original Sim." Keil argues against Original Sim by appeal to cross-category transformation studies. Preschoolers are not slaves to appearances. When asked to classify a toy bird that has been modified to have all the observable properties of a real bird, they still say that it is a toy. This is the same response that adults make, and it reflects an early appreciation of the distinction between natural kinds and artifacts.

The problem with Keil's argument is that basing a case for nativism on the responses of preschool children is risky. Cultural influences and language learning may be responsible for directing children to look beyond appearances. To really test for Original Sim, we should consider children who are much younger.

Children have been studied at the earliest stages of language development. Some of the findings support Original Sim. For example, Landau, Smith, and Jones (1988) found that early nominal concepts refer to shapes, rather than natural kinds. In contrast to Keil's preschoolers, younger children often overextend animal terms to include toy facsimiles of animals. Similar observations are made by Mervis (1987).

Critics reply that the overextension of animal concepts is open to an alternative explanation. As Soja, Carey, and Spelke (1991) argue, children may use animal terms for toys only because they recognize that those toys are *representations* of animals (see Gelman and Ebeling 1998 for some experimental support). Adults too do this when they talk of teddy bears and rubber ducks. Moreover, showing that children overextend animal concepts is consistent with the claim that folk theories are innate, as stated by P3. When young children insist that toy monkeys are really monkeys, this may reflect a bad theory rather than an absence of theory.

A more direct assessment of Original Sim comes from studies by Mandler and McDonough (1996), who also find the hypothesis wanting. They demonstrate that 14-month-old infants form superordinate categories, whose instances differ perceptually. Infants are shown an action involving either a toy car or a toy dog and then presented with a collection of other toy vehicles and animals. When shown a dog-related action, they imitate it using just the other animal toys, and when shown a car-related action, they imitate it using just the other vehicle toys. These superordinate groupings are difficult to explain by appeal to superficial similarities because the toys used in the experiment differ dramatically in shape. The animal toys included a rabbit, a fish, and a swan, and the vehicle toys included a truck, a motorcycle, and an airplane. Most strikingly, the swan toy closely resembled the airplane toy in shape. Had the infants relied on mere appearances, as Original Sim predicts, they should have coclassified these two objects.

Defenders of Original Sim can reply. Despite many superficial differences, disparate members of superordinate classes share clusters of observable features. Animals typically have eyes, nostrils, mouths, legs, asymmetric postures, curved contours, and textured surfaces. Vehicles typically have wheels, windows, doors, symmetrical "postures," straight-lines, and smooth surfaces. Not all instances have all of these features, but having a few might be sufficient for passing a membership threshold. These features are highly correlated in the toys presented to the infants, and they are bimodally distributed. In the swan and airplane case, gross shape similarities may be perceptually overridden by such equally salient differences. Swans have eyes, mouths, and textured surfaces, while airplanes have windows, doors, and straight lines.

The opponent of Original Sim might concede that infants use perceptual features in classifying superordinates (what else could they use?) while maintaining that theoretical biases determine which perceptual similarities matter for classification. On this view, the role of theories is not to transcend perceptual features but to indicate which features are

most significant. Calling such biases theoretical, however, is overly generous. One can have an innate bias to classify by straight and curvilinear contours without having an innate theory that curvilinear contours
demarcate natural kinds. It seems more likely that we have an innate
similarity space that succeeds in carving things up at many of nature's
joints, and that theoretical beliefs appear later to explain and refine these
divisions. This is exactly what Original Sim says, and nothing in the
Mandler and McDonough experiments contradict it.

Original Sim emerges unscathed from the Mandler and McDonough
studies, but it may be vulnerable to an a priori attack. Keil (1994)
objects,

There is no known route from association to domain-specific theories or belief
clusters that does not build in preexisting biases to construct certain classes of
theories over others; *and those biases cannot simply be perceptually driven.*

This can be taken as a challenge. Empiricists must show how folk theories emerge out of perceptually based categorization. If they cannot, the
claim that folk theories are innate (P3) will stand.

How do we acquire folk theories? This is among the most difficult
questions facing developmental psychologists. All developmentalists
admit that *some* folk theories are learned, but there is no consensus about
exactly how that happens. One view is that learned folk theories emerge
out of previously existing folk theories (Carey 1985). But how are those
previously existing folk theories acquired? The daunting task of explaining folk-theory acquisition makes the nativist position attractive, but I
am not convinced that sufficient effort has been made to develop nonnativist alternatives. I offer a few speculations. Even when undersup-
ported and underdescribed, such speculations are a useful strategy in the
early stages of a research program.

Any plausible story of development needs to postulate a considerable
innate endowment. In explaining folk-theory acquisition, I think the
requisite endowment includes various perceptual biases and perceptually
triggered behaviors that lead us to discover information about the world.
Rather than saying the mind is prepartitioned into theories, we can say
it is prepartitioned into senses, which are attracted to particular kinds
of stimuli. Stimuli contain considerable information, which infants can
encode through experience. The world is not a booming, buzzing con-

fusion; it is an orderly network of entities interacting in systematic ways (see Gibson 1979). Why pack lots of knowledge into the mind genetically when the world is there as a teacher? Of course, one needs to know where to look. Perceptual biases direct us to particularly useful patterns, and behavioral dispositions help us learn from those patterns by imitation and exploration. Let us consider how biases and dispositions can contribute to the formation of folk theories.

First consider folk mechanics. Infants are surprised by violations of the principles enumerated above. This surprise suggests sensitivity, at least perceptual sensitivity, to those principles. Should we conclude that they are innate? That might be hasty. Much of our physical knowledge may stem from an innate bias to pay attention to motion. Moving things are probably the most important stimuli in our early environment. They are sometimes protectors, sometimes predators, and sometimes parts of ourselves. More fundamentally, motion detection grounds our ability to identify three-dimensional shapes (Kellman 1984). It also teaches us how such shapes interact. With a natural interest in motion and an ability to detect object boundaries, we can learn which patterns of motion are likely and which patterns of motion co-occur with which shape patterns. Such observations may ground our early principles of mechanics.

Return to the occlusion example from Kellman and Spelke. Infants are surprised when an occluder is removed to reveal two objects moving together rather than a single object. There is little pressure to attribute innate knowledge in this case. In an infant's environment, two objects rarely move in synchrony. Infants can discover this by observation. Notice a great disanalogy with arguments for linguistic nativism. There is no poverty of the stimulus here. Physical regularities are there to be seen. In fact, one encounter with a physical law may be enough to set up a surprise reaction to its violations. Early evidence for physical principles is simply not proof of their innateness.

One concern about this argument is that some mechanical principles take a long time to learn. For example, Xu and Carey (1996) show that children do not initially expect objects to maintain their size and shape (principle 4). Instead, they track objects by spatiotemporal trajectories. Infants younger than 10 months are unsurprised when objects change form while moving along a path. One might use this as evidence against the view that mechanical principles are learned. If infants acquire information by observation rather than by using an innate principle, they should quickly observe that objects maintain size and shape.

To take another example, there is evidence that infants lack a full sense of the effects of gravity. For example, Spelke, Breinlinger, Macomber, and Jacobsen (1992) have shown that infants do not expect objects to fall when unsupported. In one experiment, 4-month-olds show no surprise when an object is dropped behind a screen, and then the screen is removed to reveal it suspended in midair. In similar experiments, Baillargeon and her colleagues have found that 4-month-olds often expect objects to fall, but they do not fully appreciate the kind of support necessary to prevent falling. Even at 5.5 months, infants do not expect an object to fall when it has been pushed to a position that hangs 70 percent off the edge of a supporting surface (Needham and Baillargeon 1993). Despite mastery of many principles, infants have not acquired certain principles that can be easily learned through observation. Perhaps they are not learning by observation after all.

These examples suffer from a similar flaw. Shape continuity and falling objects are frequently experienced by infants, but so are objects that change shape as they move and objects that do not fall when the lose support. Consider the first category. Most living things have transient shapes. As a person or pet walks across the room, its shape changes. This may lead infants to believe that shape changes are not violations of physical principles. Over time and further observation, they discover the more subtle fact that only some changes in shape are likely. In a similar spirit, Baillargeon, Katovsky, and Needham (1995) explain infants' odd predictions about gravity by appealing to the fact that infants observe many objects that appear to be suspended midair. For example, mobiles, lampshades, and even doorknobs appear to violate gravitational principles much as the experimental displays do.

Baillargeon et al. resist Spelke's claim that we are born with a list of innate principles governing our understanding of mechanics. Instead, they think we learn about different kinds of mechanical relations separately through observation. They point out that infants master different manifestations of the same phenomenon (e.g., object permanence under different kinds of occlusion conditions) at different times, which suggests that they are not applying general principles. If general principles are ever learned, they are probably inferred from their instances (a point anticipated by Locke). Baillargeon et al. do think there are significant innate constraints on perception and perhaps an innate understanding of causal forces (addressed in chapter 7), but they are skeptical about an innate folk mechanics.

Folk biology may also have its initial basis in our tendency to observe patterns of motion. Premack (1990) and Mandler (1992) point out that certain things tend to begin moving without anything making contact with them. Those very same things also tend to move along irregular trajectories. Things that move only when contacted are more likely to follow highly regular trajectories. Premack and Mandler argue that this difference in motion patterns can be used to ground early understanding of the distinction between animate and inanimate objects. Self-propelled, irregularly moving things tend to be animate, and contact-propelled, smoothly moving things tend to be inanimate. These motion profiles can be supplemented by the kinds of perceptual features mentioned in discussing Mandler and McDonough's work above. Irregular movement trajectories are observed to be correlated with curvilinear contours, facial features, and so on. This cluster of features provides a rich perceptual prototype for identifying living things.

Mandler (1992) questions whether motion-based conceptions of animacy should be regarded as perceptual. She notes that sensitivity to animate motion patterns involves a highly schematic level of representation that filters out many superficial features. This is not a good reason for denying that those representations are perceptual. In chapter 5, I argued that all representations within dedicated input systems are perceptual representations, and in chapter 6, I said that these included high-level representations that can abstract away from many details. In fact, one does not need to go to the highest levels of visual processing to find motion detectors that function independently of other features. Cells in MT have this profile, and evidence suggests that infants' earliest visual responses are more sensitive to motion than shape (Johnson 1993).

Gelman, Durgin, and Kaufman (1995) challenge the perceptual account by arguing that motion alone cannot ground the animate/

inanimate distinction. Beliefs about whether an object is animate often precede and determine whether a motion will be interpreted as animate. These prior beliefs involve assessments of whether an object has the right source of energy (internal versus external). This in turn depends on knowing whether an object is made of the right kind of stuff to initiate its own actions. Motions are interpreted within the conceptual scheme of animate versus inanimate sources of causal energy. Gelman et al. base their conclusions on findings such as the following: infants seem to interpret motion events causally; preschoolers can make judgments related to animacy based on still pictures of animallike versus machinelike objects; and adults find certain patterns of motion ambiguous and can provide both animate and inanimate construals.

The evidence presented by Gelman et al. (1995) suggests that we bring a rich array of information to bear in making animacy judgments, but this is consistent with the hypothesis that such decisions are perceptually based. I offered a perceptual explanation of the evidence that infants make causal attributions in chapter 7. The evidence that preschoolers can make animacy judgments based on still pictures shows only that perceivable shapes enter into animacy judgments (including perception of limbs, faces, curvilinear contours, and other features mentioned above). The evidence from adult reconstruals of ambiguous motion does not refute the claim that many motion patterns can reliably predict animacy. If motion patterns do a *reasonably* good job of dividing living from nonliving, we can use them to draw an initial division, which can form a basis for subsequent discoveries that make the division more precise. Premack (1990) views movement cues as a skeleton for building later knowledge. Such later knowledge presumably includes attributions of internal versus external energy sources, which may depend on an understanding of causation and folk psychology, discussed below. If causation and folk psychology are grounded in perception, then attributing internal energy sources does not contradict the view that notions of animacy have a perceptual basis. Our initial conception of animacy may be enriched by sensitivity to subtler perceptual cues.

Of course, folk biology involves much more than the ability to perceptually identify animate things. The hallmark of folk biology is a faith in hidden essences.[7] Children and adults recognize that the properties in virtue of which something belongs to a particular biological category do not always correlate with its appearances. Keil has shown that the tendency to transcend appearances appears in very young children. How do we arrive at that point if folk-biological categories are not innate?

From very early on, children can track things in different ways. They can track objects by their trajectories through space, by their shape, by their texture, or by the verbal labels used by people around them. Perceptual systems may be predisposed to track things by one feature or another. Objects that lack solid boundaries, for example, are easier to track by texture or color. But any observable feature provides a potential method of tracking. Children also come to discover that things have insides (and features such as heredity), which are not always observable. Children see broken dolls, sliced oranges, scraped knees, and open car hoods. They learn through experience that different kinds of things have different stuff inside of them. Studies by Simons and Keil (1995) show that this knowledge is initially quite imperfect. But knowing that insides exist and can differ from surface appearances is an important cognitive advance. Knowledge of insides, an ability to track things using different kinds of features, and an ability to distinguish living things from nonliving things constitute the raw materials for essentialism.

To take the next step, children must learn that living things should be tracked by their insides (or heredity) when appearances and insides diverge. Much of this may be learned through training and linguistic experience. As Keil's (1989) studies show, kindergarten-age children think superficial features are taxonomically significant when they make judgments about transformations within categories. Subsequent teaching and observation of language patterns is surely required for learning that things like inner organs and heredity are important for natural kinds, but not for artifacts.

A more puzzling question concerns preschooler's adultlike performance on transformations that cross over ontological categories. Why do preschoolers think that toy birds transformed to look real are still toys and not real birds? One deflationary possibility is that children simply have difficulty imaging a toy that behaves just like a real bird. Ontological categories may be organized around so many perceivable differences that successful simulation of cross-ontological transformations is difficult at a young age. If one compensated for preschoolers' limited imaginations by showing them a film of a real bird and telling them that it began as a toy, they might respond differently.

Another explanation of Keil's result is that preschoolers show the early stages of essentialist thinking. Assume that preschoolers have already figured out that insides are important to classification. Assume also that they attribute the same kinds of insides to members of a single ontological category. They do not differentiate horse blood and zebra blood. Thus, in making taxonomical decisions *within* ontological categories, they must go by appearances. Now assume that children of this age attribute different insides to different ontological categories. Animals, but not toys, have blood. Thus, in making taxonomical decisions across ontological categories, they can go by appearances or by insides. Assume finally that children of this age have been taught that insides overrule outsides when conflicts arise. Thus, in making taxonomical decisions across ontological categories, they go by insides. This explanation is consistent with Original Sim. Belief in the importance of insides can be attained without innate theories, and the belief that members of the same ontological category have the same kinds of insides may be perceptually based (e.g., the blood of different animals looks alike).

To see one final example of folk-theory acquisition, consider folk psychology. In its most basic form, this is embodied in our tendency to attribute mental states to other creatures and to explain their behavior on the basis of those attributions. The tendency is quite robust. We attribute mentality to all kinds of things, from people to animals and from teddy bears to microorganisms (see Dennett 1987). This tendency seems to be manifest at an early age and has been attributed to a specialized innate capacity. Other possibilities are available, however.

One thing to note is that there are perceptual explanations for how we decide what things are candidates for mental-state attribution. We rarely ascribe beliefs to chairs. For this we prefer things that move in irregular, self-propelled trajectories (e.g., dogs and paramecia) or things that resemble those things (e.g., teddy bears). We use our perceptual methods for detecting animacy. But how and why do we attribute mental states to animate things? Other animals can detect complex motions, but there is little reason to think that they chronically ascribe mentality.

Povinelli (1999) and his colleagues find no evidence for even the most rudimentary folk psychology in chimps. Chimps do not even seem to recognize that other creatures perceive through their eyes.[8] They display visual gestures in front of people (and other chimps) whose eyes have been covered. Povinelli concludes that chimps may lack the ability to ascribe mental states to others. Thus, a mere ability to detect animate objects, surely shared with chimps and other creatures, cannot be a sufficient precondition for folk psychology.

Another precondition may begin with the infant face bias. Johnson and Morton (1991) demonstrate that neonates have a natural interest in facelike stimuli. The bias is quite dumb in that it does not discriminate between real faces and highly simplified pictures, like smiley faces. But it is clever in the evolutionary sense. By looking at facelike configurations, infants generally end up looking at faces, and by looking at faces, they end up looking at conspecifics. Conspecifics are rich sources of information and vitally important for survival.

Infants do not just look at faces. As noted in chapter 5, they have a natural tendency to imitate them (Meltzoff and Moore 1983). Infants are prewired to contort their faces into the patterns they observe. This behavior engages another innate perceptual response. Facial expressions can produce emotional experience. When we smile, we feel happy; when we frown, we feel sad (Zajonc 1985). When imitating others, it is likely that infants experience what others are experiencing. We also have a natural disposition to following the gaze of conspecifics (Butterworth 1991). This allows us to attend to what others attend to. Shared attention plus emotional contagion adds up to feeling what others feel as we look at what they see. In other words, we feel how others are reacting to things in the environment. Harris (1992) and Gordon (1995) suggest that these dumb biases and behavioral dispositions play a role in developing the ability to think about other minds.

Emotional contagion and joint attention are not sufficient for attributing mental states, however. There is a gap in the inference from feeling what others are feeling to believing that others are feeling those things. It is certainly conceivable that there could be creatures with joint attention and emotional contagion, but no ability to attribute mental states. Chimps may be such creatures. What do we have that they lack? My hunch also owes to Gordon, Harris, and other advocates of simulation-based theories of mental state attribution (see, e.g., Gordon 1986, Goldman 1989, Harris 1989; see also Currie 1996). I think humans are more active and more controlled exploiters of off-line simulators than chimps.

Our increased brain size brings with it an increased ability to imagine nonactual situations and events. This probably begins in the first person. We imagine ourselves in nonactual situations. At some point, our ability to imagine nonactual situations is integrated with our shared-attention and emotional-contagion abilities. When we see what another is seeing and feel what another is feeling, we also simulate what it would be like to be in their position. Emotional contagion and shared attention may not be absolutely necessary for this transition, but they are likely to play an important instigating role. When we catch other people's emotions and track their gaze, we feel compelled to simulate the world from their perspective. Initially, that perspective may be conceptualized as little more than a location in space, but we come to see it as a locus of mentality because in simulating experience from that space, we experience our own mental states (including those we got by emotional contagion). Once we get in the habit of simulating other perspectives as loci of mentality, we come to perceive others as loci of mentality.

It may appear that there is still a leap here. How do we go from imagining things from another person's perspective to seeing another person as an experiencer? The answer is straightforward on a simulation view. Seeing others as experiencers *just is* imagining things from their perspective. Simulation is the fundamental form of attribution. Further refinements take place after this. For example, we come to recognize that others' perspectives can be unlike ours, we realize that others can harbor beliefs that we know to be false, and we come to master propositional-attitude talk. Readers can consult the literature on mental simulation for reasonable accounts of these transitions.

In sum, the difference between humans and apes may stem from a more general difference: an enhanced ability to simulate. Simulating the mental states of others is a demanding activity. It often requires imagining mental states that are not our own from a perspective that is not our own. In cases of false-belief attribution, we must add to this a simulation of a nonactual situation. Simulation depends on the mechanisms for retrieving and manipulating information in working memory. Working memory, we have seen, is a faculty associated with the frontal lobe, which is more advanced in our species. Bigger frontal lobes may have made us better simulators, and hence capable of acquiring a folk psychology.

This view would be supported if we could find evidence for *general* limits on simulation in the great apes. Povinelli has provided such evidence. Complementing his studies of ape folk psychology, he has tested apes' ability to reason about causal relations between physical objects (Povinelli 2000). Again, the results were dismal. This can be attributed to an impoverished ability to perform simulations. If chimps could imagine how objects will interact before picking them up and experimenting, they might be better at Povinelli's tasks. The evidence is consistent with the possibilities that there is a general difference in the simulation abilities of humans and apes. This would explain our relative success without requiring highly specialized innate theories.

The present proposal fits nicely with the brand of empiricism I have been defending. The acquisition and application of folk psychology is just a special case of our abilities to reactivate perceptual systems offline. In mental-state simulation, we use perceptual systems to experience emotions and images of situations that differ from our actual perspectives. This ability is instigated by dumb biases and general simulation skills. The view contrasts with those who postulate an innate theory of the mind (or even those who postulate innate simulation abilities specialized for attributing mental states to others).

Defenders of the nativist view often defend their case by pointing to autism. Autistics are often quite impaired in their ability to attribute mental states, especially false beliefs, to others. Leslie (1994) and Baron-Cohen (1995) have argued that autism involves a malfunction in an innate theory-of-mind module. If autism is a genetic disease that selectively impairs mental-state attribution, it provides evidence for the hypothesis that folk psychology has an innate basis. But there are other explanations. It is noteworthy that autism is not exhausted by impairments in mental-state attribution. People with autism exhibit broad difficulties in socially relating to others, a lack of pretend play, executive-function limitations, repetitive behavior, and various other symptoms. In addition, serious impairments in false-belief attribution are not found in all cases of autism. Given this broader picture of the disorder, it becomes less obvious that it should be so closely associated with a limited theory of mind (Currie 1996, Boucher 1996). Instead, autism may involve difficulties with executively controlled simulation, coupled with difficulties in attention sharing and emotional contagion. The former difficulties explain the behavioral inflexibility and lack of pretense. The latter difficulties explain the general lack of social responsiveness and the tendency to lack sophisticated skills in attributing mental states to others. On this interpretation, autism does not require that we postulate innate machinery dedicated to mental-state attribution.

Though highly speculative, all of my conjectures show that the case for innate folk theories is far from decisive. There are reasonable, if embryonic, explanations of how folk theories might emerge from general biases, abilities, and behavioral tendencies. Alternatively, an empiricist can concede that folk theories are innate, while arguing that they do not contain amodal concepts. The availability of these strategies shows that arguments for folk theories are harmless against concept empiricism.

8.2.3   Fodor's Mad-Dog Nativism

In chapter 4, I briefly discussed Fodor's (1975, 1981) argument for radical concept nativism, which is designed to show that empiricist theories of concepts are untenable. I revisit the argument here and consider how empiricists might respond. The issues that have emerged around Fodor's argument provide excellent evidence in favor of empiricism.

Fodor begins his case for nativism by distinguishing two kinds of concepts and two ways in which concepts can be attained. Complex concepts are decomposed into constituent features. They are acquired by forming and testing hypotheses using those constituent features. For example, BACHELOR may be acquired by forming and confirming the hypothesis that "bachelor" means UNMARRIED MALE. This form of acquisition is "epistemic" because it rests on the formation of beliefs and the search for evidence. Primitive concepts are not decomposable into constituent features, so they cannot be acquired by hypothesis formation. If RED is a primitive concept, the best one can do is to form the trivial hypothesis that "red" means RED. Because hypotheses must be formed using preexisting concepts, this shows that RED can only be *acquired* by hypothesis formation if it is already possessed. This is a contradiction. It shows that RED is not acquired at all. It is innate. This does not mean that all primitive concepts are available for use at birth. They must often be triggered. Triggering occurs when a stimulus in the environment causes an innate concept to become available for use. The triggering process is "brute-causal" rather than epistemic. Concepts attained through triggering are innate.

Fodor's story becomes radical when he argues that almost all lexical concepts are primitive, and hence innate. The argument can be reconstructed as follows:

P1 Any concept that is not decomposable is innate.

P2 Lexical concepts rarely decompose into defining features.

P3 Lexical concepts rarely decompose into nondefining features.

P4 A decomposable concept can only decompose into defining or nondefining features.

C Therefore, most lexical concepts are innate.

Premises P2 and P3 follow from Fodor's arguments against definitionism and prototype theory respectively. As we have seen, he thinks that good definitions are scarce and nondefinitions do not combine compositionally. I take issue with the second of these claims in chapter 11. Here I follow another line of attack. But first, I want to consider the conclusion. Fodor has been called a "mad dog" nativist, but I think his claim that concepts are innate is more innocuous than it appears.

While it is fairly easy to swallow the claim that some basic sensory concepts are innate, it is seems wildly implausible that concepts such as WALRUS, CHRISTIANITY, SPATULA, and NEUTRINO are innate. If prevailing theories of evolution are true, innate representational resources must be either selected for or generated as an accidental by-product of things that were selected for. A concept like SPATULA could not have been selected for, because it would have conferred no survival advantage in the environments in which humans evolved. And it seems equally implausible to say that such concepts are mere accidents of evolution. How odd it would be if nature accidentally equipped us with innate concepts for every artifact and natural property that we are capable of inventing or discovering.

Fodor (1975, 1981) is undaunted. He claims that WALRUS, CHRIS-TIANITY, SPATULA, and NEUTRINO are all innate (see also Piattelli-Palmarini 1986 and Chomsky 1992). Many of Fodor's readers are utterly unconvinced. They regard his nativism as a reductio on atomism (see, e.g., P. S. Churchland 1986). If atomism entails radical nativism, it must be false.

On closer analysis, Fodor's radical nativism may really be a radical form of empiricism. To arrive at this reversal, consider why radical nativism seems so bizarre. I suspect that this intuition rests on a certain understanding of what the nativist is committed to. First, it would be very bizarre to suppose that our prehistoric ancestors knew what spatulas are. If having an innate concept involves knowing what something is, then there is every reason to think that such concepts are not innate. For Fodor, this is not a serious worry because he does not give a knowledge-based theory of concept possession. Having a SPATULA concept is not a matter of knowing what spatulas are; it is having an internal symbol that is under the nomological control of spatulas. Innate concepts do not entail innate knowledge.

A second source of the bizarreness intuition does raise questions for Fodor. Even if SPATULA is unstructured, one might wonder how evolution could have endowed us with some *particular* mental symbol that is predestined to track spatulas.[9] If evolution set aside some symbol for this purpose, it would have had to anticipate the invention of spatulas. Fodor has a way out here as well. If concepts are individuated by the properties that nomologically control them, then to say that I have an innate SPATULA concept is not to say that I have some *particular* mental symbol in my head at birth, much less that all people possess inner symbols of the same (syntactic) type. It is only to say that I am disposed to enlist *some symbol or other* to serve as a spatula indicator. In other words, we are not born with spatula symbols; we are born with spatula-detecting abilities, and those abilities generate spatula symbols when they are applied. Evolution does not need to anticipate the invention of spatulas; it just needs to endow us with general-purpose detection and tracking abilities. With such abilities, we come to track spatulas, walruses, and neutrinos.

This makes radical nativism seem decidedly nonradical. The most die-hard empiricist could hardly disagree with this view. Surely, we have faculties that are capable of reliably detecting spatulas. A truly radical position would claim that we have innate knowledge of what spatulas are, or innate symbols predestined for spatula tracking. These claims would fly in the face of evolution because spatulas where not around to exert selection pressures on the human genome. But Fodor's claim is just that we are born with the ability to use some mental entity, any mental entity, to indicate spatulas. This makes the conclusion to his argument harmless. If this is what Fodor's means by claiming that concepts are "innate," he will not make enemies with empiricists. On the other hand, it also shows that the conclusion to Fodor's argument must be spurious because this notion of "innateness" is not really innateness at all. Fodor's argument for nativism is undermined by his theory of concepts.

Fodor's most recent contribution to the innateness debate supports this reading (Fodor 1998, chap. 6). He now says that lexical concepts may not be innate after all. But if Fodor revokes nativism, then one of the premises in his original argument must be false. He still supports P2 and P3, and P4 is close to a logical truth. The weak link in the argument is P1. Fodor now admits that it is an error to infer innateness from primitiveness. Conceptual primitives, construed as reliable indicators, can be acquired by coming under the nomological control of the properties they represent. They do not need to be regarded as innate. On this redressing of Fodor's position, we can generate novel primitives by simply generating new symbols and coordinating them with the environment in the right way. For example, we can generate an atomic symbol and associate it with the kind of experiences we have when we see spatulas. Such experiences will cause that symbol to be tokened whenever we encounter a spatula. The symbol thereby becomes a SPATULA concept. SPATULA is primitive because it is identified with an atomic symbol, but it is not innate, because that symbol was recruited through experience and was not predestined to track spatulas.

Fodor can get around nativism in this way, but he thinks that this account of concept acquisition still faces a serious problem. It fails to explain why the concept SPATULA is acquired by means of experiences of spatulas as opposed to any number of other things, such as walruses or neutrinos. On Fodor's account, something is a SPATULA concept in virtue of being under the nomological control of spatulas. Why is it that we generate such a concept as a result of spatula experiences? Isn't it equally possible that we might acquire such a concept as a result of other kinds of experiences or by being whacked on the head?

This puzzle also threatens those who, like the earlier Fodor, think that primitive concepts are innate. Innate concepts are said to be triggered by experience, but the experiences that trigger them are not arbitrary. If you think that SPATULA is innate, you presumably think that it is triggered by spatula experiences rather than walrus experiences. Why is this so? Radical nativists and radical empiricists are both stuck with a conundrum regarding the acquisition of primitives. Fodor calls this the doorknob/ DOORKNOB problem because he uses doorknobs as his pet example rather than spatulas. (Spatulas are a cleaner example because, as Fodor notes, DOORKNOB can plausibly be decomposed into DOOR and KNOB.)

Fodor solves the doorknob/DOORKNOB problem by making a radical ontological move. He says that being a spatula (or a doorknob), like being red or being tasty, is a mind-dependent property. More specifically, being a spatula is the property that one forms the concept of as a result of experiencing typical instances. Roughly, spatulahood is the property of causing the SPATULA concept to form. If this hypothesis is correct, then the fact that experiences of spatulas cause one to acquire the SPATULA concept is no longer mysterious. They do so because doing so is meta-physically constitutive of being a spatula.

Fodor's proposal should be rejected. One problem is that Fodor provides no independent grounds for claiming that spatulas are mind-dependent. Properties like RED are presumed to be mind-dependent because it is difficult to find anything that red things have in common other than the kinds of experiences they cause us to have. In contrast, there seems to be room for reasonable proposals about what mind-independent properties constitute spatulas, to wit, their physical and functional properties. More specifically, something is a spatula just in case it has a handle and a long flat blade used for flipping or removing objects from a hot surface. One might insist that spatulas are mind-dependent in one sense: they must be *intended* for serving the functions just described. But this is a different kind of mind-dependence than Fodor invokes. Fodor's notion of mind-dependence is completely ad hoc.

Another problem is that Fodor's proposal about the metaphysical identity of spatulas includes some nonspatulas. While it might be true that experiences of typical spatulas cause one to form the SPATULA concept, typical spatula descriptions and spatula drawings would do the same. Yet these things are not spatulas.

Fodor's account of spatulahood may also exclude some spatulas. Fodor says that spatulahood is that property that we form concepts of after experiencing *typical instances*. He has to say this because very atypical spatulas do not give rise to concepts that track spatulahood in general. Experiences of typical spatulas are more likely to make us into good spatula detectors. But there is a catch. Experiences with typical spatulas do not make us good at detecting atypical spatulas.

Suppose that only typical spatulas cause me to token my SPATULA concept. In virtue of what does my SPATULA concept refer to all spatulas and not just to the property of being a typical spatula? The standard answer on an informational-semantic theory goes like this. If only typical Xs cause a concept to be tokened, then that concept will still refer to atypical Xs because, after all, atypical Xs are Xs. In other words, metaphysics picks up the slack for our limited discriminative abilities. I may only be able to recognize a good X, but in so doing, I end up with a concept that can refer to any X. Now apply this to the spatula case. If only typical spatulas cause my SPATULA tokens, then my SPATULA concept will still refer to atypical spatulas because atypical spatulas are spatulas. For this proposal to work, there must be some property, spatulahood, that typical and atypical spatulas share. For Fodor, spatulahood is the property of being something whose typical instances cause one to form the SPATULA concept. To say that atypical spatulas have this property *presupposes* that atypical spatulas belong to the same class as typical spatulas. But this cannot be presupposed. A good definition of spatulahood must explain why all spatulas belong to a common class; it cannot presuppose it. One needs an independent measure for saying that typical and atypical spatulas go together. Such a measure exists. All spatulas are unified by a common functional essence (flipping and removing, etc.). This definition allows us to say that our SPATULA concepts refer to typical and atypical spatulas even if they are reliably tokened only as a result of encounters with the former. Fodor's definition cannot make such a guarantee.

In sum, Fodor's metaphysical solution to the doorknob/DOORKNOB problem cannot be accepted. At first blush, this bodes well for those who adopt an alternative response to his original argument for nativism. The doorknob/DOORKNOB problem arose with the rejection of P1. But one might escape nativism by denying P2 or P3 instead, i.e., by endorsing the view that many of our lexical concepts are structured. As Fodor points out, the link between SPATULA acquisition and spatula experiences can be explained if SPATULA is a complex concept. The fact that SPATULA is acquired by experiencing spatulas, on this view, is a consequence of the fact that the SPATULA concept consists of hypotheses describing what it is to be a spatula, and experiences of spatulas count as evidence supporting such hypotheses. Structured concepts do not face the doorknob/DOORKNOB problem.

There is a remaining difficulty, however. As Fodor reminds us, proponents of structured concepts are committed to the existence of some primitive concepts. Decomposition must eventually bottom out. Once one gets to the level of primitive concepts, the doorknob/DOORKNOB problem rears its head again. The doorknob/DOORKNOB problem is everyone's problem because everyone must admit that some concepts are primitive, and primitive concepts, like all other concepts, are often attained by experiencing the objects that they designate.

To find an adequate solution to the doorknob/DOORKNOB problem, one must first resolve an ambiguity in its formulation. When an object causes one to attain a concept, there are three elements in the causal chain: the object, one's experience of the object, and the resultant concept. When Fodor says that is unclear why primitive concepts are attained by experiencing the objects they designate, he could mean one of two things. He means either that it is unclear why certain objects cause certain experiences or that it is unclear why certain experiences cause certain concepts. The first interpretation could not be right. The fact that objects cause experiences (i.e., perceptual states) of the kind they do has to do with how we are wired. It is a problem for psychophysics, not philosophy, to explain. The philosophical doorknob/DOORKNOB problem involves the relationship between experiences and concepts.

Formulated thus, the doorknob/DOORKNOB problem can be readily solved by concept empiricists. Empiricists identify primitive concepts with perceptual representations. For example, they identify the RED concept with stored copies of the perceptual representations that one has when one sees red things. If RED is just a stored red experience, then there is no mystery in the fact that it is acquired by having such an experience. It could not be acquired without having a red experience.[10] Similarly, if a DOORKNOB concept is just a stored copy of an experience of a doorknob, then it follows quite trivially that it is acquired by having such an experience.

Fodor cannot explain why certain experiential states cause certain concepts to be attained because he construes concepts as arbitrarily related to experiences. If concepts are copies of experiential states, the arbitrariness disappears and with it the problem.

This constitutes a third route from Fodor's views about concepts to concept empiricism. The first route uses his theory of intentionality to argue that concepts are built up from perceptual representations (chapter 5); the second route rests on the argument that his mad-dog nativism may be interpreted as a radical empiricist thesis; the final route goes from his doorknob/DOORKNOB problem to the conclusion that primitives are perceptual. Fodor's views reveal a surprising kinship with Locke's views. Mad dogs and Englishmen have much in common.

8.3 Conclusion

There is a dogma in cognitive science according to which the mind is innately equipped with numerous nonperceptual concepts. This dogma has many researchers convinced that empiricism is completely untenable. In this chapter I consider several of the most influential arguments for concept nativism and find that none of them are fully convincing. Some of these arguments even lend support to the view that concepts have a perceptual basis. I conclude that the acquisition desideratum can be met without postulating conceptual resources beyond those available to the concept empiricist.

9

Intentional Content

On the view I am defending, concepts are proxytypes. Proxytypes are perceptually derived representations used in category detection. Detection is a process involving a nomological causal relation between a detector and something detected. Such nomological relations underlie the informational atomists account of intentionality, but unlike atomism, proxytype theory identifies concepts with structured detection mechanisms, not with atomic indicators. By combining structure with informational semantics, proxytype theory hopes to achieve the best of both worlds: structure can explain such things as categorization, while nomological relations explain intentionality. But this happy merger still requires elucidation and defense. It remains to be seen exactly how a structured theory of concepts can be coordinated with informational semantics. It also remains to be demonstrated that informational semantics provides an adequate account of intentionality. I address these issues here and argue that a supplemented informational approach can adequately accommodate the intentional-content desideratum.

9.1 Philosophical Theories of Intentionality

Philosophers have developed a number of theories of intentionality over the years. Several of these are discussed in previous chapters. In addition to informational theories (associated with atomists), we encountered resemblance theories (associated with imagists), satisfactional theories (associated with definitionists), and etiological theories (mentioned in chapters 1 and 7).[1] I review objections to these latter three theories in this section.

The resemblance theory of intentionality says that a representation refers to whatever it resembles. As we have seen, this account cannot explain how concepts refer. If a DOG concept is a dog image, it resembles dogs, but it also resembles wolves and well-disguised cats. So resemblance cannot be sufficient. Nor can it be necessary, for it is unclear how an image could resemble truth or virtue. If we have concepts that refer to these things, they do not refer by resemblance.

Satisfactional theories (also called descriptivist theories) do somewhat better. Satisfying a set of defining conditions would be both necessary and sufficient for reference. But we have seen that satisfactional theorists often provide no account of how the satisfaction relation is achieved. Suppose that VIXEN refers to anything that satisfies FEMALE and FOX. Now we must ask how something satisfies the FOX concept? Why does FOX refer to foxes and only foxes? This is exactly what a theory of intentionality should explain. Satisfactional theories merely label the problem.

This complaint can be answered by supplementing the satisfactional theory with some other theory, such as informational semantics. Suppose we say that primitive concepts refer in virtue of reliably detecting their referents, and that complex concepts refer to whatever falls under all of their primitive components. For example, if FEMALE and FOX are primitive concepts and can be used to reliably detect females and foxes respectively, then VIXEN refers to the intersection of the set of females and the set of foxes. This proposal faces a dilemma. If concepts were built out of defining features, then the proposal could work, but hardly any concepts are built up out of defining conditions. If concepts were built out of nondefining features, the proposal could not work, because it would assign the wrong referents to our concepts. For example, if VIXEN decomposes into the features SMALL, ORANGE-FURRED, and QUADRUPED, then the proposed theory of reference would entail that it refers to all small, orange-furred quadrupeds. These would include Pomeranians, male foxes, certain cats, and cleverly painted raccoons. The same complaint is at the heart of Kripke's (1980) and Putnam's (1975) critiques of satisfactional theories. They argue that we manage to successfully refer to categories even when we do not know conditions that single them out.

Resemblance theories and satisfactional theories are associated with traditional philosophical approaches to concepts. They dominated philosophy until quite recently. During this period, dissenting voices periodically suggested that intentionality is mediated by some kind of causal relation (e.g., Locke 1690, Ogden and Richards 1923, and Russell 1921). Causal theories became truly popular when the etiological theory appeared on the scene (Donnellan 1972, Putnam 1975, Kripke 1980, Devitt 1981).

The etiological theory claims that reference depends on the causal history of a representation. A representation, e.g., a word or a concept, begins its career with an initial "baptism," in which it is introduced in the presence of a member of the category to which it refers. On future occasions, the representations will refer to the category of the thing tracing back by a causal chain to that original baptism. For example, if a representation is introduced when a wildebeest is presented, future tokens of that representation will refer to wildebeests.

The etiological theory offers a remedy for the problems of satisfactional theories. Even though I lack a wildebeest definition, I can refer to wildebeests because I have a concept whose history traces back to a wildebeest baptism. Baptisms can be achieved by linguistic or nonlinguistic means. Suppose that I learned the word "wildebeest" from other people, who learned the word from still other people, tracing all the way back to the person who initially coined the word while staring at a wildebeest. When I use this borrowed word, it refers to wildebeests, even if I have never actually seen one myself. Alternatively, suppose that I have never heard the word "wildebeest" but happen to see one while traveling through the Serengeti. If I form a mental representation as a result of this encounter, I can use it to refer to wildebeests on future occasions. In both cases, wildebeest reference is achieved without knowing defining conditions.

The etiological theory faces some serious objections. First, there is a concern that having a causal chain tracing back to a baptism is not necessary for reference. This is most obvious in the case of concepts of fictional or nonexisting things. We have concepts of phlogiston, unicorns, fairies, ghosts, and gods, even though none of those things exist. If these concepts refer, as intuitions suggest, it cannot be in virtue of some initial baptism. A more fanciful case is developed by Davidson (1987). He has us imagine the bizarre possibility that a lightning bolt in a swamp might spontaneously create a creature indistinguishable inside and out from an adult human being. By freak coincidence, this Swampman might be a molecular duplicate of Davidson himself. But there is an important difference. Davidson's concepts and words causally trace back to initial baptismal encounters with the objects they designate. The Swampman has no causal history, so his words and concepts do not trace back at all. If initial baptisms were necessary for contentful mental states, Swampman's entire mental life would be vacuous. This is odd because, like Davidson and the rest of us, Swampman takes himself to have thoughts that refer to the world. His mental states seem just like ours from the inside but, on the etiological theory, they represent nothing.

There are also reasons for worrying that having an etiological link to an initial baptism cannot pick out a single category. Any particular object falls under many different categories. For example, if I form a concept as a result of encountering a wildebeest, that wildebeest is also an animal, a brindled gnu (which is a subspecies of wildebeest), and a thing that lions eat. Which of these many categories does my concept designate? Devitt (1981) calls this the "qua problem." Similarly, any object that causes me to form a concept is part of a complex causal chain. The wildebeest that causes me to form a concept also causes a retinal image, activity in my optic nerve, and patterns of activity in my occipital cortex. Which of these things does my concept designate? Call this the *chain problem.*

A related worry stems from the fact that we have different sorts of concepts, designating different kinds of things. We have concepts that refer to individual objects, concepts that refer to whole kinds, and concepts that refer to appearances. Does the concept I form when I encounter a wildebeest refer to that particular wildebeest, to wildebeests in general, or to wildebeest appearances? Putnam (1975), in developing his etiological theory of intentionality, presumes that this problem can be avoided by saying that concepts contain "semantic markers," which indicate what sorts of concepts they are. A concept designating a natural kind just has a "natural kind" marker. Putnam's strategy seems right, but his solution only draws attention to the problem. What exactly are semantic markers? Are they merely further symbols in the head? If so, how do they make different concepts refer in different ways? Put differently, if our goal is to explain how concepts refer in naturalistic (i.e., nonsemantic) terms, merely saying that concepts are "marked" in different ways does not get us very far. Call this the *semantic-marker problem*.

A number of these problems can be solved if one adopts an informational theory of intentionality.

9.2   Informational Semantics

9.2.1   Advantages

Cummins (1989) credits Locke with holding the view that concepts refer to extramental objects by causally covarying with those objects. There is support for this interpretation. For example, Locke says there is a "steady correspondence" between concepts and their referents, and he says that concepts are "constantly produced" by their referents (e.g., 1690, II.xxx.2).

Locke's causal covariation approach anticipates contemporary informational theories of intentionality (e.g., Stampe 1979, Dretske 1981, Fodor 1990).[2] Informational theories echo Locke in saying that the content of a concept is what steadily causes the concept to be tokened. More accurately, informationalists say that concepts refer to the things that *would* reliably cause them to be tokened. This is often put by saying that causal covariance is a lawlike or counterfactual-supporting relation. For that reason, it is better to talk of "nomological covariance" than "causal covariance."

One can give the following definition:

NC   Xs *nomologically covary* with concept C when, ceteris paribus, Xs cause tokens of C in all proximate possible worlds where one possesses that concept.

If concepts refer to their nomological causes, then one can escape the Swampman objection that faces etiological theories (Fodor 1994). On an etiological account, there must be an actual causal connection between the concept and the things to which it refers. Swampman lacks a causal history, so etiologists must say his concepts do not refer. Informationalists can say that Swampman's concepts do refer. There are things that cause his concepts to be tokened in nearby possible worlds even though they never have caused his concepts to be tokened in the actual world. The potential is enough.

Nomological covariance can also help with the qua problem. Suppose that I form the concept W by encountering a wildebeest. Suppose that W is reliably caused by wildebeests but not by, say, dogs and turtles. Why does W refer to wildebeests and not the entire class of animals or the more specific class of brindled gnus? W does not refer to the entire class of animals because animals do not cause it to be tokened in proximate worlds where there are no wildebeests. It does not refer to brindled gnus because, while these do cause tokens of W in all proximate worlds, so do members of the other wildebeest subspecies. Since the class of wildebeests is constituted by all its subspecies, the fact that they all nomologically cause W tokens supports the claim that W refers to wildebeests and not any single subspecies. Or to put it differently, it refers to all the subspecies.

Nomological covariance also helps with the chain problem. Retinal images of the kind I had when I first saw a wildebeest do not cause tokens of W in all nearby worlds. In particular, they do not cause tokens of W in worlds where wildebeests look different than they do in the actual world. Had I been in such a world, my wildebeest encounter would have caused a different retinal image. Yet wildebeests still cause tokens of W in such worlds, and hence W refers to wildebeests in such worlds.

Advocates of informational semantics have said less about what I call the semantic-marker problem because they have focused almost exclusively on natural-kind concepts. Nevertheless, I think their approach can be helpful in solving this problem. One way to distinguish different sorts of concepts is to distinguish different ways in which concepts and objects can be nomologically related. Above, I distinguish concepts of kinds, and concepts of appearances, and concepts of individuals. Consider the following proposals for how these can be identified informationally:

C is a *kind concept* if Xs nomologically cause tokens of C and had Xs looked different than they do, they would still cause tokens of C.

C is an *appearance concept* if Xs nomologically cause tokens of C and had Xs always looked different than they do, they would not cause tokens of C.

C is an *individual concept* if Xs nomologically cause tokens of C and if an X were presented with an object that appears exactly like X, at most one of those objects would cause tokens of C.

The first two definitions are supposed to capture the idea that kind concepts track kinds, regardless of what they look like, whereas appearance concepts track appearances. Both sorts of concepts refer in virtue of nomological connections and, as I argued in chapter 5, nomological connections are mediated by the senses. Kind concepts differ from appearance concepts only in that the sensory states that matter vary across worlds.

The definition of individual concepts is designed to capture the idea that we take individuals to be unique. Again, nomological connections depend on sensory states, but we would not apply the same individual concept to two objects simultaneously, even if they produced the same sensory states in us. Instead, we might form the disjunctive thought that one or the other of those two objects falls under that concept.

Such proposals can be fine-tuned, but they serve to illustrate how nomological relations can be used in conceptual taxonomy. In this respect, informational theories have another significant advantage over etiological theories. In what follows, I focus on kind concepts and show that, despite these advantages, informational theories face a serious objection.

9.2.2   The Disjunction Problem

The central objection to informational theories can be stated succinctly: if a concept refers to whatever has the power cause it, then there can be no error. Consider my BUSH PIG concept. It is tokened as a result of my perceptual encounters with bush pigs. Bush pigs are the "rightful causes" of BUSH PIG tokens. But this concept also has a number of illicit causes. For example, although I can usually distinguish warthogs (figure 9.1b) from bush pigs (figure 9.1a) by their girth, I almost always mistake *pregnant* warthogs for bush pigs. Pregnant warthogs reliably cause my BUSH PIG concept to be tokened. Tokens of my BUSH PIG concept are also caused by encounters with wild boars because, even under optimal conditions, bush pigs and wild boars (figure 9.1c) look indistinguishable to me. In addition, tokens of my BUSH PIG concept would certainly be

Figure 9.1
(a) A bush pig. (b) A warthog. (c) A wild boar.

caused by twin bush pigs, a species on Twin Earth whose members look exactly like bush pigs but have different micro properties. If concepts refer to anything that would cause them to be tokened, then my BUSH PIG concept refers to bush pigs, pregnant warthogs, wild boars, and twin bush pigs. When I form the thought that an animal falls under my concept BUSH PIG, I am really forming the thought that it is *either* a bush pig *or* a pregnant warthog *or* a wild boar *or* a twin bush pig.

Fodor (1984) calls this "the disjunction problem." It is an embarrassment for the Lockean program because covariance was supposed to give us an account of how concepts attain their intentional contents, and intentional contents are not supposed to be wildly disjunctive. The intentional content of my BUSH PIG concept is supposed to be the class of bush pigs.

The disjunction problem has given rise to a small industry. Philosophers attracted to informational theories try to devise ways to delimit the contents of our concepts. I cannot give a systematic review of these attempts here. I limit my discussion to a look at Fodor's (1990) solution and, more briefly, Dretske's (1981) solution.

The most striking feature of Fodor's solution is its complexity. Rather than treating the disjunction problem as a single entity, he divides it into separate problems and handles each one differently. These divisions correspond to the three kinds of illicit causes just mentioned. First, there are wild causes. These are things that cause a concept to be tokened in spite of the fact that they can easily be distinguished from the rightful causes of a concept under more optimal conditions. Pregnant warthogs fall into this category in the BUSH PIG example. Second, there are Twin Earth causes. Twin bush pigs and other nonactual creatures that would be indistinguishable from actual bush pigs fall into this category. Finally, there are Earth-bound twin causes. These are duplicates that exist here on Earth. I place wild boars in this category because I really cannot distinguish them from bush pigs. A less controversial Earth-bound-twin case would involve a hypothetical scenario in which both bush pigs and twin bush pigs inhabited the Earth.

Consider how Fodor handles these cases. His solution to the wild-cause problem involves the introduction of a restricting clause in his theory of content.

If Ys and Xs are two kinds of things that both cause tokens of some concept C, then Ys *asymmetrically depend* on Xs just in case

· if Xs did not cause C-tokens, Ys would not either, and

· if Ys did not cause C-tokens, Xs would still cause C-tokens.

More succinctly, Ys would not cause Cs were it not for the fact that Xs did, but not vice versa. Fodor says that concepts refer only to causes that are not asymmetrically dependent on other cases. This disqualifies pregnant warthogs because they would not cause tokens of BUSH PIG were it not for the fact that bush pigs did. Bush pigs, in contrast, do not asymmetrically depend on any other causes of the concept BUSH PIG.

The asymmetric-dependence condition also helps with another version of the wild-cause problem. When a pregnant warthog causes a token of my BUSH PIG concept, I am making an error; I mistake the warthog for a bush pig. But there may also be nonerroneous wild causes. For example, seeing a field guide to African mammals or having a conversation about ugly creatures may cause me to think of bush pigs by association. The causes are wild because I can easily distinguish them from bush pigs, but they are not errors, because I do not mistake them for bush pigs. Fodor calls a concept's property of referring to a single class despite the fact that umpteen things are prone to cause it "robustness." Asymmetric dependence can be used to explain this property. My BUSH PIG concept refers to bush pigs and not to African field guides, because the latter would not cause BUSH PIG tokenings if bush pigs did not.

There are problems with the asymmetric-dependence proposal. The first is that it does not handle Twin Earth cases or Earth-bound twin cases. One member of a pair of duplicates cannot depend asymmetrically on the other. The trouble is that duplicates are, ex hypothesi, indistinguishable, and it is not possible for one member of a pair of indistinguishable things to cause a concept to be tokened without the other doing so as well. If one stops causing a concept to be tokened, so will the other. Therefore, Fodor needs another story (in fact two other stories) to explain twin cases. I will come to these shortly.

The failure to handle twin cases is not a sufficient reason for rejecting the asymmetric-dependence proposal, provided those cases are handled in some other way. A more fundamental problem is that asymmetric dependence does not even seem to handle wild-cause cases successfully. The objection I have in mind is similar to an argument in Cummins 1989. In order to handle the pregnant-warthog example, the following two counterfactuals would have to be true:

(1)   If bush pigs did not cause tokens of my BUSH PIG concept, pregnant warthogs would not either.

(2)   If pregnant warthogs did not cause tokens of my BUSH PIG concept, bush pigs still would.

To evaluate (1), we must consider worlds in which its antecedent is true. Under what conditions would bush pigs fail to cause tokens of BUSH PIG? Two answers are most plausible. The antecedent of (1) would be true in worlds where

i. I lack a BUSH PIG concept or

ii. bush pigs have different appearances than they do in the actual world.

In other words, we can break the bush pig/BUSH PIG relation by altering my conceptual resources or by altering bush pigs. According to a standard policy, the truth of a counterfactual is assessed by seeing whether it is true in the *most proximate* world where its antecedent is true. To make the actual world conform to (i), we would have to change only the concepts I possess. To make the actual world conform to (ii), we would have to change bush-pig appearances. Intuitively, worlds of the first kind are closer. Presuming that I lack a BUSH PIG concept is less drastic than changing the appearance of bush pigs. If so, (1) is true. In worlds where I lack a BUSH PIG concept, pregnant warthogs could not possibly cause a token of that concept in me.[3]

This raises a problem for (2). To evaluate this counterfactual, we must consider proximate worlds in which its antecedent is true. Pregnant warthogs do not cause tokens of BUSH PIG in worlds where

i.   I lack a BUSH PIG concept or

iii. pregnant warthogs have different appearances than they do in the actual world.

By the same reasoning that I gave in my treatment of (i) and (ii), worlds in which (i) is true are closer than worlds in which (iii) is true. Changing a fact about my conceptual repertoire is less radical than changing the appearance of a class of animals. Consequently, (2) should be evaluated with respect to worlds in which (i) is true. In those worlds, bush pigs do not cause BUSH PIG tokens, because I have no BUSH PIG concept to be tokened. But this reasoning, which makes (1) come out true, makes (2) false.[4] In this case at least, Fodor cannot establish an asymmetric dependence between a wild cause and a rightful cause.

Now consider Fodor's solution to the problem of Twin Earth cases. Fodor (1990) recommends adding an etiological constraint to content determination.[5] In particular, he proposes that concepts can refer only to categories whose members have *actually caused* tokenings of those concepts. Thus, my BUSH PIG concept cannot refer to nonactual creatures on Twin Earth, even though its tokens would be caused by some of those creatures if they existed. The etiological constraint is successful in barring the imaginary creatures of Twin Earth.

The problem with this proposal is that it cannot handle Earth-bound twin cases. For variety, give bush pigs a rest and consider mimicry in nature. One can find genetically distinct species that appear indistinguishable because one has evolved to look like the other in order to fool predators. For example, viceroys mimic monarch butterflies. Imagine that I form a concept by observing a monarch, and after that, tokens of this concept are caused by encounters with other monarchs but also by encounters with viceroys. Intuitively, the fact that viceroys happen to cause this concept is irrelevant. It is a MONARCH concept because it was created to detect monarchs. Viceroys only cause it to token because they happen to be monarch mimics. Compare: if I create a bear trap that also happens to catch caribou, it is not a caribou-and-bear trap. According to Fodor's etiological constraint, a concept refers to any category whose instances have actually caused (and would reliably cause) it to be tokened. If my MONARCH concept is sometimes reliably caused by viceroys, Fodor is forced to say the concept refers to both monarchs and viceroys.

Fodor simply bites the bullet in such cases, claiming that concepts whose tokens are actually caused by members of indistinguishable kinds are disjunctive.[6] I think this is a hard bullet to bite. We take our natural-kind concepts to pick out unique natural kinds, not disjunctive sets of natural kinds. I believe that my MONARCH concept refers to one kind of butterfly even if I suspect that I am frequently duped by mimics. There are, of course, cases in which we take a concept to refer to a single kind, and it turns out to be disjunctive for one reason or another (to wit, jade). What is at issue here is not the possibility of concepts with disjunctive contents. The question is whether concepts *must* be disjunctive whenever we cannot distinguish two things that reliably cause their tokenings. As Fodor admits, an affirmative answer to this question is a concession to verificationism. It violates the antiverificationist intuition that we can refer to things even when we lack knowledge that would allow us to distinguish them from look-alikes. This intuition is intimately related to the conviction, discussed in chapter 4, that we can refer to categories without knowing their essences. Research by Keil and others suggests that this conviction is widely and deeply held. If we cannot refer to monarchs without also referring to viceroys, there is reason to think that our semantic convictions are deeply mistaken. That is an affront to common sense.

The problem with Fodor's concession to verificationism is even more apparent when we consider proper names. If a kind concept cannot pick out a single member of a pair of indistinguishable kinds, it is hard to see how a proper name could pick out a single member of a pair of identical twins. Likewise, if I dub some particular tennis ball "Hector" and cannot distinguish that ball from others, Fodor is forced to say that my HECTOR concept is disjunctive. This is not a consequence we should accept. If there is a way to escape this verificationism and render our essentialist intuitions true, then it should be seriously considered.

In summary, Fodor subdivides the disjunction problem into three separate problems—wild-cause cases, Twin Earth cases, and Earth-bound twin cases—and offers a different response to each of them. His response to the first is unsuccessful, his response to the second is limited in scope, and his response to the third makes unnecessary concessions to verificationism. Divide and conquer is not the best strategy here. I propose a single way of handling these three cases.

9.3   A Hybrid Theory

9.3.1   Incipient Causes

What we need is a way of explaining why the rightful causes of my concept tokenings are rightful. Dretske (1981) comes very close to giving an adequate answer. According to Dretske, there is a critical period when a concept is first acquired during which that concept is applied with special care. Those things that would cause the concept to be tokened during this period constitute its content. Later on, the concept is applied less carefully, and other kinds of objects cause it to be tokened. But these other objects do not thereby count as part of the concept's content, because they would not have caused it to be tokened during the learning period. Dretske would say that BUSH PIG tokens do not represent pregnant warthogs, because the latter would not have caused the former during the period in which my BUSH PIG concept was acquired.

This proposal cannot work as it stands. For one thing, it is well known that children overextend their concepts during learning. For example, tokens of young children's DUCK concepts are caused by real ducks, toy ducks, swans, and geese (Mervis 1987). Even if children did not, as a matter of fact, overextend their concepts, Dretske's proposal would not work. As Fodor (1984) argues, the *mere possibility* of one's DUCK concept being caused by something other than ducks during the learning period is fatal. The problem is that Dretske states his learning-period constraint subjunctively: things that *would* cause a concept to be tokened during the learning period get included in its content. Pregnant warthogs would cause my BUSH PIG concept during learning, so that concept turns out to be disjunctive. Dretske seems to concede this point when it comes to Earth-bound twins. He says that if there were both H_2O and XYZ on Earth, my water concept would refer to both even if I have only been exposed to one during the learning period (1981, 226).[7] This may also prevent him from handling wild-cause cases. Since my WATER concept *could* be triggered by gin samples during the learning period, Dretske may be committed to the conclusion that my WATER concept disjunctively refers to both water and gin.

Still, I think Dretske is on the right track. If we eliminate the subjunctive element from the learning period proposal, we can approach a more adequate theory of intentional content. In this vein, I propose that the intentional content of a concept is the class of things to which the object(s) that caused the original creation of that concept belong. Like Dretske's account, mine appeals to learning, but what matters here is the *actual* causal history of a concept. Content is identified with those things that *actually* caused the first tokenings of a concept (what I call the "incipient causes"), not what *would* have caused them.[8] If I form a concept as a result of a perceptual encounter with monarch butterflies, that concept refers to monarchs alone, even though it is also tokened when I see viceroys. Fodor or Dretske cannot accommodate this possibility.

Another attraction of the present account in comparison to Fodor's is that it handles all three of the disjunction problems in a uniform way. Wild causes, Twin Earth causes, and Earth-bound twin causes are all excluded because they are not the causes that led to the concepts being acquired. More succinctly, they are not incipient causes. Instead of handling these cases with the divide and conquer strategy that Fodor pursues, we can kill three birds with one stone.

I do not claim that the incipient cause condition is *sufficient* for determining intentional content. That would make my account purely etiological. I agree with Locke, Dretske, and Fodor in thinking that causal covariance plays an indispensable role in content determination. A pure etiological story would be vulnerable to the qua problem, the chain problem, and the semantic-marker problem. As we have seen, the appeal to nomological relations can solve these.

Nomological covariance delimits the set of potential intentional contents. It determines what sort of concept something is and the class of look-alikes to which it would respond. Etiology then steps in and selects from this delimited set. For example, nomological covariance determines that my MONARCH concept refers to monarchs and monarch mimics but not to butterflies or retinal images, and then etiology determines that my MONARCH concept refers to monarchs and not to their mimics, because a monarch was its incipient cause. Both factors are necessary for the determination of intentional content. This account can be summarized as follows:

X is the *intentional content* of C if

IC1 Xs nomologically covary with tokens of C and

IC2   an X was the incipient cause of C.

The first clause solves the qua and chain problems and can be embellished with further detail about the nature of the nomological relations involved to solve the semantic-marker problem. The second clause solves the disjunction problem. It satisfies antiverificationist intuitions by avoiding disjunctive contents in cases where we cannot distinguish distinct kinds that happen to look alike.

9.3.2   General Objections

The incipient cause constraint, (IC2), is what distinguishes my account from other causal-covariance accounts. Let me reiterate these differences. Unlike Dretske's learning-period constraint, the incipient-cause constraint is not subjunctive. Therefore, it disallows Earth-bound twins and wild causes from entering into the contents of a concept. The incipient-cause constraint also differs from the actual-cause constraint offered in the Fodor's (1990) theory. Incipient causes are a special subset of actual causes. They are the causes on the basis of which a concept is formed, not just any causes that happen to occur in the history of a concept. On my account, the incipient-cause constraint handles disjunction problems involving twins *and* Earth-bound twins *and* wild causes. For Fodor, wild clauses are handled by asymmetric dependence, twins are handled by etiology, and Earth-bound twins are not handled at all. Having stated these differences, I will take a quick look at a few of the objections that might be marshaled against my proposal.

First, my exposition of (IC2) implies that learning is an instantaneous affair: we acquire a concept on the basis of a single perceptual experience. In actual fact, learning seems to be a gradual process: concepts slowly emerge and evolve over time. To respond, I distinguish acquisition from learning. I think there is a point at which a concept comes into being, but that does not mean that our concepts do not change over time. Once a concept has been acquired, it can continually be modified. If we call this process learning, then we should say that learning is an ongoing affair. Our concepts can even be modified on the basis of objects that do not fall under them. When we incorrectly judge that some object falls under a previously acquired concept, we can use information about that object to modify our concept. In this sense, learning, but not acquisition, is compatible with misrepresentation.

Another objection is that we can acquire a concept without being exposed to one of its instances. For example, many of us learn natural-kind concepts such as TIGER or WOMBAT by seeing pictures or being told about them. In response, I point out that these cases of acquisition involve the use of representations whose meanings have been previously fixed by others. If I acquire my TIGER concept from a picture or a description, I rely on others to fix the meaning of my concept. In a word, concepts so acquired are deferential. The acquisition story outlined above does not subsume deferential concepts, but a similar principle can be recruited. As a first stab, the intentional content of a deferential concept is the intentional content of the representation(s) from which that concept was acquired. What matters for nondeferential concepts are their incipient causes, and what matters for deferential concepts is the content of their incipient causes. An emphasis on acquisition applies to both cases.

A third objection runs as follows. Suppose that I acquire a concept on the basis of experiences with Xs, and after that, I never apply it to Xs again, but only to Ys, which are superficially similar to Xs. The etiological constraint of my theory commits me to the claim that this concept refers to Xs and not Ys, despite the fact that I only apply it to Ys. To some ears, this sounds untenable.

As it stands, this case is underdescribed. The correct response depends on *why* the concept in question is never applied to Xs after it is learned. One possibility is that the concept is not applied to Xs because it is modified so that it no longer covaries with them. Perhaps it is (by my account, erroneously) applied to a Y after it is acquired, and is modified on the basis of that encounter. Subsequently, it covaries with Ys and not Xs. Here one can say that the concept we end up with is no longer the same concept originally acquired. In that case, the intentional content of the concept we end up with depends not on the instances that prompted the original concept, but on those that caused the original concept to be modified. This kind of modification differs from what I called "learning" in response to the last objection. When modifications result in different nomological relations, they count as transformations. Instances that result in such transformations count as incipient causes, but for a different concept.

An alternative embellishment of the case in question is that the original concept is never transformed. Instead, its failure to be applied to Xs is some kind of accident. After the concept is acquired, its bearer happens never to see an X again. But she does see lots of Ys, which happen to look like Xs, and these cause her X-derived concept to be tokened. In this case, I deny that the X-derived concept refers to Ys. Suppose that Sally's mother takes her to the zoo and shows her some alligators. As a result of that encounter she acquires a concept that would be reliably caused by further alligator encounters. But as it happens, she never sees an alligator again. What she does see are lots of crocodiles, and these reliably cause the alligator-derived concept to be tokened. I do not think that these tokenings qualify as correct applications of the concept. My intuition is that Sally is making some kind of mistake when she applies her alligator-derived concept to crocodiles.

This intuition can be bolstered by an analogy. Suppose that I create an implement for swatting flies, and though it continues to be perfectly capable of serving this function, I happen to never use it for that purpose. Instead, I use it as a paperweight. This does not mean that the implement is not a fly swatter. Nor does it mean that the implement is a paperweight. The correct characterization seems to be that the implement is a fly swatter that I use as a paperweight (also recall the bear-trap example). Origins count. Concepts are a bit like artifacts. They represent what they were originally intended to represent as long as they retain the potential to serve that function. I am assuming, of course, that we can naturalize the "original intentions" corresponding to our concepts in terms of their incipient causes. In some intuitive sense, a concept acquired as a result of encounters with Xs is *originally intended* to refer to Xs. The origins of a concept can fix its identity even when that concept is never applied to the objects on the basis of which it was acquired. An appeal to intuitions is not a demonstrative argument, but to the extent that such an intuition exists, it counterbalances the intuition underlying the objection I have been considering, and thereby defuses that objection.

Following a different course, one might object that the psychological essentialism underlying the etiological constraint is too strong. Do we really believe that our concepts pick out individual kinds? And if so, why does this belief have to be true? One way to raise these questions is to consider the case of jade. Science tells us that our JADE concepts refer to a pair of distinct substances, jadeite and nephrite. If such cases occur, why should we insist on a clause that tends to prohibit these kinds of disjunctive contents? The etiological constraint implies that natural-kind concepts pick out unique kinds even when those kinds have nonidentical look-alikes. The concept JADE seems to be a counterexample.

In responding to this objection, it is important to keep in mind that JADE is an unusual kind of case. KANGAROO does not refer to wallabies, and GOLD does not refer to fool's gold. It is also important to keep in mind that JADE is a deferential concept. We accept that it picks out two distinct substances only because we defer to experts who tell us so. Together these points suggest the following story. Suppose that science, like psychology, is predisposed toward the kind of essentialism underlying my theory of content. In particular, suppose that scientists make the following two assumptions. First, they assume that the kinds they investigate have unique underlying essences. The prevalence of this assumption is supported by the fact that JADE cases are not the norm. Second, scientists work under the assumption that the content of a concept is determined by its incipient causes. These two assumptions are generally compatible, but they can come into conflict in at least four ways. The first problem is metaphysical: the incipient causes of a concept might, on occasion, have no simple essential properties that they share with many other objects. The second problem is epistemological: it is often impossible to know what the incipient causes of our concepts were. The third problem is sociological: the concepts that different members of a community associate with a given public word might have been learned by exposure to distinct incipient causes. The final problem is semantic: a single individual can acquire a concept on the basis of encounters with distinct kinds. Each of these problems can make it difficult for scientists to settle on a unique essence. Therefore, even if they begin with the assumption that concepts pick out unique kinds, they are sometimes forced to say that a concept refers to a distinctive pair of kinds. It is plausible that JADE came to be disjunctive for these sorts of reasons. If so, the fact that JADE is disjunctive accords perfectly well with the theory of content I am proposing. Even if scientists assume that my theory is correct, JADE cases will arise because of the kinds of problems I described. In deferring to scientists who abide by the same semantic rules that determine the contents of our nondeferential concepts, we are condemned to end up with a concept like JADE now and then.

Another objection involves vacuous concepts (i.e., concepts that designate nonactual things), which have traditionally been a problem for etiological theories of reference. Concepts such as PEGASUS or UNICORN cannot be grounded in causal encounters with their referents because their referents do no exist. Some philosophers have argued that concepts such as FREE WILL are vacuous as well. If they do not refer to anything, then they refer to the same thing (i.e., nothing). If they refer to the same thing, how are we to distinguish them?

The answer is that we can appeal to their constituent structure. Perhaps PEGASUS is a proxytype representing something with a horse-shaped body and wings. UNICORN may be a proxytype representing a horse-shaped body with a single-horned head. Likewise for necessarily vacuous concepts. FREE WILL might decompose into a collection of inter-related words or a schematic perceptual representation of causal power not caused by anything else. These very different mental representations can be used to explain the sense in which vacuous concepts differ from one another.[9]

The appeal to conceptual structure can also help with Davidson's Swampman. As we saw earlier, etiological theories are committed to saying that Swampman's thoughts are contentless. They lack content because Swampman has no causal history; he is a spontaneous creation. But this seems odd because Swampman takes himself to have contentful thoughts, and his behaviors can be explained by content attribution. In endorsing an etiological condition on intentionality, my theory is burdened with this oddity.

Constituent structure helps here because many of Swampman's behaviors can be explained by the fact that he has internal representations like ours. For example, the fact that he calls cows "cows" can be explained by the fact that he has a cow-shape-detecting proxytype associated with a verbal representation that makes him produce the sound "cow."

Some may worry that this is insufficient. Swampman's mental states must also refer. Those with this intuition will be satisfied by a story I tell in the next chapter. To anticipate, I argue that concepts have a second way of referring in addition to the way described in this chapter. This way of referring connects concepts not to natural kinds but rather to something like appearance kinds: things that appear alike. Swampman's concepts have referents because they refer in this second sense.

Is this enough to satisfy our intuition that Swampman's thoughts refer? I believe so. There is no good reason to insist that Swampman's concepts pick out natural kinds. Our intuitions about him (to the extent that we have any) only require that he have a contentful mental life. One might try to argue that Swampman's contents must refer to natural kinds because he would adamantly deny that his cow concept refers only to cow appearances. Earlier I took intuitions about the specificity of our concepts very seriously. I developed a theory of intentionality that would accommodate the intuition that our concepts pick out unique natural kinds even when we lack the ability to distinguish those kinds from lookalikes. If our antiverificationist intuitions on this issue can be used to dictate a semantic theory, how can we be so quick to adopt a semantic theory that does not accommodate Swampman's antiverificationist intuitions?

To answer this rejoinder, we must observe a crucial difference between Swampman and us. Unlike us, Swampman has a false belief that he has encountered instances of his concepts in the past. This could explain the falsity of his belief that his concepts pick out natural kinds. That belief is grounded on the false assumption that when he sees a member of a natural kind, it is another member of a kind that he has seen before. It is grounded in the false assumption that there is a history of encounters tracing back to an incipient cause that he could actually point to and form a new concept about, with the force of declaring that this concept will thereafter pick out one of *those* things. We can form natural-kind concepts that transcend our verification abilities by actually encountering their instances. When we falsely think we have had such encounters, we may also falsely think that our concepts refer to natural kinds. This is Swampman's predicament.

9.3.3   Concerns Involving Proxytypes

In making the case for this theory of intentionality, I have said very little about proxytypes. This is a mark of the independence of the theory: one can follow my suggestions about intentionality without adopting proxytype theory. But this should not lead one to believe that the two are in any way incompatible. One does not need to be an atomist to be an informational semanticist. Because structured concepts can be viewed as mechanisms for detecting referents, structure adds explanatory power to a theory of concepts, and, as demonstrated, structure is a valuable resource in facing various objections. Informational semantics is the backbone of an argument for concept empiricism in chapter 5. Thus, in developing a workable (if impure) version, I have strengthened the case for proxytype theory. There are, however, a few details that must be worked out.

One question concerns innateness. In the preceding chapter I said that some perceptual representations may be innate. Representations at or near the level of transduction are the least controversial examples (e.g., cells in the eyes). If innate representations exist, how do they represent? The question is a challenge for defenders of an etiological constraint. How can an innate representation have an incipient cause? Three strategies suggest themselves. One possibility is to go evolutionary. In his more recent work on intentionality, Dretske (1988) distinguishes representations that get their meaning through learning from those that get meaning through natural selection. Both methods endow representations with the function (in a teleological sense) of carrying information. Like other evolutionary approaches, his proposal cannot explain the content of innate representations that did not arise through adaptive evolution. A second possibility is that innate representations represent the first things that cause them after birth. This would make them like the parental-imprinting representations in newborn ducks. Perhaps cone cells become representations of the colors that they detect only after those colors have triggered them. One problem with this proposal is that cone cells represent whole ranges of colors, or wavelengths. It would be strange to say that they can only represent the entire range after the entire range has been seen. The third proposal does better. It exploits a resource mentioned in discussing Swampman. On the view I defend in the next chapter, there is a second form of reference that does not depend on etiology. Innate representations can refer in this way. Perhaps, through time, they can be assigned new functions that allows them to take on the kind of etiologically grounded reference discussed in this chapter.

A second question concerns the nature of motor representations. In chapter 5, I claimed that states within the motor system qualify as representations. How do these represent? On the account defended here, representation involves reliable detection of what is represented. But detection seems to be the wrong relation for handling motor representations. They do not detect motions; they cause them. Motor representations are like imperatives. It is difficult to see how to accommodate such representations without augmenting the present account. In particular, one must add to the notion of a detector a complementary notion of a transmitter. As I will use the term, a transmitter is something that represents in virtue of reliably causing something (rather than in virtue of being reliably caused). Motor representations represent movements in virtue of reliably causing such movements to take place.

One might think it problematic to claim that something can represent in virtue of causing, rather than being caused. After all, the things that our concepts detect reliably cause those concepts to be tokened. Cows reliably cause tokens of my COW concept. If reliable causes are representations, then we are stuck with the consequence that cows represent COW concepts. Representation becomes a symmetric relation. To avoid this consequence, one must work out the details of a theory of transmitters. This project is beyond the scope of the present discussion, but it is not infeasible. One difference between cows and motor commands is that the former cause all kinds of things, while the latter generally cause movement. If cows count as transmitters, they represent so much that their representational status ceases to be of interest. Another point involves etiology. Just as we appealed to incipient causes above, we can appeal here to incipient effects. Motor representations are set up to cause motions; motions are their incipient effects. Cows do not incipiently cause tokens of one's COW concept. By adding an etiological condition, a theory of transmitters may avoid the needless proliferation of representations.[10]

The next issue of concern involves my hypothesis that concepts can be temporary constructions in working memory (see chapter 6). In some cases, the temporary constructions may simply duplicate representations stored long-term memory. But what about more fleeting constructions? We sometimes form proxytypes to meet the demands of an unusual context. Consider a case in which one is told to imagine a human in a very realistic gorilla suit. To do this, one presumably forms a gorillalike proxytype. Such a proxytype would do a good job of detecting gorillas and a poor job of detecting humans. Consequently, it is unclear how my account can show that the proxytype represents a human and not a gorilla.

The resources necessary for solving this problem are actually available to any theory of concepts. When one identifies an object as falling under a concept, one must have a way of grouping the representation of that object with the representation of the concept so that it can contribute to categorization in the future. The grouping is achieved by what I called a predicative link in chapter 6. All theories need predicative links because all theories need to explain how we store the knowledge that particular exemplars fall under our concepts.

Now come back to the case of the gorilla suit. Despite representing typical gorilla features, the representation formed when we imagine a person in a gorilla suit is predicatively linked, at the moment it is formed, to human representations. The formation of a predicative link can serve as an incipient cause if it is introduced when a representation is first generated. If a gorillalike representation is predicatively linked to a human representation when it is formed, it can inherit the representational content of that representation. This is consistent with the etiological condition discussed above. The covariation condition is also met in this example. Representations of typical gorilla features covary with gorillas, but they also covary with humans in gorilla suits. A temporary gorilla-like proxytype formed when one is asked to imagine a human in a gorilla suit would represent a human in a gorilla suit because it would covary with humans in gorilla suits and be etiologically grounded in the concept HUMAN.

The final issue involves the hypothesis, proposed in chapter 6, that superordinate concepts consist of *collections* of representations. For example, the concept FURNITURE may consist of representations of a chair, a table, a desk, and so on. Proxytype theory seems to demand such a treatment of superordinates because it would be difficult to capture a polymorphic category with a single perceptual representation. This presents a problem. The representations constituting such a mongrel presumably covary with basic-level categories, not superordinates. The chair representation in the concept FURNITURE covaries with chairs. How, then, can we ever have concepts that represent superordinates?

The answer may involve special representational links. Suppose that we form a superordinate representation by linking together a group of representations of basic-level categories so that they are tokened concurrently. When we want to determine whether something is a piece of furniture, we may compare its representation to the representations of chairs, tables, and sofas, considered as a whole. This proposal solves the semantic problem. When part of a collective, a representation of chairs serves as part of the concept FURNITURE. The collective to which the chair representation belongs can be positively matched with objects that look nothing like chairs. Therefore, when basic-level representations are linked together, they can take on semantic properties that they lack when working in isolation. They can represent superordinate categories.

9.4   Conclusion

Philosophers have struggled to come up with a theory of intentionality that explains how we can refer to unique and coherent classes of objects rather than disjunctive bundles of things that happen to look alike. The belief that concepts refer to coherent classes rather than disjunctive bundles is deeply held by ordinary people from early in development. Ordinary people believe they can refer to a category even if they cannot distinguish it from another categories whose members are superficially similar. This is a fundamental antiverificationist conviction. Limits on one's ability to distinguish things should not carry limits on one's ability to refer to things. Recent philosophical efforts to find an adequate theory of intentionality can be regarded as efforts to make sense of antiverificationist convictions. A good theory makes sense of those convictions by making them come out true.

I have argued that our concepts refer to unique categories through a conspiracy of etiology and covariance. The account I propose has advantages over other theories and meets a variety of objections. It also contributes to a defense of concept empiricism by supporting an argument for empiricism presented in chapter 5 and demonstrating that proxytype theory can satisfy the intentional-content desideratum.

10

Cognitive Content

In chapter 9, I propose a Lockean theory of intentional content. Locke appreciated that intentional content is not sufficient for individuating concepts. We also need cognitive content. Various accounts of cognitive content have been proposed in recent years, but none are satisfactory. I propose a Lockean alternative.

10.1   Narrow Approaches to Cognitive Content

We often explain behavior using mental-state attributions. Such attributions advert to intentional contents. We say, for example, that Boris killed the gnu because he wanted to make gnu stew. The desire to make gnu stew is a desire about gnus. The practice of explaining behavior by appeal to the intentional contents of mental states is quite successful, but it has two important limitations. Intentional contents are sometimes too coarse for individuating mental states, and sometimes too fine. Coarseness is illustrated by Frege's Phosphorus/Hesperus case. For variety, consider a different example. Boris wants to make gnu stew but does not want to make wildebeest stew, as he fails to realize that gnus are wildebeests. Boris believes that wildebeest stew would be repugnant. The concepts GNU and WILDEBEEST have the same intentional contents. Thus, the desire for gnu stew and desire to avoid wildebeest stew have incompatible fulfillment conditions. These desires would be jointly incoherent if one were limited to intentional contents in individuating mental states.

The second limitation on individuation via intentional contents can be illustrated by Twin Earth cases. Putnam's H_2O/XYZ case is the classic example. Boris's doppelgänger, Twin Boris, lives on a planet that is just like ours except that the stuff that looks like water is XYZ not H_2O. When Boris pours a quart of water for his gnu stew, Twin Boris pours a quart of stuff with all the same superficial properties. The concepts they associate with the word "water" have different intentional contents, but they are cognitively alike and promote comparable behaviors (e.g., the desire for a quart of water leads both of them to turn on the closest faucet to release a clear, tasteless liquid).

Psychological generalizations require a method of individuating mental states that can overcome these limitations. They must individuate mental states in a way that is both finer and coarser than individuation by intentional contents. In the terminology used in chapter 1, we need a theory of cognitive content. Most philosophers generally use the term *narrow content* rather than cognitive content. Narrow content is contrasted with *wide content*, which is just what I have been calling intentional content. Wide contents are so-called because they depend on what is in the world (e.g., H_2O or XYZ). Narrow contents are so-called because they supervene on what is inside the head. Molecular doppelgängers share narrow contents, despite different environments, because their internal states are alike. Conversely, a person who fails to realize that gnus are wildebeests has distinct narrow contents because that person associates distinct internal states with these terms. Let's take a brief look at three prominent theories of narrow content and review some objections to each.

The first theory identifies narrow contents with the internal functional roles played by concepts (e.g., Field 1978, Lycan 1981, McGinn 1982, Block 1986, Loar 1988). On a standard functional-role account, the narrow content of a concept is a subset of the inferences that can be drawn from beliefs containing that concept. The narrow content of the concept WATER, may include the disposition to infer that something is wet when one believes that it is water.

To determine what functional role a concept plays (and hence the narrow content of that concept), one can use the process of Ramsification (Lewis 1970). To Ramsify, one begins with a description of a concept consisting of a list of the inferences into which it enters. Then one replaces each instance of the word corresponding to that concept with a variable and uses the resulting description to define the concept. For example, assume that the concept WATER figures in the following inferences: if something is water, it is wet; if something is water, it is found in oceans; if something is water, it is comes out of faucets; etc. The process of Ramsification would allow us to characterize WATER as the concept corresponding to x such that if something is x, it is wet, and so on for the other WATER inferences. This is only the first step. We have defined the concept WATER by its inferential role, but our specification of that role is incomplete because we have not yet defined the other concepts expressed by our description of that role. Each other concept, such as WET and OCEANS, must be Ramsified as well. They must be replaced by variables that are defined by the inferences into which they enter. We can eventually identify the functional role of every concept by replacing each with its own unique variable. The result of this global Ramsification process is an extremely abstract structure relating variables to variables.

The most widely discussed objection to functional-role theories is that it is difficult to determine which inferences matter for concept individuation (Fodor 1987, Fodor and Lepore 1992). Should the narrow content of a concept be identified with its total functional role (consisting of a Ramsified description of every inference into which it enters) or a partial functional role? If total roles are used, then no two people have concepts with the same narrow contents, because no two people draw exactly the same inferences. If partial roles are used, then one must say which inferences contribute to narrow content and which do not. Fodor and Lepore (1992) argue that this can only be done if one can come up with something like an analytic/synthetic distinction. Quine's arguments against such a distinction convince Fodor and Lepore that individuation by partial roles is untenable. This leads them to reject functional role theories. Call this the "Holism Problem."

Some functional-role theorists have responded to the Holism Problem by defending versions of the analytic/synthetic distinction. I do not review these proposals, because I think they cannot suffice. Even if there is a principled distinction to be drawn between the inferences that matter for identifying narrow contents and those that do not, narrow contents cannot be exhaustively characterized by such inferences. The problem is that functional roles are too abstract.

Block (1978) points out that because functional roles are abstract, numerous things can occupy them. The same pattern of variables might capture the relational structure of things that are not even mental. Is one thereby committed to saying that these things have the same narrow content as mental states? Should they be subsumed by the same psychological laws? That would be absurd. More alarming, it may turn out that two distinct concepts have the same abstract functional roles. Patterns of interrelations between variables are unlikely to be highly distinctive. It would be disastrous for psychology to treat these alike. A further problem is that it is unclear how to measure similarity between abstract functional roles (Fodor and Lepore 1992). Similarity is ordinarily measured by showing that two things have some of the same features; each feature in a network of variables is individuated by its role in that network; thus, if the networks differ at all, the same feature cannot appear in two distinct networks; thus, similarity cannot be measured.

To escape these "Abstractness Problems" we need to tack down functional roles somewhere (Block 1978). If there were a set of primitive concepts not identified by their functional roles, then functional roles could be identified with networks of these primitives rather than networks of variables. Nonmental states that have the same abstract structure as mental states could be disqualified because they are not built up from primitive concepts. Distinct concepts with matching abstract structure could be distinguished by the primitives they contain. And similarity between functional roles could be measured by overlapping primitives. This way of rescuing functional-role theories of narrow content requires a set of primitives that are not identified by their functional roles. That means that functional roles cannot provide a complete theory of narrow content. Functional-role theories must be either replaced or supplemented by another theory of narrow content capable of individuating primitives. I turn to such other theories now.

Fodor (1987, 1991) defends a mapping theory of narrow content. The basic idea is that narrow contents are functions from contexts to wide contents.[1] The referent of Boris's WATER concept depends on the context in which he is situated. On Earth, his WATER concept refers to H_2O. If he lived on Twin Earth, his WATER concept would refer to XYZ. The same is true for Twin Boris. If he lived on Earth, his concept would refer to H_2O. Because he is not here and Boris is, their WATER concepts refer to different substances; they have different intentional contents. But there is a counterfactual commonality. If they were in the same contexts, their WATER concepts would have the same intentional contents. Their WATER concepts can be characterized by a function that maps them onto the same intentional contents in the same worlds. Fodor says that the narrow content of a concept is its mapping function.

The main problem with the mapping theory is that internally different states can achieve the same mapping. Consider this analogy. To be a fly-killing device, something must realize a function from living flies to dead flies. The internal workings of such devices can differ significantly. There is an enormous range of things that realize the fly-killing function: fly swatters, flypaper, fly-zapping lamps, fly-sucking vacuums, and fly-eradicating gas bombs. Because these devices behave so differently, it is unlikely that there are any interesting generalizations subsuming them other than the fact that they all kill flies. Likewise, the fact that two mental states both realize the same mapping function does not ensure that they have anything else in common. When we type mental states by their mapping functions, it is likely that we coclassify states that are extremely different.

At first blush this may appear to be an advantage (see Fodor 1991). A theory of narrow content would only be worth having if it could be used in psychological laws. To be used in psychological laws, narrow contents must be shared by many individuals, and to be shared, they must abstract away from the numerous psychological differences that divide us. If mapping functions coclassify very distinct states, they may be ideally suited for playing this role. This strikes me as blind optimism. If the only thing that two states share is the mapping function they realize, then there is nothing to guarantee that they have the same influence on behavior. To make this vivid, imagine that Boris's WATER concept maps onto H_2O in this world and onto XYZ on Twin Earth in virtue of mechanisms that causally respond to clear liquids. In contrast, imagine that Natasha's WATER concept realizes the same mapping function by using mechanisms that respond to tasteless liquids. Now suppose that clarity and tastelessness are so linked that they come together in all nomologically possible worlds. If so, the mapping functions for Boris's and Natasha's concepts are the same. But the difference in mechanisms makes a difference for psychology. For instance, Boris only calls forth his WATER concept when he has certain visual experiences, and Natasha only calls forth hers when she has certain gustatory experiences. The fact that they share a mapping function overlooks this difference in their behavior. In other words, Fodor's mapping theory does not necessarily pick out states in a way that will be of any interest to psychology. Call this the "Mapping Problem."

The Boris and Natasha case is similar to Frege's Phosphorus/Hesperus case because it involves two coreferential concepts. Standard Frege cases also face the Mapping Problem on Fodor's theory of narrow content. For all Fodor has said, many coreferential concepts realize the same functions from context to content. If Boris has a GNU concept and a WILDEBEEST concept and, on Fodor's theory, these are just atomic labels, then what reason is there to think that they ever map onto different animals? (For similar worries, see Millikan 1993). Fodor does not answer this question, but he seems to concede the problem because he does not use his mapping theory to handle Frege cases. Instead, Fodor (1998) attempts to explain Frege cases by appeal to modes of presentation, which he distinguishes from narrow contents. More specifically, he appeals to the syntactic properties of concepts. I raised some concerns about this proposal in chapter 4. But even if we bracket those worries, Fodor's account can be criticized on methodological grounds. An account that could explain Frege cases and Twin Earth cases using the same construct would be preferable.

A third theory of narrow content was initially proposed by Dennett (1982) and developed further by White (1991, chap. 2). On this account, both narrow contents and intentional contents are identified with sets of possible worlds corresponding to our thoughts. The difference between intentional and narrow content is a difference in how these worlds are chosen. Intentional contents comprise the worlds that correspond to the truth conditions of our thoughts. These worlds are selected according to the external environments in which we are situated. The intentional content of my belief that water is potable is the set of worlds in which H_2O is potable. Since the actual world is among those, my belief is true. The worlds constituting narrow contents, what Dennett calls "notional worlds," correspond to how an organism takes things to be. The notional worlds for my belief that water is potable are worlds where the clear, liquid in rivers and streams is potable, whether or not it is H_2O. Notional worlds are narrow because they are selected according to what is in the organism, not what is in the actual environment.

The notional-worlds account ties into aspects of Dennett's general philosophical perspective that are beyond the scope of this discussion (e.g., his instrumentalism). I restrict myself to a single objection that does not depend on a review of Dennett's philosophy. Narrow content is supposed to provide an account of concept individuation. Notional worlds are assigned to thoughts, rather than to concepts. To individuate concepts, the notional-worlds account must be elaborated. A natural proposal is that two people share concepts only if their thoughts pick out the same notional worlds, and the constituents of those thoughts map onto the same objects in those worlds. On this proposal, I share a WATER concept with my Twin Earth doppelgänger because we both have a belief that we would express by saying "Water is potable," that belief picks out the same notional worlds (but not the same truth-conditional worlds), and in each of those worlds the WATER concepts forming our respective beliefs picks out the same stuff (i.e., the local liquid in rivers and streams). This account of concept individuation is inadequate. There is no reason to suppose that people need to share any beliefs in order to share concepts. In fact, there is no reason to think that concept possession requires having any beliefs at all. Concepts seem to be ontogenetically and semantically prior to beliefs.[2] Any account that tries to define the content (intentional or narrow) of concepts in terms of beliefs will have to prove that this priority is illusory. Call this the "Belief-Dependency Problem."

Some of my arguments against competing theories of narrow content are too swift to be decisive, but they leave little doubt that we should be receptive to alternatives. In the next section, I develop a theory that is invulnerable to the objections that I have been discussing.

10.2   Proxytypes and Cognitive Content

10.2.1   A Narrow Victory

In chapter 6, I argued that concepts are proxytypes. Proxytypes themselves can be said to constitute cognitive contents.[3] They are what we
grasp when we grasp a concept. Two people have the same cognitive
content, on this proposal, when they have type-identical proxytypes. In
this section I compare a proxytype account of cognitive content to
leading narrow-content accounts.

To satisfy the cognitive-content desideratum, proxytypes must be
capable of handling Twin Earth cases and Frege cases. For Twin Earth
cases, we need a notion of content that is shared by molecular duplicates
and others who inhabit different environments but conceptualize those
environments in the same way. Proxytypes can play that role. Boris and
Twin Boris have perceptually derived representations of the substances
they call "water" that are exactly alike. They represent the stuff in oceans
and streams as wet, clear, thirst-quenching, and so on.

Proxytypes are also equipped to explain Frege cases. These can arise
whenever two concepts have the same referent. Referents are determined,
on proxytype theory, by informational/etiological semantics. Proxytypes
refer to their nomologically related incipient causes. This allows distinct
proxytypes to pick out the same thing. There are three kinds of cases
to consider. Sometimes two proxytypes pick out the same thing by tracking different aspects of that thing's appearance. For example, the planet
Venus appears in the morning and the evening. A visual representation
of the brightest starlike light in the dawn sky can differ from a visual
representation of the brightest starlike light in the night sky. Because
these two representations differ, one might fail to realize that they track
a common object.

The second kind of Frege case arises when one object has two names.
Proxytypes can include verbal representations. A person can have one
proxytype containing a representation of the word "gnu" and another
containing a representation of the word "wildebeest." These two representations have a common referent because they verbally track the same
animals. Experts in the community to whom we defer know that wilde-

beests are gnus. But because the words can yield distinct proxytypes, a nonexpert can lack this knowledge and come to have very different gnu and wildebeest thoughts. Likewise in the case of someone who fails to realize that "Cicero" and "Tully" corefer.

A slightly more complicated case arises when the very same name is mistakenly thought to pick out two distinct individuals (Kripke 1979). In chapter 4, I give the example of a person who fails to realize that Farrakhan the violinist is Farrakhan the religious leader. Because her two FARRAKHAN concepts use the same verbal label, they cannot be distinguished metalinguistically. But other information can be used to make the distinction. A person who believes that there are two Farrakhans presumably associates distinct properties with that name. In this example, the person thinks of one Farrakhan as a violinist and the other as a religious leader. Perceptual representations of activities, such as playing the violin, and verbal descriptions, such as "the Nation of Islam," distinguish one representation from the other.

One might object that a Kripkean case can arise where no difference exists in the perceptual representations constituting our proxytypes. Perhaps someone can believe that there are two Farrakhans without having any information associated with either of them. Here the difference in concepts cannot be accounted for by a difference in proxytypes. One's two Farrakhan concepts are proxytypically identical. Does this show that proxytypes cannot serve as cognitive contents? I think not. In this case, the two Farrakhan representations could not, for lack of internal differences, ever lead to distinct behavior. They would not enter into different generalizations. This is not to say that believing that there are two Farrakhans, with no further information, is the same as believing in one. For example, having two distinct Farrakhan representations might lead one to say, "Farrakhan is not Farrakhan." The point is that any difference in Farrakhan-directed behaviors is a function of this belief in the existence of two Farrakhans, not a function of anything intrinsic to the two FARRAKHAN representations. Consequently, these two representations can be said to have the same cognitive contents. A person in this situation has distinct representations in long-term memory (think of two mental file folders without any contents), but their cognitive contents are the same. In this special case, the fact that one can be surprised to learn that Farrakhan is Farrakhan is explained by something other than cognitive contents.

The fact that proxytypes are well suited to explain cognitive content can also be demonstrated by considering their other explanatory contributions to psychology. Philosophical theories of narrow content, which presumably satisfy the cognitive-content desideratum, are often described as attempts to arrive at a method of concept individuation that can serve scientific psychology more effectively than individuation based on intentional contents (Fodor 1987). But these claims are rarely made with any effort to look at the kinds of psychological generalizations that psychologists actually offer in discussing concepts. As we have seen, psychologists typically postulate concepts to explain categorization. In chapter 6, I argue that proxytypes can explain important categorization results. None of the theories of narrow content that I reviewed above make any claim of this kind. While we can imagine how those theories might be adapted (especially the functional-role approach), proxytype theory offers the only account of cognitive content that is independently motivated by taking scientific psychology seriously.

Taking psychology seriously is not the only advantage of the proxytype approach to cognitive content. Proxytypes also escape the objections that threaten leading narrow-content theories. I discuss these in reverse order. I save the Abstractness Problems for the next subsection.

First consider the Belief-Dependency Problem, which threatens notional-world theories of narrow content. Notional worlds are determined by beliefs, so they cannot be used to ascribe cognitive contents to creatures without beliefs. Nor can they be used to establish shared cognitive contents across creatures with distinct beliefs. In contrast, one can possess proxytypes without possessing any beliefs. They are simply stored copies of representations produced in perception. Even a simple perceptual representation of the color red can serve as a proxytype.

Proxytype theory also avoids the Mapping Problem, which threatens the mapping theory. Different devices can implement the same mapping from worlds to intentional contents. This happens in certain Frege cases and in the Boris and Natasha case discussed above. I have already shown how proxytypes handle Frege cases. Proxytypes avoid the Mapping Problem because they are the detection mechanisms that implement mapping functions rather than the functions themselves. Natasha's TASTELESS LIQUID proxytype and Boris's WET LIQUID proxytype may map onto the same stuff in some worlds, but they are obviously distinct.

Now consider the Holism Problem, which threatens functional-role theories of narrow content. Functional-role theorists generally identify concepts by the inferences into which they enter. But which inferences are these? If all inferences are used, then concepts are difficult to share. The functional-role theorist must constrain the relevant set of inferences by showing that only certain inferences matter for concept individuation. This is tantamount to an analytic/synthetic distinction. Proxytype theory avoids the vexed issue of analyticity. Proxytypes consist of small sets of features that can be coactivated in working memory. There are real constraints on working-memory capacity. No dubious semantic or epistemological distinction is needed to say what makes these features special. In chapter 6, I argue that the features that get tokened on any occasion are likely to be shared.

10.2.2   Individuating Proxytypes

The major flaw of functional-role theories of narrow content is that functional roles are too abstract. Excessive abstractness allows distinct concepts (and even nonconcepts) to occupy the same functional role. Excessive abstractness also makes it difficult to explain similarity between concepts. To avoid Abstractness Problems, one needs to tack things down at the edges. Some concepts, the primitives, must be individuated by something other than functional roles.

Proxytypes face a similar problem. Two proxytypes are type identical if they are constituted by comparably weighted, perceptually derived feature representations of the same type. But what makes two features count as the same? In some cases, two features count as the same if they consist of more primitive features of the same type. But decomposition must stop somewhere. We must arrive at a set of primitives that are not type-identified by further features. Without a way to say when primitive features are identical, there is no way to say when two proxytypes are identical or to quantify similarity between proxytypes. Like functional roles, proxytypes must be tacked down.

The primitives that make up proxytypes are perceptual, so proxytypes can be tacked down by providing a theory of how primitive perceptual representations are individuated. One option is to type-identify perceptual primitives with brain states. The obvious objection to this proposal is that brain states vary too much. The neural activity underlying my ability to see red may differ from the neural activity underlying your ability to see red. And even if you and I see red with comparable neural states, other creatures may not. Individuation by brain states may sacrifice robust generalizations across individuals and species.

In response, one can note that neurophysiologists constantly identify primitive representations across organisms and across species. For example, Hubel and Wiesel (1962, 1968) find edge-detecting cells in both cats and monkeys. Perceptual primitives seem to be exactly the kinds of things that can be type-identified with brain states.

This response can work only if we individuate brain states in the right way. In mammalian brains, cells responsive to edges are similar in morphology, firing patterns, connectivity, and anatomical location. Call these pure neural properties. Similarity in pure neural properties is not necessary for having edge-detector cells. Edge detectors are so-called because of what they allegedly detect. Like mammals, octopuses may have cells that respond to edges (Sutherland 1968). These can be called edge detectors despite the fact that octopus brains differ from ours in pure neural properties. Humans and octopuses share brain states provided one individuates brain states by the distal properties that they detect (contrast Putnam 1967). This method of individuation is a common practice in neurophysiology.

Following neurophysiologists, I think we should individuate perceptual primitives by the distal properties that they detect. But what properties are these? In chapter 9, I said that detection contributes to the determination of intentional content, but I also said that detection is not sufficient. The problem is that detection is driven by appearances. A detection mechanism cannot distinguish things that look alike. For intentional contents to pick out natural kinds, the detection condition needs to be supplemented with an etiological condition. No such supplementation is needed when it comes to the individuation of perceptual primitives. Perceptual primitives should be individuated by appearances. They can be individuated solely on the basis of what they detect, and what they detect are classes of things that appear alike. Primitives can be individuated by their nomological causes.

These considerations suggest that the term "edge detector" is actually a misnomer. So-called edge detectors also respond to small cracks or other things that look like edges (Burge 1986). It would be more accurate to call them luminance-discontinuity detectors, since "luminance discontinuity" comes close to capturing the appearance properties that they detect. For short, we can call them edge-appearance detectors.[4]

What is true about edge-appearance detectors is true about primitive perceptual representations more generally. Such representations can be individuated by what they detect, where detection is defined by nomological causation. Perceptual primitives may represent edge appearances, wet appearances, furry appearances, and so on.

If the features constituting a proxytype can be individuated by appeal to detected appearances, then the proxytypes they constitute can be individuated in this way too. Specifically, proxytypes can be individuated by appeal to *sets* of appearance properties. There is one complication, however. In chapter 6, I indicated that proxytype features are weighted. A simple set of appearances cannot be sufficient for proxytype individuation because they would not capture differences in feature weights. Two mental representations composed of the same primitives can qualify as distinct proxytypes if those primitives are weighted differently. Two such proxytypes would have different detection tendencies and perhaps different intentional contents.

To get around this problem, I propose that proxytypes be individuated by sets of sets of properties rather than mere sets of properties. In particular, we can identify a proxytype as the set containing the sets of properties sufficient for causing the proxytype to exceed its critical detection threshold. For example, if a DOG proxytype includes the features FURRY, BARKS, and FETCHES and causing any two of these to be tokened is sufficient for tokening DOG, then that proxytype can be individuated as a set containing four members: the set of appearances detected by

FURRY and BARKS, the set of appearances detected by FURRY and
FETCHES, the set of appearances detected by FETCHES and BARKS, and the
set of appearances detected by all three of these representations.

This gives us a way to compare proxytypes. Two proxytypes can be
identified if they detect the same appearance sets, and two proxytypes
are similar to the extent that the appearance sets they detect overlap.
Two proxytypes can also be said to be similar if they detect similar
appearances. The appearance of red, for example, is more like the
appearance of orange than the appearance of blue. That similarity is
objective in the sense that the physical features in virtue of which we
coclassify things as red (e.g., certain reflectance properties) may be closer
to the features in virtue of which we classify things as orange than to the
features in virtue of which we classify things as blue. Such objective similarities in the magnitudes by which we perceive the world provide a basis
for measuring similarities between internal states. Thus, similarities
between proxytypes can be measured by overlapping sets of appearances
or by independently measurable similarities between members of those
sets. This contrasts with functional roles, which are too abstract to
support similarity assessments.

10.3   Nominal Content and Real Content

I claim that proxytypes can be individuated by what they detect. Putting
this differently, I might have said that proxytypes can be individuated by
their *contents*. These are contents in the same way that intentional contents are contents: they are properties in the world. Having content, in
this sense, is a synonym for having referents. Proxytypes refer to appearances, and they can be individuated by the appearances to which they
refer.

There is a puzzle in all this. In chapter 6, I said that concepts are proxytypes; in chapter 9, I said that concepts can refer to natural kinds; and
I have now said that proxytypes all refer to appearances. If proxytypes
are concepts and proxytypes refer to appearances, then concepts refer to
appearances. But if concepts refer to appearances, how can they refer to
natural kinds? The answer is simple. They refer to both.

10.3.1   Locke's Theory of Double Reference

The suggestion that concepts refer in two ways was anticipated by Locke.[5] To understand Locke's proposal, one must recall his distinction between real and nominal essences. A real essence is that in virtue of which a member of a kind has the observable properties that it does. The real essence of gold is whatever makes gold gold. Locke says that the real essence of gold is unknowable, but today we would say it is the element Au, with atomic number 79. A nominal essence is a complex idea constituted by ideas of the properties that we observe in a kind. The nominal essence of gold is the idea (or concept) GOLD, which consists of ideas (features) corresponding to the properties by which we identify something as gold (e.g., SHINY, YELLOW, MALLEABLE). Nominal essences are in the mind, and real essences are in the world.[6]

The idea of GOLD tracks the underlying properties in virtue of which gold has the superficial properties that we observe in it. More succinctly, nominal essences refer to real essences. But nominal essences also refer to something else. Locke writes that ideas of natural kinds "have in the mind a double reference: 1. Sometimes they are referred to a supposed real Essence of each Species of Things. 2. Sometimes they are only design'd to be Pictures and Representations in the Mind, of things that do exist, by *Ideas* of those qualities that are discoverable in them" (1690, II.xxxi.6).

This passage implies that nominal essences refer to the real essences of things *and* to "the qualities discoverable in them." Loosely put, our ideas refer both to things as they really are and to things as we take them to be. Adapting Locke's terminology, we can call these two kinds of referents *real content* and *nominal content* respectively. Real contents can be directly identified with what Locke call real essences, and nominal contents can be identified with the properties represented by the ideas constituting nominal essences. The relationship between these is pictured in figure 10.1.

On this story, concepts have two distinct referents. To take another example, my COW concept refers to those things that have the real essences of cows, whatever those essences happen to be.[7] It also refers to the properties on the basis of which I identify cows as such. If genetic

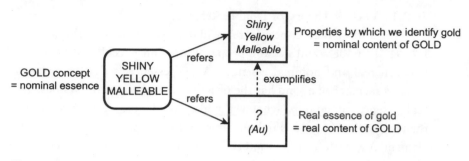

Figure 10.1
The relationship between nominal and real content.

engineers produced an entity that had reptilian innards and a cowlike appearance, it would fall under the nominal content of my COW concept, but it would not fall under the real content. Conversely, if engineers doctored something with cow innards to look like an alligator, it would not fall under the nominal content of my COW concept, but it would fall under the real content.

It should be obvious that real contents are just what I have been calling intentional contents. I recommend adopting the Lockean term and calling intentional contents "real." The term "real content" has advantages over the term "intentional content." If concepts refer in two ways, then there is a sense in which they have two kinds of intentional contents. Using the term "intentional content" for just one of these is misleading.

Nominal contents can be identified with the contents that I have said we should use to individuate proxytypes. Adopting the Lockean term is again quite useful. The term "nominal content" is more concise than the phrase "the contents used to individuate proxytypes." The Lockean term also has advantages over the term "narrow content." Nominal contents are narrow in one sense: they supervene on what is in the head. Two people who are internally alike have the same proxytypes, which detect, and are thus individuated by, the same appearances. But nominal contents are wide in another sense: they are sets of properties in the world. Using the term "narrow" is, therefore, misleading. It would be equally misleading to call proxytypes a form of narrow content. They are in the head, but they are externally individuated.

In sum, Locke anticipates my account of cognitive content, provides a precedent for thinking concepts refer doubly, and inspires very helpful terminology. We can escape the misleading division implied by "narrow" and "wide" and adopt the terms "nominal" and "real." I do that in the remainder of this chapter.

10.3.2 Reconciling the Nominal and the Real

On the theory I have been advancing, concepts can be individuated in two ways. A pair of concept tokens can be identified in virtue of sharing their real contents *or* in virtue of sharing their nominal contents. Call these "real types" and "nominal types." Any given token has both a real type and a nominal type. Sometimes our attributive practices imply that two tokens are tokens of the same concept just in case they have the same real *and* nominal contents. But this is not always the case. Doppelgängers, like Boris and Twin Boris, share concepts in virtue of sharing tokens of the same nominal type. Boris and Natasha, in the example above, share concepts in virtue of sharing tokens with the same real type. There is thus a strict sense of concept sharing, and two looser senses of concept sharing.

The distinction between nominal and real types allows me to clarify my claim that concepts are proxytypes. Each of our concept tokens is a proxytype. Those tokens can be type-individuated by their nominal contents. Since concepts can also be type-individuated this way, there is a type identity between concepts and proxytypes. As nominal types, concepts are proxytypes. But this type identity fails when concept tokens are individuated by their real contents. Distinct proxytypes can correspond to the same real contents, and distinct real contents can correspond to the same proxytypes. Nevertheless, there is an interesting relationship between proxytypes and concepts qua real types.

Imagine a person who encounters whisky for the first time. She may quickly discover a number of its core properties and form a corresponding mental representation. For example, she may discover that it is a golden, translucent liquid. This cluster constitutes a proxytype. After further investigation, she learns that this liquid also causes inebriation. Her proxytype is revised. Now the same person might have existed in a world where, because of minor environmental differences, whisky is

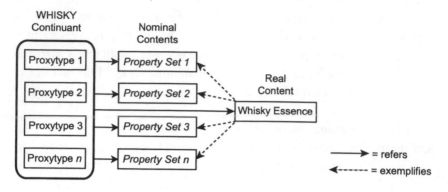

Figure 10.2
Concepts as continuants of proxytypes.

blue. In this counterfactual world, the proxytype caused by her encounters with whisky would include the feature BLUE rather than GOLDEN. Each of these three proxytypes has a different nominal content. Still, they can all be thought of as parts of a single continuant, grounded in experiences with the same substance, evolving as knowledge of that substance grows, and transforming as that substance changes from world to world. This continuant is comprised of proxytypes, but those proxytypes are bonded together by their collaboration in tracking whisky across time and worlds. Whisky is the real content of such a continuant, and of the proxytypes that compose it. Qua real type, a concept can be type-identified with the equivalence class of proxytypes that share the same real content. This basic idea is captured in figure 10.2.

These considerations help us avoid an easy confusion. Real content is determined by a combination of etiology and nomological covariance, and nominal content is determined by nomological covariance. One might think that nominal content is simply real content minus the etiological condition. This would be a mistake. The counterfactuals to which we appeal in individuating a concept by its real content do not require that the proxytypes associated with those concepts remain fixed. My WHISKY concept would covary with whisky even if whisky were blue. That is what makes it a WHISKY concept. But this can only be the case if my WHISKY concept is constituted by different proxytypes in worlds with blue whisky. If we were to subtract the etiological requirement from the account of real-content determination, these blue-whisky worlds in which our proxytypes differ would still be admissible. In contrast, when we individuate concepts by their nominal contents, we must keep their proxytypes constant. Since nominal contents are the contents by which proxytypes are individuated, the nominal content of a concept at a given time must be determined by counterfactuals in which proxytypes remain fixed.

Despite these differences between real and nominal contents, there is also an important harmony. The proxytypes that embody our concepts are responsible for mediating the relations that endow them with real contents. To ensure a steady correspondence between concepts and real contents, proxytypes must evolve in actual and counterfactual circumstances in a way that reflects features of those contents. In the WHISKY case, for example, the proxytype in a blue-whisky world has the feature BLUE. The changes in our proxytypes are dictated by features of real contents. The comparatively ephemeral nature of proxytypes reflects the fact that it is their function to track such contents. This ephemeral nature results in an interesting dynamic between nominal and real contents. There is a natural drive to reconcile the nominal and the real by adjusting our proxytypes so that their nominal contents come as close as possible to the real contents of the continuants to which they belong.

This interplay between nominal and real stems from an underlying faith in the reality of natural kinds, coupled with the fact that we must track these kinds by their appearances. To cope with this predicament, we search for appearances possessed exclusively by members of unique natural kinds. The search is limited by the perennial possibility of nonidentical indistinguishables. For example, even if we tweak a concept so that it covaries with all and only tigers in this world, there might be other worlds in which it covaries with tiger look-alikes. That is why nominal contents are hard to fully reconcile with real contents. Without an etiological grounding, they cannot decide between look-alikes. Still, because look-alikes often do not arise, nominal contents do an adequate job of helping us track natural kinds. Approximating real contents is generally enough.[8]

This raises an interesting issue concerning the relationship between sense and reference. Frege claimed that sense determines reference. We can think of nominal contents or proxytypes as successors to Frege's sense. They constitute the cognitive contents of our concepts: the kind of contents that we grasp. But if we identify nominal contents with senses, then the inverse of Frege's principle is true: reference determines sense (to some degree). Scrutinizing objects that fall under the real contents of our concepts prompts us to alter proxytypes so that their nominal contents coincide with real contents to a greater degree.

This observation helps answer an important question. Proxytypes are valuable to psychologists because they figure in psychological explanations of behavior. But what about real contents? Do psychologists ever have any reason to discuss the real contents of concepts? The preceding considerations suggest an affirmative answer. Real contents exert *normative control* over proxytypes. Proxytypes transform because they are designed to help us track real contents.[9] If psychologists want to understand why people's concepts evolve as they do, paying attention to the real contents of those concepts is invaluable. Conceptual development is a matter of fine-tuning our abilities to track real contents via appearances. Both psychological essentialism and representational maturation can be illuminated by appeal to real contents.

10.4   Conclusion

In this chapter I argued that proxytype theory can provide an account of cognitive content. Cognitive contents can be identified with proxytypes, which must be individuated by the appearances they represent. With Locke, I am committed to the view that our concepts refer in two ways: they have nominal contents and real contents.

Nominal and real contents are not wholly independent. The latter are determined by the representations that make up the former, and the former strive to approximate the latter. Together, these two species of content provide valuable explanatory tools for psychology.

11

Combining Concepts

In the preceding chapters, I showed that proxytype theory is capable of accommodating almost all of the desiderata on a theory of concepts. Only the compositionality requirement remains. In chapter 6, I indicated that proxytype theory bears a resemblance to prototype theory. Like prototypes, proxytypes are structured and nondefining. Default proxytypes consist of weighted features that are salient, typical, and diagnostic. The kinship to prototype theory may be viewed as a problem because it is widely believed that prototypes are not compositional. In a number of places, Fodor uses this allegation to challenge the adequacy of prototype theory as a theory of concepts (Fodor 1981, 1998; Fodor and Lepore 1996). Since proxytypes are closely related to prototypes, they are vulnerable to the same objection. In this chapter I defend proxytype theory indirectly by defending prototype theory. I argue that Fodor places too strong a compositionality requirement on a theory of concepts and that a weaker, more defensible requirement can be met by prototypes. I will then propose a theory of prototype combination and show that it can be adapted to proxytypes.

11.1 Confounded Combinations

According to the principle of compositionality, the content of a phrasal concept is a function of the content of its parts together with rules of combination. Fodor gives two primary arguments for thinking that concepts must be compositional.

First, without compositionality, we would not be able to explain how people are able to generate an endless variety of thoughts from finite resources. Fodor (1987) calls this the *productivity* of thought. Compositionality explains productivity because compositional systems can use a fixed set of rules and representations to generate an infinite number of novel combinations.

Second, compositionality is needed to explain the fact that the ability to possess one kind of thought is intrinsically connected to the ability to entertain another kind of thought. Fodor calls this the *systematicity* of thought.[1] In a compositional system, the rules and representations used to form one compound can often be used to form others, so if one has the ability to form one compound, one can form the others as well.

Fodor gives several arguments for thinking that prototypes are not compositional. One argument is based on the allegation that lexical concepts that have prototypes can combine to form phrasal concepts that have no prototypes. Fodor (1981) gives the following examples:

- AMERICAN CITIES SITUATED ON THE EAST COAST JUST A LITTLE SOUTH OF TENNESSEE
- CHAUCER'S GRANDMOTHERS
- GRANDMOTHERS MOST OF WHOSE GRANDCHILDREN ARE DENTISTS

In more recent writings, Fodor (1998) has made the same case using concepts generated using Boolean operations, for example:

- PINK IF IT'S A SQUARE
- OPAQUE AND A RESIDENT OF NORTH CAROLINA
- NOT A CAT

Fodor believes that none of these compounds have prototypes, even though their constituents do. Thus, prototypes are not compositional.

In a second argument against the compositionality of prototypes, Fodor acknowledges the fact that some phrasal concepts have prototypes but argues that their prototypes cannot be explained in terms of the prototypes of their constituents. Some phrasal concepts have prototypical features that are not prototypical of their parts. Fodor and Lepore (1992, 186) give us the following example:

The [prototypical] brown cow can be dangerous even though the property *dangerous* doesn't belong to the *brown* [prototype] or the *cow* [prototype]. Indeed, the [prototypical] *brown* cow can be dangerous even if the [prototypical] cow is a pussycat.

As we saw in chapter 3, the psychological literature provides many other examples. For instance, people say that Harvard carpenters are non-materialistic even though Harvard graduates and carpenters do not have this property (Kunda, Miller, and Claire 1990). Similarly, people say that pet fish live in bowls even though this is not a prototypical property of pets or fish (Osherson and Smith 1981). In a word, prototype combination generates *emergent* properties: properties that are prototypical of phrasal concepts but not of their parts. This is direct evidence that prototypes are not compositional.

In the final argument that I will consider, Fodor seems to concede that prototypes are compositional in some sense, while denying that they are compositional in the right sense. This follows from a claim originally defended in his discussions of connectionism (Fodor and Pylyshyn 1988, Fodor and McLaughlin 1990). In those discussions, he says that concepts combine in a way that is *context-insensitive*, i.e., a concept must make the same contribution to each of the phrasal concepts of which it is a constituent. Prototypes cannot meet this requirement. In some existing models of prototype combination, how a prototype is ultimately represented in a compound differs from how it is represented in isolation. In one model, for example, the concept APPLE has the feature RED when considered in isolation because apples are prototypically red, but in the compound PURPLE APPLE, the APPLE representation loses the feature RED (Smith, Osherson, Rips, and Keane 1988). In this model, concept combination is compositional in the strict sense defined above: the prototype of a compound is a function of the prototypes of its parts together with rules of combination. If Fodor is right about the context-insensitivity constraint, however, this is not compositional enough. APPLE must be represented the same way in every compound.

Fodor's argument for the claim that concept combination must be context-insensitive can be reconstructed as follows. The thought that Oscar ate the squid is systematically related to the thought that the squid ate Oscar insofar as the ability to entertain one entails the ability to entertain the other. But if SQUID were represented differently in these two compounds, this systematicity would be inexplicable because systematicity depends on the fact that the *same* representation can be used in different compounds. If representations changed form from one compound to the next, mastery of a single compound would not entail mastery of another. Thus, context-sensitive compositional systems are not compositional enough.

I share Fodor's belief that compositionality is required to explain systematicity and productivity. His arguments purport to show that prototypes are either not compositional or have the wrong kind of compositionality. If he is right, prototypes cannot be concepts. If this is true for prototypes, it is probably true for proxytypes as well. If proxytypes are not compositional or do not have the right kind of compositionality, they cannot be concepts.

11.2   Compositionality: How Much Is Enough?

In this section I answer Fodor's arguments against prototype compositionality. The first argument can be dealt with rather swiftly. The other two will require a clarification of the compositionality requirement.

11.2.1   Prototypes Lost, Prototypes Regained

In the first line of argument, Fodor cites examples of phrasal concepts that, he claims, have no prototypes despite the fact that their components do. Strangely, Fodor gives no support for this claim. To determine whether a concept has a prototype structure, one has to see how it is used and understood. For example, one must look for typicality effects and nonnecessary features. Whether a specific concept has a prototype is ultimately an empirical question, but one does not need a psychology lab to find evidence for an answer. To informally test whether a concept has a prototype, one can introspectively determine whether the concept has a graded structure. It has a graded structure if some examples are intuitively good, some are borderline cases, and some are bad. If a concept passes this test, then it probably has a prototype. In this way, we can show that all of Fodor's examples have prototypes.

It is very plausible that AMERICAN CITIES SITUATED ON THE EAST COAST JUST A LITTLE SOUTH OF TENNESSEE has a prototype because it is easy to form a typicality scale. Atlanta is an extremely good exemplar because it is a typical American city, a typical example of being situated a little south of Tennessee, and a fairly typical example of being situated on the East Coast. Charleston, South Carolina, is a worse exemplar because it is not as typical an American city and not as typical an example of being just a little south of Tennessee. Tampa is a bad exemplar because it is an atypical example of being just a little south of Tennessee and it is an atypical example of being on the East Coast. Notice that these exemplars form a scale for the composite concept, but they inherit their typicality rankings from the constituents of that composite. This suggests not only that Fodor's first example has a prototype but also that its prototype is derived from the prototypes of its constituents.

Fodor's second example, CHAUCER'S GRANDMOTHERS, also passes the test. Intuitively, a gray-haired woman that is Chaucer's grandmother by blood and who speaks Middle English is a good exemplar for CHAUCER'S GRANDMOTHERS. A gray-haired woman who is Chaucer's step-grandmother and speaks no English gets an intermediate rating. And a dark-haired woman who is the grandmother of Chaucer's wife and speaks no English does even worse. Once again, we have demonstrated that the compound has a graded structure inherited from the prototypes of its constituent concepts.

Similarly, when asked to conceive GRANDMOTHERS MOST OF WHOSE GRANDCHILDREN ARE DENTISTS, a woman with twelve grandchildren eight of whom are dentists is a worse example than a woman with twelve grandchildren eleven of whom are dentists. Prototypes are at work.

Phrasal concepts generated using Boolean operations also exhibit evidence of prototype structure. For example, PINK IF IT'S A SQUARE can inherit typicality effects from the material conditional: it is applied most readily to pink squares, less readily to pink triangles, and even less readily to blue triangles. It can also inherit typicality effects from its constituent concepts: it is applied more readily to very good squares that are colored a very common pink than to approximate squares in an unusual pink. Likewise, OPAQUE AND A RESIDENT OF NORTH CAROLINA is more readily applied to completely opaque full-time residents of North Carolina than to slightly translucent individuals who vote in North Carolina but spend most of the year in Nebraska. And finally, NOT A CAT applies most readily to noncats that are nothing like cats (e.g., egg beaters), then to noncats that are similar to cats (e.g., dogs). Confirmation of this last suggestion can be found in the fact subjects give graded typicality scales for noninstances of a category. For example, subjects will say that a worm is a very atypical inset, a bat is somewhat more atypical, and a dog is even more atypical (McCloskey and Glucksberg 1979). Noninsects vary in the extent to which they share typical features with insects. Extrapolating, one can presume that a dog is a typical noninsect, a bat is a less typical noninsect, and a worm is a very atypical noninsect. Such typicality effects suggest that Fodor's examples of Boolean compounds may be represented by prototypes after all. There is no evidence that phrasal concepts lack prototypes.

Fodor might resist this response to the NOT A CAT example. According to prototype theory, categorization is based on the proportion of typical features possessed by an object. Now imagine what a typical example of NOT A CAT might be. As I suggested, it might be an object totally unlike a cat, such as an eggbeater. The problem is that NOT A CAT cannot be represented as a typical eggbeater because things that do not share any features with the EGGBEATER prototype still get counted as noncats. Needed is a prototype that is similar to eggbeaters, dogs, and all other noncats, so that all of these can surpass its membership threshold. Such a prototype would have to contain a massive number of features. It would be far too taxing on cognitive resources to use a prototype of that girth. Therefore, if prototypes are collections of features characteristic of the members of the categories they designate, concepts such as NOT A CAT cannot be represented by prototypes. Its typicality effects must have another source.

For my response to this objection, recall a proposal from chapter 7. There I suggested that negation can be understood as an operation rather than a concept. In particular, it is an operation that changes the function used to measure similarity. Let us measure similarity by Tversky's rule:

$$\text{Sim}(I, P) = (I \cap P) - (I - P) - (P - I)$$

Then negation can be measured thus:

Recall from chapter 3 that "$I \cap P$" is shorthand for the number of features common to I and P, while "$I - P$" and "$P - I$" represent the number of features unique to I and unique to P, respectively.

$$\text{Simnegation}(I, \text{not-}P) = 2 \times \text{Threshold}(P) - \text{Sim}(I, P)$$

This rule makes similarity to a negated prototype inversely related to similarity to a prototype. Something far below the threshold for being a cat will be far above the threshold for being a noncat.

Fodor's objection was that NOT A CAT cannot be represented by a prototype because there is no concise list of typical features possessed by its instances. The reply is that there is such a list, and it is precisely the list used for the CAT prototype. The difference is that negation introduces a different similarity function. An instance will be judged to be a noncat if it fails to possess a sufficient number of cat features (e.g., if it is not fuzzy, lacks pointed ears, fails to say "meow," and so on). Put differently, we can say that something is identified as a noncat if it possesses the features NOT FUZZY, NOT HAVING POINTED EARS, and NOT SAYING "MEOW." This way of putting it shows that NOT A CAT has a prototype, which happens to contain negative features. The concept posses no threat to prototype theory.

11.2.2   Emergent Features

Fodor's second argument against the compositionality of prototypes requires a bit more discussion. Assume that we strongly associate the property DANGEROUS with BROWN COW, but not with BROWN or COW considered in isolation. Fodor thinks that this is evidence that the prototype of BROWN COW is not compositionally derived. There are three strategies that one can pursue in response to this kind of example. First, one can deny that concepts like BROWN COW are compounds. Second, one can argue that, despite appearances, the property DANGEROUS is derived from one of the constituents of BROWN COW. Third, one can argue that cases in which there are differences between the prototypes of compounds and the prototypes of their constituents are permissible exceptions to the compositionality requirement. I will consider these strategies in turn.

According to the first strategy, concepts like BROWN COW are "holophrastic": they are learned as whole units independently of their parts. Thus, BROWN COW is not a simple composite of BROWN and COW but an independent concept (which happens to have an overlapping extension). This view may be correct in some cases (e.g., UNION SUIT,

GRAY MATTER, and DUMB WAITER). There is an etymological relationship between the apparent constituent concepts and the whole, but our understanding of the whole is not derived from that connection alone. We must be taught the conventional meaning. But this cannot work in every case. If compounds were always learned independently of their constituents, we would not be able to explain the productivity of thought.

According to the second strategy, the emergent features of a phrasal concept do not emerge from outside sources. Instead, they are features of the constituents that go unnoticed when the constituents are considered in isolation. One version of this strategy is suggested by Block (1993).[2] He argues that the feature DANGEROUS, which is hypothetically attributed to the concept BROWN COW but not to BROWN or COW, may actually exist in one of the latter in the form of a conditional. Specifically, COW may have the feature DANGEROUS-IF-BROWN. If COW contains this conditional feature, then the fact that BROWN COW contains the feature DANGEROUS can be explained without violating compositionality. DANGEROUS is simply inferred from DANGEROUS-IF-BROWN and BROWN. Likewise, FISH may contain the feature LIVES-IN-A-BOWL-IF-A-PET.

The main problem with this proposal is that it is completely implausible that every feature that emerges in phrasal concepts is conditionally encoded in their constituents. We presumably believe that fish live in bowls if they are pets because we have encountered pet fish. In other words, the conditional feature is learned only because the phrasal concept is familiar. But *unfamiliar* phrasal concepts can have emergent features as well. Subjects say that carpenters who graduated from Harvard are nonmaterialistic *even if they have never thought about such individuals before*. The proposal under consideration would say that HARVARD GRADUATE contains the feature NONMATERIALISTIC-IF-A-CARPENTER. If one has never thought about Harvard carpenters before, this could not be the case.

The third reply to the emergent-feature objection begins by conceding that some features associated with phrasal concepts do not come from their constituents. They are introduced from sources that are external to the concepts being combined. There are two likely external sources of emergent features. The first is our memories of exemplars. Hampton

(1987) calls this "extensional feedback." The belief that instances of PET FISH live in bowls probably derives from our memories of actual pet-fish exemplars. The second external source is background knowledge. Why do we think Harvard carpenters are nonmaterialistic? The answer may look something like this. We believe that Harvard graduates are well educated, privileged, and successful. We believe that carpenters are blue-collar workers who do not require college degrees. General background knowledge tells us that people try to achieve their goals to the best of their ability. We then reason that if a Harvard graduate has chosen carpentry as her profession, carpentry is the best way that she can try to realize her goals. If her goal were wealth and luxury, her education would allow her to pursue a career that is better suited for achieving that goal. Therefore, wealth and luxury cannot be her goals; she is nonmaterialistic. If this kind of explanation is correct, some emergent properties derive from reasoning on the basis of background knowledge. If exemplar memories and background knowledge contribute to the prototypes of our phrasal concepts, then those prototypes are not compositional.

At first blush, this concession looks fatal for prototype theory. If prototypes of phrasal concepts are not compositional and concepts must be compositional, then prototypes cannot be concepts. Though it is consistent with what I have been saying, I want to suggest that this argument actually misconstrues the modality of the compositionality requirement. It is one thing to say that, as a matter of fact, the prototypes of phrasal concepts are not compositionally derived, and another thing to say that they cannot be compositionally derived. Similarly, it is one thing to say that concepts must *be* compositional, and another to say that they must *be capable* of compositional combination. I submit that only the latter is required.

The compositionality desideratum should be interpreted as saying that we *can* generate phrasal concepts and thoughts compositionally, not that we always do. There is no need to demand that the contents of phrasal concepts always be inherited from their constituents. Such a demand would be imprudent. Suppose that we have encountered lots of red plants, and that they have all been poisonous. Being poisonous is not prototypical of red things or of plants. Nevertheless, we would avoid hazards by including that feature in our RED PLANT prototype. Here exemplar knowledge saves the day. Now consider the concept CONCRETE HAMBURGER. We all probably lack exemplar knowledge of these, but background knowledge detects a potential hazard. In particular, we can reason that attempting to eat a concrete hamburger would cause one's teeth to break. BREAKING TEETH is not a prototypical feature of hamburgers or concrete things considered in isolation, but we would be wise to count it as a feature of our CONCRETE HAMBURGER concept.

These considerations suggest the following principle. We should derive the prototypes of phrasal concepts in a purely compositional way *only when relevant background knowledge and exemplar memories are unavailable.*[3] When these things are available, we should use them. It is simply bad cognitive policy to limit ourselves to the information contained in the constituents of our phrasal concepts when we have other relevant information at our disposal.

The principle just described is normative, and it can be defended on a priori grounds. A descriptive analog of this claim has been defended on empirical grounds by Hampton (1987) and Rips (1995). They argue that a phrasal concept cannot count as a counterexample to compositionality if we have information about the things falling under this concept. Such alleged counterexamples violate what Rips calls the "no-peeking principle." If we have "peeked" at the objects falling under a phrasal concept, we use the information so acquired in representing that concept.

Fodor and Lepore (1996) anticipate a similar objection. They consider the proposal that we combine concepts compositionally when, and only when, we are unfamiliar with the exemplars falling under them. They reject this proposal by arguing that there are cases in which a lack of exemplar knowledge fails to predict compositional combination. For example, none of us have ever seen exemplars of the concept PET FISH LIVING IN ARMENIA THAT HAVE RECENTLY SWALLOWED THEIR OWNERS. Nevertheless, this concept has emergent features. Such fish are presumably large and voracious. Therefore, noncompositional combination cannot be explained by the possession of exemplar knowledge or "peeking." On closer analysis, however, the proposal that Fodor and Lepore consider is a straw man. Noncompositional combination occurs not only when we have exemplar knowledge but also when we have relevant background knowledge. Despite our lack of familiarity with killer pet fish, we can

Table 11.1
When prototype combination gives rise to emergent features

Concept	Exemplar knowledge	Background knowledge	Emergent features
PET FISH	Yes	No	Yes
RED PLANT	Yes	No	Yes
KILLER FISH	No	Yes	Yes
CONCRETE HAMBURGER	No	Yes	Yes
COWS BELONGING TO PEOPLE WHOSE NAMES BEGIN WITH "W"	No	No	No

use background knowledge to reason that such fish will be large and voracious. We introduce these features to explain how and why they swallow their owners. The example provided by Fodor and Lepore poses no threat because the proposal I am considering predicts that compositional mechanisms will be used only when we lack *both* exemplar knowledge *and* relevant background knowledge. Compositionality is a fallback system, not a mandatory mode of operation.

This principle may appear to be untestable. When do we ever lack relevant background knowledge? Ironically, Fodor and Lepore provide us with a good example. They consider the concept COWS BELONGING TO PEOPLE WHOSE NAMES BEGIN WITH "W." It is difficult to think of any background knowledge that can be brought to bear on this compound. Therefore, the present proposal predicts a lack of emergent features, and intuition suggests that this prediction is correct (table 11.1).[4] Of course, such cases are probably rare. We generally have relevant background knowledge. When such knowledge is available, purely compositional combination is still presumably possible, but we do not exercise this possibility because doing so would be imprudent. If we are assigned the duty of capturing the pet fish that swallowed their owners, we had better take their probable size into consideration.

Thus far, I have argued that emergent features are consistent with the claim that we have the ability to combine prototypes compositionally. But why think that a mere ability is sufficient to satisfy the compositionality requirement? The answer comes from a consideration of the phenomena that motivate that requirement. First, consider productivity. People are capable of entertaining an unbounded number of novel thoughts given finite means. Compositionality explains this potential because compositional systems of representation can, in principle, generate an unbounded number of representations using a finite set of primitives and combination rules. A person can entertain a novel compound by combining two concepts she already possesses. Productivity would be impossible if each novel compound had to be learned separately. Notice the modality of this requirement and its explanation. We *can* entertain arbitrary novel thoughts because they *can* be generated by combining familiar concepts. Even if, as a matter of fact, we never generated novel phrasal concepts by simply combining their familiar components, we might still possess this ability. The fact that we use background knowledge and exemplar memories is compatible with a compositional ability, and a compositional ability is enough to explain productivity.

Likewise for systematicity. People are *able* to form thoughts that are systematically related to the ones that they are currently entertaining, but they do not necessarily exercise this ability. If I believe that Oscar ate a crab, I do not also form the thought that a crab ate Oscar. What matters is that I could form this thought. The mere existence of emergent features does nothing to cast doubt on that ability. Suppose that my EAT prototype contains the feature USING A NUT CRACKER when I form the thought that Oscar ate a crab. This feature emerges because I have experienced crab consumption, but it would not emerge if I formed the thought that a crab ate Oscar. That asymmetry makes no difference. The fact is that if I could have formed the first thought in a compositional way, then I could have formed the second thought. The ability is enough.

In sum, Fodor bases his conclusion that prototypes are not compositional on the premises that concepts are compositional and prototypes are not. But this reasoning is based on an equivocation. In saying that concepts are compositional, the strongest interpretation we can defend is that they are *potentially* compositional. In saying that prototypes are not compositional, the strongest interpretation that we can defend is that they are not *necessarily* compositional. The claim that prototypes are not necessarily compositional is consistent with the claim that prototypes are potentially compositional. Thus, the compositionality required of prototypes is modally different from the compositionality denied of prototypes. The fact that prototypes do not always combine compositionally is consistent with the claim that prototypes satisfy the strongest defensible version of the compositionality requirement.

11.2.3   Systematicity and Context Sensitivity

The preceding considerations do not undermine Fodor's argument from context sensitivity. According to that argument, even if we grant that prototypes are compositional, they are not compositional in the right way. When prototypes combine compositionally, they do so in a context-sensitive way. If combination is context-sensitive, the ability to combine concepts in one context may not carry with it the ability to combine them in another context. Systematicity is explained by the fact that the same set of concepts can be arranged in different ways using the same rules. But different arrangements produce different contexts. Therefore, prototypes cannot explain systematicity.

To respond to this challenge, one must give a negative answer to at least one of the following two questions: Is prototype combination context-sensitive when prototypes are combined compositionally? And if so, does this preclude an explanation of systematicity?

A system of prototype combination is compositional only if it can compute a new prototype from a pair of existing prototypes without bringing external information to bear. I am inclined to believe that any remotely plausible compositional system of prototype combination must be context-sensitive. An example of a non-context-sensitive system would be one that simply took all the features in a pair of prototypes being joined and grouped them together. On such a system, how a given prototype is represented would not depend on what other prototypes it is joined with, or on whether it was joined with any other prototypes at all. There seems to be little reason to adopt such a system.

First, unlike definitions, the feature representations forming prototypes do not constitute necessary conditions. Therefore, modifying them in combination is not prohibited on semantic grounds. Second, in cases like the PURPLE APPLE concept mentioned above, feature modification is obligatory on pain of contradiction (a purple apple cannot be red, even though apples are prototypically red). Third, there are plenty of psychological data suggesting that people make systematic modifications when they combine prototypes, even when there are no emergent features. For example, Smith et al. (1988) have shown that when an objects falls under both a noun concept, such as FRUIT, and an adjective-noun concept, such as RED FRUIT, it will be judged to be more typical of the latter than of the former. To explain this, they say that the weights of features and feature dimensions change when concepts combine.

These considerations suggest that the systems used for compositional prototype combination are context-sensitive. How FRUIT is represented in isolation, for example, may differ from how it is represented in RED FRUIT. If compositional prototype combination is context-sensitive, then we must determine whether it can explain systematicity.

To show that the ability to entertain the thought that Oscar ate a crab entails the ability to entertain the thought that a crab ate Oscar, two things must be established:

1. If one can entertain the first thought, one possesses its constituent concepts.

2. The rules that allow one to construct the first thought from its constituent concepts can also be used to construct the second thought.

In other words, systematicity is explained by the fact that possessing certain mental states presupposes possessing certain rules and representations that are sufficient for the ability to possess certain other mental states. The question is whether these two requirements can be met on a context-sensitive account of combination.

There is an objection to the claim that prototype theory satisfies (1). On Fodor's theory of concepts, (1) is explained by the fact that thoughts are construed as languagelike strings that literally contain their constituents as separable units. On a prototype theory, this is not the case. The RED FRUIT prototype is not a pair of independent symbols corresponding to RED and FRUIT but one complex bundle of features corresponding to fruit with a highly weighted constituent feature corresponding to red. Simply subtracting the red feature will not yield a representation of fruit as such. So there seems to be no easy road back from compound prototypes to prototypes of their constituents. Having a RED FRUIT prototype is not a sufficient condition for having a FRUIT prototype in isolation.

This allegation is consistent with the assumption that, as a matter of fact, possessing a compound prototype generally entails possession of its constituents. If there are mechanisms in place to ensure a general entailment between possessing a compound prototype and possessing its constituents, then (1) is sufficiently secure. I think such mechanisms are in place.

There are two main ways in which one can come to have a prototype corresponding to a phrasal concept such as RED FRUIT. One can get it by combining other prototypes that have been acquired (i.e., RED and FRUIT) or by directly observing red fruit. When the first method of acquisition is used, comprehension of the phrasal concept entails possession of its constituents. When the second method of acquisition is used, exposure to red fruits generally causes one to abstract representations for RED and FRUIT along with the compound. After all, prototypes are generated by abstracting feature representations. The resulting representations of RED and FRUIT may not capture the central tendency of the categories "red" "fruit," but they are adequate for tracking other instances of these categories. If a person acquires a RED FRUIT concept by observing red fruits and a BLUE CAR concept by observing blue cars, then there is good reason to think that she is also able to track red cars and blue fruits. In short, it is hard to have a phrasal concept without having representations corresponding to its constituents. Consequently, prototype theory can satisfy (1).

To satisfy (2), the rules used in generating one compound prototype must be capable of generating other compound prototypes. If this were not the case, the fact that I have a rule for deriving the thought that Oscar ate a crab from the concepts OSCAR, EAT, and CRAB would not entail that I have a rule for deriving the thought that a crab ate Oscar from the same concepts. It is difficult to see why context-sensitive combination rules would preclude multiple applications of the same rules.

As an existence proof, consider Smith et al.'s (1988) Selective Modification Model of adjective-noun prototype combination. On this model, noun concepts are formed of attribute-value sets. Attributes are assigned weights corresponding to their saliences, and values are assigned weights corresponding to their diagnosticity. Adjectives correspond to values. When an adjective is combined with a noun, three things happen: first, the appropriate attribute (the one that subsumes or would subsume the value corresponding to the adjective) is selected in the noun; second, the value corresponding to the adjective is increased to the maximum and all other values in the selected attribute are reduced to the minimum; third, the salience of the value is increased. For example, when RED combines with FRUIT, the COLOR attribute in FRUIT is selected; the RED value is increased to the maximum and all other color values are reduced to the minimum; and the salience value of COLOR in increased.

This account may be wrong in its details, but it shows that a single method of combination can be used to subsume many different cases even though it is context-sensitive. FRUIT is represented differently in RED FRUIT and SOUR FRUIT, but both of these compounds can be derived using the same rule. Therefore, the fact that a concept is represented differently in different combinations does not entail that different rules were used to construct those combinations.[5]

Before applying the lesson of the Selective Modification Model to the examples involving Oscar and the crab, it is necessary to answer an objection. If something is a purple apple, it is also purple, by logical necessity; PURPLE APPLE logically entails PURPLE. Fodor and Lepore (1996) claim that the Selective Modification Model cannot accommodate this fact. If PURPLE *simply replaces* the prototypical feature RED in the APPLE prototype, PURPLE APPLE does not logically entail PURPLE because APPLE does not logically entail RED. To make the entailment go through, the weight of purple would have to be "infinitely" increased, but this would render the account noncompositional.

This objection can be quickly defused. As I just indicated, the Selective Modification Model claims that both attribute and value weights increase when an adjective concept replaces a default prototypical feature during conceptual combination. Thus, the PURPLE in PURPLE APPLE has higher weight than the RED in APPLE. The rule can be designed to increase the weight to such an extent that PURPLE exceeds the threshold for the PURPLE APPLE prototype, and so the entailment goes through.

The prototype theorist can also object that Fodor and Lepore misdiagnose the source of the entailment in question. They assume that the inference from PURPLE APPLE to PURPLE is necessarily true because it is a consequence of the logical form of PURPLE APPLE. There is another explanation. One can ague that something qualifies as a PURPLE APPLE concept only if it refers to purple apples, and that something qualifies as a PURPLE concept only if it refers to purple things. If so, PURPLE APPLE necessarily entails PURPLE on any account, no matter what one thinks of logical form. In this light, Fodor and Lepore are wrong to accuse prototype theorists of missing a logical entailment.

In response, Fodor and Lepore can reformulate their objection. On Fodor's theory, a compound generated by combing PURPLE and APPLE refers to purple apples in virtue of the fact that the reference of compound concepts is determined by the reference of their constituents together with logical form. Fodor and Lepore can argue that because prototypes lack logical form, prototype theory cannot ensure that combining PURPLE and APPLE will produce a PURPLE APPLE concept.

This objection is not compelling. The prototype theorist can stipulate that when concepts are combined by selective modification, they refer to the intersection of what their constituents refer to. On this view, combination rules function as a kind of ersatz logical form. The compound created by combining PURPLE and APPLE refers to purple apples, not in virtue of its form, but in virtue of the fact that it is generated by a certain rule.

Alternatively, the prototype theorist can adopt a semantic theory according to which compounds refer in the same way as their components. For example, one might stipulate that both compounds and simpler concepts pick out what they reliably detect. If weights are adjusted in the fashion of the Selective Modification Model, it is reasonable to predict that the compound generated by combining PURPLE and APPLE will detect purple apples quite reliably.

Both of these proposals satisfy the condition that we can get a PURPLE APPLE concept by combining PURPLE and APPLE. Therefore, the reformulated version of the Fodor and Lepore objection poses no threat.

The Selective Modification Model is designed to handle very simple cases of adjective-noun combination. One might worry that a model of this kind cannot be constructed for more complex cases. Is it really plausible that the same rule is used to construct both OSCAR ATE A CRAB and A CRAB ATE OSCAR? What might that rule be? One (very rough) proposal is that verbal concepts very schematically represent action sequences that become less schematic when the objects involved in those actions are specified. For example, EAT might include the schematic action sequence OBJECT₁ OPENS MOUTH, PUTS OBJECT₂ IN MOUTH, and MOVES JAW. When the representations of OSCAR and CRAB are combined with EAT, they are selectively modified. OSCAR is modified to include an opening mouth and a moving jaw, and the CRAB representation is modified to follow a movement trajectory into Oscar's mouth. Background knowledge may lead to further changes, but these first changes are compositional, like the changes in the Selective Modification Model.

This proposal results in context sensitivity. If OSCAR is assigned the subject role, he will be represented as moving his mouth, and if he is assigned the object role, he will be represented as moving into the crab's mouth. But such context sensitivity does not prevent the same rule from being applied to form many distinct thoughts.

The example raises a concern. I suggested that the EAT prototype contains the action OPENS MOUTH. It is likely that this feature cannot be applied to every noun concept. In particular, EAT cannot be directly applied to a noun concept corresponding to an object that has no mouth. This creates an asymmetry in some cases. We can use the rule I described to form the thought that Oscar ate an apple, but we cannot us it to form the thought that an apple ate Oscar. Prototype theories must concede that our ability to entertain thoughts of the form aRb does not always endow us with the ability to entertain the corresponding thoughts of the form bRa. One might object that prototype theory is inadequate because it exploits mechanisms of combination that are not *fully* systematic.

The objection backfires. The limitations that prototype theory places on systematicity are actually an advantage. Fodor's own language-of-thought model does not predict such limitations. If thoughts were strings of unstructured symbols, there would be no reason to predict any asymmetries between thoughts of the form aRb and thoughts of the form bRa. But such asymmetries seem to be pervasive. It is easier to conceive of a person eating an apple than an apple eating a person. Prototype theory predicts this asymmetry, and Fodor's theory does not. The limitations predicted by prototype theory coincide with the limitations of our cognitive systems. The use of context-sensitive rules does not prevent prototype theory from explaining systematicity. It merely imposes psychologically realistic constraints on systematicity.

11.3   A Three-Stage Model of Concept Combination

The preceding discussion demonstrates that arguments against the compositionality of prototypes are unsuccessful. I argued that the mere possibility of compositional combination is sufficient for explaining productivity and systematicity. This conclusion allows for the inclusion of noncompositional mechanisms in an account of concept combination. An adequate account needs to include such mechanisms (e.g., Murphy 1988, Medin and Shoben 1988, Rips 1995). In this section, I offer, in rough outline, an informal model of concept combination that integrates compositional and noncompositional mechanisms.

11.3.1   The Retrieval Stage
The model postulates three stages. In presenting them, I focus on adjective-noun and noun-noun combinations of concepts generated in response to verbal cues. The function of the first stage is to see whether information relevant to representing a compound concept is already available in memory. Suppose that someone is asked to form the concept expressed by some two-word phrase. The first thing she will do is search her memory for an appropriate representation. There are two ways. In cases where a phrase has been encountered often enough to attain its own associated concept, the subject can simply use the verbal cue to call up that concept. If the compound is not found, she can attempt a cross-listing process. Here the subject calls up the *exemplars* for the concepts corresponding to the words in the phrase and determines whether any exemplars fall under both concepts. If any exemplars can be cross-listed, they can be used to form a representation of the compound by constructing a prototype on the fly. In both of these situations, subjects do not need to compute a combination for the phrasal concept, because enough information is available in memory. I call this the *retrieval stage*.

The retrieval stage explains concepts such as PET FISH and LARGE SPOON. These are not generated by combining their constituent concepts. Instead, they are either given their own representations in memory or created by online cross-listing. PET FISH is a likely candidate for the former. We may form a PET FISH concept that is independent of our PET and FISH concepts as a result of our numerous encounters with pet fish.

This concept will be a prototype abstracted from experiences of just those fish that are pets, rather than the whole set of fish experiences. We might first identify something as a pet fish by identifying it as a PET and as a FISH, but once it has been identified as both of these things, a PET FISH representation is formed, which can be used to identify future instances. If we repeatedly encounter objects that fall under the same two concepts, we can avoid having to go through a concept-combination process by creating a separate representation for the compound. On this analysis, we say that pet fish live in bowls because our PET FISH concept is abstracted from encounters with fish that typically live in bowls even though our FISH concept is not.

LARGE SPOON is less likely to be stored as such in memory, but it can be generated by cross-listing. When asked to conceptualize "large spoon," we call up memories of SPOON exemplars and search them to see if any qualify as large. In doing this, we do not combine LARGE with SPOON, we simply search for SPOON-exemplar representations that have LARGE as a feature. If we find any, we use them to abstract a prototype that can represent the compound. Most of the exemplars thus retrieved are wooden, so we include WOODEN as a feature of our LARGE SPOON concept, even though it is not a typical feature of SPOONS or LARGE THINGS. If we created a LARGE SPOON concept by simply adding the feature LARGE to a SPOON prototype, we would not expect this feature to emerge. Cross-listing allows us to represent the categories designated by phrasal concepts more accurately than a combination process would because it relies on memories of the exemplars of those categories.

Postulating a retrieval stage predicts that phrasal concepts with whose instances we are relatively familiar will generate emergent features because they are not constructed compositionally (Hampton 1987, Rips 1995, Gray and Smith 1995). The prediction is borne out by the two examples just considered. Murphy (1988) provides many others: yellow jackets are judged to be worn by fishermen; overturned chairs are said to be on tables; and casual shirts are said to be pulled over your head. All these examples suggest that phrasal concepts with familiar instances can be represented by recalling those instances, or prototypes of those instances, from memory. For this reason, such concepts are not really counterexamples to compositional theories of concept combination.

11.3.2   The Composition Stage

If the retrieval stage is unsuccessful, we attempt to join a pair of concepts by applying combination rules. Some of these rules are compositional. They can be applied without the help of exemplar memories or background knowledge. The information contained in the concepts being combined is enough.

The Selective Modification Model of Smith et al. (1988) is an example of this. As we have seen, selective modification works by first identifying an attribute dimension in one concept and then replacing its default value with another concept (and adjusting weights). We can call these steps alignment and integration respectively. In the cases that Smith et al. examine, the adjective concepts appear as features of the nouns they modify before combination takes place. As a result, the alignment process is especially easy. To represent RED FRUIT, one has no difficulty finding a dimension in FRUIT to align RED with because RED is already a constituent of FRUIT. One merely increases the importance of RED in FRUIT by making appropriate adjustments to the feature weights. In other cases, the adjective feature does not exist in the noun concept, but an obvious attribute dimension does. Consider STRIPED APPLE. The feature STRIPED is not stored as an optional value in our APPLE concept. Yet if APPLE has a surface pattern attribute, STRIPED APPLE can be represented by adding STRIPED to that attribute and making the requisite adjustments in the weights.

Like RED, STRIPED may be unidimensional. It does not decompose into a structured collection of features. Sometimes both of the concepts being combined are multidimensional. The model of Smith et al. is not designed with such cases in mind, but it can be adapted to accommodate them.[6] One example of this was the EAT case described above. Consider the concept SQUIRREL SNAKE, an example used by Wisniewski (1997) in developing a different model of conceptual combination. This is a novel compound to most of us, but we can come up with interpretations. One common interpretation is that a squirrel snake is a snake that eats squirrels. One can arrive at this interpretation by alignment and integration. To align SQUIRREL and SNAKE, one looks for a dimension value in SNAKE that is most similar to SQUIRREL. Suppose that SNAKE has the attribute DIET, describing what snakes typically eat. This attribute may have a number of default values, including MICE. Since squirrels have more in common with mice than with other things represented in the SNAKE concept, SQUIRREL is aligned with the diet dimension and replaces MICE.

The SQUIRREL SNAKE example works in essentially the same way as the RED FRUIT example. The main difference is that RED FRUIT can be said to pick out objects that fall under both of its constituent concepts, whereas SQUIRREL SNAKE cannot. A red fruit is a fruit that is also red, but a squirrel snake is not a snake that is also a squirrel. The same basic process can thus lead to different kinds of compounds. Wisniewski calls the processed used in forming the SQUIRREL SNAKE concept "relation linking" because the two concepts are combined by identifying a relation that links them together. This term conceals the parallels between the SQUIRREL SNAKE case and the RED FRUIT case. I coin the term "aligntegration" to name the process of aligning and integrating that underlies both examples.

Wisniewski presents another group of examples that may derive from a special case of aligntegration. He calls these cases of "property construction." Here concepts are combined by aligning a *small subset* of the features in one concept with an attribute dimension in another concept. For example, a ZEBRA TIE might be interpreted as a tie with zebralike stripes on it.[7] The ZEBRA pattern is placed under the tie-pattern slot, while other features are dropped. The pattern attribute may be selected because being striped is a default value for ties and the most salient feature of zebras. Once the ZEBRA pattern is in place, the rest of the ZEBRA features are dropped. This process may be part of the third stage in the combination process, to be described below.

Aligntegration can be used to explain a process that Langacker (1987) calls accommodation. Langacker speculates that we represent the action of running differently when we represent quadrupeds running as opposed to bipeds running. To explain this, assume that RUNNING includes the attribute dimension RAPID-LEG-MOVEMENTS. This dimension affects two leg representations when combined with HUMAN and four leg representations when combined with LION. Different concepts align with the same dimension but are integrated differently. This process is perfectly compositional, but highly context-sensitive.

Aligntegration does not always work. When combining two concepts, there are sometimes no obvious dimensions in the modified concept under which the features of the modifying concept can be placed. There are other ways of combining concepts that do not depend on alignment. For example, consider a model of concept combination developed by Hampton (1991). On this model, the features of two concepts are simply pooled together. After features are pooled, adjustments are made as follows: features that are highly weighted in either concept retain high weights in the compound; next, the remaining features are assigned weights as a function of their importance for both concepts (e.g., by averaging); finally, features with very low weights are dropped from the representation. I call this process "feature pooling."

Feature pooling can be used to explain a class of examples that Wisniewski (1997) describes as cases of hybridization. The concept HOUSEBOAT, for example, may be understood even by those who have never encountered a houseboat if they follow a procedure like the one Hampton describes.[8] The most important features of HOUSE and BOAT are retained, while other features (e.g., BACKYARD and SAILS) are dropped.

Feature pooling and aligntegration are sometimes applied under the influence of background knowledge or exemplar knowledge. For example, two concepts may be aligntegrated by using external information to create a new attribute dimension. A SUSHI TILE may be interpreted as a tile on which sushi is served, even if neither TILE nor SUSHI contain a serving surface dimension. The dimension is added with the help of the exemplar knowledge that sushi is sometimes served on unusual surfaces. But aligntegration can be applied in a purely compositional way. For example, TILE may have a COVERS-A-SURFACE dimension, which is filled by different default values, such as BATHROOM FLOOR. Using this dimension, we may interpret SUSHI TILE as tile that is used to cover the surface of sushi. Departures from compositionality are common but not obligatory. Both aligntegration and feature pooling can compute compounds without introducing features or dimensions that are external to the concepts being combined.

One might wonder how one chooses between combination strategies. When does one use aligntegration, and when does one pool features? Wisniewski (1996, 1997) suggests that similarity plays an important role. When two concepts represent things that are very dissimilar, aligntegration is used (e.g., HORSE HOTEL may be a place where horses stay for the night). When they are very similar, feature pooling is more likely (e.g., HORSE GOAT may be a hybrid of a goat and a horse). But the decision is not fixed. In most cases, either process could work (e.g., a horse hotel may be a hotel shaped like a horse, and a horse goat may be a goat that follows horses around). Wisniewski proposes that different combination strategies compete against each other in parallel. This makes sense. While one strategy may be especially easy, and hence more likely to win such a competition, there is little reason not to attempt multiple strategies at once.

I believe that aligntegration and feature pooling are both attempted in parallel after one has unsuccessfully attempted to locate a compound concept in memory. They make up the second stage in the process of conceptual combination. This stage can be purely compositional. For that reason, I call it the *composition stage*.

11.3.3   The Analysis Stage

The composition stage is succeeded by a third stage in concept combination. After combining a pair of concepts, we *analyze* the new collection of features to see whether it is coherent. Gaps must be filled in, inferences must be drawn, and apparent inconsistencies must be eliminated or explained. This *analysis stage* is quite open-ended. This is where we bring background knowledge to bear in conceptual combination. The result is a departure from compositionality. When background knowledge is used to evaluate and embellish compounds generated in the compositional stage, features that were not constituents of the combined concepts can be introduced. My characterization of the reasoning involved in arriving at emergent features for HARVARD CARPENTER typifies the process I have in mind. A conflict between the components of this compound is resolved by adding the feature NONMATERIALISTIC. Other examples are easy to multiply, and they are pervasive in the literature. Considering a few of them will be helpful.

The analysis stage is closely related to what Murphy (1988) calls elaboration. Let us look at a couple of his examples. First, Murphy found that "apartment dogs" are judged to be small, quiet, and well behaved even though these features are not associated with either component of this compound. One explanation is that subjects first use aligntegration and simply interpret APARTMENT DOG as designating dogs that live in apartments. Then subjects analyze the new compound and discover a conflict: the typical features of dogs (e.g., big, loud, rambunctious) clash with typical features of apartments (e.g., small, close to other apartments, filled with breakable things). Deciding what counts as a conflict and how to resolve it calls on background knowledge. We need background knowledge to know that rambunctious behavior can cause fragile things to break. We reason that the conflict can be eliminated if apartment dogs are well behaved.

To take another example, Murphy observes that the feature RUSTY emerges from ANCIENT SAW. This concept may be initially created using simple feature pooling: the feature ANCIENT is simply added to the collection of features making up SAW. In the analysis stage, this addition invites an inference. Saws are typically metal; ancient things are old; and old metal is typically rusty; therefore, an ancient saw must be rusty as well. The third premise in this reasoning introduces background knowledge.

The analysis stage is also comparable to what Hampton (1991) calls a "consistency checking procedure." He thinks such a procedure occurs after features are pooled. For example, once we pool features together to create the concept PET SKUNK, we discover a conflict between the skunk feature MALODOROUS and the pet feature PLEASANT-TO-CUDDLE-UP-WITH. Hampton suggests that the concept is resolved by presuming that pet skunks have been surgically altered to eliminate their odor. This is an emergent feature. Hampton also thinks that the consistency check can explain why some adjectives have a negating affect on the nouns they modify. When we use feature pooling to form STONE LION, for example, we discover a conflict between being made of stone and being a living thing. This conflict is resolved by eliminating the latter feature. Stone lions are not living things, and hence not lions.

11.3.4 The RCA Model Summarized

I can now summarize my three-stage model. Concept combination begins with the retrieval stage. When two concepts are brought together, one first attempts to look for an appropriate representation in memory. This can be done by locating a stored compound concept or by locating

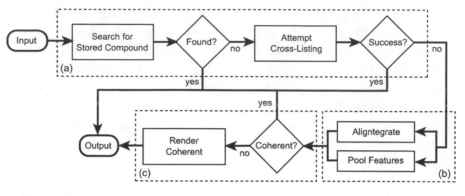

Figure 11.1
A flow chart representing the components of the RCA model: (a) the retrieval stage, (b) the compositional stage, and (c) the analysis stage.

exemplar representations that can be cross-listed under both of the concepts being combined. If this stage is unsuccessful, it is followed by the composition stage. Here, a pair of concepts is compositionally combined by aligntegration or feature pooling. Once a compound is generated, the collection of features that constitute it must be analyzed. In the analysis stage, apparent conflicts or gaps are resolved by eliminating, modifying, and introducing features. I call this the RCA model (for retrieval, composition, and analysis). The stages of the RCA model are illustrated in figure 11.1.

The RCA model borrows from several of the theories of concept combination that are currently being explored by psychologists. It incorporates, at least provisionally, aspects of Hampton's Composite-Prototype Model, Murphy's Specialization and Elaboration Model, Smith et al.'s Selective-Modification Model, and Wisniewski's Comprehensive Model. Each of these theories can contribute to our understanding of the many processes involved in concept combination. The RCA model incorporates these processes into a single model.

There are some empirical findings that can be used to argue against the sequence of stages postulated by the RCA model. Springer and Murphy (1992) demonstrate that emergent properties are sometimes accessed as fast as or faster than properties that arise through composition. This suggests that analysis cannot come after the composition stage.

Several replies are available. First, the fact that emergent features are reported as fast as or faster than features derived through composition does not prove that they are derived first. If analysis is the final stage in the combination process, it is also the one that comes closest in time to our verbal descriptions of newly derived compounds. Emergent features may be reported first because they are the most recently derived. The speed with which emergent features are reported can be explained by the fact that they are the most surprising. Like other surprises, they may attract attention. If you are asked to describe a picture of a man with a black suit and clown shoes on, you may see his black suit first, but you will probably report the shoes more quickly. I suspect that if response deadlines were pushed up, so that subjects have less chance to notice surprising novel features, inherited compositional features would be reported faster.

I must also reiterate that the RCA model does not always predict that emergent features are derived last, because some are derived during the retrieval stage, which precedes the composition stage. The belief that pet fish live in bowls is an example. The RCA model predicts that access to such features will be quite fast. Springer and Murphy (1992) anticipate this response. They correctly reason that familiar compounds are not counterexamples to theories that postulate composition before analysis, because familiar compounds may be stored in memory. To provide good counterexamples, Springer and Murphy try to restrict themselves to unfamiliar compounds by ruling out cases that subjects rate as familiar. This technique for excluding familiar cases is inadequate. As my description of cross-listing emphasizes, a compound can have familiar instances even if the phrase that designates it is unfamiliar. Springer and Murphy did not adequately control for this. As a result, they have not refuted the claim that composition precedes analysis.

Springer and Murphy's results can also be accommodated by concession. I conceded that aligntegration can involve the introduction of attribute features not contained within the pair of concepts being combined. The rules applied during the compositional stage can make use of relevant category knowledge. Therefore, features can emerge during the composition stage. Furthermore, it is possible that the analysis stage overlaps with the composition stage, kicking in just after composition begins. This proposal construes the RCA stages as cascading rather than proceeding serially. If analysis overlaps with composition, some emergent features appear at least as early as composition features.

To conclude, let me reiterate how the RCA model satisfies the compositionality requirement. In the last section, I argued that the compositionality requirement is satisfied by a theory that postulates a compositional *potential*. We must *be able* to combine concepts compositionally, even if we do not do that all the time. The RCA model complies. Consider a case in which a person has no exemplar memories or background knowledge relevant to a pair of concepts she wishes to combine. After an unsuccessful memory search in the retrieval stage, she moves on to the composition stage. Here feature pooling and aligntegration compete and compositionally produce some combination of features. She then subjects this combination of features to analysis. Lacking any relevant background knowledge, she makes no revisions. The result is derived by purely compositional means. When memories and background knowledge are unavailable, one falls back on unadulterated composition. Compositional mechanisms allow us to successfully combine concepts even when we are ignorant and inexperienced. In ordinary adult humans, this situation is probably rare because we have an abundance of background knowledge and exemplar memories.

The RCA model allows one to count on pure compositionality when in a pinch. That is all we need to explain productivity, systematicity, and the hypothetical cases in which combination occurs without backgrond knowledge or memories. To demand more, i.e., to demand that concept combination is always purely compositional, is both unnecessary and implausible. If we did not use background knowledge and memories during conceptual combination, feature emergence would be inexplicable, and our ability to avoid dangers and negotiate the environment would be greatly impaired. We would break our teeth on concrete hamburgers and succumb to poisonous red plants.

11.3.5 Combining Proxytypes

The RCA model of prototype combination can be effortlessly appropriated by proxytype theory. Consider what happens when a conceptual combination is elicited verbally, as when an experimenter asks someone to describe a large spoon or to describe an apartment dog. As with prototype combination, I propose that the first step is searching for a stored representation of the compound. If one finds a single exemplar in memory answering to both concepts in the named compound, the proxytype called into working memory is a representation of that exemplar. If several exemplars are found, the proxytype may be an extemporaneously generated representation of their central tendency. If no representations of the compound are found, one begins by calling up default proxytypes for each of the named concepts. These are usually very much like prototypes. The default proxytypes are then combined by one or more compositional rules. Finally, the newly combined representation is subjected to analysis in which conflicts are detected and resolved. As with prototypes, proxytype combination is purely compositional when both retrieval and analysis come up empty.

Proxytype theory actually has a couple of advantages over prototype theory when availing itself of the RCA model. First, prototype theorists insist that concepts must be prototypes. Representations of exemplars, causal-explanatory features, or words are not conceptual. When this kind of information comes to bear in the combination process, a prototype theorist must admit that combination relies on nonconceptual information. Proxytype theory is more ecumenical. All this information belongs to the long-term memory networks from which concepts are constructed. The fact that this information contributes to the combination process is not a departure from how proxytypes are formed in the first place, and it does not qualify as an intrusion of nonconceptual information.

Second, the perceptual nature of proxytypes allows for a rich range of ways in which concepts can be aligned. Wisniewski (1997) gives the example ROBIN CANARY. Subjects may interpret this as a canary that is red, like a robin's breast, rather than yellow. In so doing, they may assume that the red color is uniform throughout the canary's body, rather than restricted to its breast. How do they know where to spread the color? Prototypes are usually defined as structured feature lists. If a CANARY prototype has just a generic COLOR attribute with a default value of YELLOW, subjects' specific beliefs about color placement go unexplained. If, instead, CANARY is identified with a perceptual representation with uniform color, specific beliefs about placement are actually predicted.

11.4   Conclusion

Fodor's initial critique of prototype theory appears as a lemma in his argument against empiricism (Fodor 1981). He says that the main difference between empiricists and rationalists is that empiricists admit far fewer primitive concepts. For empiricism to succeed, all concepts have to be constructed out of a small repertoire. There are exactly two options for constructing compound concepts out of primitives: one can build compounds out of defining features or out of nondefining features. Fodor rejects the former option on the grounds that there are few good definitions. Here I agree. He rejects the latter option on the grounds that nondefinitional compounds cannot be compositionally combined. This chapter demonstrates otherwise. I show that a mere potential for compositional combination is enough to explain productivity and systematicity, and I outline a model of concept combination that can satisfy the requirement for compositional potential. I also show that this model can apply to proxytypes, which are perceptually based. Fodor's argument against empiricism is undermined.

Compositionality was the final hurdle. I have completed my demonstration that proxytype theory can satisfy each of the desiderata on a theory of concepts. This success distinguishes it from all its major competitors. Critics of empiricism sometimes think they are flogging a dead horse. Actually, empiricism is just a dark horse, whose surprising performance should make it a frontrunner in the search for an adequate theory of concepts.

Conclusion: Back to Our Senses

English language fairy tales end with the words "And they lived happily ever after." It would be nice to conclude that concept empiricism can now live happily ever after. The traditional German fairy tale ending is, characteristically, less rosy: "Wenn sie nicht gestorben sein, leben sie noch heute." Literally, if they have not died, they are still alive today. Likewise, my arguments may be seen as showing that if concept empiricism has not been refuted, it is still a viable possibility. That would be trivial.

The real moral of this fairy tale can be summarized by saying, *since* concept empiricism has not been refuted, it is still a viable possibility. Arguments presumed to undermine empiricist accounts fall short of their mark. Empiricism should be included when surveying competing theories of concepts. I hope to have also convinced readers of something stronger. When competing theories are surveyed, empiricism actually comes out ahead. More specifically, one version of empiricism, which I call proxytype theory, promises to satisfy more desiderata on a theory of concepts than any of the theories that have dominated recent debate.

Rather than dwelling on the flaws of other theories or retracing the successes of proxytype theory, I want to review what proxytype theory borrows from its rivals.

Informational atomism provides the most promising account of intentionality among the theories I considered. When coupled with an etiological condition, nomological covariation successfully explains how concepts refer to things in the world. Intentionality is an extremely important property. It provides an overarching framework for thinking about what concepts are. On the view I recommend, concepts are mechanisms of detection, which allow us to track things, and which enable us to simulate them when they are not impinging upon our senses.

The leading psychological theories of concepts (prototype theory, exemplar theory, and the theory theory) all provide useful clues about the kinds of information that people associate with categories. This information is invaluable for understanding how concepts are used in categorization (which is essential for detection) and how they combine (which is essential for forming simulations). It is often assumed that one must pick and choose between psychological theories. Concepts must encode information either about central tendencies, or about category instances, or about causal/explanatory principles. The view I defend is more ecumenical. It allows all this information to enter into concepts. Having a diverse repository of information permits flexibility, which helps concepts serve as mechanisms of detection and simulation.

Imagism contributes something equally important. Far too little attention has been paid to the question of primitives. Imagism offers the alluring idea that concepts are built up from perceptual representations. Recent findings support this possibility. Modality-specific resources can be found throughout the brain, and there is considerable evidence that we use perceptual representations in cognitive tasks. It is possible that conceptual abilities evolved through the emergence of structures that allow us to store, group, and reactivate perceptual states offline.

If one combines informational atomists' views about how concepts hook up to the world, psychologists' views about the kinds of information that our concepts encode, and imagists' views about the kind of media in which that information is encoded, one arrives at proxytype theory. Proxytype theory appropriates ideas from all these other accounts. But it is coherent because all of the appropriated elements contribute to the unifying idea that concepts are mechanisms of detection.

Critics may complain that my defense of proxytype theory is incomplete. In arguing that proxytype theory can satisfy the desiderata on a theory of concepts, I rely on a few promissory notes. Rather than explaining how every concept is represented, I offer strategies for handling hard cases. Rather than saying exactly how collections of perceptual states can form thoughts, I point to the idea of simulation as an alternative to strings of amodal symbols. Rather than proving that no amodal representations are innate, I raise doubts about popular arguments for strong forms of nativism. Rather than explaining exactly how concepts combine compositionally, I show that compositional combination is compatible with emergent features and context sensitivity.

Until the details are worked out, it is safest to conclude that proxytype theory *may* be able to satisfy all of the desiderata. This is a significant discovery. Other theories are unable satisfy all the desiderata. If proxytype theory may be able to, then it is the best current contender. My goal has been to show that concept empiricism is worthy of consideration. We should seriously investigate the possibility that our cognitive resources are couched in codes that originated in the service of perception. This hypothesis is not new. The history of philosophy has been a series of pendulum swings between empiricism and rationalism. It is time for the pendulum to swing back to our senses.

Notes

Chapter 1

1. I use small capital letters to designate concepts.

2. "To token" is a piece of philosophical jargon that means to produce a token of. A token is an instance. The AARDVARK concept that enters into my current thought that aardvarks are nocturnal is a token of the same type as the AARDVARK concept that entered into my thought last week that aardvarks live in burrows. Other cognitive scientists sometimes use the verb "to activate" where philosophers use "to token." In more ordinary language, my AARDVARK concept is tokened when I am thinking of aardvarks or experiencing something that brings aardvarks to mind.

3. See, for comparison, the "nonnegotiable conditions" presented by Fodor (1998).

4. It may be more accurate to say the concepts refer to properties, e.g., the property of being a frog or "froghood." The set of frogs is unified by the fact that all frogs have this property. The set of things we take to be frogs excludes some frogs and includes some things that are not frogs.

5. It is often also assumed that concepts must be syntactically compositional. The vehicles of compound concepts must contain the vehicles of their constituent concepts as real parts. This has been the subject of controversy. Some connectionists have argued that one can achieve the kind of compositionality necessary to explain productivity and systematicity without syntactic compositionality in this sense (e.g., van Gelder 1990). I do not want to get embroiled in this debate.

6. By "language" and "linguistic" I will be referring to public languages, the languages that we speak, rather than a special languagelike code used only in thought. Fodor defines a language of thought as a system of mental representation with a combinatorial syntax and semantics. Compositionality, at least in its semantic form, is already a desideratum on a theory of concepts, so it would not be surprising to find that concepts must be languagelike in this minimal sense.

Chapter 2

1. One might complain that such descriptions are not truly definitional, because they are not strictly necessary and sufficient. If the rivers and streams were drained and refilled with vodka, vodka would not be water.

2. If this view is right, philosophical analysis is more like science than introspective psychology. It discovers principles unifying entities that were initially grouped by superficial resemblance.

Chapter 3

1. Unlike most of her followers, Rosch prefers to use the term "prototype" for a behavioral effect or property of nature rather than a class of mental representations (Rosch 1978). Rosch thinks that it is risky to infer facts about the structure of inner states from how subjects respond during experiments. I think that she is overly cautious. Researchers who treat prototypes as mental representations are, like all good scientists, postulating unobservables to systematically explain a range of data.

2. To simplify exposition, I will use the word "feature" to refer to features of objects represented by concepts, or to mental representations of those features, or to words designating those features on feature lists. Context should disambiguate.

3. A sibling category is one with the same parents on a categorization tree. For example, goats and hogs are siblings under the category of animals.

4. For sophisticated accounts of how prototypes combine, see, e.g., Smith, Osherson, Rips, and Keane 1988, Hampton 1988, and chapter 11 below.

Chapter 4

1. Fodor (1981) defines a lexical concept as one that is expressed by a single word in a natural language like English, as opposed to one expressed by a phrase.

2. Fodor appeals to form in discussing Frege cases. He actually has another account of cognitive content, which he introduced to handle Twin Earth cases, namely, his mapping theory of narrow content. I will postpone discussion of the latter till chapter 10, but some of the objections below apply to this proposal as well. The fact that Fodor requires two devices to handle cognitive content is a shortcoming of his account.

Chapter 5

1. In some writings Skinner allows talk of inner states and denouncing operationalist strictures on public observability. But these inner states were construed

as covert internalizations of behavior, not as inner representations or mental images (see Skinner 1953, chap. 17).

2. Although ultimately untenable, this was a welcome antidote for the eugenics craze.

3. Note that mere temporal priority can be dismissed as too weak. If sensory states just happened to occur at some time before conceptual representations with no further link, empiricism would be devoid of interest as a thesis about the nature of concepts.

4. There may, however, be nonempirical arguments against empiricism. For instance, one might argue that sensation, or at least perception, always involves placing something under a concept. On this line, it might look as if there is no way to ground conception in perception without entering a vicious circle. This kind of worry is addressed below.

5. Locke (1690), somewhat confusingly, uses the term "idea" for both sensory states and the concepts they engender. Hume (1739, 1748) uses the term "perceptions" for both such states, but he distinguishes between "impressions" and "ideas."

6. In the limiting case, one might suppose that larger perceptual representations are used to represent larger objects, but isomorphisms can be more abstract. For example, the neural representation of the relation "X is redder than Y" may be isomorphic with a real color relation, but redder objects are certainly not represented by redder brain states.

7. In response, one might note that perceptual systems often exhibit isomorphisms in places where language does not. For example, the physical similarity between a dog and a wolf is plausibly mirrored by our perceptual representations of these animals, but it is not mirrored by the words "dog" and "wolf." Perhaps some isomorphisms are obligatory in perceptual representation and optional in other kinds of representational systems. If this contrast can be used to capture what is distinctive about perceptual representations, one must specify which isomorphisms are obligatory. It seems we can only do that by first saying what features of the world our perceptual representations represent. But, once we have an account of what perceptual representations represent, we may already have an adequate account of what makes them distinctive. In other words, the isomorphism proposal can be saved only be introducing another proposal, which may itself be sufficient.

8. I use "sense," "sensory system," "perceptual system," "input system," and "modality" interchangeably. There are a handful of philosophical discussions of how to identify senses. These include Grice 1962; Armstrong 1968, 211 ff.; Austin Clark 1993; Tye 1995; and Keeley, forthcoming. I am especially indebted to Keeley, forthcoming.

9. See also Keeley, forthcoming, for a slightly different discussion of dedication.

10. To a first approximation, two codes are the same if they include symbols that represent the same things, have the same syntactic properties (e.g., methods

of combination), and can be manipulated in the same way. A more complete theory of codes is beyond the scope of this project.

11. I voice some doubts about the James-Lange theory in Prinz, forthcoming, but defend a successor account that is equally consistent with my analysis of sense modalities.

12. Schwanenflugel's own explanation is that abstract words need extra context because they may be less familiar than concrete words and because they may be used in a wide range of contexts. Rarity and wide applicability may itself reflect a low level of imageability.

13. The developmental case complicates things by introducing the issue of innateness. Evidence against intermodal transfer in infancy would not count against a common code (because that code could be acquired later in development), but evidence for intermodal transfer in infancy would count in favor of an amodal code.

14. Modern genetics and neurobiology have also taken us light years beyond the seventeenth century, but I will focus on the lessons of behavioral techniques, which, for all there comparative simplicity, have been even more revealing.

Chapter 6

1. Milner and Goodale (1995) criticize Ungerleider and Mishkin (1982), arguing that posterior parietal regions are involved in visually guided action rather than location discrimination. They do not deny that there are spatial processing areas, however. These may be somewhere in the inferior parietal or temporal cortex.

2. We sometimes say things like "Helms thinks that abortion is wrong" when Helms is not actually entertaining that thought. This may mean something like "Helms regularly has the occurrent thought that abortion is wrong."

3. Proxytype theory is not to be identified with connectionism, which also departs from orthodoxy in cognitive science (see Bechtel and Abrahamsen 1992). The two approaches may be compatible. Hummel and Biederman (1992) use a connectionist net to implement geon-based recognition, and Andy Clark (1993) argues that nets are ideal for context-sensitive conceptual representations. But compatibility is different from identity. First, proxytypes can be implemented using nonconnectionist architectures. Thus, proxytype theory is not threatened by arguments against connectionism (e.g., Fodor and Pylyshyn 1988). Second, connectionists have not been concerned with showing that concepts are perceptually based. Connectionist nets are used to model perceptual tasks and to model conceptual tasks, but they have not been used to model conceptual tasks by means of perceptual representations (Barsalou 1999, Prinz and Barsalou 2001).

4. I choose not to use the term "perceptual symbol" because some researchers presume that symbols are amodal by definition, e.g., Newell and Simon (1976) and Haugeland (1985).

5. We also appeal to experts in thinking about dogs, screwdrivers, and string beans (Putnam 1975). But here we only defer if we want a specification of the metaphysical conditions for belonging to these categories. We do not need experts to tell us how to form the kinds of concepts used in ordinary string-bean thoughts.

6. The only exceptions are cases in which we encounter objects that are not quite above the threshold for any basic-level category. When I see a tapir for the first time, I can identify it only as an animal because I have no stored basic-level representation for it.

Chapter 7

1. Notice the role that realism is playing here. It is assumed that we can refer to a whole category by representing features that allow us to pick out a few salient exemplars. The fact that these exemplars belong to a real, mind-independent category allows us to refer to that category even thought we might have no knowledge of its essence. If categories were mind-dependent, reference would be constrained by epistemology; we could not refer to classes of things grouped together by hidden essences.

2. Scientists and lay people may supplement their knowledge of electrons with other knowledge that helps them reason about electrons or relate electrons to other theoretical objects. For example, many of us understand electrons by means of a solar-system metaphor. They are like little celestial bodies orbiting the nucleus (Gibbs 1994).

3. Other proposals have been developed by Barsalou and his colleagues (Barsalou 1993, Olseth and Barsalou 1995, Barsalou and Prinz 1997, Barsalou 1999) and by Lakoff (1987) and Lakoff and Johnson (1980).

4. Barsalou (1999) offers an account of lofty concepts that combines imagined event sequences with emotions. The account of truth that follows is a variant, without the emotional component, of the kind of story he tells.

5. The point is not that Damasio's work confirms Hume's theory of morality, only that it lends support to his theory of moral concepts. Sentiment may enter into how we think of morality even if it is not constitutive of morality. If causal semantic theories and some form of moral realism are true, sentiments might enable us to confer content to VIRTUE, even if the production of sentiments is not a necessary property of virtuous acts. (For more on the relation between emotion and moral concepts, see Prinz, forthcoming.)

6. Mentally represented words are not necessarily linked to their referents by a single expert at the end of a deferential chain. They may track their referents in virtue of a more collective practice of use. Consider country concepts, like the concept FRANCE. For most people, FRANCE may be grounded in images of maps, or in French foods, words, and landmarks that allow us to detect when we are in France. These contingent features of France can put is into a reliable causal

relation with that country. But in cases of countries whose maps and landmarks are less familiar, like Luxembourg, we may defer to the collective practice of a whole population of language users. LUXEMBOURG may refer to Luxembourg for me because I mentally represent the word "Luxembourg," an analog of which is used by members of Luxembourg's population when they express the thought "This here is Luxembourg" or "I am in Luxembourg now." Such thoughts, actual and possible, can delineate the region known as "Luxembourg." There may be an authoritative treaty that marks these borders as well, but it only refers to the region of Luxembourg because people abide by it. Deference here is to the collective.

7. Other empiricist proposals have also been explored. Resnik (1982) argues that we acquire mathematical knowledge through the experience of patterns, and Maddy (1990) argues that we can literally perceive sets. Below I suggest that this may not be far from the truth.

Chapter 8

1. Samuels (forthcoming) tries to save the metapsychological view by supplementing it with a canalization condition. This fix inherits the problems that face canalization accounts. To these problems Samuels has interesting replies.

2. See Bechtel and Abrahamsen 1992 for a discussion of the relationship between connectionism and classical associationism.

3. Fodor (1981) attributes this thesis to empiricists. He says that empiricists and rationalists both admit innate concepts; they only disagree about the size (and nature) of the innate conceptual base. For empiricists, there is a small set of primitives all of which are perceptual.

4. Fodor (1983) also compares language to sensory systems. His analog rests on the claim that they are both modular.

5. A nice strategy would be to construct neurally plausible models of systems involved in motor sequencing and rapid auditory response and then use those models to parse linguistic inputs.

6. Keil sometimes uses the university analogy.

7. Other aspects of folk biology, such as our understanding of death and digestion, are explored in Carey's (1985) work. These, she argues, initially depend on knowledge from other domains. I focus on essentialism because that is the component of folk biology that Keil seems to regard as least amenable to nonnativist treatments.

8. Uller and Nichols (2000) argue that chimps can attribute goals. Using a preferential-looking paradigm, they habituate chimps to a computer display of a block leaping over a barrier and then hitting a ball. Then the barrier is removed, and chimps either see the block follow a direct path to hit the ball or follow the same leaping path that it had followed when the barrier had been in

place. Chimps find the leaping path more surprising, which suggests to Uller and Nichols that they attribute to the block a goal of hitting the ball (in the most direct available way). The chimps' response can be interpreted without goal attribution, however. For one thing, the chimps may simply be surprised to see a moving object follow a leaping trajectory when there is no obstacle in place. This is not a commonly experienced event, nor is it a feature of the experimental habituation.

9. By "mental symbol" I mean an internal vehicle, tokens of which are realized by (or identical with) brain states.

10. Ostensibly, this proposal entails Fodor's metaphysical solution. If red is the property of causing red experiences and the concept RED is a red experience, then red is the property of causing RED to be tokened. This inference can be blocked by denying that red is the property of causing red experiences. On my view, mind-dependent properties are optional rather than obligatory. It is plausible to suppose that red is the property of causing red experiences, but it would be implausible to suppose this of other properties designated by primitive concepts (e.g., circularity).

Chapter 9

1. In addition to these, there are teleological theories, which explain intentionality by appeal to evolved functions (e.g., Millikan 1984, Dretske 1988, Papineau 1987). Discussing these would take a chapter of its own. Rather than writing such a chapter, I simply defend a nonteleological theory and hope that its success makes appeals to evolution unnecessary.

2. The term "informational" comes from Dretske (1981), who draws on ideas from Shannon and Weaver's information theory. Information theory provides formal techniques for quantifying how much information a signal carries. Dretske adapts some of their ideas to provide an account, not of how much information a signal carries, but of what a signal represents.

3. If worlds of the second kind were closer, (1) would come out false.

4. Some might think that worlds in which I have a different conceptual repertoire cannot be used in evaluating asymmetric dependence relations. The argument can be preserved if we replace worlds that conform to (i) with worlds in which the psychophysical laws relating bush pigs to tokens of BUSH PIG are different.

5. Fodor has since abandoned this proposal.

6. See Fodor's (1990) reply to Baker, where he considers a world containing both XYZ and H_2O but it just so happens that a person in that world has never seen XYZ. Fodor says that such a person's WATER concept would be disjunctive. If concepts are disjunctive in cases like this, they are certainly disjunctive in cases where a person sees both XYZ and H_2O yet fails to distinguish them.

7. Dretske (1981, 227) claims that my WATER concept does not refer to XYZ if there is no XYZ on Earth. To make sense of this, we must interpret Dretske's subjunctive formulation of the training-period constraint as restricted to the actual world. His position is that concepts refer to whatever actual, Earth-bound things could have caused them to be tokened during the training period. This is trouble enough.

8. I am not suggesting that we must remember the incipient causes of our concepts. The actual identity of incipient causes fixes content, not our memories of them.

9. Fodor (1990) also considers the strategy of explaining vacuous concepts by the features that constitute them, but it would be awkward for him to go this route, because he thinks most lexical concepts are unstructured. It is a cheat to claim that all lexical concepts *other than* vacuous concepts are unstructured.

10. I should add that there is nothing intrinsically wrong with proliferating representations. Any project that naturalizes intentionality should be unsurprised to find it popping up throughout the natural world. The main goal of a theory of intentionality should be to get the paradigm examples of representations to represent what we think they do. At the same time, we do not want to trivialize representation to a point where it ceases to be explanatory.

Chapter 10

1. This echoes Kaplan's (1988) definition of character. See also White 1982 for another Kaplan-inspired account.

2. One might respond by saying that concepts consist of beliefs. To say that a WATER concept contains the feature POTABLE might be taken as saying that it contains the belief that water is potable. This interpretation is not obligatory. Something is a belief only if it plays a certain functional role. That role may differ from the minimal role necessary for being a conceptually constitutive feature. It seems coherent to say that I conceptualize snakes as dangerous even though I do not believe they are.

3. Fodor defends a related theory in an unpublished manuscript (Fodor 1985). There he suggests that we might think of narrow contents as perceptual prototypes. See also Putnam's (1975) stereotype theory, which launched the debate about "narrow" content.

4. Burge (1986) argues that we should use the term "edge detectors" because the cells in question were designed, by evolution, to detect edges. The fact that they are responsive to other things only shows that they sometimes fire in error. Unlike Burge, I think we need a finer form of individuation for certain forms of psychological explanation. In any case, who is to say that the cells in question did not evolve to detect luminance discontinuities (which happen to demarcate edges)?

5. Accuracy of interpretation is not my primary goal. Locke is a source of inspiration.

6. Locke thinks that in some cases, nominal and real essences coincide. When that happens, the real essence of something is nothing more than our idea of that thing. Locke (1690, III.iii.18) includes simple ideas and modes in this category. The example he gives is the idea of a triangle.

7. There is considerable debate among biologists about what constitutes the essence of a species or even whether species have essences. I assume (without defense) that cows have essences, but I use the term "essence" more loosely than it is sometimes used in the philosophical literature on essentialism. With Boyd (1989), I allow the possibility that there are borderline cases of cows (fuzzy essences) and disjoint sets of properties that are sufficient for being a cow (disjunctive essences).

8. Fodor (1998, chap. 7) suggests that our concepts may begin by designating classes grouped by the features that we can recognize and then, with the advance of science, come to designate classes grouped by underlying essences. On my view, these two methods of carving things up are concurrent not sequential. I also reject the claim that science is required to make our concepts carve things up by their essences. Concepts do that via real content from the start. Science simply reveals those essences.

9. An element of teleology has been introduced here. Proxytypes may be designed by natural selection to transform in ways that help us track natural kinds. This invocation of Darwin does not entail that my semantic theory is teleological, however. Neither nominal nor real contents depend on teleology. Something could enter into a content-conferring relation without having been a product of natural selection.

Chapter 11

1. Fodor also talks of the systematicity of inference. Arguments in this chapter can be adapted to accommodate this form of systematicity.

2. Block actually states his proposal as a defense of inferential role semantics, not of prototype theory. The following is an adaptation.

3. By "relevant background knowledge" I mean knowledge that allows one to detect and resolve conflicts between the constituent features of the concepts being combined.

4. The argument that Fodor and Lepore (1996) construct is actually slightly different from what I have suggested. The principle that we generate prototypes compositionally when we lack exemplar knowledge cannot be right, they claim, because it is irrational. If this principle were right, emergent features would be less likely to occur in the case of very complex compound concepts because we are less likely to have exemplar knowledge involving such concepts. But these

concepts are also most likely to have emergent features (as the killer-pet-fish case suggests). So the principle predicts that we will combine concepts compositionally when compositional combination is least appropriate. The fallacy of this argument can be seen in Fodor and Lepore's own examples. Both of the examples cited in the text are equally complex but only one has emergent features. Therefore, emergence is a function not of complexity but of exemplar knowledge and background knowledge, as I have proposed.

5. Further evidence for the compatibility of compositionality and context sensitivity comes from the study of metaphor. Stern (2000) gives the following example. We can interpret "Juliet is the sun" and "Achilles is the sun" equally readily, but in the former case, the predicate is understood to mean something like "life sustaining," and in the latter, it means something like "has devastating force." Both of these features are components of our SUN concepts, but in different metaphorical contexts, different components are selected. Despite this fact, Stern argues that metaphorical interpretation is productive.

6. Smith et al. (1988) describe a possible extension of their model that would accommodate some multidimensional adjectives.

7. Examples given by Wisniewski (1997) include CATFISH and CHERRY TOMATO. These examples are not ideal because they have been lexicalized and can be called up during the retrieval stage without a combination process.

8. Wisniewski (1997) also offers SINGER SONGWRITER and TOASTER OVEN as other lexicalized examples.

References

Allen, S. W., and L. R. Brooks. 1991. Specializing the Operation of an Explicit Rule. *Journal of Experimental Psychology: General* 120: 3–19.

Alston, W. P. 1964. *Philosophy of Language*. Englewood Cliffs, N.J.: Prentice-Hall.

Anderson, J. R. 1978. Arguments Concerning Representations for Mental Imagery. *Psychological Review* 85: 249–277.

Ariew, A. 1996. Innateness and Canalization. *Philosophy of Science* 63: S19–S27.

Aristotle. 1961. *De Anima, Books II and III*. D. W. Hamlyn, trans. Oxford: Oxford University Press.

Armstrong, D. M. 1968. *A Materialist Theory of Mind*. London: Routledge.

Armstrong, S. L., L. R. Gleitman, and H. Gleitman. 1983. What Some Concepts Might Not Be. *Cognition* 13: 263–308.

Aydede, M. 1998. Fodor on Concepts and Frege Puzzles. *Pacific Philosophical Quarterly* 79: 289–294.

Ayer, A. J. 1940. The Foundations of Empirical Knowledge. London: Macmillan.

Ayers, M. 1991. *Locke*. London: Routledge.

Baillargeon, R., L. Kotovsky, and A. Needham. 1995. The Acquisition of Physical Knowledge in Infancy. In D. Sperber, D. Premack, and A. J. Premack, eds., *Causal Cognition: A Multidisciplinary Debate*. New York: Oxford University Press.

Baron-Cohen, S. 1995. *Mindblindness: An Essay on Autism and Theory of Mind*. Cambridge: MIT Press.

Barsalou, L. W. 1983. Ad Hoc Categories. *Memory & Cognition* 11: 211–227.

Barsalou, L. W. 1987. The Instability of Graded Structure: Implications for the Nature of Concepts. In U. Neisser, ed., *Concepts and Conceptual Development: Ecological and Intellectual Factors in Categorization*. Cambridge: Cambridge University Press.

Barsalou, L. W. 1989. Intra-concept Similarity and Its Implications for Inter-concept Similarity. In S. Vosniadou and A. Ortony, eds., *Similarity and Analogical Reasoning*. New York: Cambridge University Press.

Barsalou, L. W. 1990. On the Indistinguishability of Exemplar Memory and Abstraction in Category Representation. In T. K. Srull and R. S. Wyer, eds., *Content and Process Specificity in the Effects of Prior Experiences*. Hillsdale, N.J.: Lawrence Erlbaum Associates.

Barsalou, L. W. 1991. Deriving Categories to Achieve Goals. In G. H. Bower, ed., *The Psychology of Learning and Motivation: Advances in Research and Theory*. San Diego, Calif.: Academic Press.

Barsalou, L. W. 1993. Flexibility, Structure, and Linguistic Vagary in Concepts: Manifestations of a Compositional System of Perceptual Symbols. In A. Collins, S. Gathercole, M. Conway, and P. Morris, eds., *Theories of Memory*. Hillsdale, N.J.: Lawrence Erlbaum Associates.

Barsalou, L. W. 1999. Perceptual Symbol Systems. *Behavioral & Brain Sciences* 22: 577–660.

Barsalou, L. W., and C. R. Hale. 1992. Components of Conceptual Representation: From Feature Lists to Recursive Frames. In *Categories and Concepts: Theoretical Views and Inductive Data Analysis*. New York: Academic Press.

Barsalou, L. W., and J. J. Prinz. 1997. Mundane Creativity in Perceptual Symbol Systems. In T. B. Ward, S. M. Smith, and J. Vaid, eds., *Conceptual Structures and Processes: Emergence, Discovery, and Change*. Washington, D.C.: American Psychological Association.

Barsalou, L. W., K. O. Solomon, and L.-L. Wu, 1999. Perceptual Simulation in Conceptual Tasks. In M. K. Hiraga, C. Sinha, and S. Wilcox, eds., *Cultural, Typological, and Psychological Perspectives in Cognitive Linguistics: The Proceedings of the 4th Conference of the International Cognitive Linguistics Association*, vol. 3. Amsterdam: John Benjamins.

Barsalou, L. W., W. Yeh, B. J. Luka, K. L. Olseth, K. S. Mix, and L.-L. Wu. 1993. Concepts and Meaning. *Chicago Linguistics Society* 29: 23–61.

Bates, E. A. 1999. Plasticity, Localization, and Language Development. In S. H. Broman and J. M. Fletcher, eds., *The Changing Nervous System: Neurobehavioral Consequences of Early Brain Disorders*. New York: Oxford University Press.

Bauer, M. I., and P. N. Johnson-Laird, 1993. How Diagrams Can Improve Reasoning. *Psychological Science* 4: 372–378.

Bechtel, W., and A. Abrahamsen. 1992. *Connectionism and the Mind: Parallel Processing, Dynamics, and Evolution*. Oxford: Blackwell.

Bennett, J. 1971. *Locke, Berkeley, Hume: Central Themes*. Oxford: Oxford University Press.

Berkeley, G. 1710. *A Treatise Concerning the Principles of Human Knowledge*. J. Dancy, ed. Oxford: Oxford University Press, 1998.

Berlin, B., and O. Kay. 1969. *Basic Color Terms: Their Universality and Evolution*. Berkeley: University of California Press.

Bickerton, D. 1990. *Language and Species*. Chicago, Ill.: University of Chicago Press.

Biederman, I. 1987. Recognition-by-Components: A Theory of Human Image Understanding. *Psychological Review* 94: 115–147.

Biederman, I. 1990. Higher-Level Vision. In D. N. Osherson, S. M. Kosslyn, and J. M. Hollerbach, eds., *An Invitation to Cognitive Science*, vol. 2: *Visual Cognition and Action*. Cambridge: MIT Press.

Biederman, I., and G. Ju. 1988. Surface vs. Edge-Based Determinants of Visual Recognition. *Cognitive Psychology* 20: 38–64.

Block, N. 1978. Troubles with Functionalism. In W. C. Savage, ed., *Perception and Cognition: Issues in the Foundations of Psychology*. Minneapolis: University of Minnesota Press.

Block, N. 1986. Advertisement for a Semantics for Psychology. In P. A. French, T. E. Uehling Jr., and H. K. Wettstein, eds., *Studies in the Philosophy of Mind*, Midwest Studies in Philosophy, no. 10. Minneapolis: University of Minnesota Press.

Block, N. 1993. Holism, Hyper-analyticity and Hyper-compositionality. *Mind & Language* 8: 1–26.

Booth, M. C., and E. T. Rolls. 1998. View-Invariant Representations of Familiar Objects by Neurons in the Inferior Temporal Visual Cortex. *Cerebral Cortex* 8: 510–523.

Boucher, J. 1996. Simulation-Theory, Theory-Theory, and the Evidence from Autism. In P. Carruthers and P. K. Smith, eds., *Theories of Theories of Mind*. Cambridge: Cambridge University Press.

Boyd, R. 1989. What Realism Implies and What It Does Not. *Dialectica* 43: 5–29.

Brooks, L. R. 1978. Nonanalytic Concept Formation and Memory for Instances. In E. Rosch and B. B. Lloyd, eds., *Cognition and Categorization*. Hillsdale, N.J.: Lawrence Erlbaum Associates.

Brown, R. 1958. How Shall a Thing Be Called? *Psychological Review* 65: 14–21.

Bruner, J., J. Goodnow, and G. Austin. 1956. *A Study of Thinking*. New York: Wiley.

Brunswik, E. 1956. *Perception and the Representative Design of Psychological Experiments*. Second edition. Berkeley: University of California Press.

Buckley, M. J., D. Gaffan, and E. A. Murray. 1997. Functional Double Dissociation between Two Inferior Temporal Cortical Areas: Perirhinal Cortex versus Middle Temporal Gyrus. *Journal of Neurophysiology* 77: 587–598.

Burge, T. 1979. Individualism and the Mental. In P. A. French, T. E. Uehling Jr., and H. K. Wettstein, eds., *Contemporary Perspectives in the Philosophy of*

Language, Midwest Studies in Philosophy, no. 2. Minneapolis: University of Minnesota Press.

Burge, T. 1986. Individualism and Psychology. *Philosophical Review* 95: 3–45.

Butterworth, G. 1991. The Ontogeny and Phylogeny of Joint Visual Attention. In A. Whiten, ed., *Natural Theories of Mind: Evolution, Development, and Simulation of Everyday Mindreading*. Oxford: Basil Blackwell.

Cantor, N., and E. Mischel. 1979. Prototypes in Person Perception. In L. Berkowitz, ed., *Advances in Experimental Social Psychology*. New York: Academic Press.

Carey, S. 1985. *Conceptual Change in Childhood*. Cambridge: MIT Press.

Chomsky, N. 1968. *Language and Mind*. San Diego: Harcourt, Brace, Jovanovich.

Chomsky, N. 1975. *Reflections on Language*. New York: Pantheon Books.

Chomsky, N. 1986. *Knowledge of Language: Its Nature, Origin and Use*. New York: Praeger.

Chomsky, N. 1991. Linguistics and Cognitive Science: Problems and Mysteries. In A. Kasher, ed., *The Chomskyan Turn*. Oxford: Blackwell.

Chomsky, N. 1992. Language and Interpretation: Philosophical Reflections on Empirical Inquiry. In J. Earman, ed., *Inference, Explanation, and Other Philosophical Frustrations*. Berkeley: University of California Press.

Churchland, P. M. 1988. Perceptual Plasticity and Theoretical Neutrality: A Reply to Jerry Fodor. *Philosophy of Science* 55: 167–187.

Churchland, P. S. 1986. *Neurophilosophy: Toward a Unified Science of the Mind/Brain*. Cambridge: MIT Press.

Clark, Andy. 1993. *Associative Engines*. Cambridge: MIT Press.

Clark, Austin. 1993. *Sensory Qualities*. Oxford: Oxford University Press.

Cowie, F. 1998. *What's Within? Nativism Reconsidered*. Oxford: Oxford University Press.

Cummins, R. 1989. *Meaning and Mental Representation* Cambridge: MIT Press.

Currie, G. 1996. Autism as Mind-Blindness: An Elaboration and Partial Defense. In P. Carruthers and P. K. Smith, eds., *Theories of Theories of Mind*. Cambridge: Cambridge University Press.

Damasio, A. R. 1989. Time-Locked Multiregional Retroactivation: A Systems-Level Proposal for the Neural Substrates of Recall and Recognition. *Cognition* 33: 25–62.

Damasio, A. R. 1994. *Descartes' Error*. New York: Grosset/Putnam.

Damasio, H., T. J. Grabowski, D. Tranel, R. D. Hichwa, A. R. Damasio. 1996. A Neural Basis for Lexical Retrieval. *Nature* 380: 499–505.

Davidson, D. 1987. Knowing One's Own Mind. *Proceedings and Addresses of the American Philosophical Association* 60: 441–458.

Davies, M. 1989. Tacit Knowledge and Subdoxastic States. In G. Alexander, ed., *Reflections on Chomsky*. Oxford: Blackwell.

Deacon, T. W. 1997. *The Symbolic Species: The Co-evolution of Language and the Human Brain*. New York: W. W. Norton & Co.

DeCasper, A. J., and M. J. Spence. 1986. Prenatal Maternal Speech Influences Newborns' Perception of Speech Sounds. *Infant Behavior & Development* 9: 133–150.

Dehaene, S. 1997. *The Number Sense: How Mathematical Knowledge Is Embedded in Our Brains*. Oxford: Oxford University Press.

Dehaene, S., G. Dehaene-Lambertz, and L. Cohen. 1998. Abstract Representations of Numbers in the Animal and Human Brain. *Trends in Neurosciences* 21: 355–361.

Dehaene, S., E. Spelke, P. Pinel, R. Stanescu, and S. Tsivkin. 1999. Sources of Mathematical Thinking: Behavioral and Brain-Imaging Evidence. *Science* 284: 970–974.

Dennett, D. C. 1982. Beyond Belief. In A. Woodfield, ed., *Thought and Object: Essays on Intentionality*. Oxford: Clarendon.

Dennett, D. C. 1987. *The Intentional Stance*. Cambridge: MIT Press.

Descartes, R. 1637. *Meditation on First Philosophy, with Selections from the Objections and Replies*. J. Cottingham, trans. Cambridge: Cambridge University Press, 1996.

Devitt, M. 1981. *Designation*. New York: Columbia University Press.

Donnellan, K. S. 1972. Proper Names and Identifying Descriptions. In D. Davidson and G. Harman, eds., *Semantics of Natural Language*. Dordrecht: Reidel.

Dretske, F. I. 1981. *Knowledge and the Flow of Information*. Cambridge: MIT Press.

Dretske, F. I. 1988. *Explaining Behavior: Reasons in a World of Causes*. Cambridge: MIT Press.

Dummett, M. 1981. *Interpretation of Frege's Philosophy*. Cambridge: Harvard University Press.

Edelman, G. M. 1992. *Bright Air, Brilliant Fire: On the Matter of the Mind*. New York: Basic Books.

Ellefson, M. R., and M. H. Christiansen. 2000. Subjacency Constraints without Universal Grammar: Evidence from Artificial Language Learning and Connectionist Modeling. In *Proceedings of the Twenty-Second Annual Conference of the Cognitive Science Society*. Mahwah, N.J.: Lawrence Erlbaum Associates.

Elman, J. L. 1991. Incremental Learning, or The Importance of Starting Small. In K. J. Hammond and D. Gentner, eds., *Proceedings of the Thirteenth Annual Conference of the Cognitive Science Society*. Hillsdale, N.J.: Lawrence Erlbaum Associates.

Elman, J. L., E. A. Bates, M. H. Johnson, A. Karmiloff-Smith, D. Parisi, and K. Plunkett. 1996. *Rethinking Innateness: A Connectionist Perspective on Development*. Cambridge: MIT Press.

Erhard, P., T. Kato, P. Strick, and K. Urgurbil. 1996. Functional MRI Activation Pattern of Motor and Language Tasks in Broca's Area. *Abstracts of the Society of Neuroscience* 22: 260–262.

Estes, W. K. 1994. *Classification and Cognition*. Oxford: Oxford University Press.

Evans, G. 1982. *The Varieties of Reference*. Oxford: Clarendon.

Fauconnier, G. 1985. *Mental Spaces*. Cambridge: MIT Press.

Field, H. 1978. Mental Representation. *Erkenntnis* 13: 9–61.

Fodor, J. A. 1975. *The Language of Thought*. Cambridge: Harvard University Press.

Fodor, J. A. 1981. The Current Status of the Innateness Controversy. In J. A. Fodor, *Representations*. Cambridge: MIT Press.

Fodor, J. A. 1983. *The Modularity of Mind*. Cambridge: MIT Press.

Fodor, J. A. 1984. Semantics, Wisconsin Style. *Synthese* 59: 231–250.

Fodor, J. A. 1985. Narrow Content and Meaning Holism. Manuscript.

Fodor, J. A. 1987. *Psychosemantics*. Cambridge: MIT Press.

Fodor, J. A. 1990. A Theory of Content, I & II. In J. A. Fodor, *A Theory of Content and Other Essays*. Cambridge: MIT Press.

Fodor, J. A. 1991. A Modal Argument for Narrow Content. *Journal of Philosophy* 88: 5–25.

Fodor, J. A. 1994. *The Elm and the Expert: Mentalese and Its Semantics*. Cambridge: MIT Press.

Fodor, J. A. 1998. *Concepts: Where Cognitive Science Went Wrong*. Oxford: Oxford University Press.

Fodor, J. A. 2000. There Are No Recognitional Concepts—Not Even RED. In J. A. Fodor, *In Critical Condition: Polemical Essays on Cognitive Science and the Philosophy of Mind*. Cambridge: MIT Press.

Fodor, J. A., M. F. Garrett, E. C. Walker, and C. H. Parkes. 1980. Against Definitions. *Cognition* 8: 263–367.

Fodor, J. A., and E. Lepore. 1992. *Holism: A Shopper's Guide*. Oxford: Basil Blackwell.

Fodor, J. A., and E. Lepore. 1996. The Red Herring and the Pet Fish: Why Concepts Still Can't Be Prototypes. *Cognition* 58: 253–270.

Fodor, J. A., and B. P. McLaughlin. 1990. Connectionism and the Problem of Systematicity: Why Smolensky's Solution Doesn't Work. *Cognition* 35: 183–204.

Fodor, J. A., and Z. W. Pylyshyn. 1988. Connectionism and Cognitive Architecture: A Critical Analysis. In S. Pinker and J. Mehler, eds., *Connections and Symbols*. Cambridge: MIT Press

Frege, G. 1893. On Sense and Meaning. M. Black, trans. In P. Geach and M. Black, eds., *Translations from the Philosophical Writings of Gottlob Frege*. Oxford: Blackwell, 1953.

Gauker, C. 1994. *Thinking Out Loud: An Essay on the Relation between Thought and Language*. Princeton: Princeton University Press.

Geach, P. T. 1957. *Mental Acts*. London: Routledge.

Gelman, R., F. Durgin, and L. Kaufman. 1995. Distinguishing between Animates and Inanimates: Not by Motion Alone. In D. Sperber, D. Premack, and A. J. Premack, eds., *Causal Cognition: A Multidisciplinary Debate*. New York: Oxford University Press.

Gelman, S. A., and J. D. Coley. 1991. Language and Categorization: The Acquisition of Natural Kind Terms. In J. P. Byrnes and S. A. Gelman, eds., *Perspectives on Language and Thought: Interrelations in Development*. Cambridge: Cambridge University Press.

Gelman, S. A., J. D. Coley, and G. M. Gottfried. 1994. Essentialist Beliefs in Children: The Acquisition of Concepts and Theories. In L. A. Hirschfeld and S. A. Gelman, eds., *Mapping the Mind: Domain Specificity in Cognition and Culture*. Cambridge: Cambridge University Press.

Gelman, S. A., and K. S. Ebeling. 1998. Shape and Representational Status in Children's Early Naming. *Cognition* 66: B35–B47.

Gibbs, R. W. 1994. *The Poetics of Mind: Figurative Thought, Language, and Understanding*. Cambridge: Cambridge University Press.

Gibson, J. J. 1979. *The Ecological Approach to Visual Perception*. New York: Houghton Mifflin.

Glenberg, A. M. 1997. What Memory Is For. *Behavioral and Brain Sciences* 20: 1–55.

Gold, E. 1967. Language Identification in the Limit. *Information and Control* 16: 447–474.

Goldman, A. 1989. Interpretation Psychologized. *Mind and Language* 4: 161–185.

Goldman-Rakic, P. S. 1998. The Prefrontal Landscape: Implications of Functional Architecture for Understanding Human Mentation and the Central Executive. In L. Weiskrantz, A. C. Roberts, and T. W. Robbins, eds., *The Prefrontal Cortex: Executive and Cognitive Functions*. New York: Oxford University Press.

Goldstone, R., and L. W. Barsalou. 1998. Reuniting Cognition and Perception: The Perceptual Bases of Rules and Similarity. *Cognition* 65: 231–262.

Goodman, N. 1976. *Languages of Art: An Approach to a Theory of Symbols*. Indianapolis, Ind.: Hackett.

Gopnik, A., and A. N. Meltzoff. 1996. *Words, Thoughts, and Theories*. Cambridge: MIT Press.

Gordon, R. 1986. Folk Psychology as Simulation. *Mind and Language* 1: 158–171.

Gordon, R. M. 1995. Sympathy, Simulation, and the Impartial Spectator. *Ethics* 105: 727–742.

Gray, K. C., and E. E. Smith. 1995. The Role of Instance Retrieval in Understanding Complex Concepts. *Memory & Cognition* 23: 665–674.

Graziano, M. S. A., and C. G. Gross. 1995. The Representation of Extrapersonal Space: A Possible Role for Bimodal Visual-Tactile Neurons. In M. S. Gazzaniga, ed., *The Cognitive Neurosciences*. Cambridge: MIT Press.

Grice, H. P. 1957. Meaning. *Philosophical Review* 3: 378–388.

Grice, H. P. 1962. Some Remarks about the Senses. Reprinted in H. P. Grice, *Studies in the Ways of Words*. Cambridge: Harvard University Press, 1989.

Hammond, K. J. 1989. *Case-Based Planning: Viewing Planning as a Memory Task*. San Diego: Academic Press.

Hampton, J. A. 1979. Polymorphous Concepts in Semantic Memory. *Journal of Verbal Learning and Verbal Behavior* 18: 441–461.

Hampton, J. A. 1981. An Investigation of the Nature of Abstract Concepts. *Memory and Cognition* 9: 149–156.

Hampton, J. A. 1987. Inheritance of Attributes in Natural Concept Conjunctions. *Memory & Cognition* 15: 55–71.

Hampton, J. A. 1988. Overextension of Conjunctive Concepts: Evidence for a Unitary Model of Concept Typicality and Class Inclusion. *Journal of Experimental Psychology: Learning, Memory, and Cognition* 14: 12–32.

Hampton, J. A. 1991. The Combination of Prototype Concepts. In P. J. Schwanenflugel, ed., *The Psychology of Word Meanings*. Hillsdale, N.J.: Lawrence Erlbaum Associates.

Hampton, J. A. 1992. Prototype Models of Concepts. In J. van Mechelen, J. A. Hampton, R. Michalski, and P. Theuns, eds., *Categories and Concepts: Theoretical Views and Inductive Data Analysis*. London: Academic Press.

Hampton, J. A. 1995. Testing the Prototype Theory of Concepts. *Journal of Memory & Language* 34: 686–708.

Hampton, J. A. 1997. Psychological Representation of Concepts. In M. A. Conway, ed., *Cognitive Models of Memory*. Cambridge: MIT Press.

Harris, P. L. 1989. Children and Emotion: The Development of Psychological Understanding. Oxford: Basil Blackwell.

Harris, P. L. 1992. From Simulation to Folk Psychology: The Case for Development. *Mind & Language* 7: 120–144.

Haugeland, J. 1985. *Artificial Intelligence: The Very Idea*. Cambridge: MIT Press.

Heider, E. R. 1972. Probabilities, Sampling, and the Ethnographic Method: The Case of Dani Colour Names. *Man* 7: 448–466.

Hilbert, D. 1964. On the Infinite. In P. Benacerraf and H. Putnam, eds., *Philosophy of Mathematics*. Englewood Cliffs, N.J.: Prentice-Hall.

Hogg, D. 1983. Model-Based Vision: A Program to See a Walking Person. *Image and Vision Computing* 1: 5–20.

Holyoak, K. J., and A. L. Glass. 1975. The Role of Contradictions and Counter Examples in the Rejection of False Sentences. *Journal of Verbal Learning and Verbal Behavior* 14: 215–239.

Hubel, D. H., and T. N. Wiesel. 1962. Receptive Fields, Binocular Interaction, and Functional Architecture in the Cat's Visual Cortex. *Journal of Physiology* 28: 229–289.

Hubel, D. H., and T. N. Wiesel. 1968. Receptive Fields and Functional Architecture of Monkey Striate Cortex. *Journal of Physiology* 195: 215–243.

Hume, D. 1739. *A Treatise of Human Nature*. P. H. Nidditch, ed. Oxford: Oxford University Press, 1978.

Hume, D. 1748. *Enquiries Concerning Human Understanding and Concerning the Principles of Morals*. P. H. Nidditch, ed. Oxford: Oxford University Press, 1975.

Hummel, J. E., and I. Biederman. 1992. Dynamic Binding in a Neural Network for Shape Recognition. *Psychological Review* 99: 480–517.

Huttenlocher, J., L. V. Hedges, and S. Duncan. 1991. Categories and Particulars: Prototype Effects in Estimating Spatial Location. *Psychological Review* 98: 352–376.

Jackendoff, R. 1983. *Semantics and Cognition*. Cambridge: MIT Press.

Jackendoff, R. 1987. *Consciousness and the Computational Mind*. Cambridge: MIT Press.

Jackendoff, R. 1990. *Semantic Structures*. Cambridge: MIT Press.

Jackendoff, R. 1995. *Patterns in the Mind: Language and Human Nature*. New York: Basic Books.

James, W. 1884. What Is an Emotion? *Mind* 9: 188–205.

Janssen, P., R. Vogels, and G. A. Orban. 2000. Selectivity for 3D Shape That Reveals Distinct Areas within Macaque Inferior Temporal Cortex. *Science* 288: 2054–2056.

Jiang, W., F. Tremblay, and C. E. Chapman. 1997. Neuronal Encoding of Texture Changes in the Primary and the Secondary Somatosensory Cortical Areas of Monkeys during Passive Texture Discrimination. *Journal of Neurophysiology* 77: 1656–1662.

Johnson, M. 1987. *The Body in the Mind: The Bodily Basis of Meaning, Imagination, and Reason*. Chicago: University of Chicago Press.

Johnson, M. H. 1993. Cortical Maturation and the Development of Visual Attention in Early Infancy. In M. H. Johnson, ed., *Brain Development and Cognition: A Reader*. Oxford: Blackwell.

Johnson, M. H., and J. Morton. 1991. *Biology and Cognitive Development: The Case of Face Recognition*. Oxford: Blackwell.

Johnson-Laird, P. N. 1983. *Mental Models*. Cambridge: Harvard University Press.

Johnson-Laird, P. N. 1996. The Process of Deduction. In D. M. Steier and T. Mitchell, eds., *Mind Matters: A Tribute to Allen Newell*. Hillsdale, N.J.: Lawrence Erlbaum Associates.

Johnston, J. R. 1997. Specific Language Impairment, Cognition, and the Biological Basis of Language. In M. Gopnik, ed., *The Inheritance of Innateness of Grammars*. Oxford: Oxford University Press.

Jolicoeur, P., M. A. Gluck, and S. M. Kosslyn. 1984. Pictures and Names: Making the Connection. *Cognitive Psychology* 16: 243–275.

Jusczyk, P. W. 1997. *The Discovery of Spoken Language*. Cambridge: MIT Press.

Kamp, H., and B. Partee. 1995. Prototype Theory and Compositionality. *Cognition* 57: 129–191.

Kant, I. 1783. *Prolegomena to Any Future Metaphysics That Can Qualify as a Science*. P. Carus, trans. La Salle, Ill.: Open Court, 1902.

Kaplan, D. 1988. Demonstratives. In J. Almog, J. Perry, and H. Wettstein, eds., *Themes from Kaplan*. Oxford: Oxford University Press.

Katz, J. J., and J. A. Fodor. 1963. The Structure of a Semantic Theory. *Language* 39: 170–210.

Kaye, K. L., and T. G. R. Bower. 1994. Learning and Intermodal Transfer of Information in Newborns. *Psychological Science* 5: 286–288.

Keeley, B. L. Forthcoming. Making Sense of the Senses: Individuating Modalities in Humans and Other Animals. *Journal of Philosophy*.

Keil, F. C. 1979. *Semantics and Conceptual Development: An Ontological Perspective*. Cambridge: Harvard University Press.

Keil, F. C. 1989. *Concepts, Kinds, and Cognitive Development*. Cambridge: MIT Press.

Keil, F. C. 1994. The Birth and Nurturance of Concepts by Domains: The Origins of Concepts of Living Things. In L. A. Hirschfeld and S. A. Gelman, eds., *Mapping the Mind: Domain Specificity in Cognition and Culture*. Cambridge: Cambridge University Press.

Keil, F. C., and N. Batterman. 1984. A Characteristic-to-Defining Shift in the Development of Word Meaning. *Journal of Verbal Learning and Verbal Behavior* 23: 221–236.

Kellman, P. J. 1984. Perception of Three-Dimensional Form by Human Infants. *Perception & Psychophysics* 36: 353–358.

Kellman, P. J., and M. E. Arterberry. 1998. *The Cradle of Knowledge: Development of Perception in Infancy*. Cambridge: MIT Press.

Kellman, P. J., and E. S. Spelke. 1983. Perception of Partly Occluded Objects in Infancy. *Cognitive Psychology* 15: 483–524.

Knowlton, B. J. 1997. Declarative and Nondeclarative Knowledge: Insights from Cognitive Neuroscience. In K. Lamberts and D. R. Shanks, eds., *Knowledge, Concepts, and Categories*. Cambridge: MIT Press.

Knowlton, B. J., and L. R. Squire. 1993. The Learning of Categories: Parallel Brain Systems for Item Memory and Category Knowledge. *Science* 262: 1747–1749.

Komatsu, L. K. 1992. Recent Views of Conceptual Structure. *Psychological Bulletin* 112: 500–526.

Kosslyn, S. M. 1980. *Image and Mind*. Cambridge: Harvard University Press.

Kosslyn, S. M. 1994. *Image and Brain: The Resolution of the Imagery Debate*. Cambridge: MIT Press.

Kripke, S. A. 1979. A Puzzle about Belief. In A. Margalit, ed., *Meaning and Use*. Dordrecht: Reidel.

Kripke, S. A. 1980. *Naming and Necessity*. Cambridge: Harvard University Press.

Kruschke, J. K. 1992. ALCOVE: An Exemplar-Based Connectionist Model of Category Learning. *Psychological Review* 99: 22–44.

Kuhn, T. 1962. *The Structure of Scientific Revolutions*. Chicago: University of Chicago Press.

Kunda, Z., D. Miller, and T. Claire. 1990. Combining Social Concepts: The Role of Causal Reasoning. *Cognitive Science* 14: 11–46.

Lakoff, G. 1972. Hedges: A Study in Meaning Criteria and the Logic of Fuzzy Concepts. *Chicago Linguistic Society* 8: 183–228.

Lakoff, G. 1987. *Women, Fire, and Dangerous Things*. Chicago: University of Chicago Press.

Lakoff, G., and M. Johnson. 1980. *Metaphors We Live By*. Chicago: University of Chicago Press.

Landau, B., L. B. Smith, and S. Jones. 1988. The Importance of Shape in Early Lexical Learning. *Cognitive Development* 3: 299–321.

Langacker, R. W. 1987. *Foundations of Cognitive Grammar*. Vol. 1: *Theoretical Perspectives*. Stanford: Stanford University Press.

Langacker, R. W. 1991. *Foundations of Cognitive Grammar*. Vol. 2: *Descriptive Application*. Stanford: Stanford University Press.

Lange, C. G. 1885. On the Mechanisms of Emotion. In C. G. Lange, *The Classical Psychologists*, B. Rand, trans. Boston: Houghton Mifflin, 1917.

Lashley, K. S. 1950. In Search of the Engram. *Symposium of the Society for Experimental Biology* 4: 454–482.

Leibniz, G. W. 1765. *New Essays on Human Understanding*. J. Bennett and P. Remnant, trans. Cambridge: Cambridge University Press, 1996.

Leslie, A. M. 1994. ToMM, ToBy, and Agency: Core Architecture and Domain Specificity. In L. A. Hirschfeld and S. A. Gelman, eds., *Mapping the Mind: Domain Specificity in Cognition and Culture*. Cambridge: Cambridge University Press.

Leslie, A. M., and S. Keeble. 1987. Do Six-Month-Old Infants Perceive Causality? *Cognition* 25: 265–288.

Levenson, R. W., P. Ekman, and W. V. Friesen. 1990. Voluntary Facial Action Generates Emotion-Specific Autonomic Nervous System Activity. *Psychophysiology* 27: 363–384.

Lewis, D. 1970. How to Define Theoretical Terms. *Journal of Philosophy* 67: 427–446.

Loar, B. 1988. Social Content and Psychological Content. In R. Grimm and D. Merrill, eds., *Contents of Thought*. Tucson: University of Arizona Press.

Locke, J. 1690. *An Essay Concerning Human Understanding*. P. H. Nidditch, ed. Oxford: Oxford University Press, 1979.

Lycan, W. G. 1981. Toward a Homuncular Theory of Believing. Revised and reprinted in W. G. Lycan, *Judgment and Justification*. Cambridge: Cambridge University Press, 1988.

Maddy, P. 1990. *Realism in Mathematics*. Oxford: Oxford University Press.

Malt, B. C. 1994. Water Is Not H_2O. *Cognitive Psychology* 27: 41–70.

Malt, B. C., and E. C. Johnson. 1992. Do Artifact Concepts Have Cores? *Journal of Memory & Language* 31: 195–217.

Mandler, J. M. 1992. How to Build a Baby. II: Conceptual Primitives. *Psychological Review* 99: 587–604.

Mandler, J. M., and L. McDonough. 1996. Drinking and Driving Don't Mix: Inductive Generalization in Infancy. *Cognition* 59: 307–335.

Markman, E. 1989. *Categorization and Naming in Children: Problems in Induction*. Cambridge: MIT Press.

Marr, D. 1982. *Vision: A Computational Investigation into the Human Representation and Processing of Visual Information*. San Francisco: W. H. Freeman.

Marr, D., and H. K. Nishihara. 1978. Representation and Recognition of the Spatial Organization of Three Dimensional Structure. *Proceedings of the Royal Society of London* B 200: 269–294.

Marsolek, C. J. 1995. Abstract Visual-Form Representations in the Left Cerebral Hemisphere. *Journal of Experimental Psychology: Human Perception & Performance* 21: 375–386.

McCarthy, R. A., and E. K. Warrington. 1990. *Cognitive Neuropsychology: A Clinical Introduction*. San Diego: Academic Press.

McCloskey, M., and S. Glucksberg. 1979. Decision Processes in Verifying Category Membership Statements: Implications for Models of Semantic Memory. *Cognitive Psychology* 11: 1–37.

McDermott, K. B., R. L. Buckner, S. E. Peterson, W. M. Kelley, and A. L. Sanders. 1999. Set- and Code-Specific Activation in the Frontal Cortex: An fMRI study of encoding and retrieval of faces and words. *Journal of Cognitive Neuroscience* 11: 631–640.

McGinn, C. 1982. The Structure of Content. In A. Woodfield, ed., *Thought and Object: Essays on Intentionality*. Oxford: Clarendon.

McGinn, C. 1989. *Mental Content*. Oxford: Basil Blackwell.

Medin, D. L., and A. Ortony. 1989. Psychological Essentialism. In S. Vosniadou and A. Ortony, eds., *Similarity and Analogical Reasoning*. Cambridge: Cambridge University Press.

Medin, D. L., and M. Schaffer. 1978. A Context Theory of Classification Learning. *Psychological Review* 85: 207–238.

Medin, D. L., and P. J. Schwanenflugel. 1981. Linear Separability in Classification Learning. *Journal of Experimental Psychology: Human Learning and Memory* 7: 355–368.

Medin, D. L., and E. Shoben. 1988. Context and Structure in Conceptual Combination. *Cognitive Psychology* 20: 158–190.

Meltzoff, A. N., and R. W. Borton. 1979. Intermodal Matching by Human Neonates. *Nature* 282: 403–410.

Meltzoff, A., and M. K. Moore. 1983. Newborn Infants Imitate Adult Facial Gestures. *Child Development* 54: 702–709.

Mervis, C. B. 1987. Child-Basic Object Categories and Early Lexical Development. In U. Neisser, ed., *Concepts and Conceptual Development: Ecological and Intellectual Factors in Categorization*. Cambridge: Cambridge University Press.

Mervis, C. B., J. Carlin, and E. Rosch. 1976. Relationships among Goodness-of-Example, Category Norms, and Word Frequency. *Bulletin of the Psychonomic Society* 7: 283–284.

Merzenich, M. M. 1998. Optimizing Sound Features for Cortical Neurons. *Science* 280: 1439–1444.

Michotte, A. E. 1946. *Perception of Causality*. T. R. Miles and E. Miles, trans. New York: Basic Books, 1963.

Mill, J. S. 1843. A System of Logic, Ratiocinative and Inductive: Being a Connected View of the Principles of Evidence and the Methods of Scientific Investigation. New York: Longmans, 1959.

Millikan, R. G. 1984. *Language, Thought, and Other Biological Categories: New Foundations for Realism*. Cambridge: MIT Press.

Millikan, R. G. 1993. White Queen Psychology, or The Last Myth of the Given. In R. G. Millikan, *White Queen Psychology and Other Essays for Alice*. Cambridge: MIT Press.

Millikan, R. G. 1998. A Common Structure for Concepts of Individuals, Stuffs, and Real Kinds: More Mama, More Milk, and More Mouse. *Behavioral and Brain Sciences* 21: 55–100.

Milner, A. D., and M. A. Goodale. 1995. *The Visual Brain in Action.* Oxford: Oxford University Press.

Mineka, S., M. Davidson, M. Cook, and R. Keir. 1984. Observational Conditioning of Snake Fear in Rhesus Monkeys. *Journal of Abnormal Psychology* 93: 355–372.

Mitchell, W. T. 1990. *The Logic of Architecture: Design, Computation, and Cognition.* Cambridge: MIT Press.

Montoya, P., and R. Schandry. 1994. Emotional Experience and Heartbeat Perception in Patients with Spinal Cord Injury and Control Subjects. *Journal of Psychophysiology* 8: 289–296.

Morrow, D. G., S. L. Greenspan, and G. H. Bower. 1987. Accessibility and Situation Models in Narrative Comprehension. *Journal of Memory and Language* 26: 165–187.

Mufwene, S. S. 2001. *Ecology of Language Evolution.* Cambridge: Cambridge University Press.

Murphy, G. L. 1988. Comprehending Complex Concepts. *Cognitive Science* 12: 529–562.

Murphy, G. L., and D. L. Medin. 1985. The Role of Theories in Conceptual Coherence. *Psychological Review* 92: 289–316.

Nagarajan S., H. Mahncke, T. Salz, P. Tallal, T. Roberts, and M. M. Merzenich. 1999. Cortical Auditory Signal Processing in Poor Readers. *Proceedings of the National Academy of Science* 96: 6483–6488.

Needham, A., and R. Baillargeon. 1993. Intuitions about Support in 4.5-Month-Old Infants. *Cognition* 47: 121–148.

Newell, A., and H. A. Simon. 1976. Computer Science as Empirical Inquiry: Symbols and Search. *Communications of the Association for Computing Machinery* 19: 113–126.

Newport, E. 1990. Maturational Constraints on Language Learning. *Cognitive Science* 14: 11–28.

Nosofsky, R. M. 1986. Attention, Similarity, and the Identification-Categorization Relationship. *Journal of Experimental Psychology: General* 115: 39–57.

Ogden, C. K., and I. A. Richards. 1923. *The Meaning of Meaning.* London: Harcourt.

Olseth, K. L., and L. W. Barsalou. 1995. The Spontaneous Use of Perceptual Representations during Conceptual Processing. *Proceedings of the Seventeenth Annual Meeting of the Cognitive Science Society.* Hillsdale, N.J.: Lawrence Erlbaum Associates.

Osherson, D. N., and E. E. Smith. 1981. On the Adequacy of Prototype Theory as a Theory of Concepts. *Cognition* 9: 35–58.

Paivio, A. 1986. *Mental Representations: A Dual Coding Approach*. Oxford: Oxford University Press.

Palmer, S. E. 1978. Fundamental Aspects of Cognitive Representation. In E. Rosch and B. B. Lloyd, eds., *Cognition and Categorization*. Hillsdale, N.J.: Lawrence Erlbaum Associates.

Papineau, D. 1987. *Reality and Representation*. Oxford: Basil Blackwell.

Passingham, R. E. 1973. Anatomical Differences between the Neocortex of Man and Other Primates. *Brain, Behavior & Evolution* 7: 337–359.

Peacocke, C. 1992. *A Study of Concepts*. Cambridge: MIT Press.

Perruchet, P., and C. Pacteau. 1990. Synthetic Grammar Learning: Implicit Rule Abstraction or Explicit Fragmentary Knowledge? *Journal of Experimental Psychology: General* 119: 264–275.

Piattelli-Palmarini, M. 1986. The Rise of Selective Theories: A Case Study and Some Lessons from Immunology. In W. Demopoulos and A. Marras, eds., *Language Learning and Concept Acquisition: Foundational Issues*. Norwood, N.J.: Ablex Publishing Corp.

Poeppel, D. 1996. A Critical Review of PET Studies of Phonological Processing. *Brain & Language* 55: 317–351.

Posner, M. I., and S. W. Keele. 1968. On the Genesis of Abstract Ideas. *Journal of Experimental Psychology* 77: 353–363.

Potter, M. C., J. F. Kroll, B. Yachzel, E. Carpenter, and J. Sherman. 1986. Pictures in Sentences: Understanding without Words. *Journal of Experimental Psychology: General* 115: 281–294.

Povinelli, D. J. 1999. Social Understanding in Chimpanzees. New Evidence from a Longitudinal Approach. In P. D. Zelazo, J. W. Astington, and D. R. Olson, eds., *Developing Theories of Intention: Social Understanding and Self-Control*. Hillsdale, N.J.: Lawrence Erlbaum Associates.

Povinelli, D. J. 2000. *Folk Physics for Apes: The Chimpanzee's Theory of How the World Works*. Oxford: Oxford University Press.

Premack, D. 1990. The Infant's Theory of Self-Propelled Objects. *Cognition* 36: 1–16.

Preuss, T. M. 2000. What's Human about the Human Brain? In M. S. Gazzaniga, ed., *The New Cognitive Neurosciences*, second edition. Cambridge: MIT Press.

Price, H. H. 1953. *Thinking and Experience*. London: Hutchinson's Universal Library.

Prinz, J. J. 2000a. A Neurofunctional Theory of Visual Consciousness. *Consciousness and Cognition* 9: 243–259.

Prinz, J. J. 2000b. The Duality of Content. *Philosophical Studies* 100: 1–34.

Prinz, J. J. Forthcoming. *Emotional Perception*. New York: Oxford University Press.

Prinz, J. J., and L. W. Barsalou. 2001. Acquisition and Productivity in Perceptual Symbol Systems. In T. Dartnall, ed., *Creativity, Cognition, and Knowledge*. Westport, Conn.: Praeger.

Putnam, H. 1967. The Nature of Mental States. Reprinted in H. Putnam, *Philosophical Papers*, vol. 2: *Mind, Language, and Reality*. Cambridge: Cambridge University Press, 1975.

Putnam, H. 1975. The Meaning of "Meaning." In H. Putnam, *Philosophical Papers*, vol. 2: *Mind, Language, and Reality*. Cambridge: Cambridge University Press.

Pylyshyn, Z. W. 1978. Imagery and Artificial Intelligence. In C. Wade Savage, ed., *Perception and Cognition: Issues in the Foundations of Psychology*, Minnesota Studies in the Philosophy of Science, no. 9. Minnesota: University of Minnesota Press.

Quine, W. V. O. 1951. Two Dogmas of Empiricism. Reprinted in W. V. O. Quine, *From a Logical Point of View*. Cambridge: Harvard University Press, 1953.

Quine, W. V. O. 1960. *Word and Object*. Cambridge: MIT Press.

Quine, W. V. O. 1969. Natural Kinds. In W. V. O. Quine, *Ontological Relativity and Other Essays*. New York: Columbia University Press.

Resnik, M. D. 1982. Mathematics as a Science of Patterns: Epistemology. *Noûs* 16: 95–105.

Rey, G. 1983. Concepts and Stereotypes. *Cognition* 15: 237–262.

Rey, G. 1985. Concepts and Conceptions: A Reply to Smith, Medin, and Rips. *Cognition* 19: 297–303.

Rey, G. 1994. Concepts. In S. Guttenplan, ed., *A Companion to the Philosophy of Mind*. Oxford: Blackwell.

Rips, L. J. 1989. Similarity, Typicality, and Categorization. In S. Vosniadou and A. Ortony, eds., *Similarity and Analogical Reasoning*. New York: Cambridge University Press.

Rips, L. J. 1995. The Current Status of Research on Concept Combination. *Mind & Language* 10: 72–104.

Rosch, E. 1973. Natural Categories. *Cognitive Psychology* 4: 328–350.

Rosch, E. 1975. Universals and Cultural Specifics in Human Categorization. In R. Brislin, S. Bochner, and W. Honner, eds., *Cross Cultural Perspectives on Learning*. New York: Halsted.

Rosch, E. 1978. Principles of Categorization. In E. Rosch and B. B. Lloyd, eds., *Cognition and Categorization*. Hillsdale, N.J.: Lawrence Erlbaum Associates.

Rosch, E., and C. B. Mervis. 1975. Family Resemblances: Studies in the Internal Structure of Categories. *Cognitive Psychology* 7: 573–605.

Rosch, E., C. B. Mervis, W. D. Gray, D. M. Johnson, and P. Boyes-Braem. 1976. Basic Objects in Natural Categories. *Cognitive Psychology* 8: 382–439.

Russell, B. 1919. Propositions: What They Are and How They Mean. *Proceedings of the Aristotelian Society*, suppl. vol. 2: 1–43.

Russell, B. 1921. *The Analysis of Mind*. New York: Macmillan.

Russell, B. 1927. *The Analysis of Matter*. London: Harcourt, Brace.

Russell, B. 1940. *An Inquiry into Meaning and Truth*. London: George Allen & Unwin.

Ryle, G. 1949. *The Concept of Mind*. New York: Harper Collins Publishers.

Samuels, R. Forthcoming. Nativism and Cognitive Science. *Mind and Language*.

Samuels, R., S. P. Stich, and S. Nichols. 1999. Rethinking Rationality: From Bleak Implications to Darwinian Modules. In E. Lepore and Z. Pylyshyn, eds., *What Is Cognitive Science?* London: Blackwell.

Savage-Rumbaugh, E. S. 1991. Language Learning in the Bonobo: How and Why They Learn. In N. A. Krasnegor, D. M. Rumbaugh, N. A. Krasnegor, M. Studdert-Kennedy, R. L. Schiefelbusch, and D. M. Rumbaugh, eds., *Biological and Behavioral Determinants of Language Development*. Hillsdale, N.J.: Lawrence Erlbaum Associates.

Schwanenflugel, P. J. 1991. Why Are Abstract Concepts Hard to Understand? In P. J. Schwanenflugel, ed., *The Psychology of Word Meanings*. Hillsdale, N.J.: Lawrence Erlbaum Associates.

Searle, J. R. 1992. *The Rediscovery of the Mind*. Cambridge: MIT Press.

Semendeferi, K., H. Damasio, R. Frank, and G. W. Van Hoesen. 1997. The Evolution of the Frontal Lobes: A Volumetric Analysis Based on Three-Dimensional Reconstructions of Magnetic Resonance Scans of Human and Ape Brains. *Journal of Human Evolution* 32: 375–388.

Senden, M. von. 1932. *Raum- und Gestaltauffassung bei Operierten Blindgeborenen vor und nach der Operation*. Leipzig: J. A. Barth.

Shi, R., J. F. Werker, and J. L. Morgan. 1999. Newborn Infants' Sensitivity to Perceptual Cues to Lexical and Grammatical Words. *Cognition* 72: B11–B21.

Simons, D. J., and F. C. Keil. 1995. An Abstract to Concrete Shift in the Development of Biological Thought: The *Insides* Story. *Cognition* 56: 129–163.

Singleton, J. L., and E. L. Newport. In press. When Learners Surpass Their Models: The Acquisition of American Sign Language from Inconsistent Input. *Cognitive Psychology*.

Skinner, B. F. 1953. *Science and Human Behavior*. New York: Macmillan.

Sloman, S. A. 1993. Feature-Based Induction. *Cognitive Psychology* 25: 231–280.

Smith, E. E. 1989. Concepts and Induction. In M. Posner, ed., *Foundations of Cognitive Science*. Cambridge: MIT Press.

Smith, E. E., and D. L. Medin. 1981. *Categories and Concepts*. Cambridge: Harvard University Press.

Smith, E. E., D. L. Medin, and L. J. Rips. 1984. A Psychological Approach to Concepts: Comments on Georges Rey's "Concepts and Stereotypes." *Cognition* 17: 265–274.

Smith, E. E., D. N. Osherson, L. J. Rips, and M. Keane. 1988. Combining Prototypes: A Selective Modification Model. *Cognitive Science* 12: 485–527.

Smith, E. E., and D. N. Osherson. 1989. Similarity and Decision Making. In S. Vosniadou and A. Ortony, eds., *Similarity and Analogical Reasoning*. New York: Cambridge University Press.

Smith, E. E., E. Shoben, and L. Rips. 1974. Structure and Process in Semantic Memory: A Featural Model for Semantic Decisions. *Psychological Review* 81: 214–241.

Smith, E. E., and S. A. Sloman. 1994. Similarity-versus Rule-Based Categorization. *Memory & Cognition* 22: 377–386.

Soja, N. N., S. Carey, and E. S. Spelke. 1991. Ontological Categories Guide Young Children's Inductions of Word Meaning. *Cognition* 38: 179–211.

Spelke, E. S. 1990. Principles of Object Perception. *Cognitive Science* 14: 29–56.

Spelke, E. S., K. Breinlinger, J. Macomber, and K. Jacobson. 1992. Origins of Knowledge. *Psychological Review* 99: 605–632.

Springer, K., and G. L. Murphy. 1992. Feature Availability in Conceptual Combination. *Psychological Science* 3: 111–117.

Stampe, D. 1979. Toward a Causal Theory of Linguistic Representation. In P. A. French, T. E. Uehling Jr., and H. K. Wettstein, eds., *Contemporary Perspectives in the Philosophy of Language*, Midwest Studies in Philosophy, no. 2. Minneapolis: University of Minnesota Press.

Stein, B. E., and M. A. Meredith. 1993. *The Merging of the Senses*. Cambridge: MIT Press.

Stein, L. A. 1994. Imagination and Situated Cognition. *Journal of Experimental and Theoretical Artificial Intelligence* 6: 393–407.

Sterelny, K. 1990. Animals and Individualism. In P. P. Hanson, ed., *Information, Language, and Cognition*. Vancouver: University of British Columbia Press.

Sterelny, K., K. Smith, and M. Dickenson. 1996. The Extended Replicator. *Biology and Philosophy* 11: 377–403.

Stern, J. 2000. *Metaphor in Context*. Cambridge: MIT Press.

Stich, S. P. 1983. *From Folk Psychology to Cognitive Science: The Case against Belief*. Cambridge: MIT Press.

Streri, A., E. Spelke, and E. Rameix. 1993. Modality-Specific and Amodal Aspects of Object Perception in Infancy: The Case of Active Touch. *Cognition* 47: 251–279.

Sutherland, N. S. 1968. Outline of a Theory of Visual Pattern Recognition in Animals and Man. *Proceedings of the Royal Society of London* B 171: 297–317.

Talmy, L. 1983. How Language Structures Space. In H. Pick and L. Acredolo, eds. *Spatial Orientation: Theory, Research, and Application*. New York: Plenum.

Talmy, L. 1988. Force Dynamics in Language and Cognition. *Cognitive Science* 12: 49–100.

Tarr, M. J., and S. Pinker. 1989. Mental Rotation and Orientation-Dependence in Shape Recognition. *Cognitive Psychology* 21: 233–282.

Thompson-Schill, S. L., G. K. Aguirre, M. D'Esposito, and M. Farah. 1999. A Neural Basis for Category and Modality Specificity of Semantic Knowledge. *Neuropsychologia* 37: 671–676.

Titchener, E. B. 1910. *A Text-Book of Psychology*. New York: Macmillan.

Tomasello, M. 1992. *First Verbs: A Case Study of Early Grammatical Development*. New York: Cambridge University Press.

Tootell, R. B. H., M. S. Silverman, E. Switkes, and R. L. De Valois. 1982. Deoxyglucose Analysis of Retinotopic Organization in Primate Striate Cortex. *Science* 218: 902–904.

Tversky, A. 1977. Features of Similarity. *Psychological Review* 84: 327–352.

Tversky, B., and K. Hemenway. 1985. Objects, Parts, and Categories. *Journal of Experimental Psychology: General* 113: 169–193.

Tye, M. 1991. *The Imagery Debate*. Cambridge: MIT Press.

Tye, M. 1995. *Ten Problems of Consciousness: A Representational Theory of the Phenomenal Mind*. Cambridge: MIT Press.

Uller, C., and S. Nichols 2000. Goal Attribution in Chimpanzees. *Cognition* 76: 1–8.

Ungerleider, L. G., and M. Mishkin. 1982. Two Cortical Visual Systems. In D. J. Ingle, M. A. Goodale, and R. W. J. Mansfield, eds., *Analysis of Visual Behavior*. Cambridge: MIT Press.

Vaina, L. 1983. From Shapes and Movements to Objects and Actions: Design Constraints on the Representation. *Synthese* 36: 3–36.

Van Gelder, T. J. 1990. Compositionality: A Connectionist Variation on a Classical Theme. *Cognitive Science* 14: 355–384.

Vargha-Khadem, F., K. Watkins, K. Alcock, P. Fletcher, and R. Passingham. 1995. Praxic and Nonverbal Cognitive Deficits in a Large Family with a Genetically Transmitted Speech and Language Disorder. *Proceedings of the National Academy of Science* 92: 930–933.

Waddington, C. H. 1940. *Organizers and Genes*. Cambridge: Cambridge University Press.

Wertheimer, M. 1961. Psychomotor Coordination of Auditory and Visual Space at Birth. *Science* 134: 1692.

White, S. L. 1982. Partial Character and the Language of Thought. *Pacific Philosophical Quarterly* 63: 347–365.

White, S. L. 1991. *The Unity of the Self*. Cambridge: MIT Press.

Wisniewski, E. J. 1996. Construal and Similarity in Conceptual Combination. *Journal of Memory & Language* 35: 434–453.

Wisniewski, E. J. 1997. When Concepts Combine. *Psychonomic Bulletin & Review* 4: 167–183.

Wittgenstein, L. 1919. *Tractatus Logico-philosophicus*. D. Pears and B. McGuinness, trans. London: Routledge.

Wittgenstein, L. 1953. *Philosophical Investigations*. G. E. M. Anscombe, trans. New York: Macmillan.

Wu, L.-L. 1995. *Perceptual Representation in Conceptual Combination*. Doctoral dissertation, University of Chicago.

Xu, F., and S. Carey. 1996. Infant Metaphysics: The Case of Numerical Identity. *Cognitive Psychology* 30: 111–153.

Zajonc, R. B. 1985. Emotion and Facial Efference: A Theory Reclaimed. *Science* 228: 15–21.

Zeki, S. 1992. The Visual Image in Mind and Brain. *Scientific American* 267: 69–76.

Index

Abrahamsen, A., 320 (n. 3), 322 (n. 2)
Acquisition, 42, 56, 66–67, 80–81, 94–95. *See also* Nativism
by hypothesis testing, 228–229
introduced, 8–9, 26–27
of language, 198–212
proxytype theory and, 211–212, 218–228, 234–235
by triggering, 229
versus learning, 252
Allen, S. W., 42
Alston, W. P., 165
Amnesia, anterograde, 71–72
Amodal symbols. *See* Language of thought; Rationalism
Analyticity, 33–34, 40–41, 87, 265–266, 273
Anderson, J. R., 118
Animals, 16, 18, 19, 21, 186, 198, 224–227, 274, 322–323 (n. 8)
language skills in, 199, 203–204, 210–211,
Ariew, A., 190
Aristotle, 25
Armstrong, D. M., 319 (n. 8)
Armstrong, S. L., 10, 39, 58, 63
Arterberry, M. E., 135
Artifacts, 3, 33, 59, 76, 79–80, 84–85, 127, 216, 224, 230, 233
Associationism, 194, 322 (n. 2)

Asymmetrical dependence. *See* Disjunction problem, Fodor's solution to
Attribute-value frames, 53, 297–299, 303–305, 311
Austin, G., 35
Autism, 227–228
Aydede, M., 15, 97
Ayer, A. J., 126
Ayers, M., 25

Background knowledge, 157, 158, 291–293, 300, 308–310, 325 (n. 3), 326 (n. 4)
Baillargeon, R., 220–221
Baron-Cohen, S., 227
Barsalou, L. W.
on concept empiricism, 106, 120, 129, 142, 143, 321 (nn. 3, 4)
on concepts as temporary constructions, 148–150, 152
on connectionism, 320 (n. 3)
on goal-derived categories, 58, 149
on prototype theory, 53, 71, 73
on simulation competence, 150
on variability, 62, 158
Basic-level categories, 10, 11, 28, 29, 42–43, 56, 162–163, 260, 321 (n. 6)
Bates, E., 195, 201, 203, 282
Batterman, N., 80
Bauer, M. I., 184
Bechtel, W., 320 (n. 3), 322 (n. 2)

functional-role theories of, 264–266, 272, 273

mapping theory of, 266–268, 272–273

as narrow, 278

notional-worlds theory of, 268–269, 272

Nativism, 8, 27, 39, 95, 105, 109–110, 126, 189–235 (chap. 8). *See also* Doorknob/DOORKNOB problem

versus antinativism, 194–197, 214

arguments for, 198–200, 212–214, 228–229

definitions of "innate" and, 190–194

empiricism compatible with, 109–110, 194–197, 199

intentionality and, 257–258

of language, 198–194

radical, 94–95, 228–235

Natural kinds, 4–5, 79, 86, 192, 216, 240, 274–275, 276. *See also* Concepts, of natural kinds

Needham, A., 220

Newell, A., 105, 320 (n. 4)

Newport, E. L., 204–205, 209–210

Nichols, S., 114, 322 (n. 8)

Nishihara, H. K., 142

Nominal content, 277–282. *See also* Cognitive content; Narrow content

Nonconceptual content, 111–112

Nosofsky, R. M., 64

Object models, 141–142, 144–145, 163

Ogden, C. K., 239

Ontological categories, 79–81, 128, 212, 223–224. *See also* Domain specificity

Original Sim hypothesis (Keil). 80, 216–218, 224

Ortony, A., 63, 79, 82

Osherson, D. N., 54, 62, 63, 285, 296, 297, 303, 308, 326 (n. 6)

Pacteau, C., 64

Paivio, A., 131–132

Palmer, S. E., 30

Papineau, D., 323 (n. 1)

Parisi, D., 195, 201, 282

Partee, B., 60

Passingham, R., 201

Passingham, R. E., 204

Peacocke, C., 6, 36–37

Perceivable properties, 22, 112–113, 169

Perceptual-priority hypothesis, 106–108

Perceptual representations, 108, 121–122, 139–144

versus concepts, 197

copies of, 108–109, 128–129

defined, 119

faculty-based definitions of, 113–119

semantic definitions of, 112–113

syntactic definitions of, 110–112

in vision, 139–142

Perceptual symbols (Barsalou), 152, 320 (n. 4)

Perruchet, P., 64

Phenomenalism, 126

Piattelli-Palmarini, M., 230

Pinker, S., 140, 209

Plato, 33, 34

Plunkett, K., 195, 201, 282

Poeppel, D., 202

Polymodal and bimodal cells, 126–137

Posner, M. I., 51, 56, 71, 73

Possible worlds, 241, 246–247. *See also* Twin Earth cases

Potter, M. C., 130

Poverty of the stimulus, 193, 199, 210, 219

Povinelli, D. J., 225, 227

Premack, D., 221–222

Preuss, T. M., 203

Price, H. H., 26, 30, 104, 181

Primitives. *See* Concepts, primitive